D0044364

NEW DIRECTIONS IN SEX THERAPY

NEW DIRECTIONS IN SEX THERAPY

Innovations and Alternatives

edited by

Peggy J. Kleinplatz, Ph.D.

USA	Publishing Office:	BRUNNER-ROUTLEDGE
		A member of the Taylor & Francis Group
		325 Chestnut Street
		Philadelphia, PA 19106
		Tel: (215) 625-8900
		Fax: (215) 625-2940
	Distribution Center:	BRUNNER-ROUTLEDGE
		A member of the Taylor & Francis Group
		7625 Empire Drive
		Florence, KY 41042
		Tel: 1-800-634-7064
		Fax: 1-800-248-4724
UK		ACCELERATED DEVELOPMENT
		A member of the Taylor & Francis Group
		27 Church Road
		Hove
		E. Sussex, BN3 2FA
		Tel: +44 (0) 1273 207411
		Fax: +44 (0) 1273 205612

NEW DIRECTIONS IN SEX THERAPY: Innovations and Alternatives

4   5   6   7   8   9   0

Printed by Edwards Brothers, Ann Arbor, MI, 2001.
Cover design by Joe Dieter.

A CIP catalog record for this book is available from the British Library.

⊚ The paper in this publication meets the requirements of the ANSI Standard Z39.48-1984 (Permanence of Paper).

Library of Congress Cataloging-in-Publication Data

New directions in sex therapy : innovations and alternatives / Peggy J. Kleinplatz, editor.
    p. cm.
  Includes bibliographical references and index.
  ISBN 0-87630-967-8 (alk. paper)
    1. Sex therapy. 2. Sexual disorders—Treatment. I. Kleinplatz, Peggy J.
RC557 .N49 2001
616.85'8306—dc21   00-066741

ISBN 0-87630-967-8 (case)

CONTENTS

ACKNOWLEDGMENTS

This book was not my idea. It resulted from about a dozen years' worth of conversations with Alvin R. Mahrer, Ph.D. I would come back from sexology conferences disappointed and visit him at the Center for Psychological Services. I would complain that much of what I had heard of the state of the art only reified the same old thing, thereby limiting all that sex therapy could accomplish. For years he encouraged me to do something about it—to try to improve the field. I responded that I was not adequate to or worthy of the task. He persisted, though, asking me about the writers I admired, had learned from, and respected. Could I bring these innovative thinkers and clinicians together, creating a forum for them to provide an alternate vision? With his encouragement, the plan for *New Directions in Sex Therapy: Innovations and Alternatives* began to take shape.

But he did not stop there: Dr. Al Mahrer held my hand every step of the way. He helped me figure out how to organize what I only dimly imagined; he eagerly read my chapters and gave helpful, useful, detailed feedback, inevitably advising me to have the courage of my convictions and to say what I believed, in simple, undisguised, lucid sentences; and, most importantly, he kept me focused on the value of the task rather than on my self-doubts surrounding my competence, or lack thereof. Without his guidance, mentoring, friendship, and faith, this book would never have come to be or have been completed.

I am very grateful to those who took a chance by agreeing to participate in this project. I am indebted to Mr. Lansing Hays, who was senior acquisitions editor at Brunner/Mazel at the time of this book's inception. His encouragement, belief in the value of this project, good humor, and wise counsel have been invaluable. I also appreciate the willingness of those who contributed chapters to this book to entrust their writing to me and to this endeavor.

I would like to thank Mr. Tim Julet, Acquisitions Editor and his staff at Brunner-Routledge, particularly Ms. Katherine Mortimer, Ms. Jill Osowa, and Ms. Sherri W. Emmons, for their unflagging support of *New Directions in Sex Therapy* and their ideas for strengthening and sharpening it.

Ms. Margaret Lubowiecka and Mr. Andy Lubowiecki's organizational skills and continuing attention made it possible for me keep my energies focused throughout the duration of this project.

I am especially appreciative of the support, encouragement, and warmth of my students at the University of Ottawa and at Saint Paul University, as well as from my fellow BESTCO members (Board of Examiners in Sex Therapy and Counselling in Ontario).

Thanks also to two extraordinary editors, Michael Barrett, Ph.D., and Thomas Greening, Ph.D., for their kindness, inspiration, and interest.

I owe heartfelt thanks to the friends and colleagues who read and reread the drafts of my chapters, providing specific, critical suggestions for improvement while also offering the nurturance that sustained me in the completion of this book. These special people are Ms. Jacqueline Cohen, Irit Sterner, Ph.D., Charles Moser, Ph.D., M.D., Ronald E. Fox, Ph.D., and Howard M. Schwartz, Ph.D. I am enriched for having them in my life.

I am humbled by the love and patience of my family in making this project a reality, even as it occupied and preoccupied me for longer than I had anticipated. My parents, Sarah and Mayer Kleinplatz, offered the original inspiration for my career in sex therapy and sex education. They taught my brothers and me that sexual intimacy is a Divine gift. Their marriage continues to instruct all who know them in the meaning of desire with commitment. My children, Miriam and Bram, have been a source of endless joy and a refuge from my work, although I cannot say that I have shielded them from this adequately. During the course of this project, I received a phone call at the end of supper. Bram, then 7 years old, assumed correctly from the gist of my end of the conversation that I had been talking with a lesbian-identified sex worker. He began asking if she had sex with men or women, or both. I explained that she was willing to exchange sex for money with whomever paid her. He continued probing issues of personal and economic freedom, the nature of desire, and questions of sexual categories versus sexual fluidity. Although I believe strongly in comprehensive sexuality education, I think you and Mel have had enough for now, Bram. The sun is still shining, I'm through working, and it's time for all of us to get on our bicycles and go for a ride.

Finally, my greatest thanks go to Howard M. Schwartz, Ph.D. When this project began, I did not know how to type—(as in, "Howie, where are the capital letters?")—let alone understand the use of "keyboard" as a verb. It was his unenviable task to bring me into the twentieth century. It was his choice to remain my best friend and confidante, even when I was a distracted bundle of agitated nerves; to share in my excitement around the various stages of this endeavor; and to love me when I was lost, engrossed in the minutiae of editing a book. Few individuals are so blessed as to share their lives with a person of such integrity and so faithful and caring a partner.

INTRODUCTION   Peggy J. Kleinplatz, Ph.D.

A Critical Evaluation of Sex Therapy: Room for Improvement

I have a love-hate relationship with sex therapy. I have been teaching Human Sexuality at the School of Psychology, University of Ottawa, since 1983, and I teach Sex Therapy at the affiliated Saint Paul University's Institute of Pastoral Studies. I am certified as a sex therapist and educator and spend most of my time in the practice of sex therapy with individuals and couples (as well as the occasional group for survivors of childhood sexual abuse). On the side, I study and write about sexuality.

I like the people I meet in the field. The students are eager to learn more about sex, for both personal and professional reasons. The clients are hoping to improve their sex lives. The educators, counselors, researchers, and therapists are generally open-minded, progressive, tolerant, and compassionate individuals who seek to broaden the acceptance of sexuality, in all of its manifold manifestations, in society. As a therapist, I am privileged to be part of a field that has had notable success in treating the presenting problems that come our way, particularly in comparison to the outcome results in psychotherapy in general. We make it our business to talk about the stuff that makes other members of our society, including other therapists, markedly uncomfortable. This is a good profession but we can make it even better.

Unfortunately, with each passing year the emphasis seems to grow toward more medical and pharmacological interventions. There is correspondingly less interest in the experiences of the individuals or couples involved. I object to the mechanistic, dehumanizing, and reductionistic approach of the prevailing paradigms. More importantly, these models presuppose an underlying conception of sexuality that is narrow, constricting, heavily performance-oriented, and centered around heterosexual intercourse. They promote sexual homogeneity and mediocrity (i.e., the status quo) at the expense of the richness and variety of erotic experience with which sex therapy should be concerned.

This book takes a critical look at the field of sex therapy and will try to improve it. (By sex therapy I am referring not only to the field's original and still predominant focus—the treatment of sexual dysfunctions—but also to what is sometimes termed *clinical sexology*. The latter includes the treatment of all sexual issues, problems, and concerns.) The contributors to this book are individuals who would like to strengthen our field. These authors suggest that the cutting edge of sex therapy may require innovations in, alternatives to, and a redefinition of sex therapy as we know it.

This book begins with a critical review of the field, covering the strengths and weaknesses in both the theory and the practice of sex therapy and highlighting areas where there may be room for improvement. This chapter also highlights some of the major problems and criticisms facing the field of sex therapy, which is the focus of Part I of this book, as well as suggesting a need for new directions, which is the focus of Part II of the book. The introduction concludes by advising readers of the book's intended contributions and audience and about the organization of the book.

There have been a few—too few—reviews of the literature in the field of sex therapy over the last 10 years or so (i.e., Leiblum & Rosen, 1989; Leiblum & Schover, 1994; Rosen & Leiblum, 1995). They provide a balanced perspective on our field, and they are certainly valuable reading. This introduction will not add to that genre. Instead, this chapter begins to make a case for the need for a critical evaluation and new directions.

There has been much scrutiny and much criticism of sex therapy (see, for example, Irvine, 1990; Jeffries, 1990; Reiss, 1990; Weeks, 1985), although it has not typically originated from within the ranks of *sex therapists* (Tiefer, 1994). We have not tended toward self-criticism (with notable exceptions, e.g., Schnarch, 1991). This chapter will offer a critical evaluation of the field of sex therapy, discussing its strengths and weaknesses but focusing on the areas in which work needs to be done in order to advance our field.

☐ The Strengths of Sex Therapy

The major strength of the field of sex therapy has been its ability to treat particular sexual problems quickly and effectively. This has provided a major improvement over its psychodynamic predecessors. Our track record in treating sexual dysfunctions is impressive when compared to mainstream psychotherapy's in treating its major targets: anxiety and depression. A brief historical sketch helps to put sex therapy's successes, as well as the origins of its deficits, into perspective.

In the beginning were the psychoanalytic approaches that regarded sexual problems as they would any other problems. They dealt with the entire life of the patient rather than focusing on the sexual problem. Transference and insight were the catalysts for change, and the process was expected to transpire slowly. The psychoanalysts were not noted for their success at improving patients' sex lives, and their services were lengthy, both time- and cost-intensive. Their legacy, an interest in deep change in the whole person, was cast aside with the founding of the new field of sex therapy.

Masters and Johnson essentially built the foundations for the new field of sex therapy in the 1960s. Their focus was on eliminating the symptoms of sexual dysfunction. They emphasized brief, intensive treatment of the symptoms, regardless of their origins. Similarly, Helen Singer Kaplan focused on reversing the symptom; it was only when the symptoms proved intractable that she saw the need to explore further and deeper along a psychodynamic path. Both were extremely effective at meeting their goals and so had little need to develop their theoretical understanding of sexuality further. Rather, their work was based on the belief that sex is natural. Their sex therapy approaches *appeared* to be largely atheoretical.

Success followed. More correctly, Masters and Johnson soon became renowned for their report of a 20% failure rate (in contrast with the usual practice of reporting one's success rate). Kaplan's success rates were similarly impressive. Results for Masters and Johnson (1970) ranged from a failure rate of 40.6% in the treatment of primary impotence to a high of virtually 100% success in the treatment of vaginismus, a rate matched by Kaplan (1974).

In general, sex therapy treats the symptoms of sexual dysfunctions, and more specifically mechanical problems in performance, very well. It is relatively successful in treating anorgasmia in women, rapid orgasm in men, the pain disorders of dyspareunia and vaginismus (but not of vulvadynia), and female sexual arousal problems (by use of artificial lubrication) so as to enable intercourse. It is also increasingly effective at controlling deviant sexual behaviors.

Over the last 25 years sex therapy has come of age. If it was regarded with suspicion in the 1960s and early 1970s, sex therapy is now regarded as a science, as a discipline with full-fledged professional credibility. The field has become respectable. It has journals, conferences, training programs, professional organizations, accreditation standards, and certification boards to guarantee that its practitioners are competent, ethical clinicians rather than voyeuristic, exploitative charlatans.

However, it is in its pathway to success as a field that the seeds of sex therapy's problems have been sown.

☐ The Foundations of the Field of Sex Therapy

In 1966 and 1970, Masters and Johnson went out of their way to reassure the public and to demonstrate to professional bodies that sexology was a science like any other. To that end, they argued that sexual behavior was a bodily function, as "natural" as "respiratory, bowel, and bladder functions" (Masters & Johnson, 1986, p. 2). (This was not only a useful political maneuver but also in keeping with Masters's background and perspective as a physician.) Together, they treated sexual performance as a bodily function and therefore subject to scientific scrutiny, prediction, and control. They helped take what had been regarded previously as a private matter, belonging to the domain of morality and religion, and bring it into the realm of science (Bullough, 1994). As sex therapists, we are (or certainly ought to be) profoundly grateful to Masters and Johnson, if only for the mere fact of having jobs today. The implications, however, of the stance these pioneers assumed in order to establish this field are far-reaching and cannot be ignored. In the name of credibility, they sacrificed the uniquely human dimensions of human sexual expression in their model. Thirty years after the introduction of sex therapy, perhaps the missing aspects can be restored to the field.

Paradoxically, another factor that advanced the status of the field while leaving deficits in its underpinnings was sex therapy's extraordinary, initial level of apparent "success." For many years it was possible to overlook any structural weaknesses in the foundations of sex therapy if only because its practitioners were so effective at attaining their own goals (i.e., the elimination or reversal of the symptoms of sexual dysfunction/disorder; whether or not these are worthy goals is another matter). In the face of the early, impressive outcome data, there was little demand to delve too deeply into the rarely articulated assumptions underlying the practice of sex therapy. It may also be worth noting that over the last 15 years, the research and outcome data in the field have been neither as extensive nor as impressive as in the 1970s (Hawton, 1992; Leiblum & Schover, 1994; Wiederman, 1998).

The Role of Theory—and Lack Thereof—in the Field of Sex Therapy

Sex therapy has now attained the professional status as a field to bear closer scrutiny and to withstand criticism. At this stage, one would hope that taking a close look at the assumptions underlying sex therapy could only strengthen the field. Ironically, when we examine the basic assumptions, questions, and answers in our field, we discover that our foundations as a science are barely there. We have not even answered such fundamental questions as, "What is sex?" or "What is sexuality?" The questions seem to be so laughably simple as to be almost absurd. And yet there are those who wrestle with them. It is noteworthy that they are not sex therapists (although some are sexologists), and their contributions do not garner much attention in the mainstream sex therapy literature. (Throughout 1999, the public discussion on the nature of sex was dominated by members of the United States Congress and an array of political pundits; given the obvious lacunae in the debate, it was disturbing to see how little sexology had contributed to the discourse, leaving a vacuum to be filled by those bearing a sex-negative agenda.) Those who do grapple with such questions may be educators, anthropologists, sociologists, humanistic–existential psychologists, sex radicals/pansexuals, or evolutionary psychologists; those writing in "queer" or gay and lesbian studies, feminist studies, cultural studies, or religious studies; postmodernists/poststructuralists or even philosophers, poets, and the writers of erotica (Buss, 1998; Butler, 1990, 1993; Califia, 1994; Christina, 1992; Dimen, 1989, 1995; Dworkin, 1987; Dychtwald, 1979; Feuerstein, 1989, 1992; Foucault, 1980; Helminiak, 1996; Hollibaugh, 1989; Irvine, 1990; Jeffries,1990; Keen, 1979, 1992; Livia, 1995; Murray, 1999; Nelson, 1978; Nelson & Longfellow, 1994; Nicolson, 1993; Reiss,1990; Richardson, 1996; Rofes, 1996, 1998; Shrage, 1999; Simon, 1996; Steinberg, 1992; Ussher, 1993; Weeks, 1985). Few sex therapists, aside from various contributors to this collection, are known to struggle with these basic theoretical questions. (They may do so, but not typically in the literature.) This seems ironic given that it is practitioners, unlike theoreticians, who most need answers to these questions or at least to have working hypotheses. It is clinicians who require a set of provisional principles in order to engage in therapy.

In the process of promoting the field of sex therapy, however, it has been swept under the rug that not only does sex therapy not have the answers to the fundamental questions in sexology that need to be addressed in order to qualify for the pretensions of being a "science," we have not even articulated those fundamental questions. That is, the field acts as if it has answers to questions that have never even been asked, and so the assumptions built into the practice of sex therapy are never articulated and remain difficult to identify, challenge, and dislodge.

These questions include: What is sexuality? What turns people on and why? What makes an experience "sexual"? What constitutes sexual experience? How are we to understand sexual experience? What is the role of the body in sexual experience? What is the basis/origin of sexual desire? What makes an act or a fantasy or stimulus "sexual"? Why do some things seem powerfully erotic to some people, abhorrent to others, and irrelevant to still others, leaving them cold? To what extent are fantasies, desires, or preferences subject to change? Are all people capable of some kind of sexual feeling? What are the possible uses of sex? What is the role of the body in sexual experience? What is "normal" sexuality? What is the relationship between "normal" and "abnormal" sexuality, and what can we learn about one from the other? What is optimal sexuality? What kinds of sex do we want to promote? How are we to conceptualize sexual problems? What is the context in which certain things come to be identified as sexual problems? What is the context in which the problem comes to be defined and come into existence? What should our goals be in dealing with sexual problems?

Conception/Conceptualization of the Nature of Sexuality and Sexual Problems

What is the predominant view of sexuality within the field of sex therapy? What is the conventional model of sex therapy? These are difficult to identify, as stated above, due to the paucity of our theoretical literature. According to Wiederman (1998, p. 95), "Sexual science too frequently is performed in a theoretical vacuum." (There are rare exceptions, such as the collection on sexual theory edited by Geer and O'Donohue, 1987, though even in that book most of the contributors are not sex *therapists*.)

It may be easier to detect the public's notions about sexuality than to identify our own. As we teach our students, when we encounter cross-cultural sexual norms that run counter to our own, it is easier to detect beliefs that deviate from our culture's than to even recognize as beliefs those that support, confirm, and conform to our own views. Our own beliefs constitute the reference point from which we identify all divergent perspectives. We do not notice our own bedrock assumptions until they are violated by others' beliefs or practices. Similarly, in the field of sex therapy, we are readily able to note the lay public's beliefs in sex myths (e.g., Zilbergeld, 1992) but rarely elucidate our own assumptions.

Hence it is easiest to identify the fundamental conceptions of sexuality within the field of sex therapy in the context of our responses to lay sex myths and as they emerge in our clinical practice.

Our Fundamental Assumptions Are Laden with Sexual Myths

Ironically, although we criticize the public's faulty beliefs, we often fail to see how our own clinical approaches contain and subtly uphold these same beliefs. That is, sex therapy claims to ostensibly reject sexual myths and stereotypes (e.g., about gender, about "normalcy") but operates as though they are true, thereby ultimately reinforcing them. We try to overcome traditional ideas about sex but end up reinforcing them in our models of sex therapy (Irvine, 1990; Kleinplatz, 1996, 1998; Reiss, 1990; Schnarch, 1991; Tiefer, 1991, 1996). Our assessment procedures, diagnostic classifications, treatment methods, goals, and outcome criteria not only fail to dispel these notions but actually perpetuate and reinforce them.

We are very clear in stating that sex is more than orgasm or intercourse, and that sexual relations are not to be performance-driven but rather focused on pleasure. Yet, if we are to judge by how sexual problems are defined, labeled, and treated and how we determine effective outcome, it seems obvious that we actually do uphold these notions. Our actual techniques, methods, operations, and objectives demonstrate an embedded, implicit assumption that whatever impedes orgasm or intercourse ought to be overcome. Psychological and interpersonal barriers to "normal" genital functioning are to be eliminated, whether by ignoring the intrapsychic processes within (e.g., "bypassing" [Kaplan, 1974, 1987]) or by biomedical intervention (e.g., Viagra™). We deny that women want prolonged intercourse in order to be sexually satisfied while simultaneously prescribing either behavioral exercises or Paxil™ to reverse rapid ejaculation. We argue that there is no "correct" amount of sexual desire while we are busy treating people with (suspiciously) high or low levels of desire, including those who say, "If I never had sex again, I wouldn't miss it."

We could argue, of course, that it is the clients who define the problems—not therapists—and that our job is merely to assist clients in attaining their own goals. We are only helping them to find sexual fulfillment, however they might define it. But this is patently untrue. Of course it is the clients who come for therapy. Of course they come for their own reasons. But together, we define the nature and parameters of the problem.

Sex therapists do not necessarily agree to treat all presenting complaints simply because patients have defined them as problematic. We are no longer in the business of trying to "convert" homosexuals to heterosexuality. Similarly, we explain to couples who are seeking simultaneous orgasm that they may be better served by some sex education and counseling than by "treatment." We tell clients that all the "shoulds" they inflict upon themselves are hazardous to their well-being—but only when we disagree with them. (We might say, "You shouldn't feel guilty about self-stimulating," but we would be very unlikely to say, "You shouldn't feel guilty about stimulating your dog's genitals.") Our own underlying conceptions of sexuality (and our values) determine our diagnoses and subsequent interventions (not unlike the process our clients undergo in bed before they decide to consult us).

Thus, if we examine sex therapy in action, it is easy to conclude that underlying our praxis are the following assumptions about sexuality: Sex is a natural, biological function, impeded by repressive socialization. Sexual functioning is a normal, natural bodily function. What is natural is good. Sexual satisfaction results from effective genital stimulation. Sexual satisfaction is equated with orgasm. There are fundamental differences between men and women's sexuality. Sex should have a sexual purpose. (The phrase "sex for a nonsexual purpose," typically used in the context of pathologizing those who engage in unusual and socially unacceptable sexual behaviors [e.g., Carnes, 1983, 1991; Hastings, 1998], says it all.) Sex should occur within a particular range of frequency (rarely articulated but imagined nonetheless). Lack of desire is necessarily problematic. Lots and lots of sexual desire is suspect at best. There is a correct amount of desire. Orgasms should be properly timed: Men should not reach orgasm too soon; women cannot soon enough. The initial public hysteria surrounding sildenafil citrate (Viagra™) suggests that we are perpetuating notions of sexuality that rest on the assumptions that intercourse is the ultimate goal of sex; sex requires a hard penis; performance is the focus—not pleasure or desire; whatever impedes orgasm or intercourse ought to be overcome; and women want prolonged intercourse to be satisfied.

Similarly, by examining the clinical practice of sex therapy we can discern some of the fundamental, if unspoken, assumptions of our treatment paradigm. These include: Problems are *either* psychogenic *or* biological in origin. Psychogenic problems can be overcome by biomedical intervention. The therapist is to be an expert on normal and pathological sexuality in general and is to be a greater authority on the clients' sexuality than the clients themselves. The proper vantage point from which to understand our patients' sexuality is from a detached, objective distance. Given that sexuality is essentially biologically based, men—including male therapists—can never fully comprehend women's sexual experience; correspondingly, women—including female therapists—can never fully comprehend men's sexual experience.

Actually, this tenet was articulated by Masters and Johnson in their original (1970) formulation of sex therapy and was the reason for their insistence on dual-sex therapy teams. The centrality of this belief was further emphasized in their later (1979) work on homosexuality, in which they posited that gay men and lesbians seem to be more effective lovers than their heterosexual counterparts due to intra-gender empathy. Masters and Johnson further explained this phenomenon in terms of same-sex lovers' firsthand experience with their own genitals. Apparently, anatomy is destiny and access to similar genital equipment provides the basis for easy entry into another's sexual experience.

Other assumptions include these: The therapist is to structure the goals, sequence, pace, and nature of treatment. The goal is to be generated a priori by virtue of the nature of the problem and the social or the therapist's sexual norms. The focus of treatment is on eliminating pathological symptoms and fixing dysfunctional bodily parts; there is little emphasis on the experience of the whole person. The goal is to attain normative performance standards. Symptom reversal is the major goal in the treatment of the sexual dysfunctions and symptom containment, management, or control in the case of the paraphilias. Treatment has succeeded when the individual or couple is able to engage in heterosexual intercourse. Outcome is to be assessed by noting changes in sexual behavior—for example, frequency tabulations of orgasm, erection, or intercourse.

Notwithstanding the Sexual Attitude Reassessment workshops that constitute a compulsory component of our training as sex therapists, we promote conventional North American ideas of sex because we remain conventional North Americans.

Adherence to These Unexamined Notions Leads to Problems

We act as though we think we have answers to questions we have not even articulated. The theoretical underpinnings are weak and unexplored. Maybe if we can sift through our implicit beliefs, we can decide which to keep and which to reject (Mahrer, 2000).

There is a gaping, invisible hole in our understanding of sexuality. It is easy to fall into. It is so well-disguised (by those who act as if the answers are already a foregone conclusion) it is hard to even notice it is there. If we stand outside this trap we are well-positioned to at least ask some basic questions and perhaps to supply answers that may generate some dialogue and prospects for research.

XX New Directions in Sex Therapy

Adhering to these poorly articulated, unexamined notions creates the underpinnings of the problems in our practice. Our narrow, biomedical ideas about sex generate problems in diagnosis, treatment methods, goals, and outcome criteria. They limit us. To the extent that sex therapy adheres and feeds into conventional ideas of sex and normative performance standards with an emphasis on heterosexual intercourse, it may create as many problems as it solves.

☐ Some Problems to Be Solved If Sex Therapy Is to Improve

Here are just a few of the problems in the field of sex therapy that arise out of our basic theoretical flaws. These are among the issues discussed in Part I of this book. The chapters in Part II endeavor to provide solutions to these problems or, even better, to circumvent them entirely.

Sex Therapy Is Based on Gender-Biased, Phallocentric, and Heterosexist Assumptions

Each semester I role-play with my graduate class in sex therapy. I ask:

> Suppose a patient walks into your office complaining about coming to orgasm at the outset of intercourse, immediately upon penetration, or at the most within a few thrusts, saying: "I hardly get to enjoy it at all. We barely get into it when I'm done. It only takes a few hard strokes and I can't control it. My partner is getting pretty frustrated and I don't know what to do." What is your approach?

After my students finish arguing the merits of the squeeze technique, the stop-start technique, and pharmacologic intervention, I point out that they have assumed the patient was male. I then ask how they might react to a woman with this "presenting problem." It is assumed that *he* is in need of treatment but that *she* should go home and count her blessings. Rapid ejaculation in males is seen as far more serious than rapid orgasm in females (Reiss, 1990), whereas delayed ejaculation in males receives scant attention in the literature.

One might argue that delayed ejaculation is seldom diagnosed, but this does not fit with the reported rate (33%) of "faking of orgasm" among young males (cited in Darling & Davidson, 1986). Sex therapists are quite aware of the rates of women's difficulties with orgasm and the social pressures that lead some to "fake orgasm," but they seem less attuned to the implications of performance pressures on men and their manifestations in therapy. Perhaps to the extent that our definitions of "normal" sexual performance correspond to the prevailing cultural standards, sex therapists fail to recognize men's sexual difficulties. Delayed ejaculation is more likely to be envied than to be judged as problematic (Apfelbaum, 1995; Reiss, 1990; Schnarch 1991). That it is seen as an indicator of manliness rather than as a condition to be treated in quite the same fashion as female anorgasmia reveals a great deal about our society's conceptions of masculinity and feminine sexuality as well as about the conceptions of sexuality adopted, accepted, and perpetuated in sex therapy.

Similarly, the frenzy upon the release of sildenafil citrate illustrates that we continue to live with phallocentric definitions of sex; erectile dysfunction is seen as an obstacle to *sex*, rather than merely as an obstacle to *sexual intercourse*. As a field, we had the opportunity to exploit the media attention on penises to emphasize our alleged belief that what is between the ears is more important than what is between the legs in creating passionate sex. For the most part, we wasted this magnificent opportunity to promote a broader definition of sex and to educate the public about how men can really satisfy their partners—please note, we also failed to mention that some men prefer male partners—with their fingers and tongues, not to mention a little heartfelt imagination.

Sex Therapy Claims to Be a Biopsychosocial Science, But Its Fundamental Conception of Sexuality Is Biologically Based

Notwithstanding current lip service identifying sex therapy as a biopsychosocial science, sex therapy often fails to give due consideration to those aspects of human sexuality that fall outside the purview of biomedical examination and treatment (e.g., the elements that makes some sex hot, erotic, and memorable [Kleinplatz, 1992]). Whereas the biological aspects comprise an integral part of our understanding of sexuality, to allow them to eclipse our view of the individual, relational, and psychosocial dimensions of sexual expression may ultimately prove stultifying to our field. We may be increasingly effective at eliminating biomedical obstacles to normal sexual functioning while contributing little else to improving the quality of sexual relations.

If the biologically based underpinnings of the prevailing sexual paradigms had been previously unacknowledged, that slant is now fully explicit. The marketing of the medical model is big business. During the 1990s, erectile dysfunction came to be defined increasingly as a medical problem, to be treated by urologists. There is a growing trend toward treating sexual problems via medical intervention notwithstanding their origins, meaning, or purpose. For example, "Sildenafil is uniquely designed to treat erectile dysfunction, regardless of etiology" (Rosenberg, 1999, p. 271). In October, 1999, the new "Female Sexual Function Forum" was established to focus on female sexual *dys*function—again, from a primarily medical vantage point.

There has been a dramatically increased focus on sexuopharmaceuticals. Viagra™ has been apparent not merely as a drug but also as a commercial and marketing strategy starring Robert Dole. Its presence has been felt conspicuously in the American Psychological Association's flagship journal, the *American Psychologist*. More importantly, Viagra™ represents an increasingly prevalent mindset, one that suggests that whatever works to produce robust sexual functioning is good, regardless of the meaning of the symptom, the context in which it comes to exist, or the consequences of treating it devoid of that context.

The Focus Is on Parts Rather Than on the People Attached

The treatments of vaginismus and erectile dysfunction provide prime examples of the underlying values of sex therapy. In each, the diagnosis, treatment methods, goals, and outcome criteria illuminate the belief that sex ought to be aimed at intercourse and that whatever interferes with or obstructs intercourse ought to be eliminated. More importantly, these approaches ignore the inner world of the client.

Vaginismus makes for a particularly interesting case in point. It is when sex therapy is most successful that we can most readily discern its underlying values and vision of sexuality. In the treatment of vaginismus, there is much speculation in the literature as to the possible causes of the problem (e.g., inability to verbalize anger [Silverstein, 1989], a history of sexual assault or abuse [LoPiccolo & Stock, 1986], and unresolved feelings of vulnerability or dependence [Pridal & LoPiccolo, 1993]). There is also a clear message that the developmental, intrapsychic, and interpersonal issues are irrelevant for therapy in that treatment is quite effective in reversing the obstacle to intercourse (Leiblum, Pervin, & Campbell, 1989). Indeed, the treatment of vaginismus is said to be virtually 100% effective in reversing the impediment to coitus. (That therapists routinely treat the obstacle to intercourse when a large proportion of women with vaginismus are easily orgasmic without penetration is a conspicuous choice.)

The treatment of vaginismus consists primarily of systematic desensitization to objects in the vagina with the use of graduated, plastic vaginal dilators. The dilators are used to teach patients mastery over their pubococcygeal muscles so that they are able to open and close their vaginas on cue. There is something obscene about this picture. It works, but along the way it conveys the beliefs that heterosexual intercourse is the ultimate end of sex, that performance is more important than feelings, and that the target of treatment is the set of "parts in disrepair" (Tiefer, 1991) rather than the persons within (Kleinplatz, 1998). This is also reflected in our outcome criteria, in which adherence to treatment and frequency tabulations are the norm but satisfaction is rarely assessed (Gregoire, 1990).

Similar arguments can be made for the conventional approach to the treatment of erectile dysfunction, although in this case, at least until recently, the values were more subtly embedded in the treatment paradigm and more difficult to detect. In the treatment of erectile dysfunction our focus tends to be on the penis—that is, on the frequency and firmness of erections rather than the context in which performance on demand is expected. Assessment of erectile dysfunction is regularly conducted without the partner even present. The assumption during the assessment process is that soft penises require treatment. The possibility that any man who functions well would and should be *unable* to get an erection given a particular set of circumstances often is barely considered. Too often, the subjective experience of arousal or lack thereof is not even discussed. If patients wish to engage in sex but do not feel subjectively aroused, why would they have erections? Unfortunately, this distinction often is missed in the assessment process. Perhaps it is not that he is ready for sex and his body is unable to cooperate but that his body may be the best judge of his readiness for sex. The issue is not whether his problem is psychogenic or organic but, rather, whether a problem exists at all. Perhaps there is only evidence of good judgment demonstrated via his body. Too many men are under the impression that they ought to be able to get erections whenever sexual opportunities present themselves. Sex therapists, of course, claim to regard such thinking as erroneous but reinforce this myth every time we treat the symptom with little regard for the message from within that this man may not really want to have intercourse.

The treatment of erectile dysfunction has often been a manifestation of the biomechanical model at its most dehumanizing: Whether by behavioral exercises, suction and constriction devices, intraurethral inserts, intracavernosal injections, or magic blue pills, the aim is to turn the man's penis into a rigid thrusting machine, capable of producing erections on demand, regardless of how he may be feeling about himself, his partner, their relationship, or the demands of the situation. Treatment may succeed in enabling intercourse rather than increasing his sexual pleasure or level of intimacy. Every time treatment succeeds in promoting erections by minimizing, overriding, or "bypassing" the experience of the man attached, we are colluding in dehumanization and reductionism, perpetuating myths we claim to reject, and propping up the phallocracy (Stock, 1988).

As such, the major criterion for effective outcome remains performance. The focus is still on parts, not people; techniques, rather than ways of being in intimate relationships. We continue to focus on symptoms rather than the context in which sex disappoints us and in which we disappoint our sexual partners and vice versa. We are, therefore, still destined to disappoint and be disappointed.

Success Eludes Us Where We Need It Most: Problems Related to Desire.

Because desire does not fit well as a component of our biologically based model of human sexuality, we are unable to get a handle on problems related to desire (i.e., very high desire, very low desire, or very unusual desire). Whatever link may exist among these problems, and particularly their origins, remains poorly understood (Moser, 1992).

Sex therapy traditionally has been weak in treating problems of sexual desire. In Masters and Johnson's initial formulation, desire did not even merit consideration as a component of sexual problems (Kaplan, 1979; Lief, 1977; Zilbergeld & Ellison, 1980). Over the last 20 years or so, lack of sexual desire has been the most common presenting complaint in the offices of sex therapists. A variety of different therapeutic modalities have been employed to deal with it, including cognitive–behavioral, systemic–object relations (Schnarch, 1991), and, most recently, pharmacological (especially hormonal) intervention. Yet low desire remains the least understood and least successfully treated of sexual problems.

This is even more apparent with regard to problems of hypersexual desire/compulsive sexuality/sexual addiction. This category is so contentious we cannot even put a name to it that is agreed upon by common consensus. Each term brings along its own conceptual baggage, including an underlying conception of the problem; its causes, treatments, mode of evaluation, and goals; and even whether or not it actually constitutes a problem. This may be true of many areas within sex therapy, but it is not always so obvious. In this area and in the related area of treatment of paraphilias, our success is limited.

In treatment of low sexual desire, we may have some limited understanding of the nature of the problem, but we do not have an impressive track record in changing it. However, when it comes to the paraphilias (i.e., strong, unusual, typically socially unacceptable, sexual desires), our situation seems to be the reverse: We can control the paraphilic behavior more readily than we can understand the accompanying fantasies or their underlying meaning. It is relatively easy to prevent unwanted sexual behaviors via pharmacological intervention (and even that remains dubious outside a controlled environment); it is much harder to change the underlying sexual desires. Pharmacological intervention may limit the patient's ability to act on his sexual fantasies and may even cut down on their frequency, thus diminishing their "obsessional" character. But the nature of the desires tends to stay the same and remains equally unwanted, even if fantasies crop up less.

Thus, there is a marked lack of success where we need it most, whether in dealing with lack of desire, an excess of desire, or a "misplaced" desire. We are also relatively weak in helping clients find erotic intimacy and fulfillment (presumably the fuel for desire), at least as compared to our level of success in reversing the symptoms of sexual dysfunction and managing, containing, or controlling symptoms of the paraphilias.

The Cutting Edge Is Really More of the Same Old Thing

I foresee two arguments in response to these criticisms: One is that sex therapy is not a monolithic entity. According to this argument, sex therapy is in a post–Masters and Johnson's era, having progressed far beyond our founders' original formulation. In this case, I am merely setting up straw men to be knocked down. Sex therapy now attends to narrative and systemic factors; it includes cognitive, solution-focused, and myriad other interventions plus a post-modern integration of various modalities. The "cutting edge" in sex therapy also involves new medical/pharmacological discoveries and treatments. These include the use of oral medication for erectile dysfunction, laser over scalpel surgery for vulvadynia, selective serotonin reuptake inhibitors, (SSRIs, such as Prozac™) for treatment of rapid ejaculation and the paraphilias, and the increasingly common use of testosterone-replacement therapy for men and women who present with a lack of sexual desire. However, the premises and overall paradigm remain the same, at least if judged by what is found in the literature (i.e., major journals and review articles; see Heiman & Meston, 1997).

The definitions of sex, underlying conceptions of sexuality, and sexual problems are unchanged; the goals of treatment remain the same; our methods of treatment have become more technologically and pharmacologically sophisticated though the major criterion for effective outcome remains performance. We continue to use the stop-start technique and plastic dilators even as we say we have changed.

Leiblum and Schover (1994) bemoan the lack of progress in sex therapy. They criticize sex therapy as a field for not having any new perspectives, any "fresh blood." Maybe the two go together; in the absence of new perspectives, there can only be marginal change in attaining the same old, performance-oriented goals.

One might argue that these criticisms are not fair—that sex therapy has responded to the increasing difficulty and complexity of the cases currently challenging us with more subtle, powerful, complex interventions. Perhaps that is even true. If so, it really ought to be reflected correspondingly in our clinical literature. It is not. While the *need* for more diversified and effective responses to current challenges is discussed widely in the hallways at our conferences, the meeting rooms purvey the same old ideas. The hunger for new models is palpable and is not being met by our literature. According to Wiederman (1998, p. 96), "Although the process of conducting sex therapy may be increasingly complex, the output of theoretical and research advances beyond medical interventions have virtually ceased [Hawton, 1992; Schover & Leiblum, 1994], as has formal theory building."

A second response to the critique above may be that this suggests a return to "general" psychotherapy. This is an attempt to revert to what Masters and Johnson rightly rejected in the 1960s. Well, what is being proposed in this book is neither a newer variation of "the new sex therapy" nor an attempt to resurrect the psychoanalytic approach that predominated in the 1940s and 1950s. It is, instead, a set of attempts, based in a variety of different theoretical perspectives, to understand and deal with sexual issues and concerns in ways that differ not only from the past but also from one another.

☐ Intended Contributions

This book attempts to articulate and examine the assumptions that provide the foundations for the implicit theory and practice of sex therapy. A series of critiques of conventional treatments will be offered, followed by new alternatives to the predominant paradigms.

The goals of this book are to identify some of the problems in the field of sex therapy and to suggest new ways of practice that may provide possible solutions. This book will examine the theoretical underpinnings of the field and aim to improve and strengthen the practice of sex therapy.

That is, this book will contribute to the literature by looking critically at existing sex therapy models and studying their foundations as well as their implications for therapy. Perhaps this collection can advance the theories and practice of sex therapy. The second major goal of this book is to look at other approaches to therapy, alternatives to conventional sex therapy, to see what they can teach us about dealing with sex. This may help to expand or broaden the field of sex therapy.

Another of the objectives of this book is to strengthen and broaden the field by building bridges across paradigms and practitioners of different theoretical orientations (e.g., feminist, experiential, systemic, common factors) and bringing this work together in one volume. There is plenty of literature representing the predominant paradigm. It is relatively difficult for clinicians to locate material that might serve their needs for new alternatives. To my knowledge, no such collection has been available previously.

Some of the advances in the field of sex therapy are not known outside the world of sex therapists. It would be nice if more of those who deal with sex in therapy—that means most therapists—knew about the impressive work being done by sex therapists beyond the cognitive–behavioral or pharmacological approaches that have garnered most of the attention about our field.

It would also be advantageous if we could expand and enrich our field by considering the work being done by expert clinicians, using a variety of therapeutic approaches, whose work lends itself to application by those who specialize in working with sexuality in therapy. We may wish to look at both the work of nonmainstream sex therapists and the work of extraordinary master clinicians whose work has important implications and applications for dealing with sex in therapy. Those outside "sex therapy" may not identify as we do but provide many of the services involving sexual and other problems. They may have a great deal to contribute about how to improve our effectiveness as clinicians. It may be possible for some of their work to be integrated while other aspects may not be compatible. Some of it may cause us to rethink our entire paradigms of sexuality and sex therapy. It may therefore be helpful to practice and practitioners.

Here is a collection of new ways of dealing with sex in therapy. Actually, some of these are not new ways at all, but are new to the field of sex therapy.

Perhaps one of the obstacles to broadening sex therapy has been the notion that it is somehow unique. The belief that dealing with sexuality is intrinsically different from dealing with other human issues and concerns has restricted our field. Perhaps this book can rectify that. In the same vein, many believe that working with gay and lesbian couples in therapy is essentially different from working with heterosexual couples. This book may well demonstrate that there are greater similarities than differences among individuals and couples in therapy regardless of sexual orientation.

One of the intended contributions of this book is that it is theoretically based. Most of the contributors were selected not for their renown in treating a particular sexual dysfunction, disorder, or paraphilia but because of their strong theoretical orientations. These authors have developed and/or applied a particular theoretical perspective to their work. Some focus on dealing with sexual issues. Others deal with broader domains and include sexuality, although not exclusively. It is how the authors conceive of sexuality or psychotherapy, or both, that distinguishes their work, rather than the way they treat a given sexual problem.

☐ For Whom Is This Book Intended?

This book is intended for therapists and counselors of all stripes who want to learn how to work with sexual issues in therapy. It is also targeted toward sex therapists who are looking for new directions in clinical practice. In addition, it may be appropriate for graduate-level courses in human sexuality or sex therapy.

Part of what leads me to believe there is a need for this book is my experience over the last 15 years in giving workshops on sexuality and sex therapy to psychotherapists in general and to sex therapists in particular. Sex therapists are often dismayed at the limited range of options available to them. They seem to have a sense that something is missing and no longer practice that which is described in the current literature, but they have little notion of what the alternatives might be. They are searching for new directions but do not know where to start or what to try. I hope this will affirm and guide them.

Other clinicians may not be particularly keen on dealing with sexuality at all, or at least tend to find the area challenging. It is, however, an everyday necessity in their clinical work. More therapists are forced to deal with problems of a sexual nature that are not necessarily defined as in need of sex therapy or where sex therapy is unavailable. These clinicians may practice marital therapy or work with survivors of sexual assault and childhood sexual abuse (in which the last element of therapy to be dealt with is often sexuality). Their clients may be people with chronic illnesses or depression, overworked two-career couples, infertile couples, those dealing with "women's" issues, and so on. More people today are using psychotropic medications, particularly the SSRIs, which affect sexual desire and functioning. Increased attention also has been focused on improving the quality of life for the disabled. The emergence of HIV/AIDS has affected anxieties, behaviors, and public perceptions of sexuality. Finally, as the baby boomers enter their 50s, we will continue to see an emphasis on sexuality in older people. As such, therapists are confronted increasingly with clients' sexual issues and concerns but often feel ill-equipped to do so. These therapists are not necessarily trained, adept, or inclined to work with such clients. Many of the clinicians I have met in workshops know just enough about conventional sex therapy to find that it does not fit with their existing practices, but they do not know what to do or even to consider instead. This book might fulfill their needs and is intended for these clinicians, too, or perhaps especially.

Finally, in an age of managed care, many clinicians are looking for practical, effective therapy models, yet also want approaches that do more than just eliminate symptoms. The emphasis on empirically validated treatments by both managed-care and our own professional bodies may ignore differences in criteria for *desirable* outcome. As Rosen and Leiblum noted, "Increased accountability and third-party monitoring of all client contacts is rapidly becoming the rule rather than the exception. On the other hand, less attention is being given to the intrinsic quality or appropriateness of treatment services" (1995, p. 14). Concerns about the appropriateness of treatment have only been magnified by the new, sexuopharmaceutical industry, which ostensibly offers rapid, cost-effective relief for sexual problems with little attention to the intrapsychic, interpersonal, and social problems they maintain and enshrine. This book is intended for therapists who have such concerns.

This book, then, is intended for both the novice and the advanced practitioner, for the generalist and specialist and for anyone who wants to work with sex in therapy or to improve his or her practice or even to clarify his or her thinking about his or her practice.

Some readers will identify as sex therapists and will be more than familiar with the jargon, concepts, and problems that are their stock in trade. Others may come from different professional disciplines and will not necessarily know the terms and assumptions common in sex therapy. We have attempted to make this book user-friendly for readers who are relatively inexperienced in dealing with sexuality in psychotherapy.

☐ Organization of the Book

This book has two parts. Immediately following this chapter is a brief look at the chapters included in Part I. The first part is more theoretical, while the second is more clinical/applied in emphasis. The introductory chapters provide critiques of mainstream models of sexuality, or sex therapy, or both. They furnish a rationale for new directions in the field. Following Part I is a preview of the 10 chapters in Part II. The second part of the book offers a series of different approaches to dealing with sexual issues and concerns in therapy. In essence, the authors of Part I will issue a challenge; the response is contained in Part II.

The six chapters that comprise Part I examine various aspects of the conventional model—for example, its goals, methods, underlying assumptions, and conceptions. They point toward and demonstrate the need for alternate paradigms. Some authors discuss the models in general (e.g., Leonore Tiefer, Ph.D., examines the existing paradigm from a feminist perspective) while others explore one specific aspect (e.g., Chapter 6 focuses on the goals of sex therapy).

The chapters in Part II consist of clinicians' descriptions of how they work with sexual issues in therapy. The focus is dealing with sexual concerns (e.g., seeking more passion, intimacy, and authenticity in sexual relationships) rather than "treating sexual dysfunctions and pathology." Some of the contributors identify as sex therapists (e.g., Marny Hall, Ph.D.) but do not practice the mainstream variety. Others, such as Alvin R. Mahrer, Ph.D., are renowned as "general" therapists (rather than card-carrying sex therapists) whose work has important implications and applications for dealing with sexual matters.

Each chapter in Part II is organized around the authors' therapeutic orientation. The clinical chapters contain brief theoretical rationales for the authors' approaches. Most discuss how their work differs from the predominant paradigm. In order to make the approach in action more readily accessible, each author has provided either a case illustration or a series of clinical vignettes of individual, couple, or group therapy. Clinical material is presented with either informed consent or with identifying details changed to protect confidentiality (see Clifft, 1986).

☐ References

Apfelbaum, B. (1995). Masters and Johnson revisited: A case of desire disparity. In R. C. Rosen & S. R. Leiblum (Eds.), *Case studies in sex therapy* (pp. 23–45). New York: Guilford.
Bullough, V. L. (1994). *Science in the bedroom: A history of sex research.* New York: Basic Books.
Buss, D. V. (1998). Sexual strategies theory: Historical origins and current status. *Journal of Sex Research, 35*(1), 19–31.
Butler, J. (1990). *Gender trouble: Feminism and the subversion of identity.* New York: Routledge.
Butler, J. (1993). *Bodies that matter: On the discursive limits of "sex."* New York: Routledge.
Califia, P. (1994). *Public sex: The culture of radical sex.* San Francisco: Cleis.
Carnes, P. (1983). *Out of the shadows: Understanding sexual addiction.* Minneapolis: CompCare.
Carnes, P. (1991). *Don't call it love.* New York: Bantam.

Christina, G. (1992). Are we having sex now or what? In D. Steinberg (Ed.), *The erotic impulse: Honoring the sensual self* (pp.24–29). Los Angeles: Putnam.

Clifft, M. A. (1986). Writing about psychiatric patients: Guidelines for disguising case material. *Bulletin of the Menninger Clinic, 50*(6), 511–524.

Darling, C. A., & Davidson, J. K. (1986). Enhancing relationships: Understanding the feminine mystique of pretending orgasm. *Journal of Sex & Marital Therapy, 12*(3), 182–196.

Dimen, M. (1989). Politically correct? Politically incorrect? In C. S. Vance (Ed.), *Pleasure and danger: Exploring female sexuality* (pp. 138–148). London: Pandora.

Dimen, M. (1995). On "Our nature": Prolegomenon to a relational theory of sexuality. In T. Domenici & R. C. Lesser (Eds.), *Disorienting sexuality* (pp. 129–152). New York: Routledge.

Dworkin, A. (1987). *Intercourse.* New York: Free Press Paperbacks.

Dychtwald, K. (1979). Sexuality and the whole person. *Journal of Humanistic Psychology, 19*(2), 47–61.

Feurstein, G. (1989). *Enlightened sexuality: Essays on body-positive spirituality.* Freedom, CA: Crossing Press.

Feurstein, G. (1992). *Sacred sexuality: Living the vision of the erotic spirit.* New York: Jeremy P. Tarcher.

Foucault, M. (1980). *The history of sexuality* (Vol. 1, R. Hurley, Trans.). New York: Vintage.

Geer, J. H., & O'Donohue, W. E. (1987). *Theories of human sexuality.* New York: Plenum.

Gregoire, A. (1990). Physical vs. psychological: A need for an integrated approach. *Sexual and Marital Therapy, 5*(2), 101–104.

Hastings, A. S. (1998). *Treating sexual shame: A new map for overcoming dysfunction, abuse, and addiction.* Northvale, NJ: Jason Aronson.

Hawton, K. (1992). Sex therapy research: Has it withered on the vine? *Annual Review of Sex Research, 3,* 49–72.

Heiman, J. R., & Meston, C. M. (1997). Empirically validated treatment for sexual dysfunction. *Annual Review of Sex Research, VIII,* 148–194.

Helminiak, D. A. (1996). *The human core of spirituality: Mind as psyche and spirit.* Albany: State University of New York Press.

Hollibaugh, A. (1989). Desire for the future: Radical hope in passion and pleasure. In C. F. Vance (Ed.), *Pleasure and danger: Exploring female sexuality* (pp. 401–410). London: Pandora.

Irvine, J. A. (1990). *Disorders of desire: Sex and gender in modern American sexology.* Philadelphia: Temple University Press.

Jeffries, S. (1990). *Anticlimax: A feminist perspective on the sexual revolution.* London, UK: The Women's Press.

Kaplan, H. S. (1974). *The new sex therapy.* New York: Brunner/Mazel.

Kaplan, H. S. (1979). *Disorders of sexual desire and other new concepts and techniques in sex therapy.* New York: Brunner/Mazel.

Kaplan, H. S. (1987). *The illustrated manual of sex therapy* (2nd ed.). New York: Brunner/ Mazel.

Keen, S. (1979). Some ludicrous theses about sexuality. *Journal of Humanistic Psychology, 19*(2), 15–22.

Keen, S. (1992). *The passionate life: Stages of loving.* New York: HarperCollins.

Kleinplatz, P. J. (1992). The erotic experience and the intent to arouse. *Canadian Journal of Human Sexuality, 1*(3), 133–139.

Kleinplatz, P. J. (1996). Transforming sex therapy: Integrating erotic potential. *The Humanistic Psychologist, 24*(2), 190–202.

Kleinplatz, P. J. (1998). Sex therapy for vaginismus: A review, critique and humanistic alternative. *Journal of Humanistic Psychology, 38*(2), 51–81.

Leiblum, S. R., Pervin, L. A., & Campbell, E. H. (1989). The treatment of vaginismus: Success and failure. In S. R. Leiblum & R. C. Rosen (Eds.), *Principles and practice of sex therapy: Update for the 1990s* (pp. 113–138). New York: Guilford.

Leiblum, S. R., & Rosen, R. C. (1989). Introduction: Sex therapy in the age of AIDS. In S. R. Leiblum & R. C. Rosen (Eds.), *Principles and practice of sex therapy: Update for the 1990s* (pp. 1–18). New York: Guilford Press.

Leiblum, S. R., & Schover, L. R. (1994). Commentary: The stagnation of sex therapy. *Journal of Psychology and Human Sexuality, 6*(3), 5–30.

Lief, H. I. (1977). Inhibited sexual desire. *Medical Aspects of Human Sexuality, 7*, 94–95.

Livia, A. (1995). Tongues and fingers. In K. Jay (Ed.), *Lesbian erotics* (pp. 40–52). New York: New York University Press.

LoPiccolo, J., & Stock, W. E. (1986). Treatment of sexual dysfunction. *Journal of Consulting and Clinical Psychology, 54*(2), 158–167.

Mahrer, A. R. (2000). Philosophy of science and the foundations of psychotherapy. *American Psychology, 55*(10), 1117–1125.

Masters, W. H., & Johnson, V. E. (1966). *Human sexual response.* Boston: Little, Brown.

Masters, W. H., & Johnson, V. E. (1970). *Human sexual inadequacy.* New York: Bantam Books.

Masters, W. H., & Johnson, V. E. (1979). *Homosexuality in perspective.* Boston: Little, Brown.

Masters, W. H., & Johnson, V. E. (1986). *Sex therapy on its twenty-fifth anniversary: Why it survives.* St. Louis: Masters and Johnson Institute.

Moser, C. (1992). Lust, lack of desire, and paraphilias: Some thoughts and possible connections. *Journal of Sex & Marital Therapy, 18*(1), 65–69.

Murray, S. O. (1999). Widely plausible deniability. *Sexualities, 2*(2), 252–255.

Nelson, J. B. (1978). *Embodiment: An approach to sexuality and Christian theology.* Minneapolis: Augsburg Publishing.

Nelson, J. B., & Longfellow, S. P. (1994). *Sexuality and the sacred: Sources for theological reflection.* Louisville, KY: Westminster/John Knox Press.

Nicolson, P. (1993). Public values and private beliefs: Why do women refer themselves for sex therapy? In J. M. Ussher & C. D. Baker (Eds.), *Psychological perspectives on sexual problems: New directions in theory and practice* (pp. 56–76). New York: Routledge.

Pridal, C. G., & LoPiccolo, J. (1993). Brief treatment of vaginismus. In R. A. Wells & V. J. Gianetti (Eds.), *Casebook of the brief psychotherapies* (pp. 329–245). New York: Plenum Press.

Reiss, I. L. (1990). *An end to shame: Shaping our next sexual revolution.* New York: Prometheus Books.

Richardson, D. (1996). Constructing lesbian sexuality. In S. Jackson & S. Scott (Eds.), *Feminism and sexuality: A reader* (pp. 276–286). New York: Columbia University Press.

Rofes, E. (1996). *Reviving the tribe: Regenerating gay men's sexuality and culture in the ongoing epidemic.* New York: Haworth Press.

Rofes, E. (1998). *Dry bones breathe: Gay men creating post-AIDS identities and cultures.* New York: Haworth Press.

Rosen, R. C., & Leiblum, S. R. (1995). The changing focus of sex therapy. In R.C. Rosen & S. R. Leiblum (Eds.), *Case studies in sex therapy* (pp.3–17). New York: Guilford.

Rosenberg, K. (1999). Sildenafil. *Journal of Sex & Marital Therapy, 25*(4), 271–279.

Schnarch, D. (1991). *Constructing the sexual crucible: An integration of sexual and marital therapy.* New York: Norton.

Shrage, L. (1999). Do lesbian prostitutes have sex with their clients? A Clintonesque reply. *Sexualities, 2*(2), 259–261.

Silverstein, J. A. (1989). Origins of psychogenic vaginismus. *Psychotherapy and Psychosomatics, 52*, 197–204.

Simon, W. (1996). *Postmodern sexualities.* New York: Routledge.

Steinberg, D. (1992). *The erotic impulse: Honoring the sensual self.* Los Angeles: Putnam.

Stock, W. (1988). Propping up the phallocracy: A feminist critique of sex therapy and research. *Women and Therapy, 7*(2/3), 23–41.

Tiefer, L. (1991). Historical, scientific, clinical and feminist criticisms of "The Human Sexual Response Cycle" model. *Annual Review of Sex Research, II,* 1–24.

Tiefer, L. (1994). Introduction: Schover and Leiblum call for reform. *Journal of Psychology and Human Sexuality, 6*(3), 1–4.

Tiefer, L. (1996). The medicalization of sexuality: Conceptual, normative, and professional issues. *Annual Review of Sex Research, VII,* 252–282.

Ussher, J. M. (1993). The construction of female sexual problems: Regulating sex, regulating woman. In J. M. Ussher & C. D. Baker (Eds.), *Psychological perspectives on sexual problems: New directions in theory and practice* (pp. 10–40). New York: Routledge.

Weeks, J. (1985). *Sexuality and its discontents.* New York: Routledge.

Wiederman, M. (1998). The state of theory in sex therapy. *Journal of Sex Research, 35*(1), 88–99.

Zilbergeld, B. (1992). *The new male sexuality.* New York: Bantam Books.

Zilbergeld, B., & Ellison, C. R. (1980). Desire discrepancies and arousal problems in sex therapy. In S. R. Leiblum & L. A. Pervin (Eds.), *Principles and practice of sex therapy* (pp. 65–101). New York: Guilford Press.

I

CRITIQUES OF CONVENTIONAL MODELS OF SEX THERAPY

☐ The Critiques and Their Implications

Bernard Apfelbaum, Ph.D., has an impressive ability to make sex therapists take a fresh and closer look at what we thought we already knew. In Chapter 1, he encourages us to look again at performance anxiety. The belief that we ought to be capable of sexual response even in the face of adverse conditions continues to affect not only our patients but ourselves. It makes it harder to detect the extent to which our patients are handicapped by the expectation of automatic performance when we share their expectations. Apfelbaum highlights how sex therapists help to reinforce rather than reduce performance anxiety by accepting conventional expectations of "normal" sexual behavior.

Apfelbaum suggests that Masters and Johnson's original attempt to combat "goal-directedness" in sex has been misunderstood and undermined by the continuing goal-directedness among sex therapists. Specifically, he critiques the work of Helen Singer Kaplan and that of the behavioral sex therapists. He claims that the subtlety of Masters and Johnson's "breakthrough" is lost today upon those who continue to focus on technique while simultaneously thinking that they comprehend Masters and Johnson. Although Apfelbaum focuses on their contributions, it is his own unique insights and subtle distinctions that merit considerable attention. He untangles the fuzzy thinking in our field about sexual performance, nonintimate sex, and sexual connection. Apfelbaum may be too humble to take credit for his own innovative perspective.

Perhaps the most powerful and persistent criticisms of conventional sex therapy come from feminist theorists and clinicians. For more than 20 years, Leonore Tiefer, Ph.D., has provided an extraordinarily articulate and incisive voice in the feminist discourse in sexology. In Chapter 2, Tiefer offers a brief history of feminist perspectives on sex therapy and the resistance within mainstream sex therapy to incorporating these ideas. She examines the cultural and political context in which sex-negative ideas have been adopted more readily than the sex-positive feminists' alternatives. It has clearly been easier for a young field courting public acceptability—not to mention funding—to assume the mantle of medicalization than to acknowledge and contend with the validity of feminist concerns. She critiques the medical model as advocating positions diametrically opposed to the interests of women. Tiefer advances a new, feminist program for our field that includes new conceptualizations, new research and applied methods, and outreach to broader audiences. In keeping with feminist principles, she suggests that if sexual problems do not merely reside in the individual but are constructed in social context, perhaps the ideal domain for feminist intervention is in our communities.

The feminist literature has been helpful in focusing attention on the social construction of female sexuality. The relative silence on the social construction of male sexuality is the focus of Gary R. Brooks, Ph.D., in Chapter 3. Brooks uses two of the major media stories of 1999 as jumping off points to illustrate his contention that the cultural context in which male sexuality exists is conspicuously absent from the dominant discourse. He begins by examining the public and professional discussions concerning Viagra™ and sexual dysfunction, and then moves on to the Clinton-Lewinsky scandal. He points out that the missing voices in these discourses tell us a great deal about the dominant conceptions of male sexuality. They reveal a public stance, sometimes found among sex therapists, in which performance demands are invoked rather than refuted. He suggests that the socialization process in which men's emotions are cut off from their sexuality creates nonrelational sexuality among men. The solution, to promote sexual integrity/integration, is obscured when we focus only on the symptoms of sexual dysfunction or on public misbehavior. Brooks argues that we must advance broad cultural change; furthermore, sex therapy must include ways to help men become aware of and respond to their needs for intimacy.

Some of the major questions with regard to human sexuality have rarely been asked, let alone answered. Just one of these questions, posed in Chapter 4, concerns the nature of distress or suffering in the realm of sexuality. What is it, exactly, that we are trying to heal? From what vantage points have we attempted to grapple with this issue? In this chapter, Christopher Aanstoos, Ph.D., suggests that we may require another perspective if we are to gain a deeper understanding of our clients' sexual disappointments, hopes, and dreams. Aanstoos argues that the mechanistic, objectifying approaches to sexuality prevalent in our field have failed to illuminate the uniquely human dimension of lived sexual experience. Sexual science has often situated the body as the unit of study with little emphasis on embodied sexuality. It is as though subjective meaning and context have been extricated from our analysis. He invites us to let go of our abstractions and reminds us of the primal nature of human touch and of the immediacy of erotic encounter. Aanstoos presents us with a phenomenological model of human sexuality. The implication for clinicians is that we may want to try to heal the diminished capacity for erotic openness, mutual resonance, and the ability to be present to and with our partners. His way of thinking about and discussing sexuality is more reminiscent of the perspectives of poets, musicians, and choreographers than it is of sex therapists and is inconsistent with most of our work. We may want to consider changing that.

One premise implicit in the existence of therapy for sexual problems is the idea that we have some notion of what is problematic and what is not. Certainly, our treatment paradigms and our classification of sexual disorders imply a solid conception of "normal" versus "abnormal" sexuality. The theoretical and clinical value of a particular category within our taxonomy of sexual pathology (i.e., atypical erotic interests) is questioned in Chapter 5. Some of the more unusual sexual behaviors (not to mention some rather popular ones) have been variously known as sins, crimes, abominations against nature, perversions, deviations, variations, eccentricities, temptations, and affronts to good taste. At present, the fantasies and urges our society finds especially distasteful are referred to collectively as the *paraphilias*. Chapter 5 deals with this construct as defined in the *DSM-IV* and questions its utility for our field. Charles Moser, Ph.D., M.D., examines the history of the concept and its presence in various incarnations in the previous and current *DSM* editions. For example, one of our assumptions is that the paraphilias constitute a unitary, discrete, and distinct entity. Moser challenges this belief, questioning the commonalities and differences among intense interests in cross-dressing, in having sex with animals, large-breasted women, and with multiple sexual partners. While acknowledging that some behaviors and desires are more disturbing than others for individuals, their partners, and society, Moser evaluates our basis for identifying them as pathological. He articulates the unacknowledged overlay of moral and legal judgments in a nosology that is allegedly value-free. His analysis concludes with a proposal for an alternate set of diagnostic criteria.

The most fundamental aspect of all therapy is almost certainly its goals. Its methods, moment-by-moment interventions, and objectives as well as its criteria for effective outcome are predicated on its ultimate aims. In Chapter 6, I will take issue with how little sex therapy seeks to achieve, arguing that the parameters of what can be accomplished in sex therapy are already circumscribed for the individual or couple before even entering the therapist's office. The limits of our work will be linked to our underlying values and vision of sexuality; our acting as agents of social stability rather than social change; our willingness to settle for reversal or control of problematic sexual symptoms rather than aiming for profound change, generated from within; our opting for normative sexual relations rather than attempting to optimize erotic potential; and our reluctance to embrace sexual diversity. I will also discuss the need for an alternate set of goals that promote discovery, uniqueness, sexual connection, and the possibility of transformation. The implications of such changes in goals for clinical practice will be suggested. I will also recommend that we increase support of comprehensive sexual education and intensify our work in social advocacy so as to change the public discourse, thereby preventing sexual problems.

Bernard Apfelbaum, Ph.D.

What the Sex Therapies Tell Us About Sex

This is the story as it has thus far unfolded of our efforts to understand sex through the systematic treatment of sex problems.

The period before the publication of Masters and Johnson's *Human Sexual Inadequacy* (1970), beginning in the 1920s, can be thought of as "the era of sexual technique." It was marked by the popularity of instructional manuals (the "marriage manuals") whose principal purpose—in reaction to then-customary, one-sided, male-dominant sex—was to promote sexual mutuality by sensitizing men to women's sexuality. The effect was to raise expectations about both female and male sexuality.

Masters and Johnson exposed the ways this technique approach made us especially vulnerable to "performance anxiety." This mild term has been fatefully misleading. It does not begin to convey the paralyzing shame and humiliation to which we are susceptible in sex, and the panic and grief at the possibility of alienating our lover or mate, perhaps permanently.

If sex does not happen in the expected way we accuse ourselves, or are accused by our lovers, of being impotent (weak, unmanly), frigid (cold, withholding), uncaring, or even hostile. This makes what happens in bed a test of our adequacy as men and women, of our love, and even of our fidelity. When we think of making love, these formidable hazards are far from our minds. Sex seems simply to be our great opportunity to luxuriate in the senses, to be intimate, and to feel loved. In their book based on sex therapy with more than 800 couples, the Zussmans wrote that in sex, "There are no standards to meet, no goals that must be reached, no rules except a responsibility to not hurt others or to allow yourself to be hurt" (1979, p. 12). Few people would question this statement.

Undoubtedly all of the Zussmans' couples experienced sex as full of standards, goals, and rules, but equally undoubtedly all of them would agree that they shouldn't have. By what trick of the mind are we able to deny the reality that in sex our adequacy is on the line? The answer is that we all think that, if we feel tested in bed, it's our own fault. *Sex* is natural, it's just that *we aren't.*

The term performance anxiety itself embodies our paradoxical thinking about sex. We think that relaxing and letting go should be all there is to it, yet if sex does not happen in the expected way, we say that the person can't *perform.* We can hardly talk about sex without referring to it as a performance. To say that a man's erection went away, rather than that he lost it, sounds odd, despite being a more objective description.

Performance anxiety means, in common usage, the fear of sexual performance failure. It should be understood, instead, to refer to anxiety created by experiencing sex *as* a performance. Most often it generates performance "success" (Apfelbaum, 1977).

Our most compelling motive is to be adequate in our socially defined roles. It is far more pressing than the motives Freud considered basic: aggression and sex. That is why, in sex, libido yields to ego. In sex there is no place to hide; we can feel that our essential nature as men or women is exposed. (I should say there is *almost* no place to hide, as there is some evidence that a majority of American women have faked orgasm.)

When Masters and Johnson brought performance anxiety to everyone's attention, the reaction was not to appreciate how stressful sex can be, but instead to think that people are ruining a good thing. Performance anxiety was treated as something to get over, rather than as a profound insight. We now had to feel ashamed of letting it affect us, creating performance-anxiety anxiety (Apfelbaum, 1984).

The authors of the sex manuals showed no awareness of the possibility that requiring men to master sexual technique could create a new test of adequacy, or that it could make women feel pressured to help men succeed. Similarly, psychotherapists of the time were unaware of the way they reinforced rather than relieved their patients' fears of sexual inadequacy. Typically, they shared their male patients' belief that erection problems signified a failure to fulfill the male role, and their female patients' belief that difficulty reaching orgasm signified a failure to fulfill the female role, stigmatizing them further by diagnosing such "failures" as signs of developmental arrests—that is, as immaturity. (A woman was to demonstrate her sexual adequacy by "surrendering" to the adequate male, who demonstrated his adequacy by sexual aggressiveness.) The recognition that it was the sex roles themselves that their patients suffered from had to await the rise of feminism and necessitated the development of a sex therapy separate from the psychotherapeutic mainstream.

Therapists had made sex problems worse, reinforcing their patients' crippling fears about themselves by confirming the belief that these symptoms represented profound character defects. The result was that a symptom such as premature ejaculation—now eminently relievable in brief therapy—was considered a deep-seated preoedipal disorder, requiring long-term intensive treatment—and, even with that, the prognosis was poor.

Performance anxiety seems obvious. Of course anyone will be anxious if he or she cannot perform. Until Masters and Johnson's work, however, no one had any way to realize that performance anxiety was the cause of sex problems, not just the consequence. It means experiencing the absence of signs of arousal as a failure. It expresses our urgent need for these signs to appear and to be sustained *as the situation calls for it*. Whether a person is feeling sufficiently aroused, passionate, or even relaxed is irrelevant. Our closely scripted expectations of ourselves and our partners are made binding by the belief that they simply reflect the natural expression of our bodily programming.

Since performance anxiety seems obvious, it is all the more difficult to grasp its subtle forms. For example, imagine a shy young man who is still a virgin because of performance anxiety—panic is a better word. A familiar, commonsense remedy would have him introduced to sex by an experienced and patient older woman. Everyone thinks this is his big chance, that he now has nothing to worry about and can simply let nature take its course.

Before Masters and Johnson, no one dreamed that this approach was fated to intensify performance anxiety. It did not occur to anyone that the young man *himself* would have to think this was his big chance, that he now should have nothing to worry about, and that he could let nature take its course. Now there is no excuse for "failure." It's now or never in his mind—the ultimate test of his manhood, his virility. If he doesn't pass the test, he's doomed.

There was no way this remedy could fail. Only the man himself could fail. If it did not succeed, as it often did not, he was written off as a failure, just as he feared.

A man who does not have erections when we expect him to is called not *potent*. This label alone makes it unmistakable that his adequacy as a man is at stake, that he is at risk for terrible shame. But how could we see that when we all shared his view?

Performance anxiety can be so subtle that it has a hold even on the thinking of many sex therapists. For example, on the lists of causes of loss of sexual desire we always see career stress, burnout, bereavement, and other psychological trauma. No one questions this. Yet I once treated a patient with a bipolar disorder who said that he desperately needed help with a sex problem because he was afraid that, without sex, he would end up back in the hospital. For him sex was the tonic needed to relieve his depression.

Sex for him meant *reassurance*, whereas for most of the rest of us it means *performance*. It represents what Masters and Johnson called a "performance demand." This was a brand new concept for the very reason that it never occurred to us to think about sex any other way. That is why we all think depression interferes with sex, rather than thinking that *if* it does, this means that sex is a demand rather than a relief from demands.

If this is not immediately convincing, think of masturbation. Does losing your job result in losing your desire to masturbate (at least if you are a man)? Possibly, but not necessarily. It is at least equally likely that you will have an increased desire to masturbate. In fact, no one has suggested that stress or depression eliminate the desire to masturbate. Why not? Because you do not have to be up for it; there is nothing to prove.

To the extent that a man is susceptible to male role expectations, he will try to avoid sex when he is depressed or preoccupied or just does not feel up to it. In other words, he will avoid sex when he needs reassurance and support. If and when he cannot find a way to avoid it, he will be "unable to perform."

Another example of how difficult it can be to detect performance anxiety is the man who is made anxious when his female partner initiates sex. A dramatic instance of this kind was presented at a conference on surrogates. A therapist said that one of the woman with whom he had attempted to work "was, curiously, *too* responsive. She was so volcanically orgasmic that she literally scared hell out of the men and they fled."

These men were seen as literally afraid of this woman's sexual responsiveness. The audience laughed when this story was told. They saw only a passionate woman, just what any man would want. What could there be to be afraid of?

These people were all in the sex field, and even they did not realize that this woman's "volcanic sexuality" created an intense performance demand. But it often is the case that people in the sex field, those who see themselves as "sex-positive" and as sexually liberated, are least able to grasp the role of performance anxiety. I think this is because they experience intense performance anxiety themselves, although of the most subtle kind. The way it manifests in them is by feeling *proud* of being sexually free. This means they would be ashamed of any hesitation to respond sexually, much less of any inhibition or sex problem.

Their preoccupation with sexual performance had blinded them to the emotional impact of this surrogate's way of relating to her patients. She was able to be volcanically reactive *despite* her patient's intense anxiety. She must have been able to completely ignore them. Otherwise, their anxiety would have been contagious. What no one notices, least of all the man himself, is the impact of being ignored.

At a sex conference in Montreal, a study was presented of a woman with sex problems who was asked to draw what she was afraid of in sex. The outcome expected from this Catholic woman was a picture of a priest, a crucifix, a confession box, a frowning parent, or possibly even a lightning bolt. Instead she drew a truck, a phone, and a stereo.

I ask therapists attending sex therapy seminars I conduct what these objects had in common—what this woman intended to signify. They invariably are puzzled.

What these objects had in common for the woman who drew them was that they were distractions. She was afraid they would disturb her concentration and turn her off sexually. The operative word here is *afraid*, although she herself would probably not have known she was suffering from performance anxiety. All she knew was that she was afraid of distractions. Clearly, for her sex was a grim struggle to avoid the stigma of inadequacy, but it is unlikely she would have realized that this itself was her problem—that she was inhibited by this fear. Like the rest of us, especially before Masters and Johnson, she would just be afraid she was inadequate.

Even supposing that her Catholicism did inhibit her, it would only be a problem if this effect was locked in by performance anxiety. If she was not feeling inadequate about being inhibited, sex would gradually become a source of reassurance, that is, assuming an unanxious partner. We owe to Masters and Johnson the insight that what we ordinarily think are the causes of sex problems are only secondarily so. They do not create sex problems unless they are *potentiated* by performance anxiety. This point is made especially clear by the following case.

☐ Marian and Debbie

Marian and Debbie were a lesbian couple seen once for a 3-hour session. Marian was a 46-year-old lawyer; Debbie was a 34-year-old elementary school teacher. They had known each other for a year and a half. Marian had lost all desire for sex just after she and Debbie began living together a year before, although she had been very active sexually up to that time.

Neither Marian nor Debbie appeared at all conflicted about their sexual orientation, although they had markedly different sexual lifestyles. Marian engaged in sex without commitment: one-night stands and multiple relationships. Debbie was strictly monogamous. Except for Marian, she had never had sex with someone with whom she was not living.

Marian: (*This is how she described her symptom, from an audiotape transcript.*) Whenever Debbie comes at me (*note her words*) it's instant anxiety and instant shut-off and fear. Otherwise everything is fine. We can say anything to one another and we give each other a lot of support. I've never been so open. I trust Debbie more than I've ever trusted anyone.

It's just all physical-contact related. I lost all desire for sex. It seemed weird for me never to even think about it. It bugged me no end. I've never not had first-rate sex. And at first it was really good with Debbie, too. We both initiated it and we both were very involved.

Debbie: Now we just go to bed and hold one another, and that's the only time we have physical contact. We've done communication exercises and sensate focus exercises, and everything we do only seems to make Marian more anxious.

Debbie added that she had not given up making overtures, but Marian always reacted the same way.

They had thought a lot about the problem and had done a lot of talking, arriving at several convincing explanations. Just before they moved in together, Marian had gotten sick and become bedridden. Debbie still wanted sex, and they had fought about it. Marian accused Debbie of being uncaring and selfish. They had had full-fledged sexual encounters only two or three times after that, and not at all since they moved in together.

They also agreed that Marian had a lot of unfinished business with her mother, and that in many ways Debbie reminded Marian of her mother. Debbie had met Marian's mother and thought she was, in fact, a lot like her, adding that she often thinks Marian is relating to her mother and not to her. She said that Marian's mother is very physical, too—always touching people—and that Marian hated being touched by her. Because of this reaction, Marian's mother accused her of being cold, selfish, and unloving. As if that was not enough, Marian's younger brother, who was seen as warm and affectionate, had been killed in an accident and sanctified.

They presented yet another explanation: Marian's fear of intimacy. All of Marian's live-in relationships had predated the last 10 years. Marian had lived alone for the past 10 years and seemed to enjoy it. She agreed with Debbie that she was afraid of intimacy and said she was panicked at the prospect of living with someone again.

They also described a pronounced clash of styles. Marian said she had a big thing about privacy and separation, whereas Debbie had a big thing about sharing everything, including the mail and the towels. Debbie was amused that Marian thought she needed a separate towel.

Marian and Debbie topped off this analytic tour de force with yet another compelling explanation. They spoke of a power struggle that went on in their sexual relationship.

Marian: I would just start doing my thing and I'd get interrupted, *boom*! It felt like a power struggle. I felt like she was being stubborn, and I complained, but Debbie said that she was just being spontaneous, and I had no answer for that. Also, I felt I'd left roles behind and now it looked like maybe I wanted the masculine role.

In other words, in their previous relationships both of them had been active and aggressive sex partners—pursuer meets pursuer. Marian gave in, but she was in an unaccustomed role. She felt frustrated and unappreciated.

These are all the facts of the case, everything you need to know to arrive at a diagnosis and a solution.

The formulation most therapists arrive at, based on this information, is that Marian's symptom was an expression of unconscious anger directed both at Debbie and at her mother. They note that Marian was angry at Debbie for "coming on to her" when she was sick, as well as for being intrusive—insensitive to Marian's boundaries—just as her mother was. Also noted is Marian's resentment of Debbie's sexual aggressiveness, and of Debbie not appreciating her as a lover.

Marian is described as being too angry at Debbie to respond sexually, or as being passive-aggressively retaliatory. Some describe her as "refusing to respond" or as "holding on" to her anger. This is the standard psychodynamic model. In the work of Helen Singer Kaplan, considered by many the dominant figure in the field of sex therapy, this preexisting model has now displaced Masters and Johnson's contribution. Kaplan's core conception of sexual apathy is of a *resistance* to responding sexually.

These interpretations take no note of Marian's experience of "instant anxiety and instant shut-off and fear." This distress is either overlooked, because it is assumed to be her natural reaction to feeling apathetic, or discounted in accordance with the psychoanalytic precept that what patients most loudly complain of is what they secretly most desire. In that perspective, Marian's anxiety about not feeling sexually responsive to Debbie is seen as the conscious denial of an unconscious wish to frustrate and deprive her.

Masters and Johnson (as well as cognitive therapists) came to recognize that the patient's distress, far from being the side effect of a problem, is the "royal road" to its cause. However, to simply announce to Marian that her problem is caused by performance anxiety would mean nothing to her and could even seem to trivialize the problem.

Marian and Debbie themselves gave little thought to Marian's acute distress when Debbie approached her sexually, assuming it was a natural alarm about feeling apathetic. They also saw no special significance in the fact, reported by Debbie that "everything we do only seems to make Marian more anxious." Performance anxiety can be right in front of you, only to be overlooked or explained away.

I needed to show Marian how performance anxiety caused her condition, being inevitably intensified by the couple's interpretations and attempted solutions. I began making my case by suggesting that all the factors they had recognized were pathogenic only insofar as they prevented Marian from responding *positively* to Debbie.

I suggested that in her previous relationships Marian had avoided this anxiety about not being able to respond positively by always being the initiator and the active partner. She had developed her identity with an eye to not being the cold, rejecting person she felt herself to be with her mother. She had tried to solve the problem by being, in effect, like her mother. It was only when Debbie forced her into the passive role ("*boom!*"), that she had to reexperience the problem she had never truly solved. Suddenly she was back where she had been with her mother. She still could not cope with feeling unresponsive.

The reason they had missed this seemingly obvious repetition of the original trauma was that they assumed Marian *had to get over it*. But Marian had spent her whole life trying to get over it. She had proved many times over that she was not the monster she felt herself to be with her mother. But she still had no way to recognize that the coldness she felt when her *mother* "came at her, boom" was in any way justified. She was far from being able to have any complaint about how her mother not only made her feel molested rather than nurtured, but also invalidated that experience. In their natural assumption that she had to get over this experience, Marian and Debbie were invalidating it, just as her mother had.

The therapeutic operation was to use the past to validate rather than invalidate Marian's experience in the present. She needed to see how her experience with her mother sensitized her to the ways Debbie ignored and abandoned her even while seeming to invite emotional contact. In a word, she needed to feel *entitled* to the experience of not responding positively to

Debbie's advances.

The one instance in which Marian did feel entitled to be unresponsive was when she was sick. Then she was able to say that Debbie was being uncaring and selfish—in effect, that Debbie was turning her off. (Notice how difficult it would be to arrive at this formulation if your diagnosis was that Marian was turning *herself* off.) Without this justification, she had to feel performance anxiety.

Marian reviewed her experience of "instant anxiety and instant shut-off and fear" in response to Debbie's "coming at her." My analysis made it possible for her to recognize what "coming at her" expressed. It was like a sudden onslaught. When Debbie approached her, Marian felt that it had nothing to do with *her*—which made her feel like a sex object. It suddenly seemed obvious to Marian that in "coming on" to her, it felt like Debbie was oblivious to her grief. Having her experience understood and validated in this way immediately animated Marian, which I took as a sign that her apathy was on its way out.

I then asked Debbie how she was able to feel aroused with Marian when Marian was feeling so unaroused and either anxious or apathetic. Why wasn't she brought down by Marian's suffering? She said she wasn't particularly aroused, but she didn't want to give up on Marian. Also she thought that by being consistently aggressive she might overcome what she thought of as Marian's resistance to being aroused. She added that Marian hardly showed her anxiety, still managing to project the warm, seductive, motherly image that had attracted Debbie to her. Marian was the parental sort, and it is this role she expected to have with Debbie, 12 years her junior.

Marian was rejecting her unwanted self, the self that felt abandoned by her mother. For Marian's apathy to lift, she needed to connect with this disowned experience. If she was to no longer feel objectified, she needed to get this experience across to Debbie and to feel that this did not dampen Debbie's ardor.

This required helping Marian to have the experience she was warding off, rather than trying to get her to have a different experience. But it is common practice to take Marian's response as simply an absence of the right response. Understood that way, the goal would have been to have her move from apathy to pleasure. This goal necessitates heavy treatment pressure, which accounts, I believe, for the widespread impression that such cases are especially difficult to treat.

The solution was for Marian to feel that her disowned experience could be included in their lovemaking. Toward this end I had her recall how she felt when she was sick and Debbie made sexual advances, and also how she felt when sexually overpowered by Debbie. We sorted this experience into sayable bits, arriving at these five statements:

"Now I'm feeling pressured."

"Now I'm afraid you'll feel rejected."

"Now I'm feeling cold and reject*ing*."

"I'm hopeless about ever getting turned on."

"I'm afraid you're going to give up on me."

Specifying her reactions in this way was relieving for Marian in itself. To feel more entitled to her experience and to have it understood, without diminishing Debbie's desire, would be much more relieving and might even create some erotic feeling. At least it would put Marian in a position to begin thinking about what was going on inside her and in this sexual relationship that was deflating her, thereby blocking the ego boost that is crucial to the experience of erotic excitement.

This was a motivated and sophisticated couple with excellent rapport, which enabled them to quickly assimilate my suggestions. On 3-month follow-up, they said that Marian had gotten a lot of relief from being able to verbalize what she felt and that her sexual interest had fully returned. I think she was susceptible to losing it again in this relationship, but she now knew how to get it back.

When all the standard causes of sexual apathy are present (instead of being absent, as they were in this case), the role of performance anxiety can be especially difficult to detect: when apathy is chronic and lifelong; when there are submerged grudges and worries in the relationship that are strongly defended against; when the quality of rapport is poor; when one partner is sexually oppressive; or when the patient lacks not only sexual interest but interest in being interested. The surprise is how relieved such patients feel when the valid reasons for their apathy are identified, a relief that then makes sexual response possible.

I find it especially necessary in such cases to not try to transform the patient's experience or to promote new experiences. I find it advisable, particularly in cases of low or absent sexual interest, to scrupulously avoid efforts at sexual enhancement or any implication that the patient should feel desire. Whatever success I have had with such cases has come through helping patients to organize and feel *entitled to* the experience they are having. This has invariably meant, as in Marian's case, bringing to the surface feelings of inadequacy and guilt toward the partner so profound as to require the patient to completely withdraw from sex, preserving an almost equally profound detachment. It sometimes is possible to bring out how apathetic patients are suffering as much or more than their partners from the lack of intimacy, in the form of their experience of a cold and unresponsive world (Apfelbaum, 1985a, 1988).

As I put this elsewhere:

All sex therapists recognise how common it is for people to feel the compulsion to fit the standard sexual script. However, the expectations that create the standard script have been narrowly construed as the foreplay mental set and a preoccupation with erections and orgasm. If we recognize that the expectation of a positive response is the crux of the standard script, then we are in a position to vastly broaden our conception of sex and of our sexual potential, rather than to fit people to what still is a compulsively restrictive version of sex.

Given what still is the dominant view of sex, we find a variety of pathogens, all of which are seen as pathogenic simply because they interfere with one's ability to respond positively, e.g., a restrictive sexual upbringing, depression, distractibility, grudges, pleasure anxiety, a negative body image, Oedipal guilt, fear of failure, and fears of being used, rejected, unloved, or abandoned. . . . This is what potentiates them, that is, makes them appear to be primary pathogens, which makes it appear to be the task of therapy to modify these pathogens, rather than *the task of sex itself.* (Apfelbaum, 1995, pp. 39–40)

☐ Masters and Johnson's Observations of Normal Couples

The popular idealization of sex conceives it as the ultimate intimacy, a unique and even sacred communion. In practice, sex partners are largely silent and emotionally isolated, falling into ritualized patterns. This was the striking finding in Masters and Johnson's observations of normal couples demonstrating their lovemaking (1979, pp. 64–81).

The women were often made uncomfortable by the rather abrupt and vigorous way their partners fondled their breasts, especially during menstrual periods. Although the women admitted their discomfort to Masters and Johnson, on only three occasions (out of thousands of observations) did a woman ask her husband to be more gentle, and no woman ever asked her husband to stop. The same problem arose over early and deep finger penetration of the vagina by their husbands, as well as overly vigorous clitoral manipulation.

When asked by Masters and Johnson why they were silent, the typical reply was, "I didn't want to disturb his concentration." The women reported that at home they were just as careful not to speak.

The husbands were, if anything, even less likely than their wives to communicate dissatisfaction. The most frequent complaint made to Masters and Johnson by husbands was that their wives did not grasp the shaft of the penis tightly enough. Not one of the men had ever mentioned this to his wife, either during the period of observation or at any other time.

The level of communication is perhaps best conveyed by the report that, although it invariably was the man who decided when to penetrate, all of the men were under the impression that it was in some sense a mutual decision because, as the investigators learned from interviewing them, they only went ahead "when she was wet." In their discussion of this finding, Masters and Johnson pointed out that lubrication signifies only the capacity for penetration, not the desire. They found that the women were often distracted and disoriented by this abrupt penetration, and that encounters often ended before they had much of a chance to recover.

In other words, sex was treated by all of these couples, without exception, as something that goes on not between partners but in one's own head. Their naiveté about the simple physical needs and reactions of their partners made this blatantly obvious. These observations were made in the 1950s and 1960s. Decades later, communication on this level may be less necessary, as we now are more familiar with men's and women's sexual needs. This makes the solitariness of partner sex less obvious, but partners may be no more connected emotionally. My impression is that this is the underlying cause of all sex problems.

☐ Bypassing: The Sex Therapy of Helen Singer Kaplan

Helen Singer Kaplan's work proceeded from an opposite assumption. In effect, she took as a given that sexual excitement, or at least sexual functioning, does not require emotional connection. After all, masturbation shows that it can be generated entirely on one's own. In Kaplan's phrase (1974), sex is "friction plus fantasy." (Your partner provides the friction.) She relied heavily on promoting *bypassing*, urging patients to focus on fantasy and sensation. She also focused on sex problems as individual issues, although in a couple context. The partner is there as a facilitator.

How is it that Kaplan could advocate as a therapy what appears to resemble the mute partners-in-parallel that Masters and Johnson observed? Part of the answer is that she was sensitive to *guilt* about bypassing, especially among women. Bypassing is the male style, and women typically feel uneasy about ignoring their partners. Also, both men and women can feel selfish about focusing on maximizing their own sensations. In other words, Masters and Johnson's observed couples would undoubtedly have experienced sex differently if each partner had been free to focus on his or her own imagery and sensations wholeheartedly and with mutual awareness.

Everyone believes that sex is the ultimate intimacy, yet everyone is aware of how much of sex is nonintimate. How do we manage this? By dismissing nonintimate sex as aberrant, immature, immoral, or (at best) partial. This has severely limited our understanding.

Because masturbation is implicitly assumed to be an ersatz gratification, we lose what it can reveal about what sex does for us. We then are stuck in a normative view of sex that denies its function as an *escape* from intimacy. "Friction plus fantasy" is one way to say it. For example Kaplan advised:

> The person who is conflict-free about sex mentally does the opposite of the inhibited one, in the sense that he does *not allow* negative feelings or thoughts or distractions to intrude upon his sexual pleasure. He arranges the weekend to be free of business intrusions; he avoids arguments with his partner—in fact, he acts so as to bring out the best in her. In order to put her in a receptive mood, he focuses only on her positive attributes—makes her feel special—all in the service of his pleasure. When he is in a sexual situation, he does not criticize his partner's taste in bedroom furniture, or see figure flaws, or comment on less than brilliant conversation. His behavior instinctively maximizes his erotic experience. (1979, pp. 84–85; emphasis in the original)

Addressing herself to women's hesitancy to block out their partners, Kaplan (1974, p. 358) counseled:

> [A] woman must learn to "shut out" the nuances of her partner's behavior, at least to the extent that it will not inhibit her sexual response; she must learn, in short, to develop a more autonomous pattern of sexual functioning.

Thus, Kaplan (1974, pp. 169, 172) spoke approvingly of a woman who was "easily multiorgastic [sic] in almost any situation" and who "was perfectly orgastic even when feeling rejected!"—citing this as evidence that "she had no sexual difficulties."

When I read this material to my audiences of therapists, it elicits terrible groans, especially from the women. I then argue that Kaplan, in her bold advocacy of "selfish" sex, was trying to liberate us to feel okay about the kind of sex in which we typically engage and that, however one might feel about it, she tore aside the veil from this aspect of sex.

When couples engage in the extravagant flattery of sex hype as foreplay, they are doing just what Kaplan described the conflict-free person guiltlessly doing. By inducing the sex-trance, couples are able to leave their troubled relationship far behind. In fact, in the early days of the sex therapy movement, wisdom had it that, in sex, you should "leave your troubles at the bedroom door."

Thus, we can recognize two functions of sex: One is relief from loneliness and the other is relief from relationships. Another way to put this antinomy is to say that there are two sexual abilities: One is being able to depersonalize your partner, to treat him or her as a body, and the other is being able to "personalize" your partner, to be in intimate contact with him or her. As I understand the relationship between these two abilities, the better you are at one the better you are at the other.

To say that lovers need to shut out the nuances, to be immune to the quality of the connection, throws down the gauntlet in favor of nonintimate sex. Kaplan's willingness to take a position so opposed to both popular and professional idealizations of sex as the ultimate intimacy is of inestimable value in offering an opportunity to open up debate in the field. As yet this opportunity has not been seized. The reason for this has to do with the way Kaplan argued that her approach, far from being opposed to the Masters and Johnson model, simply takes it to a deeper level, a development made possible by her psychoanalytic training.

Kaplan saw her contribution as integrating Masters and Johnson's "behavioral" model with her "psychoanalytic" model. As is obvious from these labels, she thought of Masters and Johnson's work as relatively superficial and of her own as deep, making this the identifying feature of her approach, as the "behavioral–analytic model" and later, simply, the "integrated model." Her presentation has been widely influential, making it possible for her to reintroduce the pre-Masters and Johnson psychotherapeutic approach to sex problems and yet become the major figure in mainstream sex therapy.

As I have elaborated, performance anxiety can appear to be a relatively superficial, conscious fear of failure in reaction to failure. This is the pre-Masters and Johnson view, but given the subtle and insidious nature of performance anxiety, this is still largely the post-Masters and Johnson view. It also is the view that forms the basis of Kaplan's integrated model.

☐ Is It a Fear of Being Inadequate, or a Fear of Being Adequate?

Kaplan's conception of performance anxiety is not only a consequence of the usual misunderstanding. She perceived performance anxiety as a *cover* for a deeper anxiety—the fear of successful performance. In other words, what looks like a fear of being inadequate is really a denial and rationalization for the fear of being *adequate*. Her classically psychoanalytic framework makes it possible to stand the problem on its head. Thus, Marian complained of sexual apathy, but in this explanatory logic the sexually apathetic patient unconsciously *"does not want to feel sexual"* (Kaplan, 1979, p. 110; emphasis in the original). Marian would be asked to answer the question, "Why am I making myself so angry that I can't enjoy sex?" (For a recent reference in which this model is taken for granted as the only one, see Polonsky, 1997.)

Given the intensity of shame and humiliation that performance anxiety represents, it staggers the imagination to consider that our most compelling need, to measure up to our social-role expectations, is actually a need to fall short of these expectations, to avoid being an adequate man or woman. But Kaplan did not conceive of performance anxiety in terms of this compelling need; and the way to comprehend her logic is to keep in mind that she considered it a superficial, conscious anxiety that could easily be understood as a cover for deeper anxieties.

Clearly, what Masters and Johnson had in mind was a grave concern that could hardly be considered a cover for some deeper fear: *"Fear of inadequacy is the greatest known deterrent to effective sexual functioning"* (Masters & Johnson, 1970, p. 12; emphasis in the original). Consequently, they had patients focus on "nondemand pleasuring" and avoid "goal directness." The idea is to become absorbed in the pleasures of the moment and to avoid working at sex. As they put it, people sacrifice sensuality for sexuality.

Kaplan contended that limiting arousal in this way simply helps patients avoid functioning, when phobic avoidance is their problem in the first place. Her key contribution is the conception of sexual disorders as phobias based on fears of intimacy, success, surrender, loss of control, or any other consequence of sexual excitement and consummation. Although her explanations are classically psychoanalytic (id analytic rather than ego analytic) and hence suggestive of long-term intensive therapy, her approach to sex therapy is to overcome the presumed fear of performing by insisting on successful performance and advocating working at sex. In so doing, Kaplan reversed all the essentials of Masters and Johnson's thinking.

Once these opposing conceptions are unburied, they offer fascinating contrasts. From the Masters and Johnson perspective, the ego inflation that I have suggested triggers erotic excitement is blocked by feelings of inadequacy. From the Kaplan perspective, erotic excitement is almost reflexive, easily generated if it is not resisted. (For the influences on Kaplan that predate Masters and Johnson's work, see Apfelbaum, 1981.) Which way one looks at it has profound implications for our understanding of sex and sex therapy.

☐ Attempts to Explain Masters and Johnson's Success Rates

Much of Kaplan's justification for asserting that Masters and Johnson's treatment works only with less difficult cases rests on her claim to have compared its effectiveness with her own treatment in cases of sexual apathy, the disorder she considered the most difficult to treat. In fact, she considered such cases to be so difficult that she presented her approach as state-of-the-art, despite a success rate apparently no better than 50% (1979, pp. xvi, 53). Her claim to preeminence is bolstered by her "estimate" of a 10% to 15% success rate for Masters and Johnson's therapy in such cases (1979, pp. xvi, 53).

But this estimate was based on Kaplan's (and her coworkers) *own* application of Masters and Johnson's therapy, a measure only of their relative success in applying an approach foreign to their own and for which they had not been trained. Further, Kaplan's publication of this finding revealed that what she referred to as Masters and Johnson's therapy in her contributions was merely the sensate focus exercises as they were sketchily presented in *Human Sexual Inadequacy*. This is a common misconception, much lamented by Masters and Johnson. (For an extensive discussion of this problem, see Apfelbaum, 1985a.)

Kolodny (1979) reported a success rate of 80% with such cases at the Masters and Johnson Institute, and in their *Textbook of Sexual Medicine* (1979)—which appeared at the same time as Kaplan's *Disorders of Sexual Desire*—Kolodny, Masters, and Johnson commented that, in their treatment of sexual apathy, "satisfactory outcomes are the rule rather than the exception" (p. 574).

Although all of these success rates must be considered soft figures, the magnitude of the differences suggests that Masters and Johnson's own application of their therapy was far more effective than Kaplan's application of their therapy, and also more effective than Kaplan's own approach.

What bolsters this conclusion is Kaplan's impression that desire disorders such as sexual apathy are the most difficult to treat. Although this impression was quickly picked up by the popular press and echoed repeatedly in professional publications, it is clear that these cases were not singled out as difficult at the Masters and Johnson Institute. It could be argued that Kaplan's approach may be least suited to cases of sexual apathy, as there are limits to how much excitement can be generated by "shutting out the nuances" of one's relationship with one's partner.

For many the question remains as to why Masters and Johnson's success rates were higher than those reported by others in the field. The often-repeated explanation noted above and first proposed by Kaplan (l979) is that their patients simply did not suffer from serious sexual difficulties. This argument has it that in the early days cases were simpler and that, as sex therapy became better known and more available, it drew patients with more difficult problems.

The only evidences for this argument were these same differences between Masters and Johnson's success rates reported in *Human Sexual Inadequacy* and those of later therapists. However, later outcome statistics reported by the Masters and Johnson Institute (Kolodny, 1981) were consistent with those reported in *Human Sexual Inadequacy*. (In my own practice, I also have seen no such shift.)

Another explanation has been that Masters and Johnson's success rates were methodologically flawed. Zilbergeld and Evans's (1980) well-known critique of these methods showed that these figures suffered from criterion problems. To adequately consider this argument, we would need to compare Masters and Johnson's approach to data analysis with that of others. For example, Kaplan's outcome statistics were simply based on averaging estimates made by her staff members, with no criteria given.

In other words, Masters and Johnson's high success rates have yet to be explained. What makes their success rates appear especially suspect is the belief that Masters and Johnson's therapy is merely an unsophisticated version of the behavioral approach, and, even at that, that it is "limited" to the treatment of performance anxiety, seen only as a superficial, conscious anxiety. Behavioral sex therapists argue that their more elegant efforts to reduce *any* anxiety about sex, not merely performance anxiety (so conceived), predated Masters and Johnson's work. Hence, Masters and Johnson are thought by many in the field to be popularizers rather than innovators, their primary contribution being to put sex therapy on the map.

This perception of their contribution is the basis of the belief that all sex therapists base their treatment on Masters and Johnson's therapy, an especially compelling reason to expect that Masters and Johnson's success rates will be consistent with the results found by others.

☐ The Masters and Johnson Breakthrough

Clearly, Masters and Johnson's contribution has been difficult to assimilate. Since performance anxiety is typically recognized only as a conscious reaction to performance failure, the clinician looks for other, "deeper" causes. This difficulty was compounded by Masters and Johnson's limited and incomplete presentation of their work in *Human Sexual Inadequacy* (1970) and, with Kolodny, in the *Textbook of Sexual Medicine* (1979). Masters and Johnson's other major clinical work, *Homosexuality in Perspective* (1979), only refers back to the previous work for "basic treatment techniques," with the unrealized promise that "there will be a detailed discussion of the . . . therapeutic format in future publications" (p. 258). At a later date, Kolodny (1981, p. 313) wrote, "We are now at work on a more detailed volume that will describe the dynamics of our approach in far more depth. Had this been written earlier, perhaps some misconceptions about our therapy mode would have been avoided." This volume was never completed. The only adequate access to Masters and Johnson's approach has been through attendance at their workshops and training programs.

Not only were Masters and Johnson's publications incomplete, they were misleading. It was nowhere stated that *Human Sexual Inadequacy* was largely a presentation of their assignments, and was not, as Kolodny (1981, p. 313) put it, the "in-depth explication of the dynamics of our methods of therapy" that their promised volume was to be. Even as authoritative a figure as Helen Singer Kaplan believed that her own use of the Masters and Johnson assignments was a test of their therapy.

Their approach was dramatically counterintuitive. It was just the opposite of what had been accepted practice before them, and the opposite of the commonsense approach. If Masters and Johnson had published a single journal article, reporting on 5 couples rather than 500, and if even 2 or 3 of these cases had had positive outcomes, this alone would have been startling news.

They avoided creating a romantic or sexy atmosphere. No soft music, no body oils. No sexy negligees. No sex toys. No vibrators. No oral sex—not even any kissing. Moreover, spontaneity was strictly limited. For such an abstinent, restrictive approach to work at all was news. In fact, those in the field who have missed the point marvel that Masters and Johnson's therapy works at all. In their view, the therapy must work *despite* this overly clinical, "uptight" approach—seemingly ample grounds for skepticism about Masters and Johnson's outcome ratings.

Think of the normal couples Masters and Johnson observed. Their emotionally withdrawn, abrupt, ritualized, and seemingly joyless sex demonstrated that the pressure to perform was as much or more a driving force than was libido. Of course, these couples were being observed, and sex was not spontaneously initiated. But they were observed often enough to become comfortable, and they also reported that what Masters and Johnson saw was not substantially different from their usual sexual encounters. And these were the normal couples.

Masters and Johnson identified what can be called the *compulsions of normal sexuality*. This was the secret of their unprecedented strategy. They deliberately blocked spontaneity, because our spontaneous sexuality tends to be compulsive. They blocked spontaneous compulsiveness in order to release spontaneous sexual feeling.

First, there is the compulsion to reciprocate when touched, kissed, or hugged. We may well want to, but even if we would rather passively enjoy the experience, we cannot afford to risk it; so we feel required to "return the favor," as Masters and Johnson put it, at some cost in erotic feeling. This is why, in their instructions, they blocked mutual caressing, even returning the favor verbally.

Next is the compulsion to go on to penetration, which Masters and Johnson identified as the "foreplay" mindset. No one had challenged the universal assumption that foreplay is indeed "before play," in that partners prep each other for penetration. Masters and Johnson proposed that it should not be "before" anything, but should be simply "pleasuring" for its own sake that might lead to penetration, or might not. (Remember that, in Kaplan's perspective, this strategy only helped patients avoid the excitement they feared. Accordingly, she reintroduced the term foreplay.)

The next compulsion is to reach orgasm, especially male orgasm (the women in their volunteer couples were even more anxious to have the men reach orgasm than were the men.) To identify this compulsion, Masters and Johnson coined the term "goal-directedness."

Another compulsion that can be identified in their work is for the man to be in control, although it was not referred to as such by Masters and Johnson. In *Human Sexual Inadequacy*, the woman is made the guiding partner, not only in the treatment of women's problems but for men's as well—with no exceptions. I would add that the fundamental compulsion, of which the others are expressions, is the compulsion to respond positively, to say yes both verbally and bodily.

Although there are other components to Masters and Johnson's therapy, its distinguishing feature and most active ingredient is its set-breaking effect, its undoing of the compulsive mindset. This was also its most revolutionary feature because, in the period before 1970, the sexual compulsions they blocked and undermined had been authoritatively reinforced.

Masters and Johnson dismantled the entire sexual system that had informed the sex counseling that preceded them. They recognized that the dominant sexual ideology was creating rather than relieving sex problems. The foreplay mindset they sought to undo had been unreservedly endorsed by the marriage manuals. Sex counselors had recommended "extended" foreplay and made orgasm "the aim, the end, and the summit of the sexual act," in the words of Theodore Van de Velde (1926), one of the major pre-Masters and Johnson figures. Orgasm was the last place anyone would have thought to look for the key to sex problems.

Sex was work. Foreplay was a methodical progression through the "erogenous zones." Even mutuality was prescribed. The best-known example is the infamous simultaneous orgasm so many lovers strained to accomplish. A lesser-known but more clearly obsessive example is Van de Velde's admonition to make kissing mutual: "The erotic kiss is mutual; it is given and received *from mouth to mouth with mutual pressure*" (1926, p. 153; emphasis in the original). This made it all the more revolutionary for Masters and Johnson to recognize and block the *compulsion* to reciprocate.

The pre-1970 period was the era of sexual technique, and it was Masters and Johnson's opposition to the technique approach that made their revision especially thorough. There was no reason to expect a revision because, despite all the jokes about the menu-driven sex manuals (it looked as if the ideal lover would be a gynecologist), no one noticed that they were a prescription for performance anxiety. For all the social critics to have missed this basic fault is the most striking evidence for its elusiveness. All of the compulsions Masters and Johnson were to identify were reinforced, but no one could see this because they formed the ground of our thinking about sex. As I have been suggesting, our picture of normal sexuality is itself performance dominated. Masters and Johnson were the first sex experts to explicitly decry the technique approach to sex:

> Acquiring mechanical or technical skill is not a major focus of therapy. For example it is important for a husband to know how to approach the clitoral area when stimulating his wife, but therapists should point out that a physical approach that is exciting for the wife today may be relatively nonstimulative or even irritating tomorrow. (1970, p. 204)

☐ The Integration of Sex Therapy and Couple Therapy

Masters and Johnson treated only couples (or individuals with surrogate partners). Nevertheless, it is a sociological curiosity that until recently sex therapy developed entirely separately from family and couple therapy, each professional organization having its own meetings, journals, and accrediting bodies and drawing from different professional disciplines. Lately there has been some movement toward integration largely if not wholly through the work of David Schnarch (1991, 1997).

Schnarch traces his theoretical lineage to systemic family therapy, especially to Murray Bowen, and the issues he has focused on are familiar to couple therapists. Unlike nearly all sex therapists, Schnarch has little to say about sexual symptoms as such, preferring to focus on the couple and individual issues he believes underlie such symptoms.

Couple therapists are faced with couple fighting, cross-complaining, cold wars, and all the ways partners blame each other for their unfulfilled needs. Schnarch deplores the solution in which couples are trained to listen empathically. He argues that this only reinforces partners' dependency on one another, their need for "other-validation." Instead, he proposes, they need to be "differentiated" (autonomous) as opposed to "fused" (dependent, clinging).

Schnarch's "sexual crucible" approach is based on the proposition that the solution to couple sexual problems is through renouncing this seemingly doomed pursuit of other-validation in favor of "self-validation." Toward this end he confronts, challenges, and taunts, goading his patients to dare to risk their partner's rejection or criticism. Yet he is an unapologetic advocate of intimate sex. What makes this possible is his view of intimacy as a celebration of autonomy. As he declared to one patient, "sharing" separates the men from the boys:

> If you want to keep your sex alive, you have to grow up—we all do. The solution involves shifting from desire out of horniness to desire for *Karen*—wanting to share something with her. It's the shift from impersonal sex, like boys have, to having sex like a man. (1997, p. 31)

The question here is whether the therapist can be encouraging without reinforcing our obsession with sex as a test of competence. Masters and Johnson were the first (and are still among the few) to argue for what they called "neutrality"—that is, for the therapist to avoid being a "cheerleader," to use Kolodny's word.

Schnarch's implicit assumption is that he must push people to overcome the inertia created by anxiety and dependency, just as Kaplan assumed she needed to actively oppose the patient's resistance to giving up neurotic gratifications. Both of these "demand" approaches (as contrasted with Masters and Johnson's nondemand approach) pressure the patient to look inward, but there the similarity ends, as Kaplan advocated the nonintimate sex that Schnarch derides as adolescent.

The parallel between Schnarch's approach and my own is that we both look to the sexual encounter itself for the solution to sex problems. For Schnarch, sex is a crucible that tests our mettle, a trial of our resolve. I see it oppositely: I believe the need for other-validation is primary, just as Marian needed not to overcome feeling ignored and abandoned—she was already doing that—but to remediate these experiences by bringing Debbie in on them. This is more like a sexual "incubator" than a crucible.

Here is another of the dramatically contrasting assumptions that typify the sex field and which can be richly productive if properly clarified and mined. Toward this end, consider the "eyes-open orgasm" that figures prominently in Schnarch's system:

> Eyes-open orgasm is more than just esoteric sex. It can be a milestone in your differentiation and a way to get there. . . . When intercourse is *really* intimate, you've reached a pinnacle of human development. That's what eyes-open orgasm can be, and what differentiation lets you do. (Schnarch, 1997, pp. 234f)

Schnarch is aware that "there's a pitfall in discussing eyes-open orgasm: it can sound like I'm suggesting you're supposed to be able to do it." He has offered this clarification (1997, p. 234): "These are not new hurdles you have to jump over; they are abilities, not dictates. You don't have to! The issue is *can* you?"

Although Schnarch is as passionate an advocate of mutuality as was Van de Velde, he would like to find a way to inspire people to transcend their boundaries—he calls it stretching their self-esteem—without reintroducing the performance demands of which Masters and Johnson made us all more aware. However this may be, nondemand interventions are obviously not at the center of Schnarch's therapy.

Here is an example from my own work in which the nondemand approach is central to the presentation of eyes-open orgasm (Apfelbaum, 1985b, p. 4):

> Most [people] have not experimented with full eye contact, including during orgasm. An interesting effect of experimenting with eye contact is that it is likely to make orgasm difficult and also to inhibit erection, making it a good demonstration of how much we depend on ignoring one another in order to function sexually. If the experiment is done with just one partner being stimulated and if there is some freedom to experience and talk about what happens, many of the doubts and insecurities behind the need to hide in sex will appear and can be relieved, and eye contact (and emotional contact in general) can make sex more exciting.

In diametric contrast to the Schnarch approach, the patient is encouraged to express "doubts and insecurities" to the partner, a highly dependent position in which partner empathy and acceptance can be powerfully relieving. This is the power of sexual vulnerability, the irony being that sexual power has, both popularly and professionally, been measured by one's ability to overcome sexual vulnerability.

☐ Conclusion: Struggling Toward Maturity

Before Van de Velde (as in contemporary non-Western cultures generally), voluntary relationships based on love, or at on least choice, had only begun to modify male-dominant sex. Sex was a confirmation of virility that often had more in common with rape than with sensual dalliance. Van de Velde thundered against this one-sidedness, assuming it could be rectified by a literal quid pro quo. Masters and Johnson revealed that, in our first efforts at reciprocal sex, both men and women were oppressed by compulsive reciprocity. They also showed how sex still was a test of men's adequacy, and now of women's as well.

Kaplan's system avoided any such consideration of this broader context, the focus being on our individual fears of being sexually selfish and our guilt about nonintimate sex—even our denial of what Masters and Johnson's observations of normal couples showed, that sex is typically nonintimate. Her limited conception of performance anxiety made it possible for Kaplan to think of it as merely a cover for the fear of being a fullfledged sexual being, with its potential to imply ruthless self-interest. Given this logic, Kaplan intensified the pressure to perform and reinforced the definition of sex *as* a performance.

This has obscured the insights about sex that informed the Masters and Johnson breakthrough, and it risks reinforcing the pressure to be adequate, to be "good in bed." Behavioral sex therapists, by treating performance anxiety as merely one more glitch in the system, also have reinforced the belief that there is no good reason to suffer from it. There is no place either in Kaplan's therapy or in the behavioral approach for developing the ability to recognize the elemental force of performance anxiety, and to appreciate what it can tell us about the human condition.

The "performance" required of us is to respond positively, to say yes in words and especially with our bodies. The penalties are severe: social scorn, humiliation, and rejection. All penetrate to the heart of our self-esteem. What usually is identified as a sex problem becomes one only to the extent that it interferes with the ability to respond positively. It is uniquely possible for intimate sex to be an "incubator" in which these kinds of distress can be relieved. Ultimately, this may be what sexual relationships are evolving toward (Apfelbaum, 1995). However, our compulsion to respond positively can turn any interference into a problem. That is what we can learn from the grand experiment that the sex therapies represent.

☐ References

Apfelbaum, B. (1977). On the etiology of sexual dysfunction. *Journal of Sex & Marital Therapy*, 3, 50–62.

Apfelbaum, B. (1981). Review: H. S. Kaplan, *Disorders of sexual desire*. *Journal of Sex Research*, 17, 182–184.

Apfelbaum, B. (1984). Ego-analytic sex therapy: The problem of performance-anxiety anxiety. In R. Segraves & E. J. Haeberle (Eds.), *Emerging dimensions of sexology* (pp. 127–132). New York: Praeger.

Apfelbaum, B. (1985a). Masters and Johnson's contribution: A response to "Reflections on sex therapy," an interview with Harold Lief and Arnold Lazarus. *Journal of Sex Education and Therapy, 11,* 5–11.

Apfelbaum, B. (1985b). Breaking sexual routines. *Sexual Well-Being* (December), 3–5.

Apfelbaum, B. (1988). An ego-analytic perspective on desire disorders. In S. Leiblum & L. Rosen (Eds.), *Sexual desire disorders* (pp. 75–104). New York: Guilford.

Apfelbaum, B. (1995). Masters and Johnson revisited: A case of desire disparity. In R. C. Rosen & S. R. Leiblum (Eds.), *Case studies in sex therapy* (pp. 23–45). New York: Guilford.

Kaplan, H. S. (1974a). *The new sex therapy.* New York: Brunner/Mazel.

Kaplan, H. S. (1974b). Friction and fantasy: No-nonsense therapy for six sexual malfunctions. *Psychology Today* (October), 76–86.

Kaplan, H. S. (1979) *Disorders of sexual desire.* New York: Brunner/Mazel.

Kolodny, R. C., Masters, W. H., & Johnson, V. E. (1979). *Textbook of sexual medicine.* Boston: Little, Brown.

Kolodny, R. C. (1981). Evaluating sex therapy: Process and outcome at the Masters & Johnson Institute. *Journal of Sex Research, 17,* 301–318.

Masters, W. H., & Johnson, V. E. (1970). *Human sexual inadequacy.* Boston: Little, Brown.

Masters, W. H., & Johnson, V. E. (1979). *Homosexuality in perspective.* Boston: Little, Brown.

Polonsky, D. C. (1997) What do you do when they won't do it? The therapeutic dilemma of low desire. *Journal of Sex Education and Therapy, 22,* 5–12.

Schnarch, D.(1991). *Constructing the sexual crucible: An integration of sexual and marital therapy.* New York: W.W. Norton.

Schnarch, D.(1997). *Passionate marriage.* New York: W.W. Norton.

Van De Velde, T. H. (1926). *Ideal marriage: Its physiology and technique.* New York: Random House.

Zilbergeld, B., & Evans, M. (1980). The inadequacy of Masters and Johnson. *Psychology Today* (August), 29–43.

Zussman, L., & Zussman, S. (1979) *Getting together: A guide to sexual enrichment for couples.* New York: William Morrow.

Leonore Tiefer, Ph.D.

Feminist Critique of Sex Therapy: Foregrounding the Politics of Sex

☐ Foreword: On Being a Feminist and Sexologist

Let us begin at the beginning: The United States is home to a permanent sex war. Sexuality is a continuous political battleground, with gender an overlapping but separate zone of action. As Rubin (1984) said, "Because sexuality is a nexus of the relationships between genders, much of the oppression of women is borne by, mediated through, and constituted within, sexuality" (pp. 300–301). But, as she went on to note, complex and interconnected as sexuality and gender are, they are not one and the same, and the interests of women's liberation are not necessarily coextensive with those of sexual liberation. Those of us attempting to ride both horses often find ourselves struggling for balance.

Sex therapists, educators, and researchers as well as their clients, students, and research participants act in a context thoroughly saturated with

---

Note added in production: Since this chapter was completed, I have inaugurated a campaign called "A New View of Women's Sexual Problems" that embraces a critique of medicalization plus a new vision of women's sexual problems. It offers a non-*DSM* classification system for women's sexual problems, and I look forward to writing about it in the next edition of this book.

political and moralistic attacks and defenses. One consequence of the politicization of sexuality is that sexology as an academic subject is under-developed, stress-laden, and stigmatized. Another is that sex therapy can-not simply be studied (or new aspects created, for that matter) as if it were biochemistry or fashion design. Recent books of autobiographical reflec-tions by sexologists have illuminated just how unusual this profession and its subject matter really are (Brannigan, Allgeier, & Allgeier, 1998; Bullough, Bullough, Fithian, Hartman, & Klein, 1997). My own story is in the Brannigan et al. book, and it offers a useful supplement to this theoretical chapter.

☐ Introduction

In every venue, feminism foregrounds women's positions, women's voices, women's perspectives, and women's problems. Feminism puts women at the center of analysis, and to do a feminist critique of anything, one starts by trying to see that subject from women's point of view. Given sexol-ogy—the study of sexuality—feminism asks, "Where are women in the concepts, the methods, and the theories? What would sexuality look like if women's interests were central?" A largely unexamined, unitary idea of "women" pervaded the early years of the women's movement; but that idea has now largely been replaced by a greater attention to the diversity of women's positions. This makes our research and theorizing more com-plex, but we must attend to the range and variety of women's sexual interests.

I have been writing feminist critique of sex therapy for at least 20 years, in one way or another (Tiefer, 1978, 1995, 1996a). So have dozens of others, from Shere Hite (1976) to the pro-sex feminists represented in *Pleasure and Danger* (Vance, 1984); from American sex therapists such as Gina Ogden, Carol Ellison, and Wendy Stock (see Cole & Rothblum, 1988) to British feminists using discourse analysis (Hollway, 1984). Women of color, who are well-represented in writings about sexuality, have yet to write about sex therapy, but lesbians have made significant critiques (Hall, 1998; Loulan, 1982, 1984, 1990; Rothblum & Brehony, 1993). Feminism as a political stance about women has changed substantially over these years, as women, political realities, and feminist understandings have all evolved, and thus the feminist critique of sex therapy is necessarily a work in process.

To lump it all together, feminist critics of sexology have claimed that sex therapy is too genital and goal oriented; that sex therapy relies on sexist sex research, language, and theory; that the nomenclature of sexual problems is sexist; that sex therapy neglects gender-related power differences; that sex therapy sacrifices pleasure for performance; that sex therapy is oblivious to subjective sexual meaning and ignorant of cultural variations; that sex therapy unintentionally (or not) has reinforced patriarchal interests and sexual double standards; that it has unintentionally (or not) supported compulsory heterosexuality; and that sex therapy historically has ignored social causes and solutions of sexual problems (see Tiefer, 1991, and its annotated bibliography). Over two decades, it seemed that the simplest and most liberal of the criticisms (e.g., the need to pay more attention to pleasure and to obvious sexist language) were accepted, just as the most liberal of political feminist criticisms (e.g., eliminating separate job ads for men and women in the newspapers) were accepted. But most of the more substantial criticisms have been dismissed as "too radical" or "merely political."

The fact that little feminist critique seemed to influence the theory, nomenclature, and conduct of sex therapy seems due to political and social-historical trends including(a) various disagreements on sexual subjects among feminists following a brief period of unity and (b) a general political climate of profound sexual confusion and conservatism that has steadily gained ground since the late 1970s. Because this conservative climate has not permitted sexology to blossom as a legitimate academic discipline, sex research and clinical theory have survived during the cultural sex wars by clinging to a protective medical model and medical language (Tiefer, 1996b).

Sexology and sex therapy resisted feminist criticisms that threatened the biomedical bubble. By incorporating just a little liberal feminist language, sexology could appear "progressive enough" and thus deflect feminist attack. Moreover, feminist voices within sexology have been weaker because of isolation from feminist and sexuality theory within history, anthropology, cultural studies, and the humanities (see Jackson & Scott, 1996). Although the field of "sexuality studies" is now developing in history and the humanities, no bridges have yet been built with feminists in clinical areas.

Beginning in the 1990s, a new chapter in the social construction of sexuality began as the pharmaceutical industry became interested in sexual problems. Political antisexualism remains strong, and many in sexology have seized on the legitimacy and funding offered by pharmaceutical research. Feminist sexologists, still catching up with new academic developments in the critical and cultural realms of sexuality studies, must stay on top of the ethical, practical, and theoretical challenges offered by the new sexual drugs.

☐ Early Feminist Critique of Sex Therapy

Sex therapy arose during the sexual revolution of the 1960s. That revolution—although its credentials as a revolution continue to be debated—brought us oral contraceptives for women; the legal right to abortion; decreased censorship in public media such as newspapers, films, and theater; no-fault divorce laws; increasing tolerance and legitimacy of homosexuality; publicity about experimental forms of nonmonogamous sexual lifestyles; and a general social attitude that sexuality for pleasure and intimacy (and not just for procreation) was important to individual freedom. Increasing social recognition of the right to sexual pleasure legitimated psychotherapy for sexual discontent. Masters and Johnson (1970) provided the initial text in the new field of sex therapy, followed soon by California sociologists/marriage counselors Hartman and Fithian (1974) and New York psychoanalyst-psychiatrist Kaplan (1974). A new field was born.

At the same time, and from some of the same social wellsprings as sex therapy and the sexual revolution, the new women's liberation movement (which would turn out to be a new phase in an old revolution) critiqued contemporary heterosexual lovemaking scripts. In now-classic pieces such as Anne Koedt's "The Myth of the Vaginal Orgasm," the new wave of feminists argued for new sexual choreographies. "What we must do is redefine our sexuality. We must discard the 'normal' concepts of sex and create new guidelines which take into account mutual sexual enjoyment" (Koedt, 1973, p. 199). No more phallocentrism. No more neglecting the clitoris. No more double standard. Feminists enthusiastically adopted Masters and Johnson's (1966) physiological sex research to support their political claims.

The feminist critique of prevailing sexual mores soon broadened beyond the demand for new choreographies and more orgasms, however, and by the end of the 1970s, feminists were foregrounding gender-based violence and victimization as sources of psychological and sexual inhibition and suffering (Heise, 1995).

☐ Resistance to Feminist Ideas About Sexuality

Throughout the 1980s, feminists within and outside sexology continued to write copiously about sexuality, but with little impact on sex therapy. I want to examine two prime sources for feminism's failure to have more impact on sex therapy: the antisexual political atmosphere, which severely limited all of sexology, and disunification within the feminist movement, which limited the power and urgency of the feminist message.

Antisexual Political Atmosphere

As I mentioned at the outset, sex education, therapy, and research are plagued by the politics of sexuality in our time. The simplest suggestions about children's sexuality, reproductive rights, or moneys for sex research are controversial, and all sexologists can tell stories of unwanted publicity, investigation, protest, or loss of funding.

Sex remains the primary battleground of a "culture war" over legitimate moral authority in public and private life (e.g., Hunter, 1991). Culture wars between advocates for progressive versus traditional values have existed throughout American history.[1] Following the brief sexual revolution of 1964–1976,[2] the successful rise of an activist and politicized Christian right wing and the triumph of conservative politics created a growing moralistic backlash against the rhetoric of sexual pleasure and freedom. Panics around "The Porno Plague" (first on the cover of *Time* magazine in 1976), horrifying sexual dangers to children (in child care centers, by neighborhood pedophiles, and now on the Internet), the contagious perversion of homosexuality (dangerous because of its assault on marriage), and sexual diseases have been unrelentingly promoted.

As a measure of this backlash, we can summarize the sexual landscape in the past 20 years like this: Few new contraceptives have been developed; abortion rights have been cut back again and again; censorship of sexual art has inhibited museums and closed exhibits on college campuses; the political reaction against sexually avant garde theater practically killed the National Endowment for the Humanities; public sex education, once at the brink of a nationwide mandate, has been pared down to abstinence education; public moneys for sex research on topics other than disease or teen pregnancy are nonexistent; hate crimes are everyday matters; and civil rights for homosexuals are contested in every district. The rise of the Herpes virus in the early 1980s and the HIV virus in the middle 1980s strengthened the backlash by emphasizing the connections between sex, shame, and suffering.

---

1. A broader analysis of the culture wars addressing this progressive vs. traditional split on issues of multiculturalism, militarism, democratic authority, and so on cannot be given here. Sexologists who want to deal adequately with the challenges of contemporary politics are well advised to acquire some grasp of the larger picture (e.g., Berlet, 1995).

2. The periodizing here is more or less arbitrary.

The positive sexual legacy of the 1960s has been reflected mostly in an unbridled commercial exploitation of sexuality and a substantial decline in the sexual double standard. Sexuality figures more openly and more prominently in the media than ever before. But, as witness the almost unbelievable saga of the impeachment and trial of President Clinton in 1998–1999, the passion of conservatives against immorality is boundless. And what of sexology? DiMauro (1995, p.11) recently assessed the field, observing:

> It is often assumed that it is not professionally legitimate to promote or conduct sexuality research for the sole or primary purpose of contributing to existing knowledge about human sexual behaviors in the social science disciplines. . . . The primary outcome of such controversy [over research on sexuality] has been the inconsistent and modest financial support for this work on the part of both the government and the private sector, as well as a hesitancy to publicly promote sexuality research.

The dearth of social science research on sexuality is one reason Schover and Leiblum (1994) argued that sex therapy was "stagnating" by the end of the 1980s. The growth of a clinical field like sex therapy requires ongoing outcome research, but the political chill that set in soon after the birth of sex therapy limited empirical sex research and theory.

It is important to remember how the conservative and antisexual political atmosphere grew throughout the 1980s. Sociologists and historians have described how conservative politicians wrung their hands about one awful sex "epidemic" after another: teen pregnancy, promiscuity, pornography, sex abuse of children, fatal disease, gay teens at high school proms, etc., etc., etc. (Wagner, 1997). And they didn't just wring their hands. In 1981, for example, a new Adolescent Family Life Act (nicknamed "the chastity bill") set up services to prevent teen pregnancy through preventing teen sexuality (see Luker, 1996, for analysis of the teen pregnancy "epidemic"). In 1982, the first of a horrific series of sexual and "satanic" scandals at daycare centers exploded onto the airwaves, resulting in the unjust imprisonment of hundreds of people (with chilling repercussions on untold others) until the conviction of Kelly Michaels was reversed in 1990. By 1986, to pick just one more landmark, the officially sanctioned *Report of the Attorney General's Commission on Pornography* put the finishing touches on the demonization of sexually explicit materials (see Demac [1990] and Strossen [1995] for legal and social analyses of contemporary bluenoses).

Opposing forces in the sex wars all wanted research to support their positions and therapists to document lasting psychological dangers. Sexology became a political football and unappealing as a career. As the editor of *The Journal of Sex Research* pointed out in 1990, academic sex research was weak: There were few programs, few tenured professors, few job ads, few research grants, and few government agencies interested in sex research (Abramson, 1990). Sexology has been constantly on the defensive, and sex therapy could hardly embrace diverse modes of practice such as those suggested by feminists. This history of rejection and stigma ultimately drove sex therapy into the arms of the medical model and the pharmaceutical industry, but more about this below.

Splits Within Feminism

Throughout this antisexual period, the same political conservatives who targeted "liberal" sex research and sex education as socially corrupting, dangerous to youth, and wasteful of public resources attacked feminism as dangerous to the family and the traditional American way of life (Berlet, 1995). You would think that feminists and sexologists, finding themselves in the same boat, would become friends. You would think that feminists would become advocates for sex education and sex therapy and that sexologists would see the advantages of incorporating a critique of patriarchy into their philosophy.

Well, that didn't happen. Ignorance and homophobia within feminism prevented feminist sexologists from participating in the rich lesbian debate about eroticism. These discussions of sexual roles (as in dialogues between "butch" and "femme" lesbians) and erotic identity (how one imagines oneself as an erotic object) showed how emotional dynamics contribute more to arousal than to sexual technique (e.g., Hollibaugh & Moraga, 1983; Newton & Walton, 1984). Sexology distorted this lesson about women and sexuality, so visible in women's romance novels (see Snitow, 1983), into claims that emotion is more important to women than physical arousal, when the point is that the two are intrinsically linked.

Another bump in the road toward a feminist–sexologist coalition came with the chronicling of global sexual violence (rape, domestic violence, child sexual abuse), exploitation (sexual harassment), objectification (the beauty myth, pornography), and commodification (prostitution, trafficking in women), directly challenging whether the sex-as-pleasure-and-freedom rhetoric of sex therapy applied to women (Heise, 1995).

Early Cautions

By 1980, caution about the revolution was being voiced by even pro-sex feminists, as in this dialogue between Gayle Rubin and Deidre English:

[Rubin:] The late sixties and early seventies saw the so-called sexual revolution. Women like me felt that it hadn't worked because it was male-dominated.

[English:] That's too simple—my recollection of it is that it was not an unmitigated disaster. The sexism was there, but women were actually having more sexual experience of different kinds and enjoying it. Women were having more sex that was not procreational, and claiming the right to it as well as paying a lower social and emotional cost. . . . Women were fighting for sexual rights and often getting them. (in English, Hollibaugh, & Rubin, 1981, pp. 45–46)

Eventually, some early pro-sex feminists even recanted their early 1970s message, as in "Ziplash: A Sexual Libertine Recants" by novelist Erica Jong: "Our society has had a decade and a half of experimentation with random sexual freedom. We have discovered that it is neither so very sexy nor so very free. My generation is disillusioned with sex as a social panacea" (1989, p. 49).

Some politically sophisticated pro-sex feminists didn't reject the signs of women's sexual progress but felt the "sexual revolution" had been misnamed because it was "only a liberalization, so of course it didn't do what we wanted" (English et al., 1981, p. 45). The distinction between reform and revolution was lost in the larger antisexual backlash.

The Feminist Antisex Position Develops

Beginning in the mid-1970s, "feminists were discovering the prevalence and intensity of male violence against women, and some of the revelations were horrifying enough to make attempts to reform male sexuality seem Pollyannaish" (Ehrenreich, Hess, & Jacobs, 1982, p. 62). Historical and statistical research produced endless documentation and testimony of sexual brutality, violence, and exploitation of women and children. Abuse of women emerged as a private weapon of domestic oppression as well as a systematic weapon of intergroup warfare. Even the sanctuary of psychotherapy was invaded by charges of sexual exploitation. Feminists agreed that women's lives were colored by sexual danger and, as the facts piled up during the 1970s and early 1980s, a consensus emerged that pornography, equated with antiwoman propaganda, was one major cause. Many feminists believed that men's oppression of women could be linked to sexual fantasies internalized from misogynistic images such as those found in pornography, which presumably taught and reinforced degradation of women as central to masculine sexuality. Feminist antipornography groups toured with shocking slide-shows and devised legislation to make pornography illegal as a violation of women's civil rights. A vocal minority of anticensorship feminists protested and even ridiculed this perspective, but they were little noticed (e.g., Ellis, Jaker, Hunter, O'Dair, & Tallmer, 1988).

Impact on Feminist Sexology

In the face of this groundswell of feminism focused on sexual violence against women, feminists trying to reform sex therapy faced enormous obstacles. First, any celebration of women's capacities for physical plea-sure and sexual self-determination suddenly seemed trivial, if not down-right disrespectful. Second, it seemed that sex therapists had been as igno-rant as the rest of the public about sexual abuse, and that they should work on uncovering its prevalence and devising treatment programs for survivors.

But, third (and most problematic), suspicion that sexology as a pro-fession actually contributed to the oppression of women grew during this period and threw feminist sexologists into tremendous conflict. Antiporn feminists criticized sex therapists' and educators' use of sexually explicit materials as ignorant and harmful. They criticized sex therapists' advocacy of sexual pleasure during intercourse as thoughtless and potentially op-pressive. Sexologists, including the few feminist sexologists, felt defensive. No wonder sexology maintained a low profile during the 1980s.

☐ The Turn Toward Medicalization in Sex Therapy

Throughout the 1980s, as sexology was attacked by the conservative right and antisex feminists, sex therapy found refuge under the umbrella of the medical model. The influential *Diagnostic and Statistical Manual of Mental Disorders (DSM)* of the American Psychiatric Association first incorporated "sexual dysfunctions" into its listing of mental disorders in 1980, identify-ing difficulties with orgasm, erection, and arousal as appropriate sources of treatment specialization and mental health insurance reimbursement. This inclusion meant legitimacy for sex therapy clinics, organizations, confer-ences, and some research.

By the late 1980s, although the political atmosphere remained poi-sonously antisexual, we began to see growing signs of interest within the world of medicine in sexual problems. In particular, the surgical subspe-cialty of urology turned its attention to men's erectile problems as a result of new diagnostic instruments and some increase in treatment options

(Tiefer, 1986). Urologists had lost some of their other subspecialty areas (e.g., kidney stones and benign prostate problems), but interest resulted also because of rising sexual expectations due to demographic and cultural shifts. It took about a decade to legitimize "impotence" as a urology subspecialty area, but the effort culminated in 1992, when the National Institutes of Health held a Consensus Development Conference on Impotence (Tiefer, 1994). This type of conference was common when clinical dilemmas, such as headache or depression, required a "consensus" to guide treatment, but the impotence meeting marked the first such conference on a sexual topic. Needless to say, it was dominated by the urological point of view.

At first it seemed that sex therapists would not benefit from this turn of events because of the "steamroller" of organic causes and treatments promoted by urologists. But, unexpectedly, clinical trials on drugs required skilled screening and measurement, and pharmaceutical manufacturers began offering well-paid consultancies to sex therapists as research and clinical collaborators. Today, a growing rapprochement is developing as urologists appear regularly at sex research conferences and sexologists are frequent coauthors of pharmaceutical treatment studies. An editorial of one sex therapy journal recently trumpeted the "pharmacological era in the treatment of sexual disorders" (Segraves, 1998).

☐ Feminism and the Medicalization of Sex Therapy

But cozy and revitalizing as this development seems for some sexologists, it raises two massive sets of problems for feminists. Let me call them problems of commission and problems of omission.

Problems of Commission

These problems include all of the consequences of medicalization that are *detrimental* to feminist concerns in sexuality and sex therapy. On the most practical level, a recent letter to the *New England Journal of Medicine* drew attention to a worrisome increase in complaints of genital irritation by middle-aged women partners of men who use drugs to enhance erectile functioning (Little, Park, & Patton, 1998). It seems that using these drugs results in a problematic quality or quantity of intravaginal penetration. The "sexuopharmacological" solution for such problems, of course, would be for the women to use hormones or other products to lubricate penetration. This could start a comical infinite regress. The man's pill needs the woman's lubricant. The woman's lubricant needs the man's penile sensory enhancer. The man's sensory enhancer needs the woman's desire additive. The woman's desire additive needs the man's energy stimulant. The man's energy stimulant needs a new mattress. A new mattress needs new sheets. And so on. This scenario is not quite as ridiculous as it sounds, since all drugs have side effects. The most popular SSRI[3] drugs for depression, for example, seem to delay or inhibit orgasm, and doctors now prescribe specific antidotes to be taken before sexual activities (Ashton, Hamer, & Rosen, 1997). Antihypertensive medications usually affect genital bloodflow, requiring antidotes, and so forth.

The obsessive genital focus of "sexuopharmacology" is its central problem of commission. Successful sexual experience, in the sexuopharmacology model, is successful genital coupling. This sex = intercourse equation brings back all the dangers of pregnancy and STDs that the 1960s separation of sex and reproduction by effective contraception was supposed to reduce or eliminate. Sexuopharmacology perpetuates genital function as the primary, the "natural," sexual experience. This construction continues to permeate sex research and sex therapy.

In the diagnostic nomenclature and treatment armamentarium, the amount of time devoted to getting the penis hard and the vagina wet vastly outweighs the attention devoted to motives, scripts, pleasure, power, emotionality, sensuality, communication, or connectedness—and medicalization will perpetuate this imbalance. A chilling recent development is the identification of new women's sexual problems such as "vaginal engorgement insufficiency" and "clitoral erectile insufficiency" (Goldstein & Berman, 1998; Park, Goldstein, Siroky, Krane, & Azadzoi, 1997). These new reductionist "female genital sexual dysfunctions" and the drugs to "treat" them promise continuing struggle over medicalization.

Problems of Omission

The obsessive focus on getting the genitals to perform properly, if not perfectly, results in the neglect of many areas of concern to feminists—medicalization's problems of omission. First on this list would be downplaying the relational aspects of sexual experience. In my 13 years of work in urology departments (1983–1996), I repeatedly, even routinely, observed

---

3. SSRIs are specific (or selective) serotonine reuptake inhibitors, such as fluoxetine (Prozac™).

extensive penis function workups by doctors and technicians who had no knowledge whatsoever of the quality of the penis-owner's sexual relationship, or even if there was a relationship at all. It was as if they were car mechanics and needed to know nothing whatsoever about the car's driver, any other passengers, or how the car was driven or to where in order to fix what was wrong.

It's the wrong model, and drug companies know it. Consider the advertising campaign for Viagra™, Pfizer Pharmaceutical Company's pill for erectile dysfunction, approved in April 1998. The safety and effectiveness strengths of this prescription-only drug claim that its mechanism of action is limited to the blood vessels of the penis. Yet the advertising campaign features a large photo of a man and woman dancing together and smiling warmly, with the prominent phrase, "let the dance begin." This appeal to romance, fun, and intimacy seems aimed at women, who are more attentive to medical problems than men and more willing to fill prescriptions. So the campaign appeals to romance, but does the pill?

This is medicalization as social control—the power of medical authorities to set priorities and, through definition and labeling, to exclude whole areas of human experience as not germane to sexual function. Thus, medicalization denies diverse realities. Most couples with sexual problems have never talked with anyone about their problems, and often not even talked with each other. Before their problems can be solved, there must be some discussion and exploration. The first empirical study I conducted in a urology setting, for example, documented discrepancies in descriptive information provided by male patients and their female sex partners in 78% of a sequential sample of 40 cases (Tiefer & Melman, 1983). Simply handing out drug prescriptions is unlikely to help couples whose sexual lives have come unraveled, but, more relevant for feminists, it is likely to silence the partner whose perspective might be different from the medical authority.

Silencing of women's perspective is one of my most serious worries. The insidious thing about "omissions," of course, is that one has no idea what's being omitted. Reading novels, books about lesbians, and early 1970s feminist writings is one way to discover what erotic and relational subjects are being silenced by the push toward reductionism in medicalization. It also worries me that neglecting the relationship bypasses any opportunity to intervene in situations of sexual violence (Heise, 1995).

The second problem of omission resulting from medicalization is disinterest in cultural variation in sexuality. Because normal genital function is said to be biologically universal ("an erection is an erection"), sexuopharmacology can demote factors such as culture or religion to minor background variables. This bypasses how meaning and motivation for sexual activity derive from cultural sexual scripts. I remember a case I once supervised of a Burmese-American woman married to an Italian-American man (Tiefer, 1996c). The presenting problems were premature ejaculation (PE) and anorgasmia, and there was a history of infertility and unsuccessful in vitro fertilization attempts. But the most substantial sexual problems involved cultural discrepancies in erotic kissing (Southeast Asians often hate it, Italians usually love it) and cultural variations in gender rules around sexual initiation, sexual expressiveness, and body comfort. The PE was a consequence of the infrequent sex, which was due to the other problems. Handing this couple a drug for PE would have delayed (at best) or suppressed (probably) their ability to resolve central cultural and gender sexual issues.

The most grievous omission, from a feminist point of view, is medicalization's neglect and, to all intents and purposes, denial of issues of power. The *DSM* (third, third-revised, and fourth editions) lists sexual problems of "the vagina" and "the penis" as if sex was a function like respiration. Equal numbers of complaints are ascribed to men and to women, and there is an assumption that, therefore, men's and women's concerns are equally represented.

But men and women do not have equal political power or, often, personal sexual power; ignoring this inequality in sex therapy is a substantial omission. For example, women's political and economic inequality is reflected in incomplete health care (limits on access to abortion and contraception); greater social pressures to marry and frequent trading of sex for socioeconomic advantages; greater burdens in homecare, childcare, and eldercare, limiting energy for sex and other pursuits of the self; limits in nonmarital sexual opportunities because of dangers to reputation and threats of sexual violence; and loss of personal sexual power as a result of child sexual abuse, poor self-esteem, and depression. Institutionalized gender inequality becomes transformed into stereotyped assumptions about men's and women's essential natures resulting in popularized sex therapy texts focusing on how men and women come from different planets and *therefore* have difficulty communicating, cooperating, or coordinating (Hare-Mustin, 1991). The unwillingness of theorists to grapple with gender and power has created a vacuum that medicalized sexology has invaded.

☐ Toward a Feminist Sex Therapy

What is the task, then, for feminist sex therapists in the current atmosphere? Remember that feminism foregrounds women's position, women's voices, women's perspectives, and women's problems. In the study of sexuality, feminism asks, "Where are women in the concepts, the methods, and the theories? What would sexuality look like if women's interests were central?" A new feminist program for sex therapy will help us respond to and resist the current medicalizing trends, and even move beyond them. The following program proposes four components: new concepts, methods, audiences, and research.

Conceptualization

Medicalizing trends in sex therapy rest foursquare on the legitimacy and propriety of the medical model approach to sexual understandings and treatments. Feminists must destabilize the complacency around sexual medicalization by challenging the medical model.

First, we need a new nomenclature of sexual problems. The current nomenclature used in teaching, clinical work, research, and for insurance reimbursement is that of the *DSM*. It relies on defining problems as deviations from "the human sexual response cycle" of arousal and orgasm as proposed by Masters and Johnson (1966). I have written at length on why the *DSM* nomenclature is both flawed and sexist, and for political purposes I think we do best by ignoring its decontextualized pseudoscience and starting from scratch with new ideas about sexual dissatisfactions and problems (Tiefer, 1995). Let's have an avalanche of qualitative research. Get focus groups together of women from different social situations. Ask what gives them trouble, what makes them unhappy, what language they are comfortable with, what language they would respond to. Identify themes, groupings, and categories that are meaningful to women. Because sexuality changes as culture changes, this "let's ask women" approach must be an ongoing project.

The current pharmaceutical push to treat women is based on publicizing high rates of women's low desire that exceed even men's complaints about erection (Laumann, Paik, & Rosen, 1999). Feminists have long tried to raise awareness about the extent of women's sexual dissatisfactions, although authors like Hite had their research methods crucified as unscientific. The recent Laumann paper, authored by sexologists who also happen to be employed as pharmaceutical company consultants, rests its analysis on a single question: "During the last 12 months, has there ever been a period of several months or more when you lacked interest in having sex (check yes or no)" (Laumann, Gagnon, Michael, & Michaels, 1994, p. 660). While feminists no doubt appreciate the attention such publicity pays to women's dissatisfactions, what can the yes/no answers to such questions actually tell us? What does "lacking interest in sex" mean? With whom? What kind of sex? How will this information be used? Feminists are properly skeptical of whether such research can benefit women.

Qualitative research enabling women to articulate their own sexual concerns is akin to work in community AIDS education as it has become clear that people from different communities label and experience sex differently. For example, a group of health educators in Los Angeles wanted unmarried Latinas who were having unprotected anal intercourse to use condoms (Landrine, 1995). But the young women viewed their sex activity as intercourse that would both please their partners and protect their virginity; they didn't relate to the decontextualized term, *anal intercourse*. They viewed condoms as birth control and thus not appropriate to what they were doing. Workshops that addressed the Latinas' dilemmas and choices using their own language became highly effective educational intervention.

Second, in addition to reformulating sexual problems, feminists must poke holes in the relationship between sexuality and the medical model. In a recent paper, I identified "core" elements of the contemporary medical model as (a) mind-body dualism, (b) an objective, universal body, (c) naturalism, (d) universal bodily sexuality, (e) individualism, (f) biological reductionism, and (g) reified diseases (Tiefer, 1996b). Feminists must attack each of these elements and show how it fails to illuminate the social, political, and phenomenological realities of women's sexuality.

For example, any gendered perspective on sexuality must attack the core medical model component of individualized illness. The individualism of medicine rests on the image of disease being in the individual body. A couple may be in a car accident, but the result will be Leslie's broken bones or Jean's whiplash. The nomenclature of diagnoses reflects problems of an individual. A conceptual shift toward recognizing the gendered construction of sexuality and sexual problems would draw us away from erection-disorder and desire-disorder toward couple-diagnoses such as desire discrepancy (Zilbergeld & Ellison, 1980) or ideas from family systems theory such as enmeshment. Schnarch (1997) unfortunately ignored gender, but he approached the treatment of sexual complaints through a thoroughly nonindividual lens, and feminists could benefit from his Bowenian analysis of sexual problems as they arise from couples' problems with differentiation.

Another way to attack the credibility of "individualism" in sexuality would be to challenge the assumption that sexuality is some kind of property or faculty in an individual, as in "my sexuality" or "President Clinton's sexuality." Rather, one could view sexuality as something created in and through interaction, like friendship. Thus, we have the sexuality created between you and your ex-husband versus the sexuality created between you and other partners. You can draw the Clintonesque analogies yourself.

Methods

Current sex therapy rests comfortably within contemporary strategies of individual and couples treatment, although clinical approaches differ substantially. Some therapists favor behavioral methods, whereas others lean toward more cognitive methods. Some therapists adore sexually explicit educational videotapes; others would never use them. Some therapists can work with individuals who are members of long-standing couples; others hold that the couple should always be the focus of work. Even when working with couples, some therapists believe sexual complaints can be the focus of work, whereas others believe that sexual problems are symptoms of other issues. But which of these or other methods would foreground women's positions, women's voices, women's perspectives, and women's problems?

When I first tried to design feminist sex therapy, I suggested five areas of "remedial and compensatory coping" that might be useful for every woman and her sexual life, not just every client/patient (Tiefer, 1996a).

1. Feminism 101 helps women understand how gender works.

2. Corrective physiology education teaches women to be thoroughly familiar with the vulva from a feminist perspective (Federation of Women's Health Centers, 1981).

3. Assertiveness training helps them overcome socialization-induced inhibitions.

4. Affirmative body work enables women to experience their bodies as sources of ability and experience, rather than as objects of looksist comparisons.

5. Finally, masturbation education teaches attitudes of sexual empowerment and entitlement.

I still think these would be useful pillars of feminist community sex education. I dream of a set of spacious, mobile sex education clinics containing libraries of circulating books and videos, computers with Internet links to sex education Websites, and regular group discussion and lecture schedules. (Sigh!) Groupwork is fundamental for feminists, because it helps protect women from being railroaded by the dominant professional paradigm. Limiting the contribution of experts would seem to offer women the best opportunity to put their issues at the center.

Masturbation education is an important element of the feminist method, not because masturbation itself is so wonderful or educational, although it can be both. Rather, masturbation is the best metaphor for women's sexual entitlement. Betty Dodson, the feminist guru of masturbation for the past quarter-century, subtitles her book "The Joy of Selfloving" and dedicates it to herself, because "without my selflove it could never have been written" (1987, p. v). This sly note of narcissism communicates pride and empowerment, and Dodson's videos have been the single most effective feminist intervention I have used in sex therapy. I highly recommend her Website (*www.bettydodson.com*), with its video information and sexuality links. Dodson does not do "therapy" in the classical sense, but she does teach women how to masturbate and have orgasms. In 1998, I participated in a study group with Dodson to learn her techniques, and I am trying to figure out how to integrate her contribution into a professional method (psychotherapy) dominated by prohibitions around nudity and physical contact.

Recent support for prioritizing masturbation education comes from a fascinating volume on the history of vibrators (Maines, 1999). Maines has learned that her subject polarizes audiences: "In mixed groups the women look uncomfortable [as] they are aware that it is a major breach of etiquette to mention in mixed company the relative inefficiency of penetration as a means of producing female orgasm" (1999, p. xiii). Uncovering women's sexual secrets is a sure sign of feminist work and points to the continuing emphasis on self-pleasure as a feminist tool.

Audiences

Another result of placing women's voices and perspectives at the center of analysis is to recognize the miniscule effectiveness of sex therapy as compared with the extent of women's sexual problems. In my 22 years of practice, how many women's sexual lives have I helped? A couple hundred, at most. This is underwhelming. If women's sexual problems are caused by gender inequalities, then they are widespread, if not universal, and a truly effective and responsible feminist sex therapy must move outside the consulting room and into the community.

There are many women who will never see the inside of a sex therapy office, because of barriers of money and time, antitherapy prohibitions of their religions and cultures, refusal of their husbands to participate, or even threats by their (threatened) husbands should they express interest in a women's sexuality discussion group. Are these women destined to suffer sexual dissatisfaction and inhibition because those of us interested in feminist sex therapy think our work is done once we have written our articles and seen our patients?

What kind of sex therapy could we deliver through educational, media, and community health settings? If we think of our audiences as women in beauty salons and prenatal clinics, women shopping in supermarkets and on-line, schoolgirls and teenagers buying their first sanitary pads, how would that change our ideas of what feminist sex therapy is or could be? At the very least, it should open our eyes to the opportunities everywhere for preventive or remedial messages. Write for local media, leave copies of feminist articles in salons and waiting rooms, offer to facilitate discussions in diverse settings (for example, host a monthly women's and girls' sex discussion at your local Planned Parenthood clinic or offer a voluntary sex education discussion at your child's school to supplement the "abstinence-only" curriculum), distribute simple bibliographies, write strong letters to officials and companies, get girls' and women's Websites linked to feminist sex information, join activist groups—the possibilities are endless. Unfortunately but not surprisingly, most communitywide outlets are commercial, attentive to the bottom line, and not too interested in radical messages of women's sexual empowerment, so we have to be creative.

Coincidentally, as I wrote this last sentence, my phone rang and a woman producer from the television newsmagazine "20/20" asked if I would like to appear on a show discussing women and Viagra™. Now this could be an excellent opportunity for a feminist to make arguments about cooptation and medicalization to a huge audience, right? But I have learned that mainstream media usually want only a sensationalized and superficial approach to the subject, and that my challenge to received wisdom and billion-dollar profits is often cut. I resisted the temptation to contribute time to "20/20" and instead am preparing a pulpit address on women and sexuality ("From Niagara to Viagra™") for my Unitarian Universalist church. The audience will be much smaller, but there will be no censorship. Opportunities for a feminist message of sexual prevention or remediation are everywhere, so think beyond individuals or couples or even groups in your private office or classes.

Research

There can be no change in sexual vision without research. Throughout this chapter, I have called for research from women's point of view—putting women's problems at the center; bypassing the "official" nomenclature; looking at concepts, audiences, and methods with a fresh eye. Much of clinical sexology rests on an illusory understanding of the "normal," which historians teach us is in continuous evolution (Freedman & D'Emilio,

1988). It seems inexorable that our current understanding of sexuality will come to seem as antiquated to future generations as the Victorians' perspectives now seem to us. The primary suggestion I can make at this point is the perennial feminist one: Challenge all assumptions; reexamine everything. Once you remember that sex research is fundamentally political, fundamentally about power, you will be better prepared for the long haul.

☐ References

Abramson, P. R. (1990). Sexual science: Emerging discipline or oxymoron? *Journal of Sex Research, 27,* 147–165.

American Psychiatric Association. (1980). *Diagnostic and statistical manual of mental disorders* (3rd ed). Washington, DC: Author.

Ashton, A. K., Hamer, R., & Rosen, R. C. (1997). Serotonin reuptake inhibitor-induced sexual dysfunction and its treatment: A large-scale retrospective study of 596 psychiatric outpatients. *Journal of Sex & Marital Therapy, 23,* 165–175.

Berlet, C. (Ed.). (1995). *Eyes right! Challenging the right wing backlash.* Boston: South End Press.

Brannigan, G. G., Allgeier, E. R., & Allgeier, A. R. (1998). *The sex scientists.* New York: Longman.

Bullough, B., Bullough, V. L., Fithian, M. A., Hartman, W. E., & Klein, R. S. (1997). *Personal stories of "how I got into sex."* Amherst, NY: Prometheus Books.

Cole, E., & Rothblum, E. (Eds.). (1988). *Women and sex therapy.* Special issue of *Women & Therapy, 7*(2/3).

Demac, D. A. (1990). *Liberty denied: The current rise of censorship in America.* New Brunswick, NJ: Rutgers University Press.

DiMauro, D. (1995). *Sexuality research in the United States: An assessment of the social and behavioral sciences.* New York: Social Science Research Council.

Dodson, B. (1987) *Sex for one: The joy of selfloving.* New York: Crown Publishers.

English, D., Hollibaugh, A., & Rubin, G. (1981). Talking sex: A conversation on sexuality and feminism. *Socialist Review, 11*(58), 43–62.

Ehrenreich, B., Hess, E., & Jacobs, J. (1982). A report on the sex crisis. *Ms.* (March), 61–63, 87–88.

Ellis, K., Jaker, B., Hunter, N. D., O'Dair, B., & Tallmer, A. (1988). *Caught looking: Feminism, pornography, & censorship.* Seattle: Real Comet Press.

Federation of Women's Health Centers. (1981). *A new view of a woman's body.* New York: Simon & Schuster.

Freedman, E. B., & D'Emilio, J. (1988). *Intimate matters: A history of sex in America.* New York: Harper & Row.

Goldstein, I., & Berman, J. R. (1998). Vasculogenic female sexual dysfunction: Vaginal engorgement and clitoral erectile insufficiency syndromes. *International Journal of Impotence Research, 10*(2), S84–90, S98–101.

Hall, M. (1998). *The lesbian love companion.* New York: HarperCollins.

Hare-Mustin, R. T. (1991). Sex, lies, and headaches: The problem is power. *Journal of Feminist Family Therapy, 3,* 39–61.

Hartman, W. E., & Fithian, M. A. (1974). *Treatment of sexual function: A bio-psycho-social approach.* New York: Jason Aronson.

Heise, L. (1995) Violence, sexuality, and women's lives. In R. G. Parker & J. H. Gagnon (Eds.), *Conceiving sexuality: Approaches to sex research in a postmodern world* (pp. 109–134). New York: Routledge.

Hite, S. (1976). *The Hite report*. New York: Macmillan.

Hollibaugh, A., & Moraga, C. (1983). What we're rolling around in bed with: Sexual silences in feminism. In A. Snitow, C. Stansell, & S. Thompson (Eds.), *Powers of desire: The politics of sexuality* (pp. 394–405). New York: Monthly Review Press.

Hollway, W. (1984). Gender difference and the production of subjectivity. In J. Henriques, W. Hollway, C. Urwin, C. Venn, & V. Walkerdine (Eds.), *Changing the subject: Psychology, social regulation, and subjectivity* (pp. 227–263). New York: Methuen.

Hunter, J. D. (1991). *Culture wars: The struggle to define America*. New York: Basic Books.

Jackson, S., & Scott, S. (Eds.). (1996). *Feminism and sexuality: A reader*. New York: Columbia University Press.

Jong, E. (1989). Ziplash: A sexual libertine recants. *Ms.* (May), 49.

Kaplan, H. S. (1974). *The new sex therapy*. New York: Brunner/Mazel.

Koedt., A. (1973). The myth of the vaginal orgasm. In A. Koedt, E. Levine, & A. Rapone (Eds.), *Radical feminism* (pp. 198–207). New York: Quadrangle Books.

Landrine, H. (1995). Introduction: Cultural diversity, contextualism, and feminist psychology. In H. Landrine (Ed.), *Bringing cultural diversity to feminist psychology* (pp. 1–20). Washington, DC: American Psychological Association.

Laumann, E. O., Gagnon, J. H., Michael, R. T., & Michaels, S. (1994). *The social organization of sexuality: Sexual practices in the United States*. Chicago: University of Chicago Press.

Laumann, E. O., Paik, A., & Rosen, R. C. (1999). Sexual dysfunction in the United States: Prevalence and predictors. *Journal of the American Medical Association, 281*, 537–544.

Little, W. N., Park, G. T., & Patton, H. M. (1998). Letter to the editor. *New England Journal of Medicine, 339*, 700.

Loulan, J. (1982). *Lesbian sex*. San Francisco: Spinsters Book Co.

Loulan, J. (1984). *Lesbian passion: Loving ourselves and each other*. San Francisco: Spinsters Book Co.

Loulan, J. (1990). *The lesbian erotic dance: Butch, femme, androgyny, and other rhythms*. San Francisco: Spinsters Book Co.

Luker, K. (1996). *Dubious conceptions: The politics of teenage pregnancy*. Cambridge, MA: Harvard University Press.

Maines, R. R. P. (1999). *The technology of orgasm: "Hysteria," the vibrator, and women's sexual satisfaction*. Baltimore, MD: Johns Hopkins University Press.

Masters, W. H., & Johnson, V. E. (1966). *Human sexual response*. Boston: Little, Brown.

Masters, W. H., & Johnson, V. E. (1970). *Human sexual inadequacy*. Boston: Little, Brown.

Newton, E., & Walton, S. (1984). The misunderstanding: Toward a more precise sexual vocabulary. In C. S. Vance (Ed.), *Pleasure and danger: Exploring female sexuality* (pp. 242–250). Boston: Routledge & Kegan Paul.

Park, K., Goldstein, I. C., Siroky, M. B., Krane, R. J., & Azadzoi, K. M. (1997). Vasculogenic female sexual dysfunction: The hemodynamic basis for vaginal engorgement insufficiency and clitoral erectile insufficiency. *International Journal of Impotence Research, 9*, 27–37.

The porno plague. (1976). *Time* (April 5), cover story.

Rothblum, E. D., & Brehony, K. A. (Eds.). (1993). *Boston marriages: Romantic but asexual relationships among contemporary lesbians*. Amherst, MA: University of Massachusetts Press.

Rubin, G. (1984). Thinking sex: Notes for a radical theory of the politics of sexuality. In C. S. Vance (Ed.), *Pleasure and danger: Exploring female sexuality* (pp. 267–319). Boston: Routledge & Kegan Paul.

Schnarch, D. (1997). *Passionate marriage*. New York: Henry Holt & Co.

Schover, L. R., & Leiblum, S. R. (1994). Commentary: The stagnation of sex therapy. *Journal of Psychology & Human Sexuality, 6,* 5–30.

Segraves, R. T. (1998). Editorial: Pharmacological era in the treatment of sexual disorders. *Journal of Sex & Marital Therapy, 24,* 67–68.

Snitow, A. B. (1983). Mass market romance: Pornography for women is different. In A. Snitow, C. Stansell, & S. Thompson (Eds.), *Powers of desire: The politics of sexuality* (pp. 245–263). New York: Monthly Review Press.

Strossen, N. (1995). *Defending pornography: Free speech, sex, and the fight for women's rights.* New York: Scribner.

Tiefer, L. (1978). The context and consequences of contemporary sex research: A feminist perspective. In T. McGill, D. Dewsbury, & B. Sachs (Eds.), *Sex and behavior: Status and prospectus* (pp. 363–385). New York: Plenum Press.

Tiefer, L. (1986). In pursuit of the perfect penis: The medicalization of male sexuality. *American Behavioral Scientist, 29,* 579–599.

Tiefer, L. (1991). Commentary on the status of sex research: Feminism, sexuality and sexology. *Journal of Psychology & Human Sexuality, 4,* 5–42.

Tiefer, L. (1994). The medicalization of impotence: Normalizing phallocentrism. *Gender & Society, 8,* 363–377.

Tiefer, L. (1995). *"Sex is not a natural act" and other essays.* Boulder, CO: Westview Press.

Tiefer, L. (1996a). Toward a feminist sex therapy. *Women and Therapy, 19,* 53–64.

Tiefer, L. (1996b). The medicalization of sexuality: Conceptual, normative, and professional issues. *Annual Review of Sex Research, 7,* 252–282.

Tiefer, L. (1996c). *Transcultural aspects of sex therapy.* Presentation at Society for Sex Therapy and Research, October, New York City.

Tiefer, L., & Melman, A. (1983). Interview of wives: A necessary adjunct in the evaluation of impotence. *Sexuality & Disability, 6,* 167–175.

U.S. Department of Justice. (1986). *Attorney General's Commission on Pornography final report.* Washington, DC: U.S. Government Printing Office.

Vance, C. S. (Ed.). (1984). *Pleasure and danger: Exploring female sexuality.* Boston: Routledge & Kegan Paul.

Wagner, D. (1997). *The new temperance: The American obsession with sin and vice.* Boulder, CO: Westview Press.

Zilbergeld, B., & Ellison, C. R. (1980). Desire discrepancies and arousal problems in sex therapy. In S. R. Leiblum & L. A. Previn (Eds.), *Principles and practice of sex therapy* (pp. 65–104). New York: Guilford Press.

3

CHAPTER

Gary R. Brooks, Ph.D.

Challenging Dominant Discourses of Male (Hetero)Sexuality: The Clinical Implications of New Voices About Male Sexuality

The tragedy of contemporary male (hetero)sexuality[1] is nowhere more apparent than in the seemingly boundless public fascination with two of the most seminal events of the late 1990s—the appearance of Viagra™ and the Clinton/Lewinsky scandal. Although media preoccupation with certain news stories can undoubtedly strain the patience of many, the media spotlight can also perform significant public service by enhancing awareness of certain critical topics. For example, the O.J. Simpson trial certainly increased attention to issues of domestic violence. The Clarence Thomas/Anita Hill confrontations heightened awareness of the multiple nuances of sexual harassment. In theory, the Viagra™ and Clinton/Lewinsky stories could similarly provoke a badly needed national conversation about the "dominant discourses" (Hare-Mustin, 1994) that shape male sexuality and ideas about sexual dysfunction.

---

1. Because the author's scholarship and clinical experience have been predominantly within the framework of heterosexual experience, this chapter is most applicable to heterosexual male sexuality. Much of it, however, seems to have relevance to the lives of gay men who have been continually exposed to the dominant values of heterosexist culture.

Sadly, this has not taken place. In fact, the major effect has been the reinforcement of most conventional aspects of this model. Much of this has taken place because a major voice has been missing from the discussion—the voice pleading for a new model (discourse) of male sexuality, a voice calling for men to embrace a more mature and relational model of sexuality, to develop "sexual integrity" (Good, 1998).

To examine closely the underlying assumptions and basic dominant discourses of male sexuality, I will review two prominent samples of the discussion about Viagra™/sexual dysfunction and Lewinsky/Clinton—articles appearing recently in the journals *Sexualities* and *Journal of the American Medical Association*. One comment must be made regarding my selection of these particular articles. The first of these has not been chosen because of singular flaws or failings, but because it can be reasonably viewed as broadly representative of the primary values and assumptions underlying this field—it is a central part of dominant discourses about male sexuality circa 1999. The second article is notable for an additional reason. Despite the enormous media fascination with the Clinton/Lewinsky affair, the event has been minimally noted in the sexuality literature. In brief, the articles have been offered to illustrate my central point. Even in the most respected and mainstream representations of contemporary thought, there is no voice being given to the need for a new view of male sexuality, a view that challenges nonrelational sexuality and calls for male sexual integrity.

☐ Basic Assumptions About Sexual Dysfunction

The basic assumptions about male sexual dysfunction can be deciphered through study of both the way the field defines the basic problem and the types of solutions proposed.

Definition of the Problem

Considerable media attention recently welcomed an article published in the *Journal of the American Medical Association (JAMA)* that suggested sexual dysfunction is relatively common and poorly treated in the United States. The article, "Sexual Dysfunction in the United States: Prevalence and Predictors" (Laumann, Paik, & Rosen, 1999) was an outgrowth of the authors' analysis of data from the 1992 National Health and Social Life Survey. Among the well-published findings were indications that (a) 43% of women and 30% of men have sexual dysfunctions, (b) persons with sexual dysfunctions tend to have poorer quality of life indicators and problematic relationships, and (c) less than 20% of women and men seek medical consultation for their problems.

It is hard to quarrel with either the methodology or important public health implications of this research. Sexual dysfunction is widespread and minimally addressed. Yet, when one attends closely to the structure and assumptions of this research, disquieting issues arise.

To begin with the most rudimentary issue, what was actually being examined? Not surprisingly, the authors adopted the standard medical definition of sexual dysfunction—the definition found in *the Diagnostic and Statistical Manual of Mental Disorders* (*DSM-IV*, APA, 1994).

According to the *DSM-IV* (p. 493), sexual dysfunction is "characterized by a disturbance in the processes that characterize the sexual response cycle or by pain associated with sexual intercourse." These processes of the sexual response cycle are *desire, excitement, orgasm,* and *resolution.* Based on the literal wording of this definition, one could infer that "sexual dysfunction" could include any type of "disturbance" in the process or any type of "pain" associated with sexual intercourse. Theoretically, this could include *too many* sexual fantasies (situations in which someone cannot function because of excessive sexual fantasies that interfere with the present sexual encounter or someone is preoccupied with sexual fantasies in inappropriate situations) or *too much* sexual excitement (erections at the wrong time). Likewise, "pain associated with sexual intercourse" could theoretically refer to *psychic pain* (anxiety or guilt during or following sexual intercourse that is inappropriate).

It would be erroneous, however, to interpret the *DSM-IV* definition in this way. When one reads on, it becomes clear that the official definition of sexual dysfunction includes only *too little* sex or *not enough* physical pleasure. Therefore, within the official way of thinking, clinicians should not attend too much to a client's sexuality in context—that is, *when* they get aroused, with *whom*, and whether the sexual activity produces anything other than *physical* pleasure.

My second major concern about this article is its reinforcement of another aspect of the dominant discourse about male sexuality: When we define sexual health and dysfunction only in terms of frequency and adequacy of sexual performance, we end up with an odd exemplar of sexual vigor—the adolescent male. Ever ready for sexual encounters, with frequent and enduring erections, the young male escapes the attention of sexual dysfunction experts, while women (43%) and older men (the bulk of the 30%) are identified as sexually unhealthy. This is consistent with age-old dominant discourses and sexual stereotypes about women as frigid or sexual repressed and older men as enfeebled, mere shadows of themselves in their sexual prime of life.

Third, this article presented an interesting argument about the relationship between a person's sexual activity and his or her life satisfaction. Although the authors "stress that concomitant outcomes cannot be causally linked as an outcome of sexual dysfunction" (Laumann et al., 1999, p. 542), they did not hesitate to make that very argument—sexual dysfunction creates a low quality of life. For example, they boldly stated that studied data suggest that "sexual dysfunction is a largely uninvestigated yet a significant public health problem" (p. 544).

It would be hard to argue with this statement, since persons who do not have sex may well be more likely to be unhappy and unfulfilled. What concerns me is what the authors did not say. They omitted any reference to the interaction between quality of life and sexual functioning. That is, wouldn't we expect that a person's sex life would suffer if he or she has very poor relationships and generally unsatisfactory life circumstances? In fact, shouldn't it be considered odd if a person could have abundant sexual activity at such a time?

The authors made the fascinating observation that, for women, high rates of partner turnover and the resultant stressful sexual encounters provide the basis for "sexual pain and anxiety" (Laumann et al., 1999, p. 542). They further noted that "young men are not similarly affected." Unfortunately, since they made no further comment, one is left with the impression that young men are more sexually resilient, while young women are somehow incapacitated by trivial questions such as, "Do I know this person?" and "Do we care about each other?"

My fear is this: When the authors failed to recognize the interaction between quality of life and sexual behavior, they ended up suggesting interventions for men that focus on only a portion of the problem. In fact, immediately after citing sexual dysfunction as a significant public health problem, they said "recent advances in therapy for erectile dysfunction may increase quality of life for some men" (Laumann et al., 1999, p. 544). However, they failed to say anything at all about how improving men's quality of life (that is, their relationships, interpersonal communication, and sexual sensitivity) might have salubrious effects on their sexuality. They also said nothing whatsoever about the dangers of having sex when one is otherwise not in a good emotional place—that is, of ignoring one's psyche, which is telling one to lay off.

Finally, there is the issue of how to deal with this public health concern. Laumann et al. (1999) were very dismayed about the low rates of help-seeking behavior, noting that "roughly 10% and 20% of these afflicted men and women, respectively, sought medical consultation for their sexual problems" (p. 542). I have no problem here, because greater attention to problems of sexuality would be beneficial. However, based on my reading of the article, it is hard to ascertain how this medical help will provide what is really needed. The authors said little, except to make reference to "the recent advances in treatments for erectile dysfunction" (p. 544). When one understands (as reported by Grady, 1999) that two of the article's authors are paid consultants to Pfizer, the manufacturer of Viagra™, it is easy to imagine what "recent advances" they are supporting.

What Medical Science Offers Men

Despite its shortcomings, the science of modern medicine has been remarkably able to meet the needs of its constituency (at least those with financial clout and political influence). This certainly applies to sexuality. According to a recent article in the *Archives of Sexual Behavior* (Rosen & Ashton, 1993), there is something timeless about the interest in increased sexual performance. "The search for an effective aphrodisiac has been a perennial pursuit of most societies throughout history" (p. 521). The authors reinforced their point about the broad interest in "prosexual" drugs by noting the following (p. 522): "In particular, the search for a perfect aphrodisiac—a drug that will heighten sexual desire, pleasure, and performance—has been a continuing cultural quest from ancient to modern times."

It is unfortunate that the authors of this article identified the preoccupation with aphrodisiacs as a "cultural quest," without noting a rather obvious fact: Male members of the culture are far more likely to perennially pursue perfect performance than are women. Over the past several decades, there has been abundant interest and enormous creativity in the search for methods to enhance *male* sexual performance. From gels and creams to external vacuum pumps, penis rings, injections, plastic supports, and implanted hydraulic pumps, medical science has relentlessly pursued an engineering solution to male sexual difficulties.

In the past few years, there has been growing dissatisfaction with this "medicalization of male sexuality" and the very problematic male sexual script that undergirds it. Zilbergeld (1978) was one of the first to harshly criticize the phallocentric model of male sexuality. By identifying common myths of male sexuality, Zilbergeld challenged ideas of male sexuality being equated with the tireless functioning of an erect penis, unencumbered by situational or relational concerns. Tiefer has also been a leading critic of this engineering approach to male sexuality and has identified multiple problems with this "pursuit of the perfect penis" (1987, p. 165). Most principally, this medicalization of male sexuality "denies, obscures, and ignores the social causes . . . helps men conform to the [problematic male sexual] script rather than analyzing where the script comes from or challenging it" (Tiefer, 1987, p.165).

Despite the challenge of a few outspoken critics, the medicalization of male sexuality has not only continued but shifted from mechanical engineering to chemical engineering. With the appearance of the new "miracle" drug sildenafil citrate (Viagra™), this approach has reached never-imagined levels of hype and potential prosperity. According to early reports (Handy, 1998, p. 50), sildenafil citrate promises to be the most popular of all new drugs, "prescribed at the rate of 10,000 scripts a day, outpacing such famous quick starters as the antidepressant Prozac . . . and the baldness remedy Rogaine."

Finally, science would provide men with what it considered most needed. Men would be given a simple method of ensuring erections upon demand—a magic cure to sexual dysfunction, without the need for examination of sex in its relational context. Sadly, amid the excitement of this medical miracle there has been no concomitant call to look at the broader picture—the problematic way that male sexuality has been constructed.

☐ The Clinton/Lewinsky Scandal

The second illustration of missing voices is found in the highly visible national conversation about the sexual relations between Bill Clinton and Monica Lewinsky. Amid the torrent of attention to this "affair," a particularly broad analysis has been offered by *Sexualities*, a journal devoted to scholarly study of contemporary sexual values and behavior. In a "Special Feature" section, the journal offered a "symposium" by "six prominent commentators" (*Sexualities*, 1999). I selected this journal and its special section for attention because it seems especially representative of my theme—that even in scholarly analyses of contemporary sexual phenomena, a critical voice is missing.

In the *Sexualities* articles, six important points of view were offered. First, Stein (1999) analyzed the Clinton/Lewinsky scandal in terms of "two clashing notions of sexual morality" (p. 248). She looked at public reaction to the Clinton-Lewinsky affair in terms of how it reflected the struggle about morality and sexual behavior.

Next, Jackson (1999) discussed the affair from a feminist perspective. She was particularly critical of how "this reveals a great deal about male (hetero)sexuality, about the ability of men to divorce body and mind, to localize their sexuality in their genitals" (p. 252).

Murray, writing as a gay American man, and Shrage, writing from her research with lesbian prostitutes (Murray, 1999; Shrage, 1999), both discussed the Clinton/Lewinsky affair in terms of how it raised issues about the definition of "what is sex?"

Stones (1999) analyzed the Clinton-Lewinski affair, as well as the public fascination with Princess Diana, in terms of the social psychological processes by which the masses become engaged in the intimate lives of public figures. Finally, Hearn (1999) linked the affair to growing interest in the topic of "sex at work," noting a welcome realization that sexuality must be recognized and studied in this context.

My brief and skimpy review of this very important, scholarly symposium does major injustice to the depth and complexity of the ideas presented. This failing, however, does not detract from my central point about a critical missing voice: Although Stein came the closest, none of these six commentators really looked at the Clinton/Lewinsky affair in terms of how dominant discourses of male sexuality frequently produce calamitous outcomes in men's lives. None seemed to provide an adequate answer to the question, "Why on earth would he do this?"

Although it certainly reveals many important issues about contemporary morality, sexism, and popular culture, the Clinton/Lewinsky affair most dramatically reveals the extent of problems with normative male sexuality at the end of the millennium. It illustrates the predictable problems and multiple penalties inherent in the dominant discourse of male heterosexuality. It screams for attention to the dysfunctional way that our culture teaches heterosexual men to relate to women and sexuality, to define sexual health and sexual dysfunction.

But public discussion of sexuality is a complex and sometimes perilous process. In early 1999, George D. Lundberg was fired as editor of *JAMA* after the journal published an article about college student attitudes on whether oral-genital contact qualified as having "had sex" (Sanders & Reinisch, 1999). Amid the furor about the timing and politics of the article, little recognition was paid to the important content of the soundly conducted research. In a somewhat similar fashion, most of the public discussion of Bill Clinton's sexual behavior with Monica Lewinsky has been insufficient, as it has focused exclusively on his moral failings and betrayal of public trust. This discussion is important, but not nearly enough. To limit discussion to Clinton's moral failings and character flaws is to buy into "aberrant male theory" (Brooks & Silverstein, 1995). According to this perspective, Clinton is considered to be an outlyer, nonrepresentative of most men. But this is simply not the case. Despite the public posturing of "holier than thou" male politicians, Clinton's behavior is far from atypical among men in power. In the past decade the American public has been exposed to seemingly endless news stories revealing sexual indiscretions by men of power and influence. From Tailhook to the White House, from the halls of the U.S. Senate to the Supreme Court, from Hollywood to the National Basketball Association, from church pulpits to college fraternities, we have been exposed to repetitions of the same troubling news story—vast numbers of men with power and influence engage in sexual behavior that is reckless and destructive to others and themselves.

It is time, then, to consider Bill Clinton (Wilbur Mills, Robert Packwood, Woody Allen, Hugh Grant, Henry Cisneros, Wilt Chamberlain) as something other than a talented man with tragic character flaws. Instead of this exclusive view, it would be far more helpful to consider Clinton's behavior as "representative" of what men have been taught, as a logical outgrowth of dominant male sexual discourse. Rather than considering him as a man who has been *undersocialized*, it would be helpful to consider Clinton as one who has been *oversocialized*.[2]

Most public reactions to and national conversations about the current crisis of male sexuality are fatally flawed by their acceptance of an anachronistic delusion or inexcusable set of lies. Whether naive self-deception or calculated disinformation, the American public has repeatedly been encouraged to accept a myth. America wants to believe that it teaches its boys and men to have sexual integrity, to be sexually responsible, to integrate their emotional and relational needs with their sexual desires. This is simply not the case. American boys and men have been shaped and maintained to hold a view of women that is both voyeuristic and objectifying. They have been taught (and reinforced for) a version of male sexuality that is irresponsible, competitive, acquisitive, and destructive of their capacity for intimacy and relationships. In brief, most American men have been conditioned to develop the "centerfold syndrome" (Brooks, 1995).

☐ The Centerfold Syndrome, Nonrelational Sexuality, and Sexual Integrity

When you define the wrong problem, you will develop the wrong set of solutions. Such is the case with the dominant views of the sexual problems of contemporary men. The highly limited view of male sexual dysfunction typified by the engineering approaches to its resolution and the overly narrow public consideration of the Clinton/Lewinsky affair typifies a tragic failure of sexual consciousness—the failure to give voice to the

---

2. I would like to acknowledge Harry Brod (1987), who first used this conceptualization and phraseology to understand male violence.

ways that normative male sexuality is harmful not just to women but also to men. Normative male sexuality, as taught to contemporary young men and regularly celebrated by many sectors of popular culture, is infected with dysfunctional messages about what is sexy and what is in men's sexual best interest. Normative male sexuality encourages a "nonrelational" view of sexuality (Levant & Brooks, 1997) and promotes the centerfold syndrome (Brooks, 1995). To counteract the destructive aspects of normative male sexuality, men must work collaboratively and assiduously to promote sexual integrity (Good, 1998).

In the following section, the core elements of the centerfold syndrome and its implications for change will be outlined briefly. Once this conceptualization is presented, it becomes much easier to recognize the missing voice in the national conversation about male sexuality—the voice calling for men to reject the centerfold syndrome and nonrelational sexuality and to adopt a model of sexual integrity.

What Is the Centerfold Syndrome?

The centerfold syndrome is a pervasive distortion in the way men are taught to think about women and sexuality. It is an outgrowth of the social construction of male sexuality and a product of men's lifelong problematic relations with women, from early life struggles with intimacy and autonomy to later problems in integrating sexuality and intimacy. In part, the syndrome is a product of the ways young men have been conditioned to relate with women. But early training alone cannot account for it, since the patterns of the centerfold syndrome are assiduously reinforced by the many destructive ways that our culture portrays women and sexuality.

There may be five relatively discrete aspects of the Centerfold Syndrome:

1. *Voyeurism*: There is little argument that "looking at" is a distinguishing feature of men's sexuality. Men expend enormous resources to gaze at women's bodies. Both everyday experience and the scientific literature support this impression.

   Knoth, Boyd, and Singer (1988), for example, found that teenage boys are far more likely than teenage girls to be aroused by visual stimuli such as nude pictures. Similarly, boys are more likely to have far more visually graphic sexual fantasies. These researchers found that girls, on the other hand, are more likely to be sexually aroused by romantic fantasies and by a partner in an emotionally intimate situation. Males are the predominant consumers of nude magazines and autoerotic materials (Michael, Gagnon, Lauman, & Kolata, 1994). Gaylor (1985) described pornography as the "largest entertainment industry in America." She further noted that six of the bestselling magazines are soft-core pornography magazines and that there are more sex emporiums than McDonald's franchises.

2. *Objectification*: Closely related to men's preoccupation with staring at women's bodies is the process of objectification of women and their bodies. The centerfold syndrome calls for men to be observers, while women are the objects of that observation. Ellis and Symons (1990) noted that "men are more likely to view *others* as the objects of their sexual desires, whereas women are more likely to view *themselves* as the objects of sexual desire" (p. 529).

   This objectification of women's bodies is closely tied to gender politics, as it is highly reflective of men's traditional power over women. Being allowed to "watch" is a political act, as only groups in power are allowed to openly observe others. The powerful watch the less powerful, while the powerless avoid eye contact and watch covertly. In patriarchal cultures only men are allowed "authorized images" (Beneke, 1990) of naked bodies of the other sex.

   Feminist pornography critics have exhaustively identified the many ways that objectification of women's bodies is used to suppress women. For example, Griffin (1984, p. 36) noted that "the very core of the pornographic mise-en-scene is the concept of woman as object . . . it produces an image of a thing." Wolf (1991) extended the concept of objectification from pornography to the worlds of fashion and the "beauty" industry. For her, the "beauty myth" and "beauty pornography" are further methods for patriarchal culture to oppress women though objectification.

3. *Masculinity validation*: Although men have typically had more economic and political power than women, men have historically been highly dependent on women to validate their masculinity. Pleck (1981) noted that the traditional masculinity code prevents men from feeling fully virile unless women "play their prescribed role of doing the things that make men feel masculine" (p. 420). One especially critical aspect of this is for women to validate men as sexually potent beings. In some very graphic ways, a young man is commonly taught that the physical responsiveness of a woman's body is a direct reflection of his masculinity. If he reads sex manuals, he is likely to become preoccupied with his

ability to produce an orgasm in women. For example, Zilbergeld (1978) noted that the prominent myths of male sexuality include the idea that men needed validation from women's bodies: "a man must take charge and orchestrate good sex; good sex is a linear progression of increasing excitement terminated only by an orgasm" (p. 44). Men have been taught that a dramatic response from a woman's body—erect nipples, gyrating hips, a shuddering orgasm—can be interpreted as unambiguous evidence of manliness. On the other hand, a cool, listless, or indifferent response is likely to leave a man feeling ineffectual, inadequate, and resentful.

4. *Trophyism*: Because the dominant masculine world view is hierarchical, men experience their masculinity in relative terms—how do I stack up against other men? Men constantly compare themselves with other men and endlessly seek tokens of manhood that are seen to be in short supply. The worthiest tokens of manhood go to the worthiest men— the winners and power brokers. Women's bodies historically have been among the most treasured of all tokens—the trophy wife goes to the highest performing male. Women's bodies become living testaments to a man's prowess as a financial success, skillful sexual performer, or fearless warrior.

This male competition for access to women's bodies begins in adolescence when boys compete to be the first to "score" with the sexiest "fox," or to put the most sexual notches on the belt. The strategy of using women's bodies as trophies is damaging enough in adolescence, but it becomes even more destructive when the sexual predator role clashes with a young man's need to find a more durable relationship and long-term partner. Although the centerfold woman remains the epitome of what men have learned to sexually desire, she is no longer available because of demands of a real relationship. Men typically want to remain faithful to one partner, yet there are so many others who are visually desirable. Not surprisingly, as some men become increasingly successful and powerful, they feel cheated because they have been forbidden access to the most cherished symbols of their success—centerfold women.

5. *Fears of true intimacy*: Young boys are conditioned to feel shame over feelings of weakness and vulnerability, encouraged to suppress their needs for sensual physical contact, and expected to develop male body armor with hard muscles and an emotionally stoic exterior. In childhood, boys learn to associate women's bodies with softness, intimacy, and sensuality, the very qualities they have been taught to reject. De-

spite being encouraged to engage in manic activity and rough play, boys crave physical closeness and sensuality, but they have neither permission to request it nor avenues to experience it.

In adolescence, young men are caught between the newly appearing waves of sexual urgency and the extreme prohibitions against emotional intimacy. The sudden hormonal pressures of sexuality and the fears of intimacy surprise most young men and pose major conflicts that are almost never adequately addressed. Commonly there is some token guidance in the advice that they should be sexually controlled (or abstinent), but young men realize this for the sham it is. Their bodies, their peers, their role models, and the media send the dominant message that sexual activity is essential, that boys should get as much sex as they can.

Unfortunately, the same young men who are encouraged to become preoccupied with sex have been encouraged to resist emotional sensitivity and pretend to be emotionally tough or stoic. They have been taught to be aggressive and competitive, and they have been discouraged from learning the skills of empathy, compassion, and interpersonal communication. Although young men need emotional intimacy, they have repressed their needs and try to substitute sexuality of the "slam-bam-thank-you-ma'am" or "get-me-some booty" variety. Sexual needs are given primacy, while sensuality needs are suppressed or ignored.

As young men learn to wall themselves off from too much emotional intimacy in sex, they develop "nonrelational" sexuality (Levant & Brooks, 1997). Subsequently, they come to sexualize all feelings of emotional and physical closeness. As a result, it becomes nearly impossible for them to experience nonsexual intimacy. They have great difficulty differentiating their emotional needs from their sexual needs because they have been raised in a culture that pays minuscule attention to men's needs for intimacy and nurturing while exalting their sexual needs. It is not surprising, then, that a man wanting to be emotionally intimate assumes that he wants sex, that he is just "horny." Sadly, many men seek sex when they really are more desirous of emotional intimacy, sensual pleasure, or physical comforting.

On the other hand, because they have been taught to disconnect their emotional state from their sexual arousal, men can also engage in sex activity with women they neither like nor respect. In fact, many men develop the dubious capacity to have sexual relations with women they despise. Sex often becomes something far different than an act of emotional connection and intimacy; instead, it is an act that expresses a range of negative emotions or meets unrelated needs. As a result, men often have sex for all the wrong reasons. They rarely experience emotional connection without sex, yet they cannot always distinguish just why they are engaged in the activity when it occurs.

☐ Clinical Implications of This New View of Male Sexuality

Contemporary men will experience far greater levels of sexual gratification when they embrace sexual integrity. Sex therapy, therefore, needs to be far more broadly defined to include more than just efforts to create erections and more timely ejaculations. Sex therapy must include efforts to help men integrate intimacy and emotional connection into their sexuality. To accomplish these objectives, changes will be needed at both the broad cultural level and in therapist's offices.

Cultural Change

Although cultural change is not the principal responsibility of therapists, their work will be greatly facilitated by heightened awareness of the need for new views about male sexuality. We desperately need a new and different national forum on male sexuality. Consciousness must be raised about the multiple shortcomings of traditional views. Men must question assertively our culture's denial of these problems. We must not become discouraged by those who insist that change is foolhardy, claiming that women and men always have and always will be so essentially different that things must always continue as they are. We must also be alert to the ploys of those who want to shift the blame to women, claiming that women enjoy tantalizing and controlling men. Finally, we must avoid being duped by those who try to perpetuate the traditional views of male sexuality by aligning them with the cause of sexual freedom. For example, there has long been a school of thought holding that any challenge to soft-core pornography is automatically antisex. Those who profit from objectification and sexual exploitation claim that their products are "sex aids"—that they *help* men to be sexual. They do. *But they help men to be sexual in the old-fashioned way that harms gender relations and debases men's sexuality.* These magazines continue to teach the values of nonrelational sexuality. The cause of sexual freedom will be served when men *choose* to reject soft-core pornography and seek intimate sexuality with real women.

What is required to get on with the process of change? First, we need to become deeply knowledgeable and respectful of the socialization processes of women and men. We need to be attentive to the women and men who are courageously challenging violent pornography, rape mythology, sexual harassment, and other forms of oppression of women's bodies.

The central point of this discourse is that the dominant messages about male sexuality are egregiously limited: They take sex out of context. They view sex as separate from the relationship between the sexual partners. Women are taught that they should simultaneously be stimulators of men's sexual arousal and gatekeepers of the sexual playground. Men are taught to objectify women, compete for the favors of the most desirable female sex objects, abandon control of their sexual arousal, and disconnect their sexuality from their psychological and relational selves.

Because the problem is fundamentally about the disconnection between sexuality and psyche, the needed sex therapy is radically different than that currently proffered. It is less about sexual performance and more about connecting sexual activity with interpersonal harmony, physical and emotional intimacy. In metaphorical terms, it is about relocating male sexuality from the penis to the "heart" and "soul." This, of course, does not eliminate the role of the penis, but it does create greater connection with men's hearts (their feelings of sensitivity, compassion, and love) and their souls (their moral and relational consciences).

The core of the approach is the conviction that the biggest sexual problems of contemporary men are those that are least attended to. They are not the problems of limp penises, but the problems of penile erections that are promiscuous, disconnected from relationships. They are about the domination of lust and the ignoring of sensuality. They are about the need to broaden sexuality from the penis to the entire male body.

This perspective on male sexuality encounters an area of extreme political sensitivity. It calls for radical challenge to *male* sexuality and to men's behavior. It is unbalanced. It seems to call primarily for only one sex to change. It is my experience that this view frequently generates hurt feelings and defensiveness: "Why are you picking on men? What's so awful about *male* sexuality?"

In response to this, I argue the following. First, I have no desire to single out men as culprits; indeed, they are victims of this deficient view of male sexual functioning. The culture at large (a culture composed of both women and men) has constructed and supported this distorted male sexuality. Over the past three decades, women have begun to challenge distortions in views of themselves as sexual beings—to own the right to be sexual beings, to be sexual initiators, to free themselves from outrageous expectations of their physical selves. There is much work yet to do, but women have begun to recognize and challenge many aversive features of the dominant discourses about female sexuality. *Male sexuality* is now singled out for change, because its is *men's* turn.

Second, I am not suggesting there cannot be a place for nonrelational sexuality, disconnected and unbridled lustiness (behaviors typically seen as part of male sexuality). I have no interest in presenting "antisex" messages or detracting from sexuality that works well for all parties. Instead, the effort is to "degender" nonrelational sexuality. This type of sexual behavior, if desired and deemed appropriate, can become part of women's sexual repertoire, but it must simultaneously become far less central to male sexuality.

Sex Therapists Helping Individual Men

Sex therapists can initiate the process of overcoming nonrelational sexuality by (a) educating men about problematic symptoms, (b) introducing healthier sexual habits, (c) improving couple communication about men's sexual heritage, and (d) helping couples integrate greater emotional intimacy into their sexuality.

Recognizing Problematic Symptoms

A first step toward sexual integrity is recognizing symptoms of nonrelational sexuality. These could include a man displaying visual obsession with women's bodies, regular use of pornography, frequenting of topless bars, inability to avoid staring at attractive women who pass by, staring at women's body parts during conversation, inability to make love without fantasies of other women, masturbatory fantasies that focus exclusively on voyeurism and never include two persons, severe sexual insecurity that requires lavish praise about sexual performance, obsession with a female partner's orgasms, and emotional withdrawal following ejaculation.

Changing Habits

Because nonrelational sexuality is supported by maladaptive habits that are conditioned through ejaculation, sex therapists need to help men relearn many sexual practices. Most important, men need to be helped to view women differently. Instead of using sexualized objects in pornography to stimulate arousal for masturbation, men can be helped to substitute more relational and emotionally meaningful fantasies. For example, instead of imaging a naked stripper or bikini-clad stranger, they can image themselves in an intimate, loving, and sensual setting with someone they care for deeply. They can learn to shift their focus from depersonalized sexual objects to their overall sensual experiences.

Also, men can be helped to change the way they have learned to think about their sexual arousal. Instead of seeing it as a powerfully urgent drive, demanding rapid expression and quick relief, they can learn to think of it as a rhythmic and natural variation, an ebbing and flowing of physical and psychological states, which they can learn to integrate into their emotional and relational realities. Sexual arousal can be seen not just as a physical urge but as an integral part of a man's emotional, relational, and spiritual state of mind.

Improving Couple's Communication

Improved communication has always been a central aspect of all efforts to enhance couple relationships, and it is critical to revamping male sexuality. Couples should make concerted efforts to understand each other's experiences and value systems. This is particularly critical with the centerfold syndrome, since the male and female experiences may be alien.

Men and women enter relationships with a lifetime of emotional baggage they rarely discuss directly. A primary agenda for couples therapy should incorporate discussion of how men's sexuality has been constructed. Each partner needs to listen carefully as the other describes how voyeurism, female body worship, trophyism, validation cravings, and male fears of intimacy have affected him or her. This communication needs to be direct and honest, even when painful.

Enhancing Sensuality and Emotional Intimacy

Once the problems of men's nonrelational sexuality have been addressed, sex therapists can work earnestly to build sensuality and emotional intimacy, areas commonly part of sex therapy programs. Books are plentiful for relationship-building, improving marital communication, and enhancing sexual functioning. For example, Zilbergeld's *The New Male Sexuality* (1992) is a generally superb book that provides a range of exercises and do-it-yourself therapies for couples. Of particular relevance here are the marvelous sensate focus exercises that help couples discover sensuality and mutual pleasuring.

To develop new channels of sexual arousal couples can focus on helping each other try new ways to experience pleasure. Couples can touch and fondle each other, openly communicating about sensations and pleasures. They can open up their sensory channels through music, massage, bathing, and hugging. To avoid maladaptive habits of emotional disconnection and stranger fantasies, a man can concentrate on looking directly into his partner's eyes, studying her facial expressions, participating intimately in her sensual pleasure. He can learn to appreciate the subtle signs of her pleasure—goosebumps, erect nipples, rapid heart rate, or labial engorgement. He can become more attuned to the corresponding sensual sensation in his own body—his breathing or his increased tactile sensitivity. Couples do well to allow time to participate leisurely in relearning sexual arousal, without needing to rush into intercourse and orgasm.

Couples are encouraged to give high priority to their intimacy needs. Special efforts are made to create both psychological and physical space for relationship maintenance.

Techniques like these are invaluable in helping couples deal with sexual and emotional baggage, including the centerfold syndrome. The sensuality and revisualizing activities are critical components in changing men's sexual arousal that has previously been dependent on voyeurism and objectification. In some ways, these exercises can be thought of as relearning, as extinguishing some old habits and replacing them with new ones.

☐ Conclusion

Although national conversation has increasingly focused on the problems of male sexuality, that conversation has been markedly diminished by a major missing voice—the voice of those calling for a revamping of the dominant discourses about male sexuality. We must not continue to promote new and better ways to achieve male sexual performance without making far greater efforts to help men incorporate their sexuality with all other aspects of their psychological and spiritual selves. We must not continue to castigate men for their sexual excesses without simultaneously examining the flagrantly dysfunctional sexual scripts that continue to be proffered to men of all ages. Only by promoting sexual integrity can we hope to develop a new vision for male sexuality that replaces irresponsible, detached, compulsive, and alienated sexuality with a male sexuality that is ethical, compassionate, and sexually empowering of women and men.

☐ References

American Psychiatric Association. (1994). *Diagnostic and Statistical Manual of Mental Disorders* (4th ed.). Washington, DC: Author.

Beneke, T. (1990). Heterosexual porn. In M. Kimmel (Ed.*)*, *Men confront pornography* (pp. 168–187). New York: Crown.

Brod, H. (1987). A case for men's studies. In M. Kimmel (Ed.), *Changing men: New directions in research on men and masculinity* (pp. 9–24). Newbury Park, CA: Sage.

Brooks, G. R. (1995). *The centerfold syndrome: How men can overcome objectification and achieve intimacy with women.* San Francisco: Jossey-Bass.

Brooks, G. R., & Silverstein, L. B. (1995). Understanding the dark side of masculinity: An integrative systems model. In R. F. Levant & W. S. Pollack (Eds.), *A new psychology of men* (pp. 280–333). New York: Basic Books.

Ellis, B. J., & Symons, D. (1990). Sex differences in sexual fantasy: An evolutionary psychological approach. *Journal of Sex Research, 27,* 527–555.

Gaylor, L. (1985). Pornography: A humanist issue. *The Humanist* (July/August), 34–40.

Good, G. E. (1998). Missing and under-represented aspects of men's lives. *SPSMM Bulletin, 3(2),* 1–2.

Graves, D. (1999). Better loving through better chemistry: Sure, we've got a pill for that. *New York Times* (February 14). *NYT Archives* (nytimes.com).

Griffin, S. (1984). *Pornography and silence.* New York: Harper & Row.

Handy, B. (1998). The Viagra craze. *Time, 151*(17), 50–57.

Hare-Mustin, R. T. (1994). Discourses in the mirrored room: A post-modern analysis of therapy. *Family Process, 33,* 19–35.

Hearn, J. (1999). Sex, lies, and videotape: The Clinton/Lewinsky saga as a world historical footnote. *Sexualities, 2(2),* 261–267.

Jackson, S. (1999). A conventional affair. *Sexualities, 2(2),* 250–252.

Knoth, R., Boyd, K., & Singer, B. (1988). Empirical tests of sexual selection theory: Predictions of sex differences in onset, intensity, and time course of sexual arousal. *Journal of Sex Research, 1*(24), 73–89.

Laumann, E. O., Paik, A., & Rosen, R. C. (1999). Sexual dysfunction in the United States: Prevalence and predictors. *Journal of the American Medical Association, 281*(6), 537–544.

Levant, R. F., & Brooks, G. R. (1997). *Men and sex: New psychological perspectives.* New York: Wiley.

Michael, R. T., Gagnon, J. H., Lauman, E. O., & Kolata, G. (1994). *Sex in America: A definitive survey.* Boston: Little, Brown.

Murray, S. O. (1999). Widely plausible deniability. *Sexualities, 2(2),* 252–255.

Pleck, J. H. (1981). *The myth of masculinity.* Cambridge: MIT Press.

Rosen, R. C., & Ashton, A. K. (1993). Prosexual drugs: Empirical status of the "new aphrodisiacs." *Archives of Sexual Behavior, 22,* 521–543.

Sanders, S. A., & Reinisch, J. M. (1999). Would you say you "had sex" if . . . ? *Journal of the American Medical Association, 281*(3), 275–277.

Sexualities (1999). Special feature: A symposium on the Clinton/Lewinsky affair. *Sexualities, 2(2),* 247–266.

Shrage, L. (1999). Do lesbian prostitutes have sex with their clients? A Clintonesque reply. *Sexualities, 2(2),* 259–261.

Stein, A. (1999). Clinton, the rightwing, and "civilized" sexual morality. *Sexualities, 2(2),* 247–250.

Stones, R. (1999). Abstract intimacies: The princess and the president. *Sexualities, 2(2),* 255–259.

Tiefer, L. (1987). In pursuit of the perfect penis: The medicalization of male sexuality. *American Behavioral Scientist, 29*(5), 579–599.

Wolf, N. (1991). *The beauty myth: How images of beauty are used against women.* New York: William Morrow.

Zilbergeld, B. (1978). *Male sexuality.* Toronto: Bantam Books.

Zilbergeld, B. (1992). *The new male sexuality: The truth about men, sex, and pleasure.* New York: Bantam Books.

CHAPTER

Christopher M. Aanstoos, Ph.D.

Phenomenology of Sexuality

And the light that shines above the heavenly vault, the support of all creation, the support of the universe, in the supreme and highest realms, is none other than the light that dwells in the human body. Its actual manifestation is the warmth that is felt when the flesh is touched. (*Upanishads*)

☐ Overture

The *Upanishads*, one of the oldest spiritual texts in the world, tells us that the energy that supports all creation manifests as the warmth that arises when we are touched. What is this energy, and what sort of touch manifests it? We can find its appearance in various forms: a mother's caress, a friend's pat on the back, even a collegial handshake. Certainly, one variation is the erotic contact. To say so is not to minimize the import of touch, but to recollect the full significance of our sexuality.

Sexuality. We are at once so saturated with it, yet often we live it so incompletely. We experience it with such drivenness, yet with such ambivalence. So much attachment, yet so little embrace. Hence the source of such suffering. What can we, as psychologists, offer to relieve this suffering, and to restore the joy of complete experiencing? In this chapter, I will strive to contribute to that restorative work by sketching a phenomenology of sexuality. I will do this by offering an example of how phenomenology can illustrate the phenomenon we are called to heal. And how, by doing so, it offers the basis for a profound revision to traditional approaches to sex therapy. Phenomenology provides us access back to experience, to the lived origins of our subject matter, from which we can ask openly the most basic and taken-for-granted questions: What is sexuality? What does it mean to be sexual? What is sexual experiencing? All subsequent work in sexology and sex therapy presuppose how these questions are understood.

☐ First Movement: The Need for a New Approach to Sexuality

Sexuality is usually, and rightfully, understood as having an intrinsic relation to embodied experience. Yet this apparently obvious insight too often does not yield the conceptual harvest one might expect. Instead, our notion of embodiment is typically conceptualized by assumptions of an objectivistic psychology whose viewpoint reduces experience to the model of objects, or things. This objectivism is rooted in a dualistic philosophical base, identified as Cartesian on account of Descartes' role in promulgating an ontological divide between an "immaterial mind" and a "material world" (of objects, including the body). This centuries-old splitting of mind and body is at core an alienation from—and a mystification of—our own deepest experience of wholeness, from which we are only now, in the late twentieth century, beginning to recover. Psychologists, following the lead of philosophers, have taken one side or the other of this chasm to be the "cause" and the other, then, the "effect" of that causation. In philosophy, the position that the material side is the cause of the mental is known as "materialism." In contrast, the position that the immaterial side is the generative one is known as "idealism." In psychology, these positions were the foundations of behaviorism and cognitivism, respectively (although, in its contemporary American version, cognitivism also presupposes an ultimately physiological—i.e., material—substructure).

Different as these positions are in some respects, both consider our embodiment only in terms of the anatomical body. For sex theory and therapy, the body thus comes to be conceived as an "objective" thing—a skin-encapsulated compilation of organs—and experience is seen as the merely "subjective." It is conceived as the epiphenomenal result of causal, mechanistically governed sequences of antecedent variables leading to behavioral effects. Under the sway of this preconception, the understanding of sexuality stands bereft of the deepest insights of its own foundations in embodied experiencing—since experience itself remains presupposed under such a framework.

For example, there is a palpable sexual energy that can be generated, amplified, and distributed in ways that can be learned, but this energy does not correspond to anatomical evidence. Taoist masters have long taught the significance of a "hollow bamboo" or channel within the body that is capable of channeling such sexual energy. Tantric practice, as well as older Hindu yogas, understood this alignment in terms of seven *chakras* or bodily centers that draw energy into it and charge it. These chakras were understood to form an alignment from the genitals to the top of the head, although again, this does not correspond with traditional, Western anatomy. Renaming this channel "the inner flute," Anand provided helpful lessons in "opening" it to the flow of sexual energy, while acknowledging that it "has not been recognized as an anatomical fact" (1989, p. 166).

Mechanistic psychology can only comprehend this sort of phenomenon in one of two ways: by reducing it either to physiology (materialism) or to representation (idealism). The problem with the former is that there is no anatomical substructure within which it can be located and, if there is no anatomical structure, how can the phenomenon be "real"? The problem for the latter is how to account for its bodily felt appearance. If it is really only a representation of a disembodied consciousness, why the indirection of "looping" the representation through the body? (Not to mention the additional dilemma of how to account for the forgetting of having done so.)

Unlike other experiences, such as the habit of picking up a pen, sexual arousal reveals clearly a primordial constituting or flow of meaning coming into existence. That is, as Langer said, sexual desire is an experience:

> . . . in which something becomes significant to the extent that it attracts our body in a movement towards it, and our body comes into existence as a body in this very movement, so that the significance of the thing and that of the body come into existence together and imply one another. (1989, p. 50)

The key to realizing this significance of sexual arousal is as obvious as the commonplace way that we may be attracted to a person to whom another is not attracted. As a 13-year-old, I found myself drawn to a girl in my class whom I saw as beautiful. My friend, on the other hand, recoiled from her, saying she had a "frog face." Although I could see what he meant, to me it was an incredibly beautiful frog face. Later in life, I again found myself in love with a woman whom I regarded as the most beautiful woman I had ever known. Friends told me, "she's not *that* beautiful," to which I could only reply, "she is to me." So we cannot conceive of sexual appeal as an objective *thing*, already constituted—as some sort of object adhering to the other person. Rather, the other's sexuality presences itself *for me*— "beauty is in the eye of the beholder," as they say. On the other hand, such beauty is not, strictly speaking, in my eye, but there, on the face of my love. It is not in some interior mental space that I encounter such an appeal, after all, but there, *in the other*. I find myself being drawn *there*, palpably there, to this other person, not to some interior representation. It is for me, but it is not my creation *ex nihilo*. Rather, it is my way of encountering an appeal to my incarnate subjectivity in the other. Sexual appeal is thus inseparable from the body of the other whom I find appealing, but it is not reducible to physicality, since this woman appeals to me, but not to you, or even to me today, but not yesterday. As Langer put it:

> In sexuality we are therefore best able to appreciate that significance is neither something given, or inert, in the manner of a traditional sense-datum, nor something simply conceived and imposed by a pure consciousness. Sexual significance is created in the living dialogue in which my body begins to exist for me in a new way in responding to another incarnate subjectivity. (1989, p. 50)

To reduce sexual attraction to either side of mechanistic theorizing fails to comprehend this significance. To conceive of it as the result of the impingement of material sensation or as the result of the imposition of representations by immaterial consciousness is, in either case, to overlook the only place such appeal resides: in the engaged, embodied experience. Phenomenology is that approach designed specifically to comprehend experience as it is lived.

☐ Second Movement: A Phenomenological Alternative

Phenomenological Method

What is phenomenology? It is the bold project to eschew conceptualization of "the real" for description of whatever presents itself as real in our deepest experience. It is, in other words, the discipline that makes the implicit meanings of lived experience explicit through description. As Heidegger (1927/1996, p. 30) said, phenomenology means "to let what shows itself be seen from itself, just as it shows itself from itself." Or, as Heidegger next agreed, this understanding of phenomenology is nothing more than what

Husserl (1912/1931), phenomenology's founder, meant by his maxim, "to the things themselves!"

Phenomenology was first formulated within philosophy by Husserl (e.g., 1912/1931, 1912/1980, 1925/1977) in the early decades of the twentieth century as an alternative to metaphysical speculation. It has gone through much subsequent development and is increasingly appropriated today as a methodology for the various disciplines of the human sciences (such as psychology, sociology, geography, pedagogy, anthropology, political science, communication, and health care). Its relevance in this chapter will be the phenomenology of the body, particularly as it contrasts with the objectivist approach in conventional sex therapy. The work of the French phenomenologists, Sartre (1943/1956) and especially Merleau-Ponty (1945/1962), will prove most helpful in this endeavor. Contemporary American phenomenologists also will be helpful to this task, particularly the work of Levin (1985) on "the body's recollection of Being," Lingis (1985) on "libido," Barral (1984) on "the body in interpersonal relations" and Dillon (1998) on "sex and objectification."

Circumscribing the Phenomenon of Sexuality

In contrast to the traditionally dualistic approaches, a phenomenology of sexuality begins with a radical fidelity to lived experience—the very dimension concealed by such dualism. This inquiry begins by circumscribing the phenomenon of sexuality by means of descriptions of specific experiences. As I consider my own, the following examples may help to sensitize us to its parameters.

> As a very young boy, of 5 or 6, I savored going into the coat closet in the front hallway, closing the door behind me, and, there in the dark, stroking my mother's fur coat. It felt so good to touch it, to caress its sublime softness, slowly, over and over, much like I later tingled while feeling my lover's furry hair between my fingers or when caressing my cat, slowly, lusciously, drawing my fingers down the length of the soft fur of her belly, sharing with her the mutual bliss of such sensuous contact. Once, when I was 9, I sobbed uncontrollably in the middle of getting my hair cut. To have my head touched just felt so good. It gave me such a deep sense of wholeness, and wellness, and at-homeness that I cried from the intense sensuous pleasure of that moment. The barber, confused, asked what was wrong. But I, only a 9-year-old boy, had no words with which to describe my experience, nor any way to explain the ecstasy of that touch. More recently, I licked and nibbled and sucked my lover's armpit, shivering with arousal at such scintillating contact. The erotic allure of that sensitive, interior space, coming forth from hiddenness—veritably a vaginal armpit.

But what is it about the irresistible softness of fur? Or about the overwhelmingly satisfying sense of having one's scalp gently massaged? And what is it about an armpit, after all, that makes licking it an arousing rather than disgusting experience? Or about the erotic appeal of any bodily orifice? We would do well to remember the utter bewilderment we felt in early adolescence when we first heard the details of "French kissing"—our amazed realization that people actually found it satisfying to have another person's tongue inside their own mouth (the same sort of confused puzzlement we may still feel, for instance, upon hearing of someone enjoying sex with a corpse). What is this erotic charge, so unmistakably palpable in a given situation, yet so elusive, even paradoxical, to conceptualize objectively? It does us no good to seek answers in the realm of "epidermal contact" explanations, for we are still left with the questions of "why this flesh, rather than that?" and "why this time, not that?" No, we have to go beyond physiology if we are ever to unravel the enigma of sexuality.

Psychoanalysis offered a step beyond the physiological. Freud gave to libido the status of an intention—a meaning—as desire. Thereby he was able to investigate its modes of appearance in relation to questions of personal motivation, and significance (conscious and unconscious). In so doing, he found that we are, indeed, "polymorphously perverse"—that any and every bodily feature can become an erogenous zone. But Freudian libidinal theory remained anchored in and justified by a biologistic entity. Hence, for Freud, a hydraulic (or steam engine) model in which excitation "built up" and was "discharged" seemed to be the governing principle of sexuality.

But, if we return to our examples, we will find that it is not the body conceived as an object that is, or can be, the basis of such meanings. Hidden beneath, or prior to, this conception of the body as an object lurks another vision: the body as we live it in our immediate experience. Armpits evoke the interiority of vaginas not in objectified bodies, but in experienced ones. An erogenous zone is not a place in objectified space, but in a place of lived experience. To apprehend this place, we must let our inquiry be directed by a phenomenological approach to embodied existence.

Phenomenology of Embodied Existence

In a previous publication, I provided a phenomenological analysis of embodied experiencing and depicted how, through the body, we embody a network of lived relations, with other people and the world. I described this intertwining nexus as a "bodying forth" (Aanstoos, 1991). That depiction, by taking seriously our embodied experiencing as it shows itself, can also help us to better grasp sexuality, and so it merits a summary here. As with any phenomenology, it begins with a suspension of belief in the traditional object-centered metaphysics of the body and, instead, takes as phenomena whatever bodily experience reveals itself. Rather than violating that experienced givenness by subjecting it to conceptual categories extrinsic to experience, we attend faithfully to what presents itself, taking it precisely *as it presents itself*. We learn to look with appreciation, wonder, and awe upon our actually lived bodily experience.

That discernment begins when we cease conceptualizing the body as an encapsulated object. We do not deny the possibility of viewing the body as an object. Indeed, such an impersonal viewpoint—which discloses the body as a mass of tissue, blood, organs, and neuronal networks—is the necessary underpinning of the surgical attitude. The fact that the body lends itself to both first-person and third-person viewpoints is of great significance to an understanding of its ontology (Merleau-Ponty, 1945/1962, 1968; Pollio, 1982, pp. 53–75; Wertz, 1987; Zaner, 1981). But we will never understand the first-person experience of one's own body by reducing it to a third-person perspective, since the body is not only the *object* of perception, but the *subject* of perception as well (Husserl, 1937/1970, pp. 178–180; Marcel, 1952; Merleau-Ponty, 1945/1962; Sartre, 1943/1956; Wertz, 1987). Husserl (1937/1970, pp. 211–212) made a key distinction, in his native German, between *korper* and *leib*. The former word refers to the body in the sense of "the physical body" (as in that of a corpse), whereas the latter means the experienced or "lived" body. This distinction is helpful for reminding us to attend to the *experience* of embodiment.

Embodiment as lived experience is a movement of the heart, reaching out to touch, to embrace—as ecstasy. To describe the body of our experience as *ecstatic* is to remember the etymological meaning of ecstasy: *ex-stasis*, to stand beyond or to place beyond. It is also to assert the body's existential character as disclosiveness, as openness onto a world. That is to say, the body reveals, through its openness, the very meaning of being human: that as human beings, we *are* this openness. And it is via the body that we open the world.

Merleau-Ponty (1968) described well this openness of the body and how it forms our deepest relational intertwining with the flesh of the world. This shared "flesh" was also evoked by Roll's (1986) use of the term "skinship" to describe our relations with one another and the world. The body has "carnal knowledge" of the flesh of the world. "All sense perception involves something like a carnal embrace" (Lingis, 1985, p. 52). In the sense that "our flesh lines and envelops all the visible and tangible things which nonetheless surround it, the world and I are within one another" (Merleau-Ponty, 1968, p. 123). Therefore, "every perception is a . . . communion . . . the complete expression outside ourselves of our perceptual powers and a coition, so to speak, of our body with things" (Merleau-Ponty,

1945/1962, p. 320). Lingis amplified this sense of intercourse by noting that "perception is an inscription of a dynamic version of the outside within and a reflection of oneself on the outside" (1985, p. 51). This analysis is most clear, Lingis pointed out, with regard to sexuality. For example:

> [T]o see someone sprawled on the bed as seductive is to feel, forming within oneself, the movements of taking him or her. The other is structured perceptibly as a surface destined for kisses and embraces, the exterior relief of one's inward lines of feeling. (Lingis, 1985, p. 51)

This ecstatic body is thus a "body of love" (Brown, 1966), a "movement of sympathy" (Levin, 1988, p. 298).

The body and the world are distinguishable, certainly, but not separable. The body–world boundary is a porous one, permitting unceasing interpenetrability. Indeed, its permeable border, far from being dualistic, is what allows for the commingling of each with the other. We can caress each other, but every caress that gives the other pleasure pleasures us as well (Lockford, 1999). There is an ontological "reversibility" between the body and the world, exemplified most keenly by the way we must be "touchable" beings in order to be "touchers" (Merleau-Ponty, 1968). This profound understanding of the nonduality of embodied consciousness and world requires more explication than is possible in this short chapter. Instead, the summaries of two commentators must suffice here. Cohen (1984, p. 330) interpreted this reversibility thesis with the aid of the metaphor of a Mobius strip, to demonstrate how:

> Insides turn into outsides and vice versa. At best these discriminations are provisional, relative . . . subject and object are not two opposed domains to be somehow united, they are both aspects of the same flesh, the flesh seeing itself, turned upon itself, overlapping itself, folded upon itself, reversible.

Similarly, Cataldi (1993) interpreted Merleau-Ponty's ontology of the flesh by indicating that his reversibility thesis reveals the flesh as "exchange" (pp. 68–69) that "deborders" the body–world boundary (p. 110). She noted that this "debordering" especially is evident in an emotional experience, adding:

> In the deepest of our emotional experiences . . . it is difficult or impossible to tell the "inside" and the "outside" apart from each other. Because they may "become" each other and "reverse," it is difficult to say "who" is perceiving and "who" is perceived. (Cataldi, 1993, p. 175)

Perhaps the most exemplary experience is falling in love. When this new relationship permeates one's being, it "changes the entire world. . . . Nothing remains the same. Colors, textures, sounds, food, all of life takes on a fresh, dazzling beginning. Rooms brighten and move . . . the world is a beautiful place" (Moustakas, 1977, p. 24; cf., van den Berg, 1972). Such experiences so evidently reveal the constitutive nature of embodied perception, as we noted above with respect to sexual desire.

Through this ecstatic embracing of the world, our embodiment discloses its *there*. This reflective bodily mode is a "locus of meaning" (Shapiro, 1985, p. 14; also see Gendlin, 1962). Leder (1990) likewise drew our attention to the body as not merely a "located thing" but "first and foremost . . . a path of access, a being-in-the-world." We embody and express this existential openness through our posture, our stance, our movement, our gait, our comportment, the gestures of our hands—every enactment of our embodied being offers us our existence as an existential openness, as our most basic human capacity of worlding a *there* (Keleman, 1975; Straus, 1966; Vassi, 1984).

Our embodiment manifests its openness in a myriad of ways, a typology of which is far from established. Openness, as our way of being, can appear across even the most diverse concrete events. The ecstatic as a "placing beyond" is, after all, particularly manifested in both orgasm and panic—and in so many variations in between. We may feel a "gut reaction," a "broken heart," "cold feet," or a "loss of face." We may feel the "chill in the air." Or we may be twinkled by the twinkle in the other's eyes, or be struck by the betrayal in the other's voice. Or we may burst into giggles, or goose pimples, or ulcers, or awe, as I felt when my 5-year-old daughter described the tooth fairy as "wings of love." I just burst open in awe. Certainly, in sexual experience we discover a prime example of this understanding of embodiment as an opening onto a meaning-filled world, as we will see next.

☐ Third Movement: Phenomenology of Sexuality

To demonstrate this phenomenological understanding of sexuality, some concrete analysis will be a useful exemplar, albeit necessarily brief and sketchy in this context. This analysis will be based on descriptions I have gathered from interviews with men and women in three countries: the United States, England, and France. For each phase of the analysis, we will begin with some illustrative quotations from these protocols to develop an explication of their essential, structural significance.

Sexuality is like an atmosphere, in the sense that it is an ever-present background—a horizon of existence as such (Merleau-Ponty, 1945/1962). Just as we *are*, we *are sexual*. In that sense, we could look for the phenomenon of sexuality in any and every experience. Even eating an orange secretes a sexual dimension and so offers us an aperture into sexuality. Nevertheless, in most moments this sexual dimension of existence is implicit, and the portal offered is quite narrow. It may be most fruitful to look for experiential manifestations of sexuality in which this phenomenon shows itself most directly: those occasions when we find our sexual being explicitly solicited. In these moments, we find ourselves spontaneously experiencing "the call of the erotic"—which will be identified as the first phase of the explicit experience of sexuality. Sometimes, this first phase will continue with additional adumbrations, which will be included here as the second and third phases of the experience.

Phase 1. The Call of the Erotic

The experience of sexuality begins with an invitation, a solicitation. The other beckons me, calls me out, arouses me, turns me on. This call need not be signaled purposefully, nor do I necessarily grasp it as purposive. Yet its appearance is felt unmistakably, even when the intentions of its sender are highly ambiguous. Some examples from the protocol data include these:

> The way he looked at me, with such deep eyes, like he could see completely through me. Now I know what it means to feel you're about to swoon. Though it was just a look, it hit me so strongly I actually felt my knees weaken.

****

> Her arm brushed ever so softly against mine as she reached across the table, and it felt so, so . . . stimulating. It was quick and vague. Did she mean anything by it? I couldn't tell, but I knew for sure its impact on me. There was no question about that.

This initial encounter with another as erotic does seem to have two discernibly distinct variations, which we could stereotypically identify as masculine and feminine—although mature adults of both genders typically experience both variations, even in a single instance. Stereotypically, the "masculine" gaze discovers the other as erotic by how she looks, whereas the "feminine" gaze finds the other as erotic by how he acts. For example, a woman told me, while looking at a man standing on the beach, "I can't tell yet whether he arouses me. I have to see him doing something first." In contrast, a man reported being immediately aroused by the shape of a woman's hips.

As noted above, however, more often both perspectives are present, overlapping and elaborating each other. For example, a woman spoke of finding a man appealing by the soft way he walked, almost as if he were half-woman. Yet she also noted how appealingly the sun shined on his bare arms as he walked, revealing their softness. Thus, it is both the other's comportment and their appearance that beckon interest and invite further exploration.

The solicitation is experienced perceptually, and thus with immediacy. That is to say, the perceived presents itself without mediation by other modalities of consciousness (such as thinking or belief). It is not a representation, but neither is it a purely mechanical connection. This call may arise from any sensory modality, for erotic perception is truly polymorphous, as Freud held; or (better) all perception is a cohabiting of sensory modes—a "sensorium commune"—as Merleau-Ponty pointed out (1945/1962). In one instance, I may be first solicited visually, say by the curve of a hip or a lip. In another, I may first experience the call aurally, by the husky sound in the other's voice or even by their breath. At another time, it may be given first by the other's smell: the delicate fragrance of perfume or the musky smell of her sweat. Or, again, it may be that touch which opens me onto the erotic profile.

> It was the way he moved that first caught my attention. There was just something so sexy in the way he walked, even in the way he moved his arm as he reached for something.

****

> I just really liked the way his mind worked, what he was saying . . . it was such a turn-on. I can't really explain it.

If we are to understand this initial description of the phenomenon, let us do so by more deeply interrogating this experience of being called by the erotic profile. The twin questions to pose are these: What calls, and who is so called? It is in attempting to answer these basic questions that much of psychology goes awry. These missteps are in either of two well-trodden paths we have already identified by the terms behaviorism and cognitivism (earlier known as empiricism and idealism, in the longer history of their philosophical roots). Phenomenologists recognize that either side of this dichotomy leads to an objectifying abstraction from our lived experience. Behaviorism reduces the erotic solicitation to a stimulus causally linked to responses conditioned onto the body conceived as a mechanism, an object-body. Cognitivism, on the other hand, conceives of the erotic as a representation posited by the intellect, and in so doing dismisses the constitutive role of the bodily-felt experience. In neither case is it possible to account for that palpable immediacy of intrinsic connection described above. A phenomenology of sexuality begins, instead, with the notion of the body as body-subject able to take up an existential project. In this depiction, erotic experience is reducible neither to mechanisms nor representations. Rather, it is approached as a manifestation of that utterly irreducible intertwining of lived-body and lived-world. So, in this first phase it is as a "body-subject" that we are solicited by the call of the erotic. A pure subject cannot be so summoned, nor can a pure object, but only the living unity of embodied subjectivity.

Phase 2. Responding to the Invitation

The first phase of experiencing the call of the erotic is followed by a second, in which we find ourselves responding to this solicitation. This response, as a continuation of the initial perception of the other as erotic, can have two sides or modes: an active and a passive synthesis. In his phenomenology of encountering another person, Sartre (1943/1956) saw perception as a form of appropriation, and in that sense emphasizes the active mode. An example of this mode is the experience of a woman who described herself passionately repeating *"I'm so hungry. I want to eat you."* But Merleau-Ponty (1945/1962), in his examination of the phenomenology of perception, called it *communion*, thereby drawing attention to the passive, or nonthematized, synthesis that perception yields. In other words, our response to the call of the erotic can take the form of either grasping or merging.

Certainly, the perception of sexual desire is an empathic immersement in the perceived other. And in this immersement, there is indeed a sort of appropriation underway. We reach out to the other with any and all of the diverse faculties available for such contact. But the person responds with the anticipation of finding a mutuality of desire in that contact. This intended fulfillment within a communion is the trajectory toward which our anticipatory responsiveness refers. Our arousal, in this sense, arcs in reference toward a future possibility. This anticipatory orientation is what Merleau-Ponty referred to as an "intentional arc."

This anticipation reveals the receptivity of the other to contact, and the shared tending toward connection. I experience this susceptibility there, in the other, and likewise in my own body, which flows outward toward that beckoning. Already there in virtuality, already underway, this responsiveness is at once anonymous and yet intimately personal and intensely idiosyncratic (Kleinplatz, 1996a). It is this virtuality that serves to arouse so intensely, our awareness of the anticipated potentiality that we are opening ourselves onto, by our own manifest responsiveness. As Kleinplatz (1996a, p. 112) said, "Thus, eroticism involves not only heightened arousal but the awareness of the potential for intense arousal and the choice of entering into it." A man noted that he felt himself to be like a flower, opening, blossoming with each word, with each caress from his lover. A woman described her delighted arousal brought about by the give and take of leaning into her lover's chest and his leaning into her own.

In the second phase, we respond to the call of the erotic by putting ourselves into the situation that beckons us. For example, we find the smooth back of our lover alluring precisely as we experience its touchability for our caress. Indeed, it is just that caressing contact we can already sense that draws us so seductively to that smooth back. In other words, beneath the body-object there is another body, as it were, already operatively engaged in the situation, already being there, with that silky skin tingling to its curving smoothness, that lights the way for our vision of it as such. "The look . . . envelopes, palpates, espouses the visible things" (Merleau-Ponty, 1968, p. 13). It is the body as expression, for, as Merleau-Ponty noted, "the body is essentially an expressive space" (1945/1962, p. 146).

The body is especially articulate, especially expressive, when it gestures: "Eros is visible in every moving gesture. We greet, we entreat, we give, we receive, we hold, we retreat, we touch and caress . . . these are gestures" (Levin, 1982–1983, p. 232). By means of such gestural potentiality, we inhabit our situation, both through our actual movement and by our insertion of ourselves into the situation through the pull of possible movements. This bodily felt capacity to project ourselves into this virtual, imaginal activity is our initial response to the summons of the erotic. In that sense, we take the position of the lover much as we take the position of the sleeper: by aligning ourselves with its possibilities in order that they may engage and "gear" us to them.

Merleau-Ponty made this clear in his analysis of the case of Schneider, a patient who could no longer become erotically engaged. His phenomenological analysis of a case of erectile dysfunction portrayed unmistakably the conceptual shortcomings of both the physiological and the cognitive approaches, while demonstrating the need for a phenomenological one. As Merleau-Ponty noted, for traditional approaches, "sexual incapacity ought to amount either to the loss of certain representations or else to a weakening of the capacity for satisfaction. We shall see this is not the case" (1945/1962, p. 155). Schneider's troubles arose first from an injury at the back of his head—an unusual variation, therefore, and one that would seemingly lend support to a medical or physiologically based approach. To discover, even in such a case, the irreducible importance of lived experience is, therefore, particularly instructive. His presentation is as follows:

> One patient no longer seeks sexual intercourse of his own accord. Obscene pictures, conversations on sexual topics, the sight of a body do not arouse desire in him. The patient hardly ever kisses, and the kiss for him has no value as sexual stimulation. Reactions are strictly local and do not begin to occur without contact. If the prelude is interrupted at this stage, there is no attempt to pursue the sexual cycle. In the sexual act intromission is never spontaneous. If orgasm occurs first in the partner and she moves away, the half-fulfilled desire vanishes. At every stage it is as if the subject did not know what is to be done. There are no active movements, save a few seconds before the orgasm, which is extremely brief. (Merleau-Ponty, 1945/1962, p. 155)

Schneider was not aroused by visual or verbal eroticism. In fact, it was only when he was being manually stimulated that his body "geared into" the sexual dimension of the situation. Schneider was able to have intercourse and orgasm, but only when his partner took all of the initiative. And, should this stimulation stop, he immediately lost his interest. What had Schneider lost, Merleau-Ponty asked? Was it some physiological functioning? No, he was still able to become aroused by manual contact. Was it then some power to represent the situation as sexual that Schneider lacked? We could show him sexually explicit images, photos, videos, and the like, yet none had the power to arouse sexual desire for him. For Schneider, all women's bodies looked basically similar, no one more physically appealing than another. In contrast, we normally do experience such distinctions and find ourselves solicited by very personal significances of the other (this is what we mean by "chemistry"). And this is so because we actively place ourselves *into* the situation, beyond its concrete appearances, and thereby experience (endow/discover) its individualized solicitation. This is what Schneider had lost: that basic existential capacity to *be there*, as a living spontaneity, within a meaningful situation (rather than merely a location) by means of an "original openness" to others, a "pre-communication" through the "warm radiance of the flesh" (Levin, 1982–1983, p. 235).

If we consult the traditional theories, the empiricist/physiological approach would assert that Schneider had lost the capacity to initiate sexual interaction and to respond to all but the most direct sexual stimulation, "some decline of normal sexual reflexes or of pleasurable states." Evidently this loss of automatic reflex apparatus (of stimulus-response) was caused by his head injury. But it is difficult to so account fully for the breakdown of sexuality in Schneider. It seems curious that only particular aspects of his sexuality were affected—and even these were context-specific—rather than a more generalized impact on his sexual functioning. He could, after all, still ejaculate. Thus, as Langer concluded, "a purely physiological account . . . is at a loss to account for a fundamental change in the very structure of erotic experience" (1989, p. 51).

On the other hand, if we consider the cognitive/intellectualist theory, the assertion is that Schneider's problem was due to the loss of representations needed for arousal. Such a position rests on the assumption that there is an association between certain ideas, mental images, or representations and the subsequent sexual arousal. This position, of course, has the conceptual problem of all associationist claims: How does an idea "associate" to something outside itself? It also has the problem of explaining why the undiminished tactile dimension is not a similarly representational source. However, the main dilemma of this approach lies in the fact that we could supply Schneider with his allegedly "missing representations"— such as pornographic images, nude bodies, and erotic descriptions—to no avail. These "do not arouse desire in him" (Merleau-Ponty, 1945/1962, p. 155).

No, Schneider's dysfunction cannot be reduced to physiology or intellect. Rather, Merleau-Ponty noted, his pathology "brings to light, somewhere between automatic response and representation, a vital zone in which the sexual possibilities of the patient are elaborated . . . there must be, immanent in sexual life, some function which ensures its emergence" (p. 156). For Schneider, "perception has lost its erotic structure":

> In the case of the normal subject, a body is not perceived merely as an object; this objective perception has within it a more intimate perception: the visible body is subtended by a sexual schema, which is strictly individual, emphasizing the erogenous areas, outlining a sexual physiognomy, and eliciting the gestures of the masculine body which is itself integrated into this emotional totality. But for Schneider a woman's body has no particular essence . . . for physically they are all the same. (Merleau-Ponty, 1945/1962, p. 156)

The body of the other is normally perceived as erotic by an "intimate perception." And what is it that launches such perceptual intimacy? Merleau-Ponty pointed to the lived body, which is the power of projecting oneself into a situation as sexual. In sexuality, we see with a desire that comprehends a situation, not intellectually, but deeper: We perceive with an intentionality or meaningfully focused orientation "which follows the general flow of existence" (1945/1962, p. 157). Erotic perception is not a pure inner mind aiming at an outer objective thing. A sight has an erotic significance for me, not when I mentally associate it to pleasure or to zones of my body—nor through some merely causal, objective physiological response—but precisely when it speaks to me bodily; but the body so addressed is one that has the power to project around itself a sexual world, and so to put itself into an erotic dimension by situating itself there. This, then, is what Schneider had lost: this intentionality of the lived body engaging a world of meaning. It was, as Merleau-Ponty punned, his "intentional arc" that had "gone slack."

This critique of sex therapy's usual mechanistic view of erectile dysfunction can be similarly extended to a more generalized critique for men, inclusive of such phenomena, as retarded (delayed) or rapid (premature) ejaculation for men; and for women, vaginismus, anorgasmia, and dyspareunia. In every case, traditional sex therapy's mistake is the fallacy of reductionism generally: the notion that experience is reducible to objective physiology, that experience is finally a matter of measurable swellings, contractions, and secretions. Again, what gets neglected is the existential meaning of the situation for the person. How is it, for example, that intercourse with *this* partner is so painful, or that at *this* point in the relationship the woman is anorgasmic? Beneath the measurements are matters of desire—an interconnected web of personally lived meanings that constellate a world and can only be addressed by attending to this experience on its own terms. To treat these "disorders" without understanding their lived, experiential meanings for the person is, inevitably, to reduce the person to a mechanism, and so fail to comprehend the fuller dimension of the situation. This, if anything, is what phenomenology reminds us to recall. No objective measurement of penile erection can ever substitute for a real understanding of the meaning of the situation in which the person, not merely the penis, is always involved in an intricate, experiential web of significations.

I should note, too, that it is not ultimately to physiology that this reduction brings us, but specifically to a cultural norm of such physiology, a critique well-articulated by Irvine (1990), Kleinplatz, (1996b), and Reiss (1990). As Irvine (1990, p. 22) pointed out, traditional sex therapy falsely universalizes a set of historical and social relations. Reiss' example (1990, pp. 169ff) of the so-called disorder of "coital anorgasmia" tellingly demonstrated the implicit cultural norms involved in such allegedly medical diagnoses.

But once we return the presupposed physiology to its cultural embeddedness, phenomenology shows us that we must go all the way and understand its ultimate inherence in lived, intentional (i.e., personally meaningful) experience. To understand this intentionality, whereby the body subjectively projects itself within a meaningful world, we must look beneath the objectivistic presuppositions of dualistic, causal thinking. We must strive to understand how a person participates simultaneously as a body *and* as a subject in constituting a situation as erotic. We must begin to ask more seriously the situated meaning of desire, not merely the length of time to erection or to orgasm. Whereas the original sex researchers (i.e., Kinsey and Masters & Johnson) were most concerned with establishing the legitimacy of the field by constructing it on the seemingly solid edifice of measurable, physiological responses, we must now understand that this pursuit of medical legitimization carries a correlative cost: the neglect—indeed, the concealment—of our lived experience.

Phase 3. Fulfillment

Sexual desire fulfills itself as a conjoining, a merging of energies, rhythms, bodies, fluids, and pulsations, culminating in such an alteration in the field of experience that at times it is no longer even clear whose sexual organs are whose, whose movement, whose tingling, whose orgasm. There is a coming in and out not only of body parts but of consciousnesses, in the sense that egoic awareness of separate personhood alternately flits in and out, as the experience of flow immerses one so fully in the immediate sensory field that there is no leftover self-reflection. The waves of pleasure sweep the lovers up in a flow that has no definite boundaries but is rich with open, tactile contours.

A woman described this open field in the following way:

> That night, making love in the cabin, I felt I was having intercourse with the lake, the cliffs, the trees, all embodied there together in my lover, and me all extended fully into that vast space.

A man likewise experienced this presubjective deformation of the "ego-other" structure very powerfully, in the following way:

> "Come all the way in," she said, and I did. Through the portals of her eyes I entered her, fully. She changed shape, her face became bird-like, then even more geometrical. And then that huge, huge expanse. It was as if we, together, were the ends of the universe, encompassing that infinite space, and yet with no distance at all.

In this third phase of the sexual encounter, we find a communion of self and other that requires a more adequate understanding of intersubjectivity than is traditionally available in objectivistic psychology. Phenomenologists have sought to describe this more primordial intersubjective matrix, but perhaps it was Buber who most radically depicted it. As Friedman summarized Buber's view, "when two individuals 'happen' to each other, there is an essential remainder that reaches out beyond the special sphere of each—the 'sphere of the between'" (Friedman, 1988, p. 124).

Merleau-Ponty related this sense of intersubjectivity to the phenomenon of embodiment. As he said, "Insofar as I have sensory functions . . . I am *already* in communication with others" (1945/1962, p. 353). This "already" available intersubjectivity, so crucial to this fulfillment phase of sexuality, is particularly evident in the phenomenon of the touch. As noted earlier, to be able to touch, we must have a surface that can be touched; that is, touching requires touch-ability, so that in touching another we are also touched by that other's touch. Merleau-Ponty spoke of a "postural impregnation" of one person by another—for example, the way that one person's smile plays across the other's face. Ultimately, he wrote "I live in the facial expressions of the other, as I feel him living in mine" (1964, p. 146). It is in this way that sexuality "expresses one's presence to the other subject and becomes the expression of the presence of the other to oneself" and the sexual body becomes "the intermediary of the immediacy and directness of human encounter . . . of human intersubjectivity" (Kovacs, 1982–1983, p. 212). This fundamental "reversibility" of the flesh opens us to the deepest possibilities of mutuality, with the consequence that, in sexual fulfillment at its best, we enter a realm far removed from any "zero sum game" in which pleasure is some quantity that belongs either to me or to you. Instead, as the excitation is reciprocally engaged, it becomes a truly shared prospect, in which the other's pleasure is simultaneously my own. As we resonate to each other's exhilaration, a veritable contagion, a "syncratic sociability" of arousal, builds and we experience an elastic bodily field of intercorporeal bliss.

This capacity of the sexual body-subject to weave back and forth between the personal and the interpersonal is an example of a more generic human capacity to do so. Csikzentmihalyi, who has studied this phenomenon for many years, called it "the flow experience," or simply "flow." A representative instance of it is his citation of the following description by a composer who was asked "how it felt when writing music was going well." His answer:

> You are in an ecstatic state to such a point that you feel as though you almost don't exist. I have experienced this time and time again. My hand

seems devoid of myself, and I have nothing to do with what is happening. (cited by Csikzentmihalyi, 1999, p. 825)

☐ Aria

As phenomenologists, we can say that the body and existence are related just as are expression and that which is expressed: two interdependent terms that together constitute the reality of which, separately, they are only abstract moments. The body is "solidified existence" and existence a "perpetual incarnation." This understanding of the body as expression helps clarify the existential significance of sexuality, a sense that appears in even its most sedimented forms.

In that sense, our existence *is* sexual. Sexuality permeates the human mode of existing; it is neither cause nor symptom, but a dimension. Therefore, we could say with equal precision that for humans sexuality is an existential project, a way of projecting our own existence as a living spontaneity. The failure to appreciate this existential dimension has been the key limitation of the traditional objectivistic approach to sex therapy, which has resulted in so stultifying that field. Of course, that tradition deserves much credit for having brought sex back from the repressed. But it did so in the same way that psychology restored consciousness from its once taboo status: by treating it as a mechanism that can be explained by the objectivistic presuppositions of a natural science. In light of the preceding phenomenology of sexuality, the cost of doing so must now be realized.

We can help that realization by recalling again that there are actually two poles of this objectivistic approach: the materialistic and the idealistic (or, in psychology, behaviorism and cognitivism). Now we may be in a better position to realize how both of these positions are abstractions from our living sexual experience. In that sense, it is not a problem simply of seeing each position as a partial truth to be complemented by the other pole (as the emerging cognitive-behavioral approach has sought to do). Adding together two abstractions in any combination does not equal one concretion. Once split apart, we do not put Humpty-Dumpty together again, not with any amount of the king's glue. Rather, to understand the *experience* of sexuality, we need to respect and approach such experiences on their own terms: as phenomena rather than as things. This distinction accounts for why no behavioral, cognitive, or physiological determinants, measures, or techniques can ever simply be substituted for a person's *actual experience*. Such determinants, as sheer objectivities, are not themselves situated within a personally meaningful world, whereas sexuality, as we have seen, essentially involves our human capacity of constituting a sexual experience by existentially putting ourselves into a situation. And that is why a gesture might be so erotic just now for Jim, but do nothing for Joe. Likewise, no technique, employed abstractly, can ever replace lived experience. The usefulness of any technique can only be as a portal, a catalyst for entering into a sexual situation. But for it to so serve as an entry point, it necessarily presupposes this human capacity to open the moment by situating oneself there, in that meaning. We do not situate ourselves in the same manner as we put a thing into a specific location, such as a coin in a jar. The jar is the *location* of the coin, but it is not its *situation*, since the coin is not intrinsically involved with the jar (i.e., the jar has no meaning for the coin). Rather, its relations with the jar are extrinsic ones. Our human capacity of calling forth a situation, on the other hand, involves an existential rather than objectivistic placing of ourselves there. Only if we meaningfully "take up residence" there does the technique have efficacy. That is, only by our actual engagement do we open experience and so live the new meanings that thereby become available to us.

Thus, even traditional sex therapy's success depends on and presupposes this dimension of our concretely lived experience. So, rather than blindly depending on that strata, it can be most efficaciously guided by a phenomenological understanding of it. Our task should be to welcome sex therapy back to its own taken-for-granted origins in lived experience, just as sex itself welcomes us back to that primordial wholeness. Or, as Moore (1998, pp. 26–27) said, in sex we "come" to come home to ourselves, "back into our world from our mental outposts," to our own most, unmediated, immediate sensory being.

☐ References

Aanstoos, C. M. (1991). Embodiment as ecstatic intertwining. In C. M. Aanstoos (Ed.), *Studies in humanistic psychology* (pp. 94–111). Carrollton: West Georgia College.

Anand, M. (1989). *The art of sexual ecstasy.* Los Angeles: Jeremy Tarcher.

Barral, M. R. (1984). *The body in interpersonal relations.* Lanham, MD: University Press of America.

Brown, N. (1966). *Love's body.* New York: Vintage.

Cataldi, S. (1993). *Emotion, depth and flesh: A study of sensitive space: Reflections on Merleau-Ponty's philosophy of embodiment.* Albany: State University of New York Press.

Cohen, R. A. (1984). Merleau-Ponty, the flesh, and Foucault. *Philosophy Today, 28*(Winter), 330.

Csikzentmihalyi, M. (1999). If we are so rich, why aren't we happy? *American Psychologist, 54,* 821–827.

Dillon, M. (1998). Sex objects and sexual objectification: Erotic vs. pornographic depiction. *Journal of Phenomenological Psychology, 29,* 92–115.

Friedman, M. (1988). Dialogue, confirmation, and the image of the human. *Journal of Humanistic Psychology, 28,* 123–135.

Gendlin, E. (1962). *Experiencing and the creation of meaning.* New York: Free Press.

Heidegger, M. (1927/1996). *Being and time* (J. Stambaugh, Trans.). Albany: State University of New York Press.

Husserl, E. (1912/1931). *Ideas toward a pure phenomenology and a phenomenological philosophy* (W. B. Gibson, Trans.). New York: Collier.

Husserl, E. (1912/1980). *Phenomenology and the foundations of the sciences* (T. Klein & W. Pohl, Trans.). The Hague: Nijhoff.

Husserl, E. (1925/1977). *Phenomenological psychology* (J. Scanlon, Trans.). The Hague: Nijhoff.

Husserl, E. (1937/1970). *The crisis of European sciences and transcendental phenomenology* (D. Carr, Trans.). Evanston, IL: Northwestern University Press.

Irvine, J. (1990). *Disorders of desire: Sex and gender in modern American sexology.* Philadelphia: Temple University Press.

Keleman, S. (1975). *Your body speaks its mind.* New York: Simon & Schuster.

Kleinplatz, P. (1996a). The erotic encounter. *Journal of Humanistic Psychology, 36*(3), 105–123.

Kleinplatz, P. (1996b). Transforming sex therapy: Integrating erotic potential. *The Humanistic Psychologist, 24,* 190–202.

Kovacs, G. (1982–1983). The personalistic understanding of the body and sexuality in Merleau-Ponty. *Review of Existential Psychiatry and Psychology, 18,* 207–217.

Langer, M. (1989). *Merleau-Ponty's phenomenology of perception.* Tallahassee: Florida State University Press.

Leder, D. (1990). *The absent body.* Chicago: University of Chicago Press.

Levin, D. M. (1982–1983) Eros and psyche. *Review of Existential Psychology and Psychiatry, 18,* 219–239.

Levin, D. M. (1985). *The body's recollection of being.* London: Routledge & Kegan Paul.

Levin, D. M. (1988). Transpersonal phenomenology and the corporeal schema. *The Humanistic Psychologist, 16,* 282–313.

Lingis, A.(1985). *Libido.* Bloomington: Indiana University Press.

Lockford, L. (1999). Personal communication.

Marcel, G. (1952). *Metaphysical journal* (B. Wall, Trans.). Chicago: Regnery.

Merleau-Ponty, M. (1945/1962). *Phenomenology of perception* (C. Smith, Trans.). New York: Routledge.

Merleau-Ponty, M. (1968). *The visible and the invisible* (A. Lingis, Trans.). Evanston, IL: Northwestern University Press.

Moore, T. (1998). An erotic way of life. *The Sun* (June), pp. 24–28.

Moustakas, C. (1977). *Turning points.* Englewood Cliffs, NJ: Prentice Hall.

Pollio, H. (1982). *Behavior and existence.* Monterey, CA: Brooks/Cole.

Reiss, I. (1990). *An end to shame: Shaping our next sexual revolution.* Buffalo, NY: Prometheus.

Roll, W. G. (1986). Personal communication.

Sartre, J.-P. (1943/1956). *Being and nothingness* (H. Barnes, Trans.). New York: Washington Square Press.

Shapiro, K. (1975). *Bodily reflective modes.* Durham, NC: Duke University Press.

Straus, E. (1966). *Phenomenological psychology*. New York: Basic Books.

van den Berg, J. H. (1972). *A different existence*. Pittsburgh: Duquesne University Press.

Vassi, M. (1984). *Lying down: The horizontal worldview*. Santa Barbara, CA: Capra Press.

Wertz, F. J. (1987). Cognitive psychology and the understanding of perception. *Journal of Phenomenological Psychology, 18*, 103–142.

Zaner, R. M. (1981). *The context of self: A phenomenological inquiry using medicine as a clue*. Athens: Ohio University Press.

CHAPTER

Charles Moser, Ph.D., M.D.

Paraphilia: A Critique of a Confused Concept

This chapter is more than a critique of the "paraphilia" construct. It is an attempt to unify several disparate sexological and psychiatric concepts. I will review the history of the concept of paraphilia, its use in the *Diagnostic and Statistical Manual* (*DSM*) of the American Psychiatric Association (APA), and the distinctive uses of the same term in both psychiatry and sexology. I also will present an alternative *DSM* classification and criteria.

For present purposes, a sexual interest is defined as the focus of an individual's sexual fantasies, urges, desires, and behaviors. Explanations of the origins of sexual interests have emphasized behaviors or urges that our society has deemed peculiar. Correspondingly, there has been little attempt to develop a theory to explain "normal" sexual interests. The resulting gap will be addressed and critiqued in this chapter.

☐ Sexual Interests

Neither sexology nor other disciplines have been able to explain how humans develop any or even particular sexual interests. The possibility (and probability) that different developmental processes can result in the same sexual interests and the same process can result in different sexual interests further complicates the question. The fact that sexual interests can have different intensities, and that these intensities can change over time, also makes theory building difficult. It seems there are some interests the individual "needs" to explore. Others are explored for the sake of curiosity, to satisfy a partner, or because the opportunity presents itself—and some are not explored by choice. It is also possible for an individual to respond negatively to a specific sexual stimulus. Sexual revulsion can be seen as the polar opposite of sexual interest. Some people like broccoli, some people do not care for it, and some people are revolted by it.

Although some attributes are more commonly eroticized than others (e.g., breasts or adult sex partners in North American society), research have yet to find an attribute that has not been eroticized. Someone, somewhere will find the most seemingly unlikely stimulus erotic. It is interesting to question why feet are more commonly eroticized than hands, or why the desire for thinner or fatter sex partners has been preferred at different points in history; all interests appear to occur at all times. Although everything can be eroticized, some individuals have not eroticized any attribute. These individuals may be among those who present with a lack of desire (Moser, 1992).

Simplistically, the general public finds some sexual interests acceptable (heterosexual coitus within marriage), some possibly acceptable (homosexual attraction), some odd (shoe fetishes), and some disgusting (pedophilia). Acceptable sexual interests vary cross-culturally and change transhistorically.

Over the last century, we have seen a relative reversal in North American societal and scientific views of masturbation, oral-genital contact, and homosexuality. Each of these was thought to be the cause, sign, or result of mental illness and all were seen as particularly dangerous to children; these behaviors are now relatively accepted. It is also thought that childhood participation in these acts increases the probability that these behaviors would become part of an individual's adult sexual pattern. It seems obvious that value judgments are an implicit aspect of this thinking process. Few objections are raised to children being exposed to adult behaviors that may become ingrained in children's developing sexual patterns, unless the behaviors in question are deemed socially unacceptable. Nevertheless, exposing children to heterosexuality does not ensure adult heterosexuality.

Since the dawn of civilization, every society has attempted to control the sexual behavior of it members. What is perceived as appropriate and normal sexual activity is socially relative, and society acts as an agent of control over aberrant sexual expression. Creation of the diagnostic category of *paraphilia*, the medicalization of nonstandard sexual behaviors, is a pseudoscientific attempt to regulate sexuality. The use of the diagnostic process to maintain and to conform to social conventions is relatively transparent. The diagnostic criteria have been written to pathologize those behaviors our society deems sexually unacceptable; when these criteria are shown not to apply to the majority of those who engage in the specified sexual behavior, the criteria are changed to include these individuals. For example, it was once thought that paraphilic ideation was "necessary" for the paraphiliac's arousal. The "necessary" criterion was seen as a clear distinction between those with healthy and those with unhealthy sexual interests, although no one seemed concerned about the "necessity" of heterosexual imagery for the masses. When it was shown that a paraphiliac could also respond sexually to nonparaphilic stimuli, instead of depathologizing those individuals, the "necessary" condition was dropped from the definition. Individuals who have nonstandard sexual interests continue to be pathologized, despite a lack of research establishing a difference in functioning between those so diagnosed and "normal" individuals. There is little evidence that they experience any distress or dysfunction except as a result of societal condemnation of their sexual desires.

Each individual has a specific, sexual pattern as unique as a fingerprint; this is the mix of various cues to which one responds erotically. Response to a particular cue or attribute can vary from lust to apathy, curiosity to revulsion. The preference for sex partners to be men or women usually is referred to as *sexual orientation*. For historical, religious, and social reasons, the sex of the desired partner has been regarded as different from other erotic interests. This is reflected in the schism in the conventional classification of sexual interests. That is, we tend to see a difference between a sexual interest in women (whether heterosexual or homosexual) and a sexual interest in women's feet, or in dressing like a woman, or in wanting to observe women surreptitiously. (It is not typically considered a sign of mental illness to watch a woman openly, on stage or in a film.) The mental health professions have been complicit in reinforcing this schism by classifying these interests separately in the *DSM*.

☐ So When Is Sex a "Problem"?

Many individuals seek out health professionals and educators because they have sexual concerns. It is appropriate that mental health practitioners respond to these concerns and provide appropriate treatment and information (Moser, 1999).

But questions surrounding whether sexual desires are normal or abnormal are beyond the purview of therapists, alone. Such determinations are influenced by (and in turn have implications for) medicine, religion, law, science, society, and culture. The clinician is not immune to these influences. When someone has more sex than is believed to be the norm, it is deemed excessive. It has been said that compulsive masturbation is diagnosed when the patient has a higher masturbatory frequency than the person making the assessment. Promiscuity is identified as having more partners than the one stating the opinion. The subjective element is always present. This is really no different from other diagnostic issues. How much sadness makes someone depressed? What is the distinction between eccentric and psychotic? What is the difference between the paranoid and someone with a "true grasp on reality"? The opinion and personal experience of the diagnostician always comes into play. Anyone who exceeds the therapist's own comfort zone is deemed sick. An alternative is to acknowledge the existence of differences in personal preferences or even tolerance limits, but to choose not to impose them on others. This ethic is actually normative within the S/M subculture. Within this subculture, the term *squicked* denotes that a given activity upsets some people, but they accept that others might enjoy it. This is not a pejorative term; the activity and the tolerance of it are seen as a legitimate part of sadomasochism, even if the individual is "squicked" by the act.

☐ "Paraphilia": History of a Confused and Confusing Construct

The term *paraphilia* was coined by Stekel (1924) and has been translated as "interest in perversion" or "love of the perverse" (Rosario, 1997). The origins of the term suggest the beginnings of confusion. The *Oxford English Dictionary* defines "para" as "other," as in paranormal, or as "demented," as in paranoia. "Philia" is defined as "fond or loving." Using the *Oxford English Dictionary* then, one could define paraphilia as either "other love" or "demented love." Thus the term is a misnomer; it should have been *paralagnia*. (The root, *lagnia*, means lust). The term paraphilia was popularized by John Money (1980, 1984) as a nonpejorative description (without prescriptive connotations) of nonstandard or unusual sexual interest. Unfortunately, it was assimilated into the *DSM-III* (APA, 1980) and subsequent editions as a diagnosis, and so it is now a classification of pathology.

The *DSM* has become the definitive resource for defining psychopathology and designating the criteria necessary to make specific psychiatric diagnoses. The *DSM* is used to determine which behaviors and desires are regarded as healthy and unhealthy, not only by mental health practitioners but also by others who rely upon it (e.g., the divorce courts and the criminal justice system). The importance and influence of the *DSM* cannot be underestimated.

It is important to view the *DSM* in its historical context. The first edition (APA, 1952) classified atypical sexual interests as "Sexual deviation" (code number 000–x63):

> This diagnosis is reserved for deviant sexuality which is not symptomatic of more extensive syndromes, such as schizophrenic and obsessional reactions. The term includes most of the cases formerly classed as "psychopathic personality with pathologic sexuality." The diagnosis will specify the type of the pathological behavior, such as homosexuality, transvestitism, pedophilia, fetishism, and sexual sadism (including, rape, sexual assault, mutilation). (pp. 38–39)

It is noteworthy that the text states, "the diagnosis will specify," thereby linking the specific behavior with psychopathology. This initial error has been carried through all subsequent editions of the *DSM*. Simply, why should the clinician specify the behavior? There is no rationale for it. The *DSM* lists obsessive-compulsive disorder, but does not differentiate between compulsive hand-washers and word-counters. Specifying the behavior should signal a unique aspect of the diagnosis. For example, the withdrawal syndrome from cocaine is different than that from opiates. There is no discernable advantage to distinguishing among the various paraphilias.

It should be noted that the above list includes both homosexuality and rape.

The *DSM-II* (APA,1968) continued to refer to nonstandard sexuality as "sexual deviations" (302), as follows:

> This category is for individuals whose sexual interests are directed primarily toward objects other than people of the opposite sex, toward sexual acts not usually associated with coitus, or toward coitus performed under bizarre circumstances as in necrophilia, pedophilia, sexual sadism, and fetishism. Even though many find their practices distasteful, they remain unable to substitute normal sexual behavior for them. This diagnosis is not appropriate for individuals who perform deviant sexual acts because normal sexual objects are not available to them. (p. 44)

This text refers to "bizarre circumstances." Surely, what constitutes "bizarre" sexuality is highly subjective and not an ideal descriptor for illness. The *DSM* may be merely pathologizing practices that many psychiatrists find distasteful. However, patients may find their sexual behavior neither distasteful nor a source of distress or dysfunction. Societal sanctions are so great, the distaste may well be for the consequences of the behavior and not for the behavior itself.

According to the text above, patients "remain unable to substitute normal sexual behavior for them." If patients are unable to find sexual fulfillment in any other way, they are deemed pathological. The emphasis is on the necessity or dependence on the particular activity or fantasy *exclusively*. The final sentence is especially important: In this edition, the implication is that the behavior per se is not sufficient for diagnosis—the motivation is important, too. If the individual is engaged in the particular activity because no one else is "available" (e.g., the proverbial man in prison, engaged in same sex contacts), he is just a "red-blooded American guy," not subject to diagnosis.

From careful reading of the definition, one may infer that oral sex and masturbation are to be classified as sexual deviations. It also is clear that this diagnosis is asymptomatic, meaning that simply engaging in the behavior is enough to warrant the diagnosis, without any other "symptoms."

In the *DSM-II* (APA, 1968), the following are listed as sexually deviant behaviors: homosexuality, fetishism, pedophilia, transvestitism, exhibitionism, voyeurism, sadism, masochism, other sexual deviation, and unspecified sexual deviation. Please note that homosexuality is still listed in 1968, and this edition allows for both "other" and "unspecified" categories. Rape is no longer specifically cited as an example of sexual deviation.

In 1980, the term paraphilia replaced sexual deviation in the *DSM*. In describing the criteria for this diagnosis, it was emphasized in the *DSM-III* (APA, 1980, p. 266) that, "unusual or bizarre imagery or acts are necessary for sexual excitement . . . [and] . . . tend to be insistently and involuntarily repetitive." Clearly, the implication is that exclusive arousal to particular fantasies or acts is judged pathological only when social norms are violated. In any case, this criterion fell apart when it was "discovered" that individuals diagnosed as paraphiliacs are also capable of sexual arousal to various, more conventional sexual interests. Further research cast doubt on the exclusivity argument as the basis of the pathology of a sexual behavior (Langevin, Lang, & Curnoe, 1998). As such, future editions of the *DSM* expanded their criteria for sexual psychopathology.

The *DSM-III-R* dropped the "necessary" condition and stated instead (APA, 1987, p. 279): "The Paraphilias . . . are characterized by arousal . . . that [is] not part of normative arousal activity patterns and . . . may interfere with the capacity for reciprocal, affectionate sexual activity." The *DSM-III-R* uses "normative sexual arousal" as its reference point. The reference to normalcy is circular, however. The meaning of normalcy and abnormality are defined relative to one another, but there are problems in defining either one. Using a statistical definition, blue eyes are abnormal. However, blue eyes are not pathological. Previous definitions have been limited by social and legal constructs of the time and place of the behavior. A sexual act between two men is a serious offense in China and illegal in Georgia, and its participants are protected from discrimination in California. If a law was passed in the United States criminalizing *heterosexual* behavior, how many previously law-abiding citizens would be able to comply? How many people could find happiness engaging in the now mandated homosexual interactions? How many individuals would engage surreptitiously in criminal heterosexual acts? Would these criminals be seen as dangerous to children and lose their parental rights? The diagnosis of paraphilia has been intertwined with social judgments of normalcy and used to deny civil rights.

The next revision, the *DSM-IV* (APA, 1994), was a major step forward in that it acknowledged the possibility that nonstandard fantasies, behaviors, and objects can be used for nonpathological purposes: "A paraphilia must be distinguished from the **non-pathological use of sexual fantasies, behaviors, or objects as a stimulus for sexual excitement**" (APA, 1994, p. 525; emphasis in the original). The essential features of the paraphilias are (APA, 1994, p.522) "recurrent, intense, sexually arousing fantasies, sexual urges or behavior." By this criterion, almost everybody qualifies for the diagnosis of paraphiliac. So, three subtypes of behavior are specified in the *DSM-IV*: The interest must involve nonhumans or nonconsenting partners or involve suffering humiliation. The "nonhuman" paraphilias listed include fetishism and transvestitic fetishism, but not zoophilia. The rationale for this omission is not elucidated.

"Suffering humiliation" refers to sadism and masochism, but what constitutes humiliation, and from whose perspective? Masochists often report that the "humiliating" activity in which they choose to engage is not humiliating to them, but is sexually exciting. Such individuals do not find random humiliation exciting. It is the context (i.e., a consensual relationship) which makes their sexual activities exciting. If the professional making the diagnosis considers the activity humiliating, this speaks to the professional's sexual and political values rather than to the mental health of those who engage in the behavior. Similarly, Freud reported that heterosexual coitus could be interpreted as an attack upon the woman, although the woman perceives no attack but, rather, a sexually exciting experience (Freud, 1905).

The inclusion of "nonconsenting partners" pertains to pedophilia, exhibitionism, frotteurism (sexual arousal by rubbing against someone else surreptitiously), and voyeurism. Inexplicably, again, rape is not included.

Other criteria used to define the paraphilias were that they are "rare," "unnatural," and "resulting from childhood trauma." These interests are found in nature and across a wide variety of different cultures, however, and so one cannot argue that they are unnatural. As for being rare, depending on one's definition, they are found in a substantial part of the population. For example, interests in sadism and masochism are relatively common (Kinsey, Pomeroy, Martin & Gebhard, 1953). The belief that a given sexual interest is the result of childhood trauma remains a popular but unproven assumption, without benefit of substantiating data.

Finally, in the *DSM-III* (1980, p. 283), *III-R* (1987, p. 296), and *IV* (1994, p. 538) under Sexual Disorder, Not Otherwise Specified, the same wording is used to describe another form of psychopathology. This entity pathologizes those who treat their partners "only as things to be used." This statement presupposes that there is a correct attitude toward one's sexual partner, and that attitude is straight out of a bad romance novel. It also could be said that an individual who uses sex to obtain some advantage (e.g., children, money, advancement, or marriage) now qualifies for a sexual diagnosis. It also pathologizes most of history. Before there was the concept of romantic love, use of one's partner was the norm. Finally, it presupposes how a psychiatrically defined "healthy relationship" should appear.

☐ Other Attempts at "Fixing" the *DSM*

This chapter is not the first critique of the *DSM* (see, e.g., Schmidt, 1995; Silverstein, 1984; Suppe, 1984; Tallent, 1977). Some have suggested adding new categories to expand the types of sexual behavior to be pathologized. Recognizing the inadequacies, flaws, and inconsistencies in the *DSM* nomenclature, several sexologists have suggested alternate diagnostic categories. Coleman (1991) created "compulsive sexual behavior disorder," while others have suggested "sexual addiction" (Carnes, 1983, 1991; Schwartz & Brasted, 1985) and "courtship disorder" (Freund, 1990; Freund, Seto, & Kuban,1997); still others have suggested that these behaviors be listed under "atypical impulse control disorder"(Barth & Kinder, 1987).

Others have criticized the concept of paraphilias as being too narrow. Kafka and Hennen (1999) suggested both "nonparaphilic hypersexuality" and "paraphilia related disorder" to expand the concept of pathological sexuality. They defined paraphilia related disorder this way:

Sexually arousing fantasies, urges or activities that are culturally sanctioned aspects of normative sexual arousal and activity but which increase in frequency or intensity (for greater than 6 months duration) so as to preclude or significantly interfere with the capacity for reciprocal affectionate activity. (Kafka & Hennen, 1999, p. 306)

Individuals who report a high frequency of sexual activity, including heterosexual coitus, would be subject to the diagnosis of "nonparaphilic hypersexuality" (Kafka & Hennen, 1999), even if they do not experience distress or dysfunction emanating from their sexual interests. The lack of subjective distress is said to indicate that the person is in denial and is displaying more severe pathology. Ostensibly, the category of nonparaphilic hypersexuality encompasses those who enjoy too much of a good thing. Clearly, there are people who are distressed by lack of control over their sexuality. There is an inherent difficulty, however, in establishing objective criteria to "diagnose" the problem. The contextual nature of this issue becomes obvious every time two people present for therapy, one of them claiming the other is a "sex addict" and the other responding with the counter-accusation that the partner is "uptight." The entire concept of hypersexuality is reflective of a sex-negative environment in which it is too easy to stigmatize those who evoke our ambivalence about high rates of sexual activity.

The construct of hypersexuality also is subject to the imposition of the therapist's values and social norms on the patient. It is understandable in this culture, which stresses monogamous marriage, that those who will not or cannot or do not wish to adhere to that goal will experience some conflict.

Therapists need to be cognizant of the societal messages they and their clients have internalized, before judging others as mentally ill. Even those individuals who are more than two standard deviations away from the perceived norm are not necessarily ill. If the trait is the ability and desire to throw a football accurately, that person is rewarded in our society. If it is the ability and desire to engage in sex multiple times a day or with multiple partners, Kafka and Hennen would consider that person mentally ill.

It is of questionable value to create new diagnostic categories that fragment further the concept of distressing or dysfunctional sexual interests, urges, desires, fantasies, or behaviors. Furthermore, any new taxonomy would be well advised to avoid accusations of built-in therapist and cultural bias. The proponents of such changes to the diagnostic categories often have treatment programs to promote as well. While any change deserves to be considered seriously, these programs (e.g., for treatment of sexual addiction) have shown neither clear diagnostic criteria nor long-term outcome data (Goodman, 1992; Moser, 1993).

Kafka and Hennen's proposal can be accused of the same moral judgments and is open to the same misuse. Theoretically, therapists are not supposed to project their beliefs into the diagnostic process. We must ask ourselves, "Why are people trying to pathologize this? And is there a pathology there to pathologize?"

☐ Sexual Orientation and the *DSM*: A "Deviation" Gets Recalled

The role of sociocultural and political influences in the classification of the paraphilias has also been apparent in the *DSM* with respect to sexual orientation. Although homosexuality was listed in the *DSM I* and *DSM II*, it was removed from the *DSM* by a vote of the APA in 1973. It was replaced by a new diagnostic category entitled "Ego-Dystonic Homosexuality" in the *DSM-III* (1980, p. 282) and categorized this way: "There is a sustained pattern of homosexual arousal that the individual explicitly states has been unwanted and a persistent source of distress." This category, too, was supposedly removed from *DSM-III-R* and subsequent editions. Of note, there was no thought of adding an "Ego-Dystonic Heterosexuality" category. Presumably, if one is to be dysphoric over one's sexual preferences, it must be because these preferences do not conform to the norm.

Ego-dystonic homosexuality was listed in the *DSM-III* under "Sexual Disorder, Not Otherwise Specified" (NOS). Although, the term ego-dystonic homosexuality was removed from *DSM-III-R* and *DSM-IV*, nearly identical wording remains in those editions, still under "Sexual Disorder, NOS." The *DSM-III-R* lists, "Persistent and marked distress about one's sexual orientation" (APA, 1987, p. 296). Similarly, the *DSM-IV* lists, "Persistent and marked distress about sexual orientation" (APA, 1994, p. 538). Thus, even though the term no longer exists as a separate category in the *DSM*, the concept continues and the diagnosis persists in a disguised form. Additionally, it would seem that the editors of the *DSM-IV* have inadvertently pathologized homophobia.

Is homosexuality a paraphilia? It was the equivalent of a paraphilia in *DSM-I* and *-II*. It was and is still seen by some as dysfunctional. So how did it come to be removed from the *DSM*? Its removal was a political act (Bayer, 1981), no more motivated by new scientific research than the inclusion and later exclusion of masturbation and oral sex. (Given the nature of our clouded thinking about sexuality, our diagnoses remain heavily influenced by social fads.) The data to support the removal of homosexuality were scant, but the data to support its inclusion were even rarer (Bayer, 1981). Neither sexology nor psychiatry can produce a research-based argument that is convincing. If the removal had been motivated by scientific considerations (i.e., the lack of evidence for homosexuality as dysfunctional), surely other paraphilias and homosexuality would have shared a common fate. The reasoning behind the inclusion or exclusion of homosexuality applies just as well or as poorly to the paraphilias. They all would and should have been removed from the *DSM* simultaneously.

Further evidence for the flaws inherent in the construct of the paraphilas becomes obvious by questioning whether heterosexuality qualifies for this diagnosis. Technically, heterosexuality cannot qualify because it is not rare or unusual. (Of course, the fact that a given sexual interest is neither rare nor unusual has not prevented its inclusion in the *DSM*.) However, the fact that the inclusion of heterosexuality was never considered seriously speaks to the context in which this taxonomy is assembled.

The APA (1994) has stated that the *DSM* is to represent the state of the science; it is not to be used to support a political or social agenda. Although its authors have demonstrated sensitivity to such issues, they have not succeeded at meeting their own goal.

Clearly, there are some problems with the bases for classification in the *DSM*, which may not be resolvable as long as we retain the current nosology.

☐ Sexual Orientation and the Paraphilias

The confusion surrounding the construct of the paraphilias in the *DSM* is mirrored in its treatment of sexual orientation; the implicit assumption that heterosexual coitus is the ideal, covertly distorts and infuses attempts to be "scientific." We have structured our investigations with a built-in bias. We view all other sexual interests as secondary to the sex of the partner. We study homosexual masochists, heterosexual shoe fetishists, and bisexual voyeurs. Although there are numerous theories on how individuals develop aberrant sexual interests, there are strikingly few attempts to explain how individuals develop a heterosexual orientation (cf., Freud, 1905; Money,1993; Storms, 1981). Most psychological theories assume that healthy sexual development will result in heterosexual orientation, and that homosexuality, bisexuality, and other sexual interests are inferior or even pathological. At present there are no convincing data to demonstrate that any sexual orientation is necessarily dysfunctional in an individual's life, except by having to overcome the societal sanctions imposed on those who do not conform. Research into the development of heterosexuality has been retarded by the governing assumption that it is natural. This underlying belief system has led to improper pathologizing of other sexual orientations and interests.

☐ A New Alternative: "Sexual Interest Disorder"

One intended contribution of this chapter is to provide an alternate diagnostic nomenclature. Mental health professionals require clear language and concepts in order to diagnose patients appropriately. The *DSM* is hopelessly confused. Minor adjustments will not succeed in helping clinicians to identify patients' sexual problems. More radical solutions are required. Given all the flaws inherent in the construct and category of the paraphilias, the entire paraphilia section should be removed from the *DSM*. The proposed alternative must be less subject to fashions in values, free of the aforementioned inconsistencies, and more parsimonious and comprehensive, unifying the problems of concern in one, inclusive category.

I proposed that a new classification, to be entitled, "Sexual Interest Disorder" (SID), be substituted in place of the paraphilias. SID would eliminate and replace the entirety of the diagnoses currently referred to as the paraphilias and sexual disorders NOS as well as the proposed constructs of nonparaphilic hypersexuality, paraphilia related disorder and other, similar categories. The emphasis in this new category would be on the effect of the interest on the individual rather than implying that people who engage in particular behaviors are inherently "sick." The SID category would have two criteria:

A: Specific fantasies, sexual urges, or behaviors cause clinically significant distress or impairment in social, occupational, or other important areas of functioning.

B: The sexual interest is not better accounted for by another Axis I disorder, not due to the effects of a general medical disorder, and is not the result of substance use, misuse, or abuse.

The primary rationale for treating patients is their distress or dysfunction. The proposed new "A" criterion features precisely that. It is a restatement of the "B" criterion common to all paraphilia diagnoses in the *DSM-IV*. This criterion is the common point that separates paraphilias from "healthy" sexual behaviors.

The proposed "B" criterion has been added because sexual interests can be the result, albeit rarely, of other medical disorders (e.g., brain damage or seizure). Treatment of the underlying medical disorder may ameliorate the distressing or dysfunctional sexual interest. Additionally, some psychiatric syndromes (e.g., drug intoxication) may affect sexual interests. Treatment of these syndromes can result in cessation of the problematic sexual interest.

As mentioned above, the singling out of specific sexual behaviors must be avoided. In the SID category, naming of the specific sexual interest would be eliminated for three reasons: First, it is a theoretical flaw to pathologize behavior. A behavior by itself is not necessarily evidence of psychopathology. People hallucinate without being psychotic, show vegetative signs without being depressed, use excess substances without qualifying for a drug abuse diagnosis, and so on. So, the sexual interest per se is not the issue, but whether or not it is the cause of distress or dysfunction in the individual's life. Therefore specifying the behavior can only confuse the clinician and draw the focus of the evaluation away from the individual's level of the distress or dysfunction. Avoiding the naming of the behavior and focusing on the psychological deficits the behavior engenders is an important aspect of any proposed diagnostic consideration.

Second, the therapist's own socialization is likely to be thrust into the evaluation. The proposed alternative requires the individual diagnosing the client to justify the diagnosis on the basis of distress and dysfunction, rather than confounding the evaluation with the therapist's personal reaction to atypical sexual behavior. It is not uncommon to hear mental health professionals make derisive comments on a patient's behavior rather than focusing on the distress or dysfunction exhibited by the patient. For example, "How could being humiliated be healthy?" or "Cross-dressing must be compulsive—why else would anyone do it?" These and similar remarks demonstrate that the therapist's own socialization is the basis of the determination of psychopathology, rather than more objective criteria.

Third, the act of specifying particular sexual behaviors as pathological has led to discrimination against all practitioners of that behavior, even when its expression is appropriate and benign. Specifying the behavior brings additional stigma to individuals who appropriately find their sexuality to be a source of enjoyment and satisfaction in their lives. Individuals have lost jobs, security clearances, custody of children, and other rights as the result of being so labeled.

It is important to note that the diagnostic criteria do not specify "treatments." It may be appropriate to reassure the client, to have the client attempt to cease the behavior and fantasies, to help the client with other underlying problems (e.g., depression), to problem-solve solutions to the client's dilemmas, among other scenarios. If an individual's sexual interest causes distress or dysfunction, the therapeutic options include the elimination of the interest or learning to express the interest in a "healthier" manner. Elimination of the interest is the parsimonious approach, as attempts to merely control the behavior require constant monitoring; transforming the interest is also possible but rarely attempted (Kleinplatz, 1996).

☐ Implications of the New Alternative: The Politics of Diagnosis

These issues are not just of taxonomic interest. Beliefs surrounding what constitutes inappropriate sexual interest have led to imprisonment, executions, personal distress, and the breakup of families, as well as other sanctions. Discomfort by both individuals and societies has led to medical and clinical sexological intervention, often with negative consequences. Historically, our treatments of nymphomania and homosexuality have not been examples of psychiatry's finest work.

It is not clear why certain kinds of unlawful behavior are seen as just that—criminal activity—while others are taken as evidence of psychopathology. For example, the commonalities between rape and pedophilia are striking. Both crimes involve sex, power, and victimization, and affect adversely the survivor's subsequent functioning. The perpetrators of both crimes are detested and scorned by society. Many perpetrators of these crimes want desperately to change their sexual patterns. The inclusion of pedophilia with the exclusion of rape in the *DSM* (since *DSM-I*) is inconsistent. Thus, the inclusion or exclusion of certain behaviors from this nosology reflect the implicit, underlying sexual values and the context in which diagnoses are delineated in the *DSM*.

The proposed new classification, sexual interest disorder, does not suggest that all sexual interests are acceptable. Some, clearly, are not acceptable. Nor does it imply that any interest should be afforded special rights or protections. It can be argued that it is especially true for heterosexuality.

I am peripherally concerned here with pedophilia, which may or may not eventuate in criminal acts. To be perfectly clear, adult-child sexual contact should not be condoned under any circumstances. Individuals who commit these crimes should be punished. That punishment should *not* be mitigated by claims of mental illness. The notion that removing pedophilia from the *DSM* is somehow defending pedophiles is confused. Rape is not listed as a paraphilia, but there are clearly individuals for whom rape is paraphilic per the *DSM-IV*. Rape was listed in *DSM-I* (1952, p. 39) as a sexual deviation, the category that contains what we now think of as paraphilias. Removal of rape from the list has not been seen as defending rapists.

Removal of pedophilia from the *DSM* would imply that those who violate the law should be punished in the criminal justice system. If someone sexually abuses a child, that person belongs in the criminal justice system, whether or not a strong preferential sexual interest in children exists. We do not care about sexual interests; we care about acts.

Conversely, "just" being a pedophile—meaning that one has a sexual interest in prepubescent children but does not ever act on it—is not necessarily a problem. Acting on it is a problem. When individuals who are neither dysfunctional nor distressed by their behavior engage in sexual activity with minors, their behavior should not be construed as evidence of mental illness. Such individuals are criminals. They have engaged in a crime.

Arousal to a given stimulus does not in and of itself imply psychopathology. "Rape" fantasies (which in no way resemble the reality of sexual assault) are common among women. But I have never met a woman who actually wanted to be raped. Fantasy and actuality are very different. Just because someone has a fantasy does not mean he or she would choose to act on it. Any sexual activity among consenting adults may be healthy but still be judged illegal or immoral. These are separate issues. Healthy individuals are able to refrain from specific sexual activity. Failure to do so when the individual wishes to refrain is a sign of dysfunction.

Although society has a responsibility and a duty to protect individuals from all types of attack, we do not include bank robbers, bigamists, and those who commit libel in the list of psychiatric diagnoses. Criminals are dealt with by the justice system; those who suffer from a mental illness should be dealt with by the mental health system.

The sociopolitical context in which the discourse surrounding sexual psychopathology exists is fraught with controversy, particularly for the sexologist. For example, Rind, Tromovich, and Bauserman (1998) published a meta-analysis of the effects of childhood sexual abuse (CSA) on college students. Their article concluded, "findings of the current review do not imply that moral or legal definitions of or views on behaviors currently classified as CSA should be abandoned or even altered" (p. 47). Although the article condemned CSA, it was nonetheless roundly criticized as defending pedophiles. The resulting controversy led to a unanimous congressional resolution to condemn and denounce the article (H. Con. Res. 107, 7/30/99) and forced a change in the editorial policies of scientific journals.

☐ Conclusion

The *DSM* is a major worldwide reference, reflecting and influencing how we think about psychiatric disorders and, in this instance, sexual disorders. By changing the *DSM* we influence the thinking of mental health professionals and the larger society. It was when homosexuality was removed from the *DSM* that the civil rights of gay people were advanced—not before. This timing is not coincidental. The civil rights of paraphiliacs are abridged routinely, and discrimination against these individuals is rampant. The psychiatric establishment is complicit in fostering this discrimination by its overly broad specification of the behavior as pathology.

People are sexual, and everything is subject to being eroticized. We do not know how any erotic interests, including heterosexual interests, develop. The strong negative responses to some interests and not to others are curious and puzzling. It appears that sexual behavior is like ethnicity and religion in the way it evokes visceral clutch. If we are to live together, we will be faced with those who are sexually different. No society has been able to control its citizens' sexual behavior, even though each has tried. To be tolerant, we will have to accept nonstandard sexualities. That does not mean we relinquish the right to protect people from sexual encroachments. Children cannot consent. Unconscious people cannot consent. If people are forced to engage in sex without consent, that constitutes rape. If, in fact, sexual assault occurs, the courts step in just as they would if someone tried to steal a wallet or break into a home. Sex among consenting adults, behind closed doors, in the privacy of one's home, however, should not be the purview of government or of unwanted mental health intervention.

Theoretically, therapists should not impose their beliefs on their patients. The *DSM*, as it currently exists, promotes our society's values and projects them onto patients. In contrast, the proposed category, sexual interest disorder, features the individual's own experience of well-being or distress and dysfunction. No classification system can claim to be value-neutral; this proposed category places a premium on the values and perspective of the client over those of the therapist. Rather than add to and complicate the present *DSM* structure, sexual interest disorder is parsimonious and elegant.

☐ References

American Psychiatric Association. (1952). *Diagnostic and statistical manual of mental disorders.* Washington, DC: Author.

American Psychiatric Association. (1968). *Diagnostic and statistical manual of mental disorders* (2nd ed.). Washington, DC: Author.

American Psychiatric Association. (1980). *Diagnostic and statistical manual of mental disorders* (3rd ed.). Washington, DC: Author.

American Psychiatric Association.(1987). *Diagnostic and statistical manual of mental disorders* (3rd ed., rev.). Washington, DC: Author.

American Psychiatric Association. (1994). *Diagnostic and statistical manual of mental disorders* (4th ed.). Washington, DC: Author.

Barth, R. J., & Kinder, B. N. (1987). The mislabeling of sexual impulsivity. *Journal of Sex & Marital Therapy, 13*(1), 15–23.

Bayer, R. (1981). *Homosexuality and American psychiatry: The politics of diagnosis*. New York: Basic Books.

Carnes, P. (1983). *Out of the shadows: Understanding sexual addiction*. Minneapolis: CompCare.

Carnes, P. (1991). *Don't call it love*. New York: Bantam Books.

Coleman, E. (1991). Compulsive sexual behavior: New concepts and treatments. *Journal of Psychology & Human Sexuality, 4*(2), 37–52.

Freud, S. (1905). Three essays on the theory of sexuality. In J. Strachey (Trans.), *The standard edition of the complete psychological works of Sigmund Freud* (vol. 7). London: Hogarth Press.

Freund, K. (1990). Courtship disorder. In W. L. Marshall, D. R. Laws, & H. E. Barbaree (Eds.), *Handbook of sexual assault: Issues, theories, and treatment of the offender* (pp. 195–207). New York: Plenum.

Freund, K., Seto, M. C., & Kuban, M. (1997). Frotteurism: The theory of courtship disorder. In D. R. Laws & W. O'Donohue (Eds.), *Sexual deviance: Theory, assessment, and treatment* (pp. 111–130). New York: Guilford Press.

Goodman, A. (1992). Sexual addiction: Designation and treatment. *Journal of Sex & Marital Therapy, 18*(4), 303–314.

House Congressional Resolution 107, 7/30/99

Kafka, M. P., & Hennen, J. (1999). The paraphilia-related disorders: An empirical investigation of nonparaphilic hypersexuality disorders in outpatient males. *Journal of Sex & Marital Therapy, 25*(4), 305–320.

Kinsey A. C., Pomeroy, W. B., Martin, C. E., & Gebhard, P. H. (1953). *Sexual behavior in the human female*. Philadelphia: W.B. Saunders.

Kleinplatz, P. J. (1996). Transforming sex therapy: Integrating erotic potential. *The Humanistic Psychologist, 24*(2), 190–202.

Langevin, R., Lang, R. A., & Curnoe, S. (1998). The prevalence of sex offenders with deviant fantasies. *Journal of Interpersonal Violence, 13*(3), 315–327.

Money, J. (1980). *Love and love sickness: The science of sex, gender difference, and pair bonding*. Baltimore, MD: Johns Hopkins University Press.

Money, J. (1984). Paraphilias: Phenomenology and classification. *American Journal of Psychotherapy, 38*(2), 164–179.

Money, J. (1993). *Lovemaps*. New York: Irvington Publishers. (Originally published 1986.)

Moser, C. (1992). Lust, lack of desire, and paraphilias: Some thoughts and possible connections. *Journal of Sex & Marital Therapy, 18*(1), 65–69.

Moser, C. (1993). A response to Aviel Goodman's "Sexual addiction: Designation and treatment." *Journal of Sex & Marital Therapy, 19*(3), 220–224.

Moser, C. (1999). *Health care without shame: A handbook for the sexually diverse and their caregivers*. San Francisco: Greenery Press.

Rind, B., Tromovich, P., & Bauserman, R. (1998) A meta-analytic examination of assumed properties of child sexual abuse using college samples. *Psychological Bulletin, 124*(1), 22–53.

Rosario, V. A., II. (1997). *The erotic imagination: French histories of perversity*. New York: Oxford University Press.

Schmidt, C. W. (1995). Sexual psychopathology and the DSM-IV. *American Psychiatric Press Review of Psychiatry* (14), 719–733.

Schwartz, M. F., & Brasted, W. S. (1985). Sexual addiction: Self-hatred, guilt, and passive rage contribute to this deviant behavior. *Medical Aspects of Human Sexuality, 19*(10), 103–107.

Silverstein, C. (1984). The ethical and moral implications of sexual classification: A commentary. *Journal of Homosexuality, 9*(4), 29–37.

Simpson, J. A. (Ed.). (1989). *Oxford English dictionary*. Oxford: Clarendon.

Stekel, W. (1924). *Peculiarities of behavior: Wandering mania, dipsomania, cleptomania, pyromania, and allied impulsive acts* (2 vols.). English translation of *Impulshandlungen* (1922) by J. S. Van Teslaar. New York: Liveright.

Storms, M. D. (1981). A theory of erotic orientation development. *Psychological Record, 88,* 340–353.

Suppe, F. (1984). Classifying sexual disorders: *The Diagnostic and Statistical Manual of the American Psychiatric Association*. In J. P. DeCecco & M. G. Shively (Eds.), *Bisexual and homosexual identities* (pp. 9–37). Binghamton, NY: Haworth.

Tallent, N. (1977). Sexual deviation as a diagnostic entity: A confused and sinister concept. *Bulletin of the Menninger Clinic, 41*(1), 40–59.

Peggy J. Kleinplatz, Ph.D.

A Critique of the Goals of Sex Therapy, or the Hazards of Safer Sex

If there is one overriding factor that seems to determine the character of sex therapy, it is the nature of its objectives. Over the last 20 to 30 years, the scope of our cases has changed, the clientele and their problems have become more complex, and our methods have become more sophisticated. Our goals, however, basically remain the same: the elimination of the symptoms of sexual dysfunction, the reversal of desire disorders, and the containment of paraphilic urges and behaviors.

There has been an alleged backlash against Masters and Johnson's style of sex therapy. We are said to be in a postmodern phase (LoPiccolo, 1992), yet older conceptions of sexuality and sexual inadequacy remain entrenched in our current practices and reified in the *DSM-IV*. This chapter will critique these conceptions and the goals that arise from them as limiting the potential outcomes of our work.

☐ Sex Therapy Emphasizes Performance Rather Than Subjective Meaning and Experience

The goals of sex therapy emphasize individual/couple performance rather than embodiment, connection, and integration. Correspondingly, "success" is measured in terms of objective, behavioral, and physiological indices rather than in terms of subjective meaning and experience.

In a sense, sex therapy has an advantage over other forms of psychotherapy. Most of the problems and solutions in our domain seem relatively discreet, well-demarcated, and readily identifiable. Whether or not one has orgasms or "erections sufficient for penetration" is more easily discerned than the comparatively amorphous concerns of patients in general psychotherapy. It would seem that the goals in treating women who present with anorgasmia or men who have been diagnosed with erectile dysfunction would be clear-cut (i.e., having orgasms or erections), especially relative to the goals in treatment of depression or anxiety. This makes it particularly easy for us to be trapped into defining the problem and the symptom as one and the same; it also means that the goal typically is defined in terms of remedying technical difficulties in performance. It makes it harder for us to distinguish between the anorgasmia and her feelings about it, or his lack of physiological signs of arousal and his subjective sense of being turned on. Zilbergeld and Ellison (1980) suggested 20 years ago that the cognitive and affective components of sexual response ought to be included in our understanding of sexual function/dysfunction. Their innovation, the incorporation of subjective aspects of arousal and the sense of satisfaction into our models, has not been given its due. As such, our models still cannot account for problems in sexual desire when performance is intact.

The following vignette illustrates the gaps in the conventional model. The couple in my office have had a high frequency of sexual activity for years. They know one another's bodies cold. He brings her to multiple orgasms regularly within minutes of commencing genital stimulation. There are no component failures here, yet, ironically, herein lies the problem. She is full of contempt as she says, "He plays my body like a violin and I am growing to hate him for it." Her desire had disappeared as she began to feel that her body was the object of his expert manipulations while the person within lay untouched (Kleinplatz, 1996b).

One night of sex with a new partner may be exciting, if only because of the possibilities to be explored. It is when we quit exploring the person within, forgoing passion and focusing instead on the more expedient goal of orgasm, that sexual problems begin. It is paradoxically in the act of repeating—relentlessly—the successes of the past that we ultimately become ineffective lovers. The consequences of participating in sex over a prolonged period without intimate sexual connection, even when the mechanical aspects of sex are satisfactory, may be the loss of sexual desire or the inability to become aroused.

In a second case, the couple's relationship seems warm and loving. There are no conspicuous marital problems and no desire disorders. The problem is in arousal, at least when she is in bed with him (as opposed to during self-stimulation, when arousal is easy). She says the problem is that he touches her genitals in order to arouse her, prior to intercourse, but that there is no use in touching her genitals until she is sexually aroused. How does she become aroused? She becomes aroused in response to either nongenital touch or the sense of erotic connection. When she is very excited, genital stimulation can bring her to orgasm relatively quickly. When she is not aroused, genital stimulation is useless at best, and irritating at worst. It is more than that: When she is sexually aroused, almost everything feels good and almost nothing is irritating. When, on the other hand, she is not aroused, she is very easily aggravated by particular acts and techniques. As long as the goal is merely producing arousal sufficient for penetration, sexual relations will eventually be disappointing. When the emphasis instead is on heightened sexual pleasure and intimacy for its own sake, the goal of sexual fulfillment is easier to attain, regardless of performance.

Such couples illustrate that when one complains about the other's technique, the partners may not be in the ideal mind-set for giving and receiving stimulation with pleasure. "He's tweaking my nipples." We hear these kinds of complaints frequently, and with them the partner's exasperated response, "No matter what I do, I can't seem to get it right. I can't seem to please her." The reason he cannot please her is because they are not sufficiently attuned to one another for him to feel her responses, or lack thereof. Because they are not on the same wavelength, she is not easily aroused to the point where whatever he does will please her.

Correspondingly, individuals who object to a given set of sexual acts may be less particular when they are so aroused that they are governed by their senses rather than by their sensibilities.

Technique had better excel when arousal is depending on it and it alone. One cannot afford any mechanical glitches when technical proficiency alone is intended to produce arousal. To create intense sexual excitement, skillful stimulation is not nearly as "effective" as eroticism. Eroticism can override an awful lot of lousy technique. In fact, erotic connection can generate sexual excitement in the absence of any physical contact at all.

This is exactly the opposite of what Kaplan (1974) suggested. She recommended that those with sexual dysfunctions learn to bypass their own thoughts and feelings in order to allow their bodies to respond "freely," that is, autonomically. But practicing to be devoid of inner cues (aside from philosophical objections about dehumanization and the partner's likely objections about not being present during sex) raises the standard for technical proficiency, because it is then the sole mechanism for reaching orgasm.

It seems so much easier to produce arousal by relying on both erotic contact and technical proficiency at physical stimulation. This requires more than hitting the right nerve endings.

Two examples illustrate the relative roles of physical stimulation and the subjective experience of erotic contact in producing arousal: First, both the anus and the perineum are loaded with nerve endings. Stimulation of these areas may be powerfully erotic for some men and women, while for others it is powerfully repulsive. The difference is related to individuals' cognitions and emotions about these areas rather than to the number of nerve endings. That is, one's response to anal stimulation is related to the meanings assigned to these areas; it is a case of mind over matter. Second, according to Masters and Johnson (1966), the contractions of orgasm are apparently strongest when the orgasm results from self-stimulation. If the strongest orgasms result from masturbation, why is it that most people prefer dyadic sex over self-stimulation? There is more to sexual fulfillment than physiologically intense orgasms. In fact, the most powerfully erotic experiences may not be subject to measurement via physiological indices.

When clients are focused on erection or orgasm, we know they are oriented at the performance level. We encourage them to stay on this plane rather than to enter the erotic dimension when our solutions target symptoms alone. Treatments for mechanical problems that encourage clients to perform on automatic may engender feelings of disconnection and disembodiment. Men who can bypass their feelings and produce automatic erections and women who can lubricate notwithstanding a lack of subjective arousal can perform, but they cannot be present. Sooner or later, either they or their partners sense it. That is when the emptiness begins, and with it a lack of desire. When they are embodied within and connected to one another as erotic beings, performance becomes far less relevant for sexual fulfillment, which takes on a whole new character.

Our goals seem aimed at treating symptoms of sexual dysfunction. The alternate goal is to augment the ability to be present and sexually accessible, in which case concerns about functioning seem to recede, even if the performance has not yet changed. This entails a shift in orientation from *doing* to *being* (L'Abate, & Hewitt, 1988). Perhaps we need to prevent the development of future problems by going beyond performance concerns, even when those are the presenting complaints, and focus instead on clients' inner and interpersonal experience.

☐ Sex Therapy Promotes One-Size-Fits-All Goals at the Expense of Appreciating Individual Uniqueness

Sex therapy treats broad categories of dysfunctions and disorders rather than the particular individual who bears the diagnosis. Our field aims to eliminate the problem without sufficient regard for the individuality of the person within (i.e., the uniqueness of the client and the role, meaning, purpose, or value of the problem for the person). Goals are thus based on insufficient data about the nature of the client's sexuality (at present or in potentia).

Part of the problem with the goals of sex therapy is that they are macro, one-size-fits-all, nomothetic objectives, when what we need are micro, individualized "interventions," highly sensitive to what lies within a given individual. Combinations of subjective, sexual/erotic meanings are as distinctive as fingerprints. They are intricate, complex, subtle, and powerful.

The *DSM-IV* offers huge categories, made useless to the clinician by their lack of specificity. The diagnostic categories are too abstract and vague to describe and identify a client's underlying phenomenology. "Pathological" behaviors may seem superficially indistinguishable, but the individual's level of sexual satisfaction or dissatisfaction will be directly linked to the extent to which particular, subjective meanings are involved. It is not the event of having an erection or engaging in intercourse or having your thigh stroked or being bound or wearing women's clothes that matters— it is the particular, unique experience it evokes, permits, and opens up that is important.

If we begin with the *DSM-IV* category, all we know is the name given to a broad rubric of behaviors, desires, urges, and fantasies; but it stays at that level—it is just a name. There is no opportunity to truly understand the nature of a given phenomenon with its corresponding label. If anything, the label may act as an obstacle by suggesting that the clinician knows enough to proceed and that there is no need to delve deeper. If, however, we develop and employ more sensitive epistemologies, we begin to understand the vast array of ways of being, sexually and otherwise, that have been lumped together.

Therapists often act as if all individuals who fit a given psychodiagnostic category are alike; once they have been diagnosed with the same pathology, they will receive the same treatment and that treatment will target the same goal. For example, in treatment of the paraphilias, the goal may simply involve controlling the unacceptable or compulsive sexual behavior, without distinguishing the significance of the desires for a particular client. In contrast, the literature by sadomasochistic participants distinguishes between sadism, dominance, and other motives for certain superficially similar behaviors. Those who participate in sadomasochistic activities at least try to clarify motives so that it is easier (to try) to find what they seek.

The approach to sadomasochism within sex therapy is markedly different from the approach of the actual participants. Sex therapy sees only the broad category of sexual sadism and sexual masochism, as listed in the *DSM-IV*. Participants (i.e., sadomasochists, sex radicals, pansexuals) conceive of a wide spectrum of behaviors under this umbrella and an even more varied spectrum of underlying goals and purposes motivating these acts. While sex therapy focuses on what is on the surface, participants are interested in the meanings that lie at a deeper level. When a professional dominatrix or even a seasoned amateur undertakes a given scene, she must first investigate, inquire, understand fully and thoroughly what her partner wants to experience and aims to attain, achieve, derive, or accomplish therein.

Telling your therapist that you have powerful and compelling cravings for bondage and discipline, that you would rather be engaging in your favorite form of sadomasochistic sexual relations than going to work in the morning, is enough to get you classified as a paraphiliac and as mentally ill. In contrast, saying this to the dominatrix is useless. It does not give her nearly enough information to know how to proceed. She would be out of business very quickly it she were to provide the identical or even quite similar services to every man who requested bondage and discipline. To satisfy her customer, she needs to know the nature of his desires precisely. Does he imagine a determined and unyielding disciplinarian? Is she to be a loving, nurturing, almost maternal figure who knows just how to take care of him? Is she to be a wild, driven, sex-crazed woman who simply will not let go of him until she's had her fill? The devil is in the details. Saying that her client is masochistic or submissive does not begin to capture it.

The dominatrix may be the ultimate phenomenologist. She interviews her submissives to get at what they want *most*. So are dominatrices better interviewers than therapists are? Do they have higher, more sophisticated goals? Perhaps they have simply validated that desires are surely more complex than what is seen on the surface, that motives are expected to be complicated, and so they implicitly normalize the idea that "sexual" behaviors are embedded with particular, unique motives.

For clinicians, the alternative to treating the category is to develop more sensitive and subtle approaches to appreciating the uniqueness of each client and to tailor our goals accordingly.

☐ Sex Therapy Marginalizes Diversity Rather Than Embracing It

Sex therapy tends to conceive of sex in the same way North American society does: It is for attractive, youthful, able-bodied, monogamous, heterosexual couples in committed relationships. We deny this, of course, providing chapters in our books that address the problems of "different" populations. However, these chapters may inadvertently reinforce the notion that "we" are talking about "them" and how to fix "their" problems. Surely, we do not deliberately aim to curtail diversity, but we may marginalize others nonetheless. These are more likely to be sins of omission than of commission. Attempts to be inclusive can go further—we can broaden our fundamental notions of sex to embrace the entire spectrum of sexuality as it actually exists.

We talk about diversity, but we continue to promote a coital, heterosexual norm. Our methods are designed to alleviate whatever impedes intercourse (e.g., dyspareunia, vaginismus, rapid ejaculation, erectile dysfunction). One might argue that, on the contrary, sex therapy often prohibits intercourse in the course of treatment so that couples can focus on sensual, nondemand aspects of mutual pleasure. Nonetheless, our actual techniques and operations (e.g., sensate focus, cognitive behavioral exercises, vaginal dilators, the squeeze technique, the prescription of paroxetine or sildenafil citrate) involve steps intended to lead toward intercourse. We frequently conclude sex therapy when intercourse has resumed, thereby communicating the implicit but powerful message that coitus is the ultimate end of sexual relations.

The techniques employed are very effective at enabling couples to achieve intercourse. We then aim to modify these exercises to better fit the needs of individuals or couples with different needs, wishes, and concerns (e.g., gay and lesbian couples, incest survivors, nonmonogamous individuals and couples, the elderly, the disabled or chronically ill, the transgendered). Sometimes these minor adaptations work; often they do not. Perhaps this is because we begin with a template that is too narrow and attempt to fit it onto all clients. This may leave individuals who live outside conventional parameters as invisible within the world of sex therapy as within our society in general.

Often mere modifications to a standardized conception of functional sex mask differences among people. We fail to distinguish that some problems do not generally pertain to lesbian couples (e.g., vaginismus). Conversely, we may not detect problems that might be unique to particular client groups. (There are rare but noteworthy exceptions, such as Rosser, Short, Thurmes, and Coleman's 1998 article, which identified the problem of anodyspareunia among gay male couples.) We may fail to train new sex therapists in how to work with elderly or disabled clients, thereby adding to the invisibility of their sexuality. (Perhaps this will change with the aging of the baby boomers.)

What does this have to do with the goals of sex therapy? Sex therapy tends to base its objectives on a norm that involves two able-bodied heterosexuals in a monogamous relationship. Problems are defined and treated in terms of such a norm, and outcome is assessed based on this image. When clients present with other characteristics (e.g., performance anxiety during group sex), we tend to accommodate our treatment from this baseline, rather than reconsider the norm. Rarely do we consider actually revising our whole definition of the norm so that it reflects alternate ways of seeing sexuality and relationships. That is, we try to stretch our sexual norms rather than learn from those we label as "other" to fundamentally question and revise our conceptions of sexuality.

It has taken a long time to understand that we can learn from those who are different from the norm. Among Masters and Johnson's (1979) greater contributions was their recognition that gay and lesbian couples are worth studying for what they can teach "us" about "their" sexuality (rather than to understand, predict, or control their "pathology"). Divergent groups can teach us about sexuality per se and how to improve it, rather than teaching us only about a particular brand of sexuality. That is, when Masters and Johnson "discovered" that gay and lesbian couples tended to be more empathic, communicative, and effective lovers than their heterosexual counterparts (1979), they were teaching us about more than one particular brand or style of sexuality; they were teaching that all individuals can learn about lovemaking by paying attention to one another, even when there seem to be superficial or even significant differences between us.

What can we learn about how power functions in most relationships by asking consensual sadomasochists? What are the constraints and implications of traditional, stereotypic gender roles, particularly for heterosexual couples, and what can the transgendered teach us about how to navigate through them? How do individuals who practice "polyamory" or "polyfidelity" manage trust and jealousy? What lessons might they have to offer therapists dealing with extramarital affairs? What can we glean about the range of healthy sexuality by exploring, examining, and celebrating the breadth of divergent modes of sexual expression? We may have a great deal to learn from and about the farther reaches of human sexuality if we can quit pathologizing whatever seems alien and embrace it instead. We can keep our goals narrow, or we can expand them to reflect not only the limits but also the full range of capacities of our patients.

☐ Sex Therapy Opts to Promote Conformity to a Toxic Norm Rather Than Social Change

When we diagnose, treat, and assess outcome among our clients we typically begin with normative performance standards as our reference points. It is deviation from these norms, defined in terms of the medical model, statistical norms, and conventional values, that serves as a major criterion for diagnosing disorder and determining the goals of treatment. We attempt to restore our patients to a level of functioning (or control, in the case of the paraphilias) that may be in neither their best interests nor those of our society. We tend to accept the social definition of the problem and treat it instead of combating it (Irvine, 1990). We aim to achieve conformity to a troubled norm (Reiss, 1990) rather than applying ourselves to changing the norm.

What is this norm? Sexologists recognize that North American sex scripts may have toxic effects on sexual development, relationships, self-image, and so on. The messages embedded in these scripts undoubtedly engender sexual problems. The emphasis on the unattainable ideal of female beauty surely contributes to the body image problems we see in our clients; yet we continue to treat the anorgasmia rather than combat the source of the self-consciousness that impedes women's pleasure. We recognize that definitions of masculinity centered on the belief that a man's worth is measured by his last erection can only impair his sexual functioning, not to mention his enjoyment; but we mention this in passing, just before we treat his erectile dysfunction. We treat the symptoms of lack of sexual desire and vaginal atrophy with hormone replacement therapy without examining the context in which older women come to be seen as dried up sexual beings. Our knowledge that these "symptoms" are related to cultural values is hardly publicized. Meanwhile, our society tries to eliminate the "symptoms" of aging, and we meekly acquiesce, rather than emphasizing how sexual patterns develop in older couples, making for different but no less pleasurable sex. We automatically treat gender identity disorder and cross-dressing when we see the early signs of nonstereotypic gender-role behavior rather than challenging the culture in which transgression of such constricting norms becomes so tantalizing.

Every time we treat patients one-on-one we inadvertently help to reinforce the status quo. That is, we take money to help this particular client resolve this presenting problem, perhaps even acknowledging in the course of therapy that our society has engendered her body image problem or his preoccupation with his erections. However, by focusing our energies in this limited fashion we keep this secret in our consulting offices

(Irvine, 1990) and fail to devote ourselves to changing society. We abet in maintaining the social context in which the problem exists.

We know all this. Sex therapists are quite aware of the deleterious impact of North American sex scripts on our society. We just are not doing enough en masse to fight it and thereby to prevent the development of sexual problems. This is not to say that we should stop helping those in distress; merely that, in addition, we should be devoting more energy to prevention of sexual problems.

The alternative may involve increased advocacy for social change and new, more public roles for sex therapists. If we are serious about not merely treating but preventing sexual problems, we have a responsibility to aim broader. We might consider augmenting the information on television and on the Internet and getting out and about in our communities, letting people, especially youth, know that it does not have to be this way. We can assist adolescents in developing effective sexual negotiation skills and teach them to become centered in their own bodies as part of their decision-making processes. We can intensify our support of sex educators and promote *comprehensive* sexuality education—not just classes on reproductive biology. We can fight encroaching censorship in the classrooms; work with government agencies, religious groups, youth groups, parenting groups, and rehabilitation programs; and train fellow health professionals (e.g., in occupational therapy and physiotherapy programs). We must resist leaving sex education in the hands of the right wing or those (such as talk-show hosts) who profit from keeping our sexual discourse salacious. We can revolutionize attitudes toward sexuality so that we no longer assist in reifying sexual dysfunctions, disorders, and compulsions. We will know that we have succeeded when we have made ourselves obsolete.

The other alternative to promoting the status quo is to treat patients based on their best interests, aiming for personal growth independent of social conventions; this may entail a revolution in our goals, making them more individualized, based on individual potential—not normalcy—and with an eye toward discovery.

☐ Sex Therapy Promotes a priori Solutions Rather Than Change Generated from Within

The goals of sex therapy stop at the level of normative, standard functioning, whereas what lies within the individual is what ought to guide and direct what this person can become in therapy. We aim merely to restore clients to a predetermined functional state, even though what this particular individual has the potential to become is not merely symptom-free—it is also unique and distinct from all other clients (Mahrer, 1996). To the extent that our goals (and, correspondingly, our methods) foreclose on the possibility of discovery of unknowns and of change generated from within the client, we will never discover all that our clients can aspire to and become. That is, the narrowness of our goals limits the extent of possible changes. If all we aim to achieve is symptom reversal, we will never discover all that each individual can become; we will be oblivious to how different the outcome of therapy can be, even though a series of clients may all begin with the same diagnosis.

Consider the differences in outcome in the following three clinical vignettes; although each man was referred for treatment of erectile dysfunction, the disparate kinds of change sprang from what lay within each individual.

He enters therapy because of erectile dysfunction and depression. His erectile dysfunction feeds his depression and his depression feeds his erectile dysfunction. Is the therapist to treat the depression? Should the therapist target the erectile dysfunction? The alternative is to work with the whole person. We begin at a moment when he is aware of feeling despondent, hopeless, and never being good enough. All his energy is bound up in evaluating himself and not measuring up. It was at its worst that day she brought home the antique pocket watch she had recently inherited. Before she had a chance to put it away for safekeeping, though, he picked it up and examined it, appreciating the fine detail and getting lost in the intricate craftsmanship. It was when she entered the room that he became startled and dropped the watch, breaking it. As usual, he was overwhelmed by feelings of guilt, his sense of being a loser—impotent—and of ruining everything. In the process, he banished the sense of fascination that had so enveloped him just moments before.

But as he allows himself to revel in how it might feel to be entranced, to be in full reverie, to let go of self-consciousness and focus all of his attention on something special and utterly compelling, a new possibility arises. (It is by entering this new way of being that emerges from within that change is effected [Mahrer, 1996, 1999]. In this instance, it is the ability to immerse himself in something or someone utterly fascinating.) He is transfixed by his wife. He lies between her legs, his face barely inches from her genitals, enraptured by her beauty. All his energy is upon her. He is quietly fascinated by her. Every fold in her vulva is captivating. He is absorbed by the texture of her skin and how it shifts from coarse to velvety and delicate to slippery. "I've never really felt free to look at her this way before." As he says these words, he is no longer the depressed person he had been earlier, and his erectile dysfunction has conspicuously evaporated, too.

This is neither the cure for spectatoring prescribed by Masters and Johnson (1970) nor the dereflection recommended by Frankl (1963, 1967), even though in this case it had the same end point (i.e., a shift in focus, concurrent with resolution of sexual dysfunction). This was not my objective; rather, the change was one that sprang from my client. The result was that not only the sexual dysfunction but also the feelings of inadequacy, incompetence, and self-consciousness were gone. In their place was the capacity to lose himself in erotic union with his wife.

A second client, too, comes to therapy because of erectile dysfunction. He, too, is depressed. For him, the problem begins when they are in bed, ready to make love. The peak moment is when she says to him, "I want you inside me right now." For him, this is hell. His attention, however, is not on her—it is on his penis. In fact, his penis is so riveting it seems to have a life of its own. Be the penis, I suggest. Allow it to speak from its vantage point. Listen to its message. "Quit nagging me. You can't tell me what to do," is the response. "You are too busy performing to enjoy. I want attention. I want to be wanted." He had been in the habit of going through the motions even though his partner had been relatively passive and expressed little overt desire for him. He begins to giggle as he imagines playing hard to get. The session concludes with the stirring of an erection. By the following session, he has given voice to his newly discovered capacity to bask in concerted sexual attention and the desire for pure pleasure (instead of being stymied by his formerly uncooperative, dysfunctional penis). He reports having had a great time in bed with his lover, who, much to his surprise, is absolutely thrilled to caress and stroke his penis, which now "functions" quite well. He also reports that his writer's block has dissipated.

A third client explains that his arousal level literally goes up and down. He and his partner spend so much time worrying about his wavering penis while attempting to have sex and between times that they have lost interest in sex. Each attempt has become so stressful that it is just not worth the effort. It would be easy for the sex therapist to diagnose erectile dysfunction and spectatoring and to prescribe exercises to buttress his soft penis. The cognitive behavioral techniques really work and, when they falter, there is always Viagra™. The trickier part is getting the partners to acknowledge what would make it worth their while to be fully present to one another, even without the guarantee of a rigid erection. If they could do that, the penis would take care of itself; or, to put it another way, the problem of the penis' rigidity or lack thereof would disappear. They have attempted to have sex when they have barely reached the threshold of excitement required for minimal functioning, let alone the level of desire required for intense erotic connection.

When they venture within, each discovers that precisely the fantasies they have construed and warded off as most taboo, dangerous, vola-tile, and explosive—they have it half-right—are the ones that harbor the potential to make them feel whole, intimate, connected within and to one another. He discovers an inner strength, a respectful forcefulness, and a capacity for controlled power. For her, coexisting with her genuine inde-pendence of spirit is a wish to become the irresistible object of his desire, to captivate him and then to surrender to his will, allowing herself to be possessed. These two individuals begin to thrive as they explore role-play-ing dominance and submission. Their lovemaking is now so explosively charged that their relationship simmers and sizzles even when they are washing the dishes. Their sexuality is no longer focused on whether they can get physically aroused enough to get through intercourse but on play-ing together to enhance mutual growth. Their "disorders" evaporate si-multaneously.

From the vantage point of the therapist, there is something tremen-dously exciting and enlightening about starting at a given place and not knowing where we will arrive. The alternative to a priori solutions is to discover what each individual can become, respectfully enabling the client to grow in that direction and expanding the client's limits as far as he or she so chooses (Mahrer, 1996, 2001).

This not only means a change in our goals but necessitates a shift in methods to meet these new objectives. Sex therapists will have to envi-sion, borrow, and/or create techniques suited to accomplishing such goals.

☐ Sex Therapy Stops Too Soon and Settles for Too Little

If many people have lousy sex lives, one reason is that so many settle for too little in bed. It is as though they come to the table intent only on satisfying their hunger (Schnarch, 1991). Sex can be about so much more. Great sex can be like great therapy: Each involves aspiring high and not stopping for as long as each of the participants is ready, willing, and able to continue. Each can provide a means to touch, reach, play with, explore, probe, penetrate, and transform all that is within. Many people do not get what they want in bed because they are not really honest about it. They speak in vague generalities about the kinds of sex they want rather than acknowledging aloud, to self and partner, what they truly crave. They are so afraid of having to look closely at and admit (as if it were a crime) what they really want. Their partners let them get away with it. Sometimes their partners do not know any better. We, as sex therapists, let them get away with it but should know better; we have no excuse. We know that individuals will not get any more out of sex than they are prepared to request. Part of our jobs is or should be to help clients figure out why they are dissatisfied, what they ultimately want, and what it would take to satisfy them. We are to help them figure out how to divulge what they want. Like many lovers, many therapists settle at the level of vague generalities and, as such, do not gather the necessary information to keep the customer not just satisfied but happy.

Great therapy can be like great sex. The possibility is for utter transformation in the hands of someone who is willing to reach all the way inside and help bring forth all that one can be. This requires an enormous commitment not merely to being honest but also to being open and opened, transparent, genuine, authentic, vulnerable, and defenseless. Correspondingly, lousy therapy can be like lousy sex. Both are predicated on participants who are willing to stop too soon and settle for too little. They settle for effective functioning and bodily satisfaction. Many want more but dare not aspire to more or admit to their desires. Some delude themselves about being ready to proceed without ever having to acknowledge what the stakes are and how high they might be. If they proceed in a fog, they remain safe, shrouded in and condemned to invisibility. But if they dare to be known and chance exposing the places that are most tender, sore, aching, and sensitive, they risk judgment, rejection, being misunderstood or worse—being understood accurately and then rejected. They risk being hurt as well as the possibility of fundamental change.

The poets already know the transformative power of sexual experience. The pornographers, spiritual leaders, and disciples already know that sex can be therapeutic. It is only therapists who will not venture there. We stop short. Instead of facilitating human growth in the context of sexual relations, we merely attempt to eliminate problematic symptoms. Most of us, however, want more than merely to be free of sexual inadequacy (Schnarch, 1991). We want to be touched, reached, felt, understood. If we conceive of bodies as merely physiological organisms, subject to breakdown and repair, we miss all the joy our bodies can experience, claim, and reclaim. Our bodies are the repositories for memories, fears, secrets, hopes, and dreams. If you touch me in my secret places, will I lie to you? Will I lay myself bare and let you feel my joy? Why stop at orgasm when we can aim for ecstasy (Ogden, 1994)?

Maybe we really ought to consider learning from those who aim high—from those who aim to get all they can out of their sexual encounters and refuse to settle for perfunctory sex. They aim to use sex as a vehicle for personal growth and transformation and interpersonal intimacy. If the means they use are outside the conventions and constraints of ordinary sexual relations, so too are their goals extraordinary.

Instead, we aim to return dysfunctional clients to a hypothetical bio-logical norm—a regression to the mean. We promote sexual safety and stagnation rather than risk the dangers of all-out eroticism. We stay away from the potentially volatile, even though that is where the power for sexual change and growth lies. The transformative power of the erotic (Kleinplatz, 1996a, 1996b; Leonard, 1989; Morin, 1995; Ogden, 1988, 1994; Rofes, 1996; Steinberg, 1992) is largely absent from our discourse.

This is never more so than in the case of our work with incest survi-vors. In the face of their history of suffering, we help them to endure sex better rather than transform their pain. Much of the clinical literature on child sexual abuse is filled with cases of low sexual desire. Similarly, much of the literature on low desire is linked to histories of child sexual abuse. In the treatment of incest survivors, sexuality seems almost an afterthought (Price, 1994). We are to focus on anger, betrayal, trust, powerlessness, guilt, and so on, but dealing with the client's sexuality is hardly a priority. Perhaps it is assumed that once all the other (presumably underlying) is-sues are dealt with, sexuality will take care of itself. Sometimes that is exactly the case. (The omnipresent assumption that sex is a natural pro-cess that will assert itself once impediments to its expression are removed pervades even the incest literature.) In other cases, it does not follow that way. The client deals with all other issues and still feels no sexual desire.

Survivors are wounded in their sexuality. They typically want to deal with the past but do not know how. Common attempts to deal with sexu-ality in therapy aim to reduce clients' anxiety by heightening control. Thera-pists often support survivors in circumventing the triggers (i.e., setting, timing, and positions) for flashbacks (e.g., dark room, late at night, being flat on his or her back or belly) and arranging instead for sex in the after-noon, in a bright sunny room in a different position. However, this is not a solution—it is just a way of not dealing with the problem. Each time some concession is made, another need for accommodation becomes salient: Kisses must be dry; no wetness is allowed; no raising her breasts up and together; no moaning and groaning, or other spontaneous exclamations of sexual passion. There are ways, of course, to avoid evoking the bad memories, but not without evoking a sense of the sexual world having been diminished or narrowed in the name of taking control over the past.

But what if the survivor is seeking freedom from the past? What if he or she does not want to exist in a world that is no longer dangerous—it is now dreadfully safe—but is not yet free? In the name of empowerment (rather than only control), in the name of freedom (not just safety), and in the name of eroticism rather than tolerable sex, there is an alternative. What if we, as therapists, accompany our clients to precisely the places where it hurts and touch them, stroke and play with them until they pro-vide an avenue toward transformation? Why not use the power embedded in these memories to open a pathway to change and erotic freedom? Then the solution may involve going directly into whatever scares a client and confronting it fully rather than avoiding it (Mahrer, 1996).

Ms. Walsh presents for sex therapy with anorgasmia and a history of incest. She had been in various forms of therapy for 15 years. During that time, phobias dominated increasingly large chunks of her life, becoming debilitating and narrowing her world. The therapy goals had been to deal with effects of the abuse on her sexuality and to produce orgasms. Therapy had focused on issues common to incest survivors (e.g., shame, anxiety, control, low self-esteem). It had also involved traditional cognitive-behavioral exercises designed to treat anorgasmia. The problems persisted because the goals (and methods) aimed merely to make sex possible (i.e., mediocre) rather than create an avenue for healing and the full flowering of her eroticism. The guiding assumption had been that the incest had left her afraid, unable to let go, even or especially in bed. Making her surroundings and sexual relations increasingly safe had become stultifying rather than liberating. Furthermore, it is the assumption of the sheer horror of the past that prevented her and her therapists from getting at deeper, transformative feelings.

It is only by entering her inner world that we discover it is not the victimization per se that stands in her way. It is the unacknowledged, buried peace she experienced after each assault ended, when she lay with her ear against his chest, feeling the peace of listening quietly to the rhythm of his heartbeat as it slowly returned to normal, feeling the safety of being Daddy's little girl again and the certainty that all was well in the world. It is when she begins to tap into the powerful, life-affirming memory of intimate connection in an absurd, horrific context that she is enabled to reappropriate her own sexuality. As a consequence, her world begins to open with sexual and other choices and she is freed to experiment with new options, springing from within.

The alternative to promoting safely mediocre sex is to go to the core of our clients' pain and joy, the sources of hope and despair, and to aim for optimal and transformative sexual experience.

☐ Sex Therapy Opts for Controlling Paraphilic Behavior Rather Than Aiming for Fundamental Changes in Desire

The major approach to the treatment of the paraphilias involves either cognitive-behavioral therapy or, with increasing predominance, pharmacologic treatment (primarily with anti-androgens or the SSRIs), or a combination of both. The goal of such treatments is to control the unacceptable behavior and reduce the frequency of the associated impulses or compulsions. The individual is taught to keep the fantasies at bay and to stay away from whatever stimuli might trigger his or her (typically his) behaviors. The pharmacologic component is intended to lower his overall level of sexual desire or response. In parallel with the treatment of sexual dysfunctions, the prevailing treatment approach to the paraphilias targets the symptom while leaving the source of the problem unexplored. The focus is on reducing the impetus to act on unacceptable urges, but the nature of the desires themselves is left unchanged (Pfafflin, 1992). A series of review articles on the treatment of the paraphilias cites reports of patient noncompliance, high dropout rates, long-term treatment failures, and the need for treatment to continue indefinitely, if not for life (Abel & Osborn, 1996; Barbaree & Seto, 1997; Berlin, Malin, & Thomas, 1996; Brown, 1996; Gijs & Gooren, 1996; Maletzky,1997). These difficulties may be related to the emphasis on behavioral management rather than profound change in the underlying fantasies.

The longer fantasies are hidden away and kept remote from conscious exploration, the more monstrous, dangerous, and taboo they seem to become. It is as though they are kept in an opaque bubble, impervious to penetration. When they are kept distant, they become increasingly ego alien, foreign, removed, and strange. Unfortunately, this may be the result of the conventional attempts at containment of paraphilic desire. The paradox is that, as long as therapists (or their patients) do little more than attempt to keep symptoms in check, they grow like mushrooms in the dark. To the extent that we are successful in controlling behavior, we help to fuel the alienation from within and thereby make the sexual desires, shrouded in secrecy, seem more compelling and menacing. It is only by entering into the heart of these desires that there may be any hope for transformation. The closer one gets to the core, the more it becomes understandable, takes on a human face and softens, becomes less obsessional in character, less insistent, burdensome, and frightening and becomes more friendly and alive, albeit no less intense.

Certainly, as a society, we are entitled to deem certain conduct unacceptable; those who engage in such behaviors, particularly when they violate others' rights, should be incarcerated. However, as therapists, we can go beyond attempts to regulate behavior. Instead, we can help individuals who so choose to change their underlying desires. Such a goal involves more fundamental shifts than merely reducing the frequency of the fantasies or even their intensity or the ability to enact them. The alternative to managing paraphilias is transforming the very nature of the core desires.

He presents with compulsive, masochistic desires that have spun out of control. He can no longer function at work or at home because he is unable to concentrate on anything but his fantasies. His proclivities involve asphyxiation. On one level, he is able to find the partners he seeks, as long as he can afford to pay for them. On a deeper level, he wonders why he rarely gets quite the satisfaction he craves even with them, and he is left instead with feelings of disappointment, emptiness, and shame. He recognizes that his hobby is costly, and not just in terms of the money required to pay for his partners and the intricate constriction devices involved; it also poses considerable risk to his health. Masturbatory reconditioning did not help for long. SSRIs reduced the frequency of his desires but not their nature. Similarly, group therapy aimed at controlling his urges only made him feel defective and ashamed.

The alternative solution begins by entering into his desires more fully rather than attempting to contain them (Mahrer, 1996). Specifically, he focuses in therapy on the edgy, jittery, restless feelings that precede his urges to be restrained and enclosed tightly. Whereas he typically feels driven to act on these rising feelings, if only to quell the mounting agitation and painful sense of chaos, in this session he is encouraged to enter into them more fully and to let them grow. When he allows them to intensify long past the point at which he would normally release them through orgasm, he begins to experience a new, peaceful sense of floating, of being suspended, accompanied by a warm, energized glow. As he imagines sharing these harmonious feelings in his sexual relations, his superficially self-destructive urges are replaced by the ability to meld with another, to be so intimately connected that there is no space between them, fully permeable in quiet union. As such, following this session, not only his behavior changes, permitting him to bond deeply with his partner, but so do his persistent images, urges, and fantasies.

The alternative to aiming merely for containment of the paraphilic symptom involves fundamental changes in the client's desires. Paraphilias involve highly stigmatized and often illegal behaviors; by fostering deep-seated change the therapist is better positioned to support the client without acting as an agent of social control (Pfafflin, 1992).

☐ Why Not Just Do What Works? What's the Catch?

If the squeeze technique, vaginal dilators, and sidenafil citrate work, why object? These treatments have been proven to be highly effective, at least short-term, in reducing or eliminating the symptoms of rapid ejaculation, vaginismus, and erectile dysfunction, respectively. A useful tool is just that—

a fine thing to have available in our arsenals. Whether and when to use these tools are decisions to be made by clinicians and their clients.

It is a question of which approach this individual or couple will find most helpful in meeting his/her/their wishes. These wishes may well be for symptom reversal or control, in which case either brief, cognitive-behavioral treatment or medical intervention may fit the bill. However, if we present our patients with only these options, we may miss those who seek entirely different kinds of resolutions to their problems. Perhaps they want to refrain from intercourse, or to refrain from sex with their current partner(s); perhaps they prefer same-sex partners or a time of celibacy; perhaps they would prefer to be assertive enough to decline sexual intercourse verbally and directly rather than with their seemingly uncooperative bodies; perhaps they would prefer to focus on the dysfunctional relationship, in which case "normal" sexual functioning would constitute a betrayal of the self; or perhaps they want to use the symptom, regardless of its origins, as an opportunity for individual or interpersonal growth, to deepen the relationship, to heighten the chance for inner change, or to optimize sexual (or other) potential. Not all patients would choose to avail themselves of these options. Some just want the symptom to go away. That choice deserves to be honored. But it is not much of a choice if it is the *only* possibility offered. We owe it to our patients to present them with more (and, for some, better) options. Increasingly, market-driven forces will make such a position difficult, although all the more crucial, to sustain.

The concern is that economic pressures from managed care have led to treatment decisions that are not necessarily in the best interests of clinicians and their patients. Patient welfare is not the priority in decision making. In medicine, this has resulted in increased out-patient surgery for major procedures, reduced hospital stays after surgery, and forcing women out of the hospital within 24 hours postpartum. Similar agendas with parallel consequences have surfaced in mental health care. Current controversies surround the possible overprescription of antidepressants to adults and Ritalin™ to children, without sufficient exploration of side effects or alternate treatment approaches (Cohen & Jacobs, 2000; Duncan & Miller, 2000; Duncan, Miller, & Sparks, in press). In the same fashion, the presence of expedient, efficient treatment modalities for the symptoms of sexual problems may provide a welcome weapon in our armamentarium. However, the economic pressures brought to bear upon us may ultimately make the most expedient solution appear the most attractive, rather than merely one option among many (Fox, 1995, 1999–2000). Managed care often aims for the fastest route to symptom reversal or containment, even when the underlying problem remains unchanged (i.e., band-aid therapy).

Sometimes our hands are tied by the demands of insurance companies forcing us to treat only pathology rather than to improve or enhance sexuality. We stop when the goal of "normalcy" has been attained, even though achieving merely this may eventually engender other sexual problems. (For example, "successful" treatment of vaginismus may engender lack of sexual desire.) This limits us to working only with those who have diagnosable disorders or dysfunctions. Furthermore, the politics of the situation demand that we continue to classify individuals seeking therapy as pathological; otherwise, they will not be reimbursed by insurance providers. The conflict created for therapists and their clients is illustrated in cases of transgendered individuals, who may disagree with labels of psychopathology but are unable to access clinical services unless their differences are first certified as pathological (Califia, 1997).

We are thus limited in our abilities to help our clients. As soon as patients are no longer officially sick, we are supposed to terminate treatment, even though we may now be ideally positioned to help them optimize their sexual potential. We tend to go along with the managed care agenda rather than combating the whole notion that therapy should aim no higher than ameliorating disorder.

Furthermore, the alleged advantage of such treatments within the realm of psychotherapy per se can be highlighted and made to look impressive by their easy measurability. Health maintenance organizations (HMOs) encourage and emphasize empirically validated treatments. Some treatments lend themselves more readily to assessment than others. That such treatments are easy to study because they target only symptoms makes them look very "scientific." What they attempt to achieve is narrow and discrete, so whether or not they succeed in attaining these goals is (relatively) easily measurable. It may, however, make broader sets of goals seem less scientific because measuring them is more complex (Bohart, O'Hara, & Leitner,1998). Other sets of deeper, more comprehensive goals may be more valuable but may look less attractive, relative to discrete, expedient treatment of troublesome symptoms. It may be increasingly difficult to fight for comprehensive, relational, transformative, holistic goals when treatment of symptoms alone looks so cost-effective and scientifically supported.

Sometimes therapists are aware that this limited goal is problematic but are caught in the financial straits imposed on them by HMOs (Fox, 1995). In Canada, we have been spared the worst ravages of managed care. Surely, it is a matter of time before we, too, are subject to American-style health "care."

It is incumbent upon us to put forth alternate, broader agendas that aim to keep the best possible solutions and most satisfying outcomes at our disposal. Otherwise, we will lose access to the highest goals when they are most appropriate.

☐ Conclusions

The focus of sex therapy today is on sexual functioning/dysfunction and behavior rather than on subjective experience. The predominant goal of our work is eliminating or controlling symptoms rather than understanding the person within, aiming for deep-seated change, and enabling the individual to become all that he or she can be. We tend to settle for sexual mediocrity and stagnation rather than risking erotic transformation. Our field inadvertently maintains the status quo, supporting the conventional sex script by quietly treating its casualties, even though this set of norms engenders the sexual problems we aim to treat; instead, we must intensify our work in social advocacy to change our public discourse, thereby preventing sexual problems. Sex therapists may want to consider suspending the conventional objectives and adopt an alternate set of goals. This involves expanding our aims in depth, to work with the whole person/couple; in breadth, for greater inclusiveness; and in height, to aim for optimal erotic potential.

☐ References

Abel, G. G., & Osborn, C. A. (1996). Pedophilia. In G. O. Gabbard & S. D. Atkinson (Eds.), *Synopsis of treatments of psychiatric disorders* (2nd ed.; pp. 821–828). Washington, DC: American Psychiatric Association.

Barbaree, H. E., & Seto, M. C. (1997). Pedophilia: Assessment and treatment. In D. R. Laws & W. O'Donohue (Eds.), *Sexual deviance: Theory, assessment, and treatment* (pp. 175–209). New York: Guilford Press.

Berlin, F. S., Malin, H. M., & Thomas, K. (1996). Nonpedophilic and nontransvestic paraphilias. In G. O. Gabbard & S. D. Atkinson (Eds.), *Synopsis of treatments of psychiatric disorders* (2nd ed.; pp. 811–820). Washington, DC: American Psychiatric Association.

Bohart, A. C., O'Hara, M., & Leitner, L. (1998). Empirically violated treatments: Disenfranchisement of humanistic and other psychotherapies. *Psychotherapy Research.* 8(2) 141–157.

Brown, G. R. (1996). Transvestism. In G. O. Gabbard & S. D. Atkinson (Eds.), *Synopsis of treatments of psychiatric disorders* (2nd ed.; pp. 829–836). Washington, DC: American Psychiatric Association.

Califia, P. (1997). *Sex changes: The politics of transgenderism.* San Francisco: Cleis Press.

Cohen, D., & Jacobs, D. (2000). A model consent form for psychiatric drug treatment. *Journal of Humanistic Psychology, 40*(1), 59–64.

Duncan, B., & Miller, S. (2000). *The heroic client.* San Francisco: Jossey-Bass.

Duncan, B., Miller, S., & Sparks, J. (in press). The myth of the magic pill. *Psychotherapy in Australia.*

Fox, R. E. (1995). The rape of psychotherapy. *Professional Psychology—Research and Practice, 26*(2), 147–255.

Fox, R. E. (1999–2000). The dark side of evidence-based treatment. *Practitioner Focus, 12*(2), 5.

Frankl, V. E. (1963). *Man's search for meaning.* New York: Simon & Schuster.

Frankl, V. E. (1967). *Psychotherapy and existentialism.* New York: Simon & Schuster.

Gijs, L., & Gooren, L. (1996). Hormonal and psychopharmacological interventions in the treatment of paraphilias: An update. *Journal of Sex Research, 33*(4), 273–290.

Irvine, J. A. (1990). *Disorders of desire: Sex and gender in modern American sexology.* Philadelphia: Temple University Press.

Kaplan, H. S. (1974). *The new sex therapy.* New York: Brunner/Mazel.

Kleinplatz, P. J. (1996a). The erotic encounter. *Journal of Humanistic Psychology, 36*(3), 105–123.

Kleinplatz, P. J. (1996b). Transforming sex therapy: Integrating erotic potential. *The Humanistic Psychologist, 24*(2), 190–202.

L'Abate, L., & Hewitt, D. (1988). Toward a classification of sex and sexual behavior. *Journal of Sex & Marital Therapy. 14*(1), 29–39.

Leonard, G. (1989). Erotic love as surrender. In G. Feuerstein (Ed.), *Enlightened sexuality: Essays on body-positive spirituality* (pp. 79–81). Freedom, CA: Crossing Press.

LoPiccolo, J. (1992). Postmodern sex therapy for erectile failure. In R. C. Rosen & S. R. Leiblum (Eds.), *Erectile disorders: Assessment and treatment* (pp.171–197). New York: Guilford Press.

Mahrer, A. R. (1996). *The complete guide to experiential psychotherapy.* New York: Wiley.

Mahrer, A. R. (1999). The doorway into the inner deeper world is the instant of peak feeling in the scene of strong feeling. In J. Rowan & M. Cooper (Eds.), *The plural self* (pp. 213–237). London: Sage.

Mahrer, A. R. (2001). *The complete guide to self-transformation.* Palo Alto, CA: Bull Publishing.

Maletzky, B. (1997). Exhibitionism: Assessment and treatment. In D. R. Laws & W. O'Donohue (Eds.), *Sexual deviance: Theory, assessment, and treatment* (pp. 40–74). New York: Guilford Press.

Masters, W. H., & Johnson, V. E. (1966). *Human sexual response.* Boston: Little, Brown.

Masters, W. H., & Johnson, V. E. (1970). *Human sexual inadequacy.* New York: Bantam Books.

Masters, W. H., & Johnson, V. E. (1979). *Homosexuality in perspective.* Boston: Little, Brown.

Morin, J. (1995). *The erotic mind.* New York: HarperCollins.

Ogden, G. (1988). Women and sexual ecstasy: How can therapists help? *Women and Therapy, 7,* 43–57.

Ogden, G. (1994). *Women who love sex.* New York: Pocket Books.

Pfafflin, F. (1992). What is in a symptom? A conservative approach in the therapy of sex offenders. *Journal of Offender Rehabilitation, 18*(3/4), 5–17.

Price, M. (1994). Incest: Transference and countertransference implications. *Journal of the American Academy of Psychoanalysis, 22*(2), 211–229.

Reiss, I. L. (1990). *An end to shame: Shaping our next sexual revolution.* New York: Prometheus Books.

Rofes, E. (1996). *Reviving the tribe: Regenerating gay men's sexuality and culture in the ongoing epidemic.* New York: Haworth Press.

Rosser, B. R. S., Short, B. J., Thurmes, P. J., & Coleman, E. (1998). Anodyspareunia, the unacknowledged sexual dysfunction: A validation study of painful receptive anal intercourse and its psychosexual concomitants in homosexual men. *Journal of Sex & Marital Therapy, 24*(4), 281–292.

Schnarch, D. (1991). *Constructing the sexual crucible: An integration of sexual and marital therapy.* New York: W.W. Norton.

Steinberg, D. (1992). *The erotic impulse: Honoring the sensual self.* Los Angeles: Putnam.

Zilbergeld, B., & Ellison, C. R. (1980). Desire discrepancies and arousal problems in sex therapy. In S. R. Leiblum & L. A. Pervin (Eds.), *Principles and practice of sex therapy* (pp. 65–101). New York: Guilford Press.

II

NEW ALTERNATIVES/ INNOVATIONS IN SEX THERAPY

 New Clinical Alternatives and Innovations

The development of Viagra™, extensive media coverage of its release, consumer demand for prescriptions, and reactions to it provide a window on sexual and gender politics in motion. In Chapter 7, Wendy Stock, Ph.D., and Charles Moser, Ph.D., M.D., provide a variety of case illustrations demonstrating how and when Viagra™ may be advantageous or detrimental to couples in dealing with erectile dysfunction. They show how Viagra™ can be used to clarify or to obfuscate the individual and relational issues that bring couples into sex therapy. They offer both a brief medical resume on how sildenafil citrate works and a psychosocial analysis of the context in which it is sought. Rather than remaining ensnared, however, in political diatribes about the value of Viagra™ or lack thereof, Stock and Moser provide an assessment protocol from a feminist perspective to guide clinicians on when to prescribe Viagra™.

Among their six clinical examples is that of a gay couple wrestling with the effects of AIDS on their relationship and the role of Viagra™ in helping to reestablish sexual intimacy. The sheer presence of this case illustration in Chapter 7 is striking; it highlights the absence of such couples in the sex therapy literature. Stock and Moser's inclusion of this couple in their material helps to redress the invisibility of marginalized groups among us.

In Chapter 8, Carol Rinkleib Ellison, Ph.D., refers to the mindset that dominates our society and our field as the "manufacturing orgasms" sex script. Ellison describes her alternative approach as an intimacy-based sex therapy in which her role is to assist couples in choreographing their sexual relations. That is, she aims to help them structure their busy lives and relationships so as to enhance the quality of their sexual intimacy, whether or not it includes erections, intercourse, or orgasm. Unlike Masters and Johnson's or Kaplan's paradigm of sex therapy, nongenital intimacy is not merely a stage in the therapy process, leading to the resumption of "normal" sexual functioning; for Ellison, it may be of value in and of itself. In her approach, the goals of sex therapy are mutual erotic pleasure, intimacy, satisfaction, and self-esteem. Her methods typically include homework assignments, but the nature of these "experiments" is generated by the clients rather than by the therapist.

Ellison questions notions such as "sex should be natural and spontaneous" and offers guidelines for creating opportunities for intimacy, the foundation for mutual erotic pleasure. She suggests that therapists and their clients should attend to the subtleties of sexual initiation and refusal. For example, she offers the commonsense but uncommonly asserted observation that a sure way to kill sexual desire is to proffer or accept sexual invitations half-heartedly. Her emphasis on mutual consent rather than an unspoken sense of obligation to go though the motions provides a refreshing antidote to the sex-as-performance model. Unlike those who would encourage clients to ignore inner or interpersonal conflicts and to focus on sensation, Ellison encourages clients to discuss whatever may be on their minds, sexual or otherwise, that might prevent them from wanting to connect sexually.

One of the consequences of the early attempts to achieve credibility for the discipline of sex therapy as a science has been the relatively dry tone of much of the literature in the field. It is as though we have attempted to convince our readers that our interest in sex is purely scientific rather than reflective of any enthusiasm we may hold for the subject matter personally. As such, the person of the therapist has often been conspicuously absent from the public record of our work. (This is in marked contrast to the field of psychotherapy in general, wherein discussion about the therapist is relatively common.) In Chapter 9, Jeanne Shaw, Ph.D., has taken the bold step of discussing how the therapist's own experience and growth as an individual relates to her or his clinical work. Shaw has the courage to acknowledge how the therapy process is gauged and advanced in the person of the therapist—in this instance, as the session begins to cook, Shaw literally gets hot—rather than in allegedly "objective" indicators of progress. She demonstrates how the therapist's own experience and level of development contribute to sex therapy progress.

Shaw also demonstrates how research in sexology can be relevant and useful for broadening sex therapy. Whereas most research into sexuality tends to be removed from the world of the practicing therapist, her chapter illustrates how the astute and curious clinician may be drawn to doing research by her observation of a surprising phenomenon in therapy and how her data may, in turn, influence her practice. Her research and clinical interests meet as Shaw illustrates how the differentiation of the mature therapist can enhance the growth of the elderly couple in sex therapy to levels that surpass the common stereotypes of older individuals (including therapists) as dried up, neutered, sexual has-beens.

Sex therapy originally developed as a form of brief, intensive, behaviorally oriented intervention(s) targeted to treat specific sexual symptoms. It grew as an alternative to and distinct from the field of psychotherapy in general. However, in being separate from the rest of the field of psychotherapy, sex therapy has perhaps also become insular, unable to benefit from the developments in the broader domain. Karen Donahey, Ph.D., and Scott Miller, Ph.D., bring their combined expertise in sex therapy and psychotherapy outcome research, respectively, to their discussion of "'What Works' in Sex Therapy." They point out that there has been a parallel in the evolutions of the fields of psychotherapy per se and sex therapy in particular. Both fields began with enormous enthusiasm and hope, fueled initially by exciting outcome data. Donahey and Miller note that, with time, research, and sober reflection, doubts have been cast on the effectiveness of the various modalities. They trace the research on psychotherapy outcome and apply it to working with individuals and couples who present with sexual concerns. Specifically, they identify four common factors found in effective treatment strategies, regardless of clinical model, and apply these elements to sex therapy. Donahey and Miller suggest that sex therapists should consider incorporating and emphasizing these ingredients of effective psychotherapy in our work. Their work also makes clear that sex therapists must be engaged in the ongoing evaluation of our practice if our field is to continue to grow.

Clinicians who focus their practice on working with sexuality in therapy but who criticize the assumptions of the conventional paradigm or want to aim for deep and substantive change may wish to consider Experiential Psychotherapy. The model described in Chapter 11 circumvents the vexing problems facing our field (e.g., gender bias, narrow and constricting goals, and mind-body dualism). Alvin R. Mahrer, Ph.D., and Donald Boulet, Ph.D., are not sex therapists, but their chapter is highly instructive for those who wrestle with difficult problems manifest in either bodily symptoms or disappointing intimate relations. Experiential Psychotherapy does not merely aim to solve the "presenting problem," sexual or otherwise; its aim is to radically transform the person, based on whatever lies deep within, freeing him or her of the painful feelings and situations along the way. Therapy is targeted neither at the body of the client nor at his or her psyche, behaviors, or external world (i.e., significant others). Rather, the work is directed at and by the whole being; the assumption in Experiential Psychotherapy is that, when the changes are profound enough, they will be manifest in every domain, including the client's emotions, cognitions, body, and ways of relating to him- or herself and others.

Mahrer and Boulet's clinical illustration involves a man who might be described by the average sex therapist as being depressed and having hyposexual desire. While many therapists would be arguing about which of the two disorders is primary and which to treat first—or, even worse, if prescribing SSRIs would further diminish the client's desire—Experiential Psychotherapy proclaims the entire dimension of psychopathology and its diagnosis as irrelevant to achieving its goals. The focus of this approach is neither treating depression nor treating desire disorders but a search for whatever is deeper within this man during the moments he finds most painful (or sometimes most joyful). When this inner experiencing is integrated and actualized, both the desire problem and the depression evaporate. Mahrer and Boulet invite us to suspend our murky preconceptions momentarily so that we can consider a genuinely new way to not only meet but surpass our own goals in a radical, respectful, and effective manner.

There is, unfortunately, a huge market for the growing literature on childhood sexual abuse, its consequences, and their treatment. It seems striking that, while a variety of issues are the focus of immediate clinical attention (e.g., betrayal, anger, guilt, trust, or self-esteem), sexuality seems to be almost an afterthought. It seems odd that the site of one's wounds should be of such low priority in treatment. Corresponding to the disproportionately low emphasis on sexuality in the incest literature is the lack of attention paid to the needs and concerns of this large population in the sex therapy literature. Sex therapists are more than aware of the pervasiveness of child sexual abuse. Although such clients inevitably comprise a significant segment of the clientele in sex therapy practices, considerations particular to working with such patients are often overlooked. In Chapter

12, Wendy Maltz, M.S.W., attempts to remedy the splits in these two divergent sets of literature and practice with her work on sex therapy with survivors of sexual abuse. Maltz approaches therapy with survivors using an eclectic/integrationist framework and provides 10 recommendations for sexual healing. She blends conventional sex therapy with strategies and techniques borrowed from other therapeutic modalities to create a hybrid aimed at "healthy sexual intimacy" (i.e., sex that is passionate rather than merely tolerable). Her approach may prove instructive for clinicians of any orientation.

The literature on desire in long-term relationships tends to be pretty dismal, suggesting that sexual interest tends to decline over time, with sex therapists having minimal success in dealing with low desire or desire discrepancy in sex therapy. The picture is, if anything, even more demoralizing in the literature on lesbian couples. Marny Hall, Ph.D., is among the rare therapists who specialize in working with the sexual aspects of lesbian relationships. In Chapter 13, she describes her use of narrative therapy in dealing with sexual desire discrepancy in lesbian couples. Her goal is not necessarily to equalize the level of sexual desire in the relationship so much as to assist the couple in making meaning of and honoring the differences between them. Her chapter teaches techniques therapists can employ to help lesbian clients, among others, shift their sexual and romantic narratives.

According to Hall, postmodern perspectives may be particularly appealing in dealing with marginalized populations in therapy. She states that most "sex and gender renegades . . . have already stumbled upon the mutable nature of personal reality" (p. 280). Her work involves helping those who have defied conventional sex scripts to rewrite their sexual stories in alternate, more congruent ways. Her approach also may be appealing to anyone willing to eschew one-size-fits-all solutions and to be attuned to the uniqueness and complexity of any given individual or couple. The clinical illustration presented here has much to teach all therapists about the power of being understood in soothing sorrow and alienation. If therapists, or lovers, want to promote the vulnerability that facilitates sexual intimacy, it is to their advantage to develop the exquisite sensitivity to subjective meaning that Hall demonstrates in this case.

It is most difficult to find literature about the sexual concerns of gay men in couples therapy, particularly in relation to HIV status. Most of the literature in this area over the last 15 years has either been psychoeducational in orientation, with the goal of curbing gay men's sexual expression (thereby promoting safer sex practices), or clinical material that focuses on helping gay men deal with loss and the inevitable grief. Unprotected sexual activity among gay men often is automatically pathologized with little attention or attempt to comprehend the subjective meaning or value ascribed by the participants. The notion that gay men may actually be in need of or might benefit from services *facilitating* their sexual expression is unheard of. In Chapter 14, Alex Carballo-Diéguez, Ph.D., and Robert Remien, Ph.D., address this gap in our clinical literature. They describe their work with serodiscordant gay couples (i.e., couples in which one man is HIV-positive and the other is HIV-negative). Their approach offers an excellent illustration of truly integrated, multilayered care for couples who present with sexual difficulties in the face of chronic illness. Carballo-Diéguez and Remien provide an overview of the medical, emotional, and social concerns that must be considered in working with serodiscordant gay couples. They also demonstrate the need for therapists to be attuned to alternate group norms, (e.g., values related to monogamy), whether these are the norms of another culture or those of a sexual minority group.

Gina Ogden, Ph.D., begins with the premise that many individuals want more from sex, whether or not they qualify as dysfunctional. Ogden suggests that science has barely begun to identify what many clients seek, let alone how to help them in attaining it. Her goals involve no less than integrating splits between mind and body, sexuality and spirituality. The work she describes in Chapter 15 promotes freedom from rather than reinforcement of cultural imperatives. Her approach involves leaving the traditional office setting and offering intensive, weekend workshops for women. Here, the focus is on sexual safety, creativity, healing, and growth rather than on interventions designed to treat problems localized to the genitals. Ogden rejects the role of therapist as authority figure (part of the legacy of Masters and Johnson's approach). Instead, she attempts to minimize the hierarchical dynamic inherent in most therapy approaches via the group format and to empower the participants through use of peer relationships and modeling. The techniques she employs—the use of touch, ceremony, mystical experience, and sensuality—signal a radical departure from the white-coat sterility of her predecessors. She presents us with a challenge: We can either dismiss her approach as irrelevant for clinicians or contemplate the possibility that the current popularity of spiritually oriented approaches represents a hunger for an alternative to dehumanizing, reductionistic, medicalized models.

In Chapter 16, I will present 10 conclusions drawn from the criticisms, proposed alternatives, and innovations suggested in this book. I will also recommend future directions for clinical practice and research. The choice is clear, and it is the same one that confronts our clients: Either we risk stagnation, or we risk fundamental change in the hope of future growth. I invite you to join those who wish to change and strengthen the field of sex therapy.

Wendy Stock, Ph.D.
Charles Moser, Ph.D., M.D.

CHAPTER 7

Feminist Sex Therapy in the Age of Viagra™

Pharmacological treatments of sexual dysfunction have opened a new and exciting area for clinical sexology and sex therapy. Used correctly they can help people to overcome fears of and actual sexual dysfunction. Used incorrectly, they can wreak havoc in the relationship or with the individual. The recent pharmaceutical debut of sildenafil citrate (Viagra™), and the ensuing stampede by male consumers to obtain it, is a significant historical moment in our collective sexual history. The advent of a medication that reduces the vulnerability of erections to some psychological and even medical causes of impairment provides many men with a "bionic" insurance policy against shame regarding their sexual performance. Undoubtedly, many men and their partners are well-served by sildenafil citrate (Goldstein, Lue, Padma-Nathan, Rosen, Steers, & Wicker, 1998). Such couples are unequivocally delighted at the remission of erectile problems, enjoying their regained ability to lose themselves in the sexual encounter without worrying about erections. For other couples, sildenafil citrate uncovers relational dilemmas, revealing the inadequacy of the medicalized construction of sexuality. The impact of any new medical innovation that makes it easier for men to have erections and thus to have penetrative sex must be understood within the relational and social context.

Fueled by the media and the anonymity and accessibility of the Internet, millions of patients are requesting pharmacological solutions for erectile dysfunction. Clearly, not all individuals who would benefit from sildenafil citrate are availing themselves of it; conversely, many inappropriate prescriptions have been written. Our clients and the public in general will not be well-served if sildenafil citrate is used indiscriminately. Any intervention, including psychotherapy, can be misused or abused. Pharmacotherapy is no different. Sildenafil citrate is just the first in a series of drugs that will treat various sexual concerns. Sex therapists should familiarize themselves with the uses, abuses, and misuses of these drugs. Some patients will seek out a nonphysician to avoid confronting a physical defect or problem. The opposite is also true—patients who want to deny a psychogenic etiology of their dysfunction will present to a physician. The solution to this dilemma involves helping both sex therapists and physicians to incorporate these new medications in social and relational context.

☐ Feminist Sex Therapy

Feminist sex therapy has led the field in recognition of the costs of dismembering of sexuality from relational context. Tiefer (1981) identified the influences of the positivist approach and of biologically based explanations of human sexuality in the misdirection of sex therapy's focus away from sex-role, relational, or psychological issues. Seidler-Feller (1985) questioned the adequacy of sex therapy from a feminist perspective, citing the tendency to implicitly reinforce normative sex roles (Stock, 1983) and the power differential between the sexes that underlies them (Seidler-Feller, 1976). Tiefer (1988) also critiqued the *DSM-III* (1980) sexual dysfunction nomenclature as focusing exclusively on physical performance while omitting empirically based information on what women consider important in sexual life, including intimacy, negotiation, and communication. Tiefer (1988) adapted Reissman's (1983) analysis regarding the negative consequences of medicalization for women's sexuality, pointing out the processes of mystification, moral neutrality, and individualization of sexual problems inherent in the medicalized, traditional approach.

Mystification places definitions of "normal and healthy" sexual functioning in the hands of officially sanctioned experts rather than self-defined enjoyment, more often reflecting these experts' reality rather than women's. When medical science alone defines the norms for sex, an objective reality is assumed, leading to a stance of *moral neutrality* in which "sex is no longer a human arena for negotiation, but an arena where there is an objective standard against which performance can be measured" (Tiefer, 1988, p. 17). McCormick (1994) further identified the "nonconscious equation of sexual activity with reproductive potential" that influences clinicians to equate sexual dysfunction with "physical failures in the performance of intercourse" (p. 188). In *individualizing* sexuality and sexual problems, medicalization denies and obscures the effects of social contributions to people's sexual complaints, including rigid sex roles, unrelenting standards of performance, relationships of unequal power, and histories of sexual victimization.

Tiefer (1996, p. 53) recommended that feminist sex therapy include "corrective genital physiology education, assertiveness training, body image reclamation, and masturbation education." McCormick (1994) also recommended that therapists treat individuals and couples for deficits in tenderness, poor communication, sexual selfishness, disinterest in oral sex, and unwillingness to cuddle, although she noted that deficits in these areas have not been assigned formal psychiatric diagnoses. A feminist approach to sex therapy uses existing scientific knowledge about biology, medical approaches, and empirically validated treatment techniques while adding the following ingredients:

1. Recognition of social and cultural gender inequality;

2. Recognition of the influence of this power differential in relationships, and a willingness to intervene at this level;

3. Valuing equally the subjective and affective aspects of sexuality, relative to physical performance;

4. Recognition of traditional sex roles as etiologic of many sexual problems, and a willingness to intervene at this level; and

5. Recognition of the unique experiences of men and women regarding sexual socialization, experiences of sexual coercion, sexual decision making, and the influence of relational factors in sexual dysfunction.

☐ How Sildenafil Citrate Works

Sildenafil citrate facilitates erections in men with psychogenic, diabetic, vasculogenic, traumatic, and surgical causes of erectile dysfunction (Goldstein et al., 1998). It is not an "orgasm pill," does not increase desire, and does not facilitate erection in the absence of psychological or tactile stimulation. Nevertheless, all these factors are interrelated; indirect effects are probably observed. Simplistically, erection is the process of sequestering blood within the penis to increase its size and rigidity (see Melman &

Gingell, 1999, for a complete discussion of the erectile mechanism). Tactile or psychological stimuli, or both, can initiate or sustain the process.

The blood is predominantly sequestered in the corpora cavernosa, two connected spongelike bodies in the penile shaft. The corpora cavernosa comprise a network of arteries, veins, nerves, smooth muscles, and sinusoids (i.e., the spaces that actually fill with blood). The tunica albuginea is a thick, fibrous bilayer sheath that surrounds the corpora cavernosa. As the corpora cavernosa fill with blood, the tunica albuginea stretches to its capacity. The veins that drain the corpora cavernosa are compressed against and between the layers of the tunica albuginea, preventing outflow. The bulbocavernous muscles at the base of the penis contract, which raises the pressure above systemic blood pressure and results in a rigid penis.

The lining of the corpora cavernosa and some penile nerves produce nitric oxide (NO). The NO induces the production of cyclic guanosine monophosphate (cGMP), which specifically causes penile smooth muscle relaxation. In a process that is still not completely understood, smooth muscle relaxation leads to the trapping of blood in the corpora cavernosa. The NO also causes the arterioles (small arteries) to dilate, increasing the blood flow into the corpora cavernosa. The cGMP is degraded by phosphodiesterase type 5 (PDE5), an enzyme predominantly found in the penis. When the cGMP is degraded, the smooth muscle returns to its resting (contracted) state, the outflow of blood increases, and the erection resolves.

Sildenafil inhibits the action of PDE5, allowing smaller amounts of cGMP to produce an erection and for that erection to last longer (Goldstein et al.,1998). Similarly, less NO is needed to produce an equivalent amount of cGMP.

Sildenafil has been approved only for use in men; research on its effects in women is ongoing. Preliminary results are conflicting. Initial investigations reported that Sildenafil increased lubrication, genital sensation, ability to achieve orgasm, and sexual satisfaction among women with complaints of sexual dysfunction (Berman, Berman, Lin, & Goldstein, 1999; Berman, Berman, Werbin, & Goldstein,1999). Application of topical Sildenafil was reported to improve arousal, genital sensation, and ability to reach orgasm in a small sample of women (23) with sexual dysfunction (Kaminetsky, 1999). Others, however, have found little evidence thus far that sildenafil is useful in the treatment of sexual dysfunction in women. Kaplan, Reis, Kohn, Ikeguchi, Laor, Te, and Martins (1999, p. 483), for example, concluded, "Our data do not support the use of sildenafil in treating postmenopausal women with sexual dysfunction." Its effects and uses for women remain to be fully elucidated. In addition, sildenafil for women carries the same risks of misuse as for males.

There have been some reports of the usefulness of sildenafil in the treatment of SSRI-induced sexual dysfunction in both women and men (Ashton & Bennett, 1999; Balon, 1998,1999; Rosenberg, 1999a, 1999b). Men under treatment with SSRI antidepressant medications may experience an incidence of sexual dysfunction as high as 50%. Women also report orgasmic dysfunction, decreased genital sensation, and diminished sexual desire as a result of SSRIs.

Sildenafil citrate is well-tolerated with only minimal interactions with other drugs. The one major interaction is with nitrates (primarily used in the treatment of heart disease), resulting in serious and sometimes even fatal blood pressure decreases. One form of nitrate can be obtained over the counter: isobutyl nitrate, known on the street as "poppers." Its illicit use involves inhalation of the fumes during sexual activity. It reportedly acts as a sexual stimulant (theoretically as another source of nitric oxide). Patients should be specifically warned against the use of sildenafil with any inhaled, recreational drug agent. It is important for the patient to tell the physician of any sildenafil use.

A high-fat meal will decrease the total absorption and delay the onset of sildenafil citrate. Taking one's partner out for a romantic (high-fat) dinner and then taking sildenafil with dessert is unlikely to achieve the desired reaction. The most common side effects include headache (16%), flushing (10%), upset stomach (7%), and nasal congestion (4%; Pfizer, 1998). Abnormal vision also has been reported, predominately a bluish tinge to vision, but also blurred vision and sensitivity to light. All of these are mild, resolve with cessation of the drug, and rarely cause the discontinuation of the drug.

☐ Erectile Dysfunction and Sildenafil Citrate: Assessment and Treatment

Medical Considerations in Assessment and Treatment

Patients (and often their sex therapists) assume a sexual dysfunction must be psychogenic, if a recent medical evaluation has not revealed any likely cause. This reasoning is just as error-prone as when patients assume their dysfunctions must be organic because they have a "good" relationship. Not all the causes of erectile dysfunction are known, and we have a limited ability to demonstrate any factor as causative. When in doubt, erectile dysfunction is assumed to be multifactorial.

The therapist should first ascertain if the client's physician was aware of the sexual dysfunction, so that a focused examination could be performed. An undirected examination is unlikely to uncover the cause of the "unknown" sexual dysfunction. The sex therapist should know what constitutes an appropriate medical evaluation and suggest specialty evaluation when indicated. Even when the dysfunction is clearly situational or the result of psychogenic factors, a medical evaluation is the standard of care.

One concern of the present chapter is when and under what circumstances sildenafil may be appropriately prescribed. The following are our guidelines for the appropriate initiation of sildenafil:

- Rule out medical contraindications for the use of sildenafil. An exercise stress test may be appropriate to demonstrate that the patient can safely tolerate the physical exertion inherent in being sexual. Patients who are using nitrates even on an as-needed basis should *not* receive sildenafil.

- Rule out medical conditions that may present with erectile dysfunction. Finding reversible causes of sexual dysfunction is important, but identifying and treating chronic medical problems whose first symptom may be erectile dysfunction is equally important. The diagnoses of most concern are diabetes mellitus, hemochromatosis, hypercholesterolemia, hypogonadism, kidney disease, liver disease, prolactinoma, sleep apnea, thyroid disease, and vascular disease. The presentation of erectile dysfunction should always prompt an exploration of alcohol, tobacco, and drug use, with a strong recommendation to quit. Bicycle riding is also associated with erectile dysfunction; this includes stationary exercise bicycles (Solomon & Cappa, 1987).

- Rule out effects from medications or treatments prescribed for other conditions.

- Rule out other sexual dysfunctions or mental health problems that the patient may present as erectile dysfunction. This is meant to include both individual and relationship problems. Substance misuse, as well as substance abuse, can be a major factor in the etiology of erectile dysfunction.

- Sildenafil is readily available from many physicians, over the Internet, and from the black market. Patients often will turn to other sources if the physician refuses to provide sildenafil citrate without a clear medical reason. It is often prudent to give a small prescription of sildenafil while the more intensive evaluation is in process. In addition, the response or lack of response to sildenafil can have diagnostic implications.

- Erectile dysfunction alters relationships, even when the cause is clearly organic. A referral to a sex therapist should be given in all situations. The patient should be urged to inform and include his partner in the decision to use the drug. Sildenafil has potential for use in sex therapy to help a patient confront the issues that the dysfunction allows him to avoid.

- Avoid open-ended prescriptions. Patients often stop using sildenafil citrate even when it is effective.

- See both partners together whenever it is feasible.

Feminist Considerations in Assessment and Treatment

What would a feminist approach to sex therapy add to the notion of a screening protocol for use of sildenafil citrate? The subjective and interpersonal aspects of erectile dysfunction are sometimes overlooked in the diagnostic process. Assessment should always include a detailed exploration of the context and process of sexual initiation, sexual behaviors, typical duration, and physical and affective comfort levels for the activities and for communication with each other about these activities (Kaplan, 1974). A feminist assessment protocol for any sexual dysfunction, including sexual or relationship problems related to the use of sildenafil citrate, might include the questions below. This assessment includes some standard questions used in conventional sex therapy, but it emphasizes issues of communication, negotiation, initiation/refusal, power dynamics, eroticism (genital and nongenital), and meaning. These are concepts that sometimes are given short shrift when the emphasis is on technical aspects of sexual functioning and when a purely medical approach to diagnosis and treatment is taken.

History

- Assess individual psychological functioning for each individual, including general mental status, recent functioning, overall history, and sexual history.
- Relationship history: how the couple met, course of relationship.
- Are there unresolved power issues in the relationship?

Pain/medical conditions

- Are intercourse or sexual relations not desired, physically painful, or problematic for either partner?
- Does either partner suffer from any medical conditions that would make penetration or sexual activity painful?

Meaning of sexual functioning/dysfunction

- Role of sex in the relationship:What functions does it serve?
- What is the meaning of erections/intercourse to the individual, to the partner, in the couple's relationship?
- Why do they want sildenafil citrate, and what are their expectations?
- How much do both partners care about erections, intercourse?
- What would the meaning be of restored erectile functioning in this relationship?

Communication, sexual and otherwise

- How does the couple talk about sex?
- What are they thinking about when engaging in sex with each other?
- Are they able to share their thoughts and feelings with one another during, prior to, and after sex?
- To what degree do they each feel they must "function" to please one another and hide thoughts or feelings that might distract from the focus on "completing" the sexual "act"?
- To what extent is each partner able to be fully "present," cognitively and emotionally, during sex?
- What priority is placed on having a sense of connection in relationship, emotional intimacy, sexually, and otherwise?

Initiation and refusal of sex/affection

- Can both partners easily initiate and refuse sexual relations?
- Can both partners express nongenital physical affection easily?

Passion and eroticism

- What is the experience of eroticism in relationship? Do the partners have the ability to touch erotically/sensually?

- What is the quality of tenderness and emotional connection?

- Do the partners experience sexual passion with each other? Did they in the past?

Even if significant deficits are reported in the couple's relationship, sildenafil citrate is not necessarily contraindicated. Rather, all of these areas should be assessed, and the intervention should be directed accordingly to encompass the range of deficits, not limited to physical sexual functioning.

☐ The Gender Politics of Sildenafil Citrate, Part I: Social Context and Historical Precedent

The social impact of the birth control pill in the late 1960s is an historical precedent worth examining in regard to sildenafil citrate. In freeing women from the risk of pregnancy, the pill removed a reason for women not to engage in sex. In a culture that did not, at the time, grant women an internalized sense of sexual agency, many women felt unable either to initiate desired sexual activity or to refuse unwanted sexual activity. With the removal of the risk of pregnancy, women lost their major external justification for sexual refusal. Invoking the fear of becoming pregnant had been the last, and sometimes the only, stopgap women felt they had in verbally resisting unwanted sexual intercourse.

During the sexual revolution of the late 1960s, the new norm dictated that to refuse sex on a date was evidence of sexual "uptightness" or outmoded prudery. It was not the oral contraceptive itself, of course, that was responsible for this change, but the gender politics surrounding sexuality. Women had never been seen as having a true internal locus of control regarding their sexuality. Although the feminist movement of the late 1960s and 1970s succeeded in introducing the concepts of control of one's body, sexual choice, sexual harassment, and marital and date rape into the social vocabulary, these notions have continued to compete with those spawned by the sexual revolution. In the presence of an aroused male with an erection, women are still seen, and often view themselves, as responsible for both causing and remedying the male's sexual tension. Clinical approaches that have ignored the social context of gender inequality have often backfired, hurting the very populations that they were intended to help.

Many women in our culture continue to engage in unwanted sex that is not physically or emotionally satisfying and is sometimes physically uncomfortable. According to Laumann, Paik, and Rosen (1999) one-third of women (compared to one-sixth of men) said they are uninterested in sex. One-fifth of the women (but only one-tenth of the men) said sex gave them no pleasure. Most women can have orgasms easily by masturbating, and their sexual complaints are not generally due to a physical inability to enjoy sex, but are "psychological" in origin. It is clear that, since solitary sexual pleasure is possible for most women, it is sex in heterosexual relationships (in the majority of cases) that is problematic or nonpleasurable to many. Women in lesbian relationships report more frequent orgasms with partners and higher levels of sexual satisfaction compared to heterosexual women (Coleman, Hoon, & Hoon, 1983), but also report a lower frequency of genital sexual contact (Blumstein & Schwartz, 1983; Loulan, 1988) compared to heterosexual women. In contrast, older heterosexual women, whose male partners are more likely to use sildenafil citrate, are more likely to have lower levels of sexual desire than their partners, and may also have a preexisting lower level of sexual satisfaction relative to their partners. In this context, sildenafil citrate may function (like the birth control pill) as a double-edged sword in the sex lives of many heterosexual women and men, by providing a welcome return of sexual intercourse for some while increasing demands for sex without pleasure for others.

Clinical Illustrations of Treatment of Viagra™-Related Sexual and Relationship Problems

Feminist therapists who work with heterosexual or homosexual couples will likely encounter, at some point, a relational or sexual conflict related to the use of sildenafil citrate. How might the presence of sildenafil citrate play out in relational contexts? What issues will this pose for the feminist therapist, and how does feminist theory inform our treatment of such cases? The following examples highlight different therapeutic presentations of couples in which the male partner may be prescribed sildenafil citrate. These six clinical illustrations are intended to demonstrate a range of cases that might typically present for sex therapy, as well as the range of possible outcomes involving sildenafil citrate.

Positive Outcomes Examples

Ben and Elaine. The first example illustrates a nonproblematic and positive outcome. This couple exemplifies the ideal situation in which prescription of sildenafil citrate has only positive implications.

Ben and Elaine, both in their late 50s, present as a couple for sex therapy, reporting that Ben has had difficulty achieving and maintaining erections since the onset of his medical condition, diabetes mellitus. Based on their responses during initial assessment to the questions suggested above, it becomes apparent that Ben and Elaine have always had good communication, a mutually satisfying history of sexual functioning, and currently have no major areas of ongoing conflict. Elaine has always enjoyed their sexual relationship and is able to experience sexual pleasure and orgasm through manual and oral stimulation, as well as occasionally during intercourse. Both Ben and Elaine have been able to ask for what they want during sex, and both can freely initiate or decline sexual activity. This type of case represents that most likely to have a positive outcome. Sildenafil citrate is highly successful in assisting men with impaired erectile capacity who are in relationships in which they can experience subjective and physiological sexual stimulation and arousal with a partner who desires and enjoys sexual intercourse.

The positive effects sildenafil citrate can have include these:

- Men who have erectile problems can become very focused on getting and keeping erections. As long as technical competence is the major goal, the affection, tenderness, and communication that enhance sexual intimacy often are diminished. The partner may see the man as more concerned with erectile success than with mutual pleasure. By assuring a man of a lasting erection that will not fade after a few minutes of foreplay, sildenafil citrate allows him to attend to his partner, physically and emotionally, and to become more immersed in sexual activities as emotional experience. (As such, the fact that sildenafil citrate takes 30 to 60 minutes to work is an advantage.)

- Men with erectile problems may rush to insertion, fearing that if the erection is lost, they will not be able to attain another. This is a real fear, especially for middle-aged and older men who may experience a secondary refractory period—that is, the inability to obtain a subsequent erection after a prior one subsides without orgasm (Masters & Johnson, 1966; Moser, 2000).

- In the same way that sildenafil citrate may free men from the distraction of self-monitoring their erections, it may free their partners from this concern. Many partners of men with erectile difficulties also constantly monitor the status of their partners' erections, worrying that they are not doing enough, feeling powerless (or impotent) themselves in their inability to help attain or maintain erections, or doubting their sexual skill or attractiveness.

- Perelman (1998) suggested that many men avoid condoms because of fear of erectile failure. By restoring sexual capacity, sildenafil citrate could result in increased condom use.

In the case of Ben and Elaine, the role of a feminist sex therapist would be largely psychoeducational—providing information, discussing possible etiologies of Ben's erectile dysfunction, and suggesting how sildenafil citrate may affect their relationship as a couple. This approach is consistent with the fundamental beliefs of feminist therapy, which are to demystify the change process, to engage with the clients as equal participants in the change process, and to avoid the role of omnipotent "expert" by acknowledging the clients' abilities to make informed decisions and use information themselves (Enns, 1997, p. 16). Following the institution of sildenafil, the therapist should continue to track the couple's progress and adjustment to Ben's renewed erectile functioning.

Lou and Jay. The second positive outcome involves a male couple. Lou and Jay have been in a committed relationship for 17 years. Lou is a 47-year-old entrepreneur who now owns a successful business. Jay is 52 years old, has his own consulting firm, but primarily works in Lou's business. Both have AIDS, a history of AIDS-related cancers, and numerous opportunistic infections. Despite receiving state-of-the-art antiretroviral drug "cocktails," both have detectable viral loads. Both have been in treatment for AIDS for more than 10 years.

Lou and Jay are both very knowledgeable about their disease, often bringing copies of the latest studies downloaded from the Internet to their appointments. As can be expected, the stresses from the disease, along with the more mundane stresses from their business and relationship, led both into individual and couple therapy. Each has his own individual therapist and they sporadically see a relationship therapist.

Lou has a history of clinical depression, but he is no longer taking an antidepressant. He does not meet the diagnostic criteria for depression presently. Both partners report a history of erectile dysfunction, mostly difficulty maintaining erections; less frequently, getting erections and lack of desire are also problems. Lou has been much more concerned about his erectile difficulties. A complete diagnostic work-up was done without finding a treatable etiology, although it is not surprising in light of his numerous medical problems.

Lou followed the development of sildenafil citrate and called the day it was approved by the FDA. He was clearly disappointed when told that it was not in the pharmacies yet. When the first shipment of the drug had arrived, both Lou and Jay came in for a joint appointment to discuss how to use sildenafil citrate, its likely effects, and its possible side effects. A prescription for six sildenafil citrate tablets was given, one of the first prescriptions written.

Lou requested a refill the next day. Clearly, if he had taken sildenafil citrate as prescribed, he would not need a refill yet. When questioned, Lou confessed that the first pill was an amazing success. He gave a pill to Jay, who had an erection "like I was a teenager." Like two kids in a candy store, they called another couple they knew and shared their supply of sildenafil.

While sharing prescription medication is inappropriate, illegal, and dangerous, it points out the importance for clients of regaining their functioning. Jay did come in for a complete work-up and was eventually given his own prescription. Both have refilled their prescription several times, Lou more frequently than Jay. They say they no longer share prescriptions.

Lou and Jay have seen several positive effects from their sildenafil citrate use: It has clearly drawn them closer together; performance anxiety has decreased; both report impromptu sex without the use of sildenafil citrate. Lou's mood is clearly more upbeat and his self-esteem has increased. Jay has been more subdued. His health has been deteriorating, but he jokes about having to put on more weight to keep up with Lou.

The most notable effect has been a recommitment to the relationship. With both partners battling fatal diseases, there are obvious strains on the relationship. It seems they were drifting apart prior to the institution of sildenafil citrate; they now seem to have been drawn closer together. Both report an increase in the intimacy of the relationship. Both individual therapists and their relationship therapist report that the therapies are progressing well.

It is a truism that emotional intimacy leads to sexual intimacy. It is also true that sexual intimacy can lead to emotional intimacy. For whatever reasons a couple stops having sex, it generally leads to and may reflect other problems in the emotional aspects of the relationship. Part of the reparative process of the relationship is the reestablishment (or establishment in more severe cases) of the sexual component. Although renewing the sexual relationship too early can be an error, waiting too long can also be problematic.

Problematic Couple Relationships Presenting with Erectile Dysfunction

This second category exemplifies more problematic situations, in which the male's erectile dysfunction is symptomatic of unresolved relational issues that underlie his lack of subjective arousal with his partner and are expressed in his inability to have erections in sexual interactions. Quite often in such cases, the nature of the erectile dysfunction is highly situational, and these men are capable of achieving erections and ejaculation during self-stimulation as well as with other sexual partners. Many such clients are highly reluctant to discuss their feelings with their partners or to enter couples or sex therapy and explore their feelings in that context. Below are examples of three couples who might seek sex therapy with the complaint of erectile dysfunction. Considerations for assessment and treatment are included.

Joe and Barb: Fears of Intimacy and Loss.   Joe, age 52, has had difficulties achieving and maintaining erections since Barb's mastectomy the previous year. He had always been aroused by the sight and touch of Barb's body, particularly her breasts. The prospect of Barb's death from cancer, from which she is currently in remission, deeply frightened him. He did not want to contend with the prospect of life without her. He has not discussed his feelings and reactions with Barb, feeling ashamed and unmanly for having them. Barb has kept her nightgown on from the waist up during subsequent attempts at sexual intercourse, based on her own discomfort with her body and her impressions of Joe's possible reactions. Joe has withdrawn emotionally from the relationship in response to his fear of loss, vulnerability, and confusion over how to support Barb.

In the age of Viagra™, Joe might receive a prescription without ever being asked to describe the relational context of his erectile difficulties, let alone his feelings about them. In his attempts to produce and maintain erections, Joe has learned to avoid looking at Barb's torso and to focus intensely on penile sensations. Apfelbaum (1977) described such effective sexual functioning as a defensive style called *bypassing*, identifying two subtypes: spontaneous and effortful bypassing. The latter, represented by Joe's approach to Barb, is seen as motivated by performance anxiety, indicating that the client "has the motivation and ability to narrow down their [sic] consciousness at will, to hold an exclusive focus on sensation, tuning out any discordant notes in the relationship" (p. 60).

Apfelbaum (1977) noted that such clients more often present for therapy for postcoital depression than for sexual dysfunction. Sildenafil citrate will likely facilitate Joe's ability to produce an erection and decrease the physiological impact of his distracting thoughts, thereby allowing Joe to ignore and override his conflicted feelings about having sex with Barb. Ironically, Joe's circumvention of actually being emotionally present during the sexual encounter is an heroic attempt to preserve sexual intimacy as this couple once knew it. Sildenafil citrate can be seen as a *chemical bypass*, a third subtype of Apfelbaum's (1977) bypassing strategies, providing a powerful pharmaceutical boost when the male's ability to bypass psychologically falls short of a full erection. Sildenafil citrate could allow this couple to continue "functioning" sexually around the specter of Barb's cancer through a combination of psychological and medically assisted contortions.

Both Joe and Barb may suffer from believing they "should" be able to "get over" Barb's cancer and that, with enough effort, they should be able to "get around" this. These beliefs become apparent during assessment, when both partners describe what they are silently telling themselves during each sexual encounter. A crucial aspect of assessment is to help the partners articulate their respective subjective thoughts and feelings during lovemaking, to themselves and to each other. Assessment here serves dually as intervention, as both may begin to experience increased empathy for the other, as well as a learning process of sharing what was previously censored.

Joe and Barb do not know how to have a conversation about the impact of Barb's cancer and mastectomy on their sexual relationship. Both have engaged in a mutually self-protective dance of avoidance intended to save one another from further pain. Therapy can facilitate the sharing of grief, anger, fear, and insecurity that are elicited specifically in each sexual encounter. A feminist approach also can provide a context in which to examine the cultural hinging of female self-worth on physical appearance, and of male self-worth on strength and mastery. Barb's cancer has thrown a monkey wrench into the genderized cognitive schema of self-concept for both partners. Joe's sexual "dysfunction" could serve as a call to attend to these issues, rather than simply bypassing them by using sildenafil citrate. Sex therapy could allow this couple to use a very stressful and tragic event to push them toward a new and deeper level of emotional intimacy.

Ted and Alice: Power, Status, and Erectile Problems.   Ted and Alice present for sex therapy with the specific complaint of Ted's difficulty maintaining an erection. His erections typically subside shortly after vaginal penetration. Two years ago, Alice completed her degree in computer science, was hired by a rapidly growing company, and had quickly advanced to a high-paying executive position. Ted now earns half of Alice's salary. His previous role was as sole economic supporter of the family, and he had made most of the major economic decisions. Alice now participates more equally in these decisions. Ted has experienced a growing resentment of her that strikes him as illogical and childish. Alice is now working in a predominantly male environment. Ted, who considers her quite attractive, has begun to feel threatened by her close working relationships with several men, as well as feeling sexually inadequate.

As in the case of Barb and Joe, Alice and Ted do not know how to talk with each other about the impact of the reversal in their economic status in their relationship and Ted's fear of loss of power. In spite of his conscious belief that sharing decision-making power with Alice does not make him less of a man, Ted is beset by lingering doubts. Exploring the meaning to Ted of his loss of role as primary breadwinner, and his resultant feeling of superfluousness and shame, would set the stage for assessing the meaning of Ted's erectile difficulties to him. Ted's loss of erections after penetration is likely linked to concerns with his sexual performance, and the extreme pressure he places on himself to be competent sexually, in contrast to his feelings of uselessness in other aspects of his relationship. A great deal more rides on the success of each sexual encounter for Ted now than in the past.

During the assessment process, Ted shares his embarrassing fears of being found lacking by Alice and then being abandoned or replaced sexually. Sex was the only area in which Ted felt he had something to offer in this relationship; it represented an opportunity to regain his sense of worth as a man, which paradoxically became unattainable once his erections became imbued with so much importance. In each sexual encounter with Alice, Ted had been trying to act as if he felt confident and in control, although the opposite was true.

Alice has felt sympathy for Ted in his predicament, but she also has begun to feel increasingly frustrated, impatient, and disappointed. She feels guilty and selfish that her success has come at such a high price for Ted. She also reluctantly admits that she is angry she cannot have both success in work and happiness in her relationship. She feels almost punished for stepping out of role by Ted's inability to have erections sufficient for intercourse. Having intercourse with Ted makes Alice feel she is loved and sexually desirable. Alice, like Ted, has also been trying to behave as if nothing was wrong during their sexual encounters. When Ted loses his erection and they cannot continue with intercourse, she experiences it as a rejection of herself as attractive and lovable, and as a painful double-bind in having to pay a price for her success.

If Ted had received a prescription for sildenafil citrate, it is likely his ability to maintain his erections would be enhanced. This would allow him to feel bolstered by his ability to perform sexually, and it would allow Alice to avoid sexual frustration and the sense of being punished for her success. In this case, the timing of when sildenafil citrate is used might be essential, as its use might not be inherently harmful to the couple. If prescribed initially, the motivation to explore and discuss the issues that likely resulted in Ted's erectile problems would be vastly decreased. It is quite possible that although Ted's erectile dysfunction might be ameliorated, it could be replaced by another symptom of his emotional distress—for example, hypoactive sexual desire, a somatic complaint, or some acting-out behavior.

Even in the absence of "symptom substitution," Ted and Alice will likely have to confront the underlying issues of power and status in their relationship, or they probably will find the emotional gulf between them expanding. Premature prescription of sildenafil citrate might preclude this essential work. A feminist approach to sex therapy with this couple would encourage and teach Ted and Alice to talk about the issues precipitating Ted's erectile problems, and to develop facility in sharing their anxiety about sexual encounters. This type of conversation may decrease much of the self-pressuring this couple does to "act as if" and, when articulated, can demystify the largely unspoken couple and cultural mythology about the importance of Ted's erections. The couple also can be encouraged to explore the many other ways they can help each other experience sexual pleasure, which might begin to seem more exciting once erections are seen with a different perspective.

A hallmark of feminist therapy is the reframing of seemingly dysfunctional behaviors as having functional or survival value. The effect is to depathologize the symptom and to understand its meaning in the relationship. Another aspect of a feminist approach is the explicit intent to help the client gain freedom from assigned gender roles and recognize roles that are confining, restrictive, or oppressive for both men and women (Enns, 1997). It must be emphasized that feminist sex therapy would not automatically discount the use of sildenafil citrate for couples in treatment, but would pay close attention to the timing of its implementation. It would not be assumed that a return of sexual functioning would automatically help to mend the relationship, and clients would be encouraged to attend to the message the symptom of erectile dysfunction might have conveyed.

Bob and Carole: Keep It Down, or a Strike Against Alienated Working Conditions. Bob and Carole present for sex therapy due to Bob's inability to maintain erections during sexual interactions with Carole.

He reports achieving erections during masturbation, often when fantasizing about other women. This couple has had very traditional gender roles in their relationship almost from the beginning. Although it was the initial intent for both to complete their degrees and work, Carole decided to quit before finishing, and then decided she wanted to have children, which was not their initial understanding. Bob felt unable to influence Carole directly in these decisions, and he has never felt he could express himself fully or represent himself well in discussion or conflict with Carole. Although he was in disagreement and resented Carole's unilateral style, he shouldered the financial responsibility of supporting a family, afraid to rock the boat and endure further discussion and conflict. At the time of therapy, Bob feels trapped and resentful, although he still cares for Carole and their children.

Bob feels (accurately) that he does not have equal power or control in the relationship. He feels manipulated and trapped by his own sense of responsibility. Although he may not immediately articulate this, he likely experiences rage toward Carole for creating a situation in which she always has her way. He may also experience rage at himself for not better representing his own interests in the relationship. Bob's erectile dysfunction could be seen as a "strike against working conditions" (Seidler-Feller, 1985) in his relationship. What emerges during assessment is that previous to the onset of erectile dysfunction, Bob would become "depressed" immediately following a sexual encounter with Carole. He would be in a bad mood for at least half a day. Carole had noticed this effect, but had not wanted to rock the boat, as most of her needs were being met.

In Bob's case, it is possible that, if provided with a prescription for sildenafil citrate, he might be reluctant to use it. Wise (1999) described two cases with similar dynamics, in which the husband was angered by his wife's challenge to his power. Similarly, Althof (1998) cited dropout rates of 20% to 50% in the medical treatment of erectile dysfunction, suggesting the strong need for sex therapists to be attuned to the complex individual and interpersonal factors that may determine resistance to drug treatment. The introduction of sildenafil citrate that is not sensitive to the relational context can have destructive consequences to a relationship, even if the sildenafil citrate remains in the bottle (Wise, 1999).

In the complex cases above, an immediate prescription of sildenafil citrate would likely preclude these couples from addressing the important issues described. The use of sildenafil citrate in such cases is not overtly inappropriate, but instead speaks to the more insidious encroachment of medicalization of sexuality into our relationships, offering a ready panacea for sexual dysfunction at the cost of emotional connection. These cases point to the need for multidisciplinary assessment and the appropriate timing of the introduction of sildenafil citrate.

Sildenafil Citrate: A Medicalized Escape from Intimacy

Many men and women hope that a medical etiology for their sexual problems will provide a cure without sex therapy. In our culture, erectile dysfunction has tremendous power to threaten masculine identity, affecting a man's self-esteem and sense of human worth. As Zilbergeld (1992, p. 22) pointed out, "The concern of being considered a non-man keeps men in a state of almost perpetual vigilance and anxiety." As Masters and Johnson (1970, pp. 187–188) noted, "Every sexually inadequate male lunges toward any potential physical excuse for sexual malfunction."

Prior to the advent of sildenafil citrate, the presence of erectile dysfunction often served as a therapeutic lever to impel the couple to address relational issues that otherwise would have been overridden or denied. In the cases above, one view is that partial erectile functioning provided by sildenafil citrate would make the critical difference in whether these men seek out sex therapy. Another view is that the failure of sildenafil citrate would demonstrate the psychogenic component and propel them into sex therapy. The skill of the prescriber is probably the deciding factor. These men might be prescribed sildenafil citrate as a primary intervention, most likely without any involvement of the partner. The economics of managed care support the use of medical treatments over relational treatments for sexual problems. Many insurance providers have removed marital and sex therapy from their coverage policies, leaving it an option for only a select few. Sildenafil citrate provides one way to shore up the crumbling foundation of the traditional male role, allowing men to continue to function as machines in their presumably intimate relationships. For men, having to function sexually regardless of their physical or psychological states or the quality of intimacy with their partners is considered a "natural" part of the male sex role (Levant & Brooks, 1997). To function sexually within this mindset may require a nonrelational orientation to sexuality, which the use of sildenafil citrate certainly can facilitate. In this manner, the mechanization of sexual problems risks obscuring what our bodies may be revealing about our relationships.

Tom and Nicole: "I Thought I Was Done Providing Sex."   Tom and Nicole are a couple in their mid-60s who have not engaged in sexual intercourse or other dyadic sexual activity for 5 years. Nicole, who is postmenopausal, has experienced a decrease in sexual desire related to hormonal changes, as well as decreased vaginal lubrication and atrophy of vaginal tissues that now renders sexual intercourse painful. Nicole had never experienced significant sexual pleasure or satisfaction in her 35-year marriage to Tom, and she has little or no interest in exploring these issues now. She was secretly relieved when Tom developed erectile dysfunction, and was pleased at the cessation of sexual pressure and demands. Although she is vaguely sorry for Tom, he has not been sensitive to her sexual needs or needs for nonsexual affection over the years in their marriage. Both Tom and Nicole have come to accept a basically distant marital status quo. The quality of the relationship is not sufficient to sustain Nicole's desire to engage sexually with Tom, which otherwise might motivate her to pursue medical remediation for her postmenopausal sexual symptoms.

Women in general, and particularly older women, are often undiagnosed and underserved by medical and psychotherapeutic practice in the area of sexual difficulties; they are also frequently reluctant and embarrassed to act as their own advocates with medical professionals and therapists. With regard to sildenafil citrate, one group of urologists noted that 15 female spouses (55 to 75 years old) of male patients prescribed this drug had developed frequent, urgent, burning urination, diagnosed as cystitis (Little, Park, & Patton, 1998). Although "honeymoon cystitis" is not necessarily a sign of an unwilling or unhappy partner, it further demonstrates the need for involvement of both partners in treatment.

Men experience age- and illness-related decrements in their erectile ability. With sildenafil citrate, men like Tom may want to renew sexual intercourse. If Tom is prescribed sildenafil citrate, he may assume that because Nicole provided him with sexual intercourse in the past, she will again now. If she does not want to lose Tom, because of either emotional or economic factors, Nicole may reluctantly cooperate again with nonrewarding, often painful sexual intercourse in response to Tom's sexual pressure.

If Tom and Nicole enter couples sex therapy, they may be presented with more beneficial options. For better or worse, the availability of sildenafil citrate has created a crisis that may lead to the dissolution or the reinvigoration of their relationship. The couple must be helped to determine if sufficient motivation exists, or can be developed, to create the conditions under which they would want to have an improved sexual relationship. This requires first addressing broader relationship issues of reciprocity, mutuality, and empathy for the other's position. If the couple is prepared to do this work, they may be able to approach the previously abandoned arena of their sexual relationship. If either partner refuses to engage in this work, Tom will have to choose between foregoing a sexual relationship, seeking extramarital sexual outlets, or leaving the relationship entirely. These alternatives, however painful, should be addressed as part of therapy. In the best of outcomes, the introduction of sildenafil citrate could serve as a catalyst for change, presenting a challenge and an opportunity for both partners to move toward creating a more intimate relationship.

This type of case presents the therapist with an ethical dilemma. The therapist must avoid colluding with the heterosexual imperative, or the "cult of intercourse" (Hite, 1976), and also avoid joining with the male partner and cultural context in pressuring the female partner to explore or engage in unwanted sexual contact. On the other hand, the therapist cannot ignore the desire of the male partner to be able to express his sexuality. It is incumbent upon the sex therapist to be aware of the cultural and possible economic pressures already bearing on Nicole, in the case above, to submit to unwanted intercourse as her "wifely obligation." Because this context is so common and pervasive that it may recede as "ground" rather than emerge as "figure," the therapist must swim against the tide of the couple's taken-for-granted social reality, as well as the therapist's own internalized socialization. Even if economic circumstances cannot be changed in therapy, identifying and naming the money issue as a variable that may dramatically impact Nicole's options is appropriate and necessary within the scope of feminist sex therapy. Medical treatment for Nicole's physical symptoms presents a potentially seductive pseudosolution to the therapist. Hormone replacement therapy, the application of topical estrogen cream, and the use of lubricant could provide a remedy for Nicole's physical discomfort, and the advantages and disadvantages of these options can certainly be discussed when appropriate. But the therapist must first and foremost consider and ask the couple, "Why would (or should) Nicole want to engage in sex with Tom?" and "Must sex include sexual intercourse?" There is considerable social pressure on the therapist to try to "fix" Nicole, yet it is imperative that the therapist resists this pressure, while helping the clients to articulate their choices and the reasons they might have for making them.

☐ The Gender Politics of Sildenafil Citrate, Part II: Effects on Heterosexual Relationships

Although men have generally welcomed sildenafil citrate as a panacea for erectile problems, references to the ambivalence felt by some women have begun appearing anecdotally. Erectile dysfunction may function in some relationships as the "canary in the mine" of relationship problems, a somatic marker of individual or relational distress, as vaginismus or orgasmic dysfunction might for some women. Now men can produce erections in situations where in, the past, they might have wilted. Pharmaceutically enhanced erections can increase the ability to disconnect from affect, thereby obscuring relational disconnection, or they can spotlight that tendency.

The presence of erectile dysfunction changes the dynamics of communication and affection in a relationship beyond the reduction or cessation of sexual intercourse. Men with erectile problems often refrain from any expressions of tenderness for fear of raising false hopes in their partners. Women may do likewise to avoid inducing pressure or guilt in their partners.

The implications for sex therapists of the larger cultural context of sildenafil citrate's introduction demand that we remain acutely aware of the positioning of this drug in our clients' lives and in the larger culture. We need to be cultural resisters rather than accomplices to these trends as we conduct our therapy with individuals and couples. Women's psychological and physical health have not, to date, been well-served by the medicalization of sexuality.

☐ Summary

Sildenafil citrate is a boon for couples in which the male's erectile difficulties are not symptomatic of relational distress. However, when lack of emotional intimacy, power struggles, or failure to create the conditions that would generate sexual desire characterize relationships, sildenafil citrate may delay attending to relational intimacy. Although a common, cultural male fantasy is to be able to function like a machine, as the sexual equivalent of the Energizer bunny, both men and women lose something if medical interventions allow us to function without the necessity of emotional connection. By lowering the threshold for physical or psychological stimulation to result in the physical ability to have sexual intercourse, are we improving sexuality or increasing our alienation from one another? Is the ability to perform like a sexual machine desirable, individually or on a cultural scale? What does this medically augmented ability of the body to function even in the presence of relational disengagement do to the subjective experience and deeper meanings of sex? Sildenafil citrate may well function as yet another double-edged sword on the frontier of both women's and men's sexual development and exploration. We must continue to pose these questions, in our theory building and in our practice, to counteract the potential for alienation and mechanization of sex. Instead, we must seek to foster a model of sexuality as having the potential for a human, connective experience.

□ References

Althof, S. E. (1998). New roles for mental health clinicians in the treatment of erectile dysfunction. *Journal of Sex Education and Therapy, 23*(3), 229–231.

Apfelbaum, B. (1977). On the etiology of sexual dysfunction. *Journal of Sex & Marital Therapy, 3*(1), 50–62.

Ashton, A., & Bennett, R. (1999). Sildenafil treatment of serotonin reuptake inhibitor-induced sexual dysfunction. *Journal of Clinical Psychiatry, 60*(3), 194–195.

Balon, R. (1998). Fluvoxamine-induced erectile dysfunction responding to sildenafil. *Journal of Sex & Marital Therapy, 24,* 313–317.

Balon, R. (1999). Sildenafil and sexual dysfunction associated with antidepressants. *Journal of Sex & Marital Therapy, 25,* 259–264.

Berman, J., Berman, L., Lin, H., & Goldstein, I. (1999). *Effects of sildenafil on subjective and physiologic parameters of the female sexual response: A two-phase pilot study.* Podium 32, Proceedings, New Perspectives in the Management of Female Sexual Dysfunction, Boston University School of Medicine Continuing Medical Education, October 22–24.

Berman, L., Berman, J., Werbin, T., & Goldstein I. (1999). *Effects of sildenafil on female sexual response as assessed by the female intervention efficacy index (FIEI).* Podium 23, Proceedings, New Perspectives in the Management of Female Sexual Dysfunction, Boston University School of Medicine Continuing Medical Education, October 22–24.

Coleman, E., Hoon, P., & Hoon, E. (1983). Arousability and sexual satisfaction in lesbian and heterosexual women. *Journal of Sex Research, 19*(1), 58–73.

Enns, C. (1997). *Feminist theories and feminist psychotherapies: Origins, themes, and variations.* New York: Harrington Park Press.

Goldstein, I., Lue, T., Padma-Nathan, H., Rosen, R., Steers, W., & Wicker, P. (1998). Oral sildenafil in the treatment of erectile dysfunction. *New England Journal of Medicine, 338,* 1397–1404.

Hite, S. (1976). *The Hite report.* New York: Macmillian.

Kaminetsky, J. (1999). *Preliminary results of a topical formulation of sildenafil in the treatment of female sexual dysfunction.* Poster session 37, Proceedings, New Perspectives in the Management of Female Sexual Dysfunction, Boston University School of Medicine Continuing Medical Education, October 22–24.

Kaplan, H. S. (1974). *The new sex therapy.* New York: Brunner/Mazel.

Kaplan, S., Reis, R. B., Kohn, I. J., Ikeguchi, E. F., Laor, E., Te, A. E., & Martins, C. P. (1999). Safety and efficacy of sildenafil in postmenopausal women with sexual dysfunction. *Urology, 53,* 481–486.

Laumann, E., Paik, A., & Rosen, R. (1999). Sexual dysfunction in the United States: Prevalence and predictors. *Journal of the American Medical Association, 281*(6), 537–544.

Levant, R. F., & Brooks, G. R. (1997) *Men and sex: New psychological perspectives.* New York: Wiley.

Little, W., Park, G., & Patton, H. (1998). Letter to the editor. *New England Journal of Medicine, 339*(10), 700.

Loulan, J. (1988). Research on the sex practices of 1566 lesbians and the clinical applications. *Women & Therapy, 7*(2/3), 221–234.

Masters, W., & Johnson, V. (1966). *Human sexual response.* Boston: Little, Brown.

Masters, W., & Johnson, V. (1970). *Human sexual inadequacy.* Boston: Little, Brown.

McCormick, N. (1994). *Sexual salvation: Affirming women's sexual rights and pleasures.* Westport, CT: Praeger.

Melman, A., & Gingell, J. C. (1999). The epidemiology and pathophysiology of erectile dysfunction. *Journal of Urology, 161,* 5–11.

Moser, C. (2000). *The effect of sildenafil citrate on middle-aged "normal" men*. Unpublished manuscript.

Perelman, M. (1998). Commentary: Pharmacological agents for erectile dysfunction and the human sexual response cycle. *Journal of Sex & Marital Therapy, 24*, 309–312.

Pfizer, Inc. (1998). *Viagra description*, May. New York: Pfizer Labs.

Reissman, C. (1983). Women and medicalization: A new perspective. *Social Policy, 14*, 3–18.

Rosenberg, K. (1999a). Sildenafil citrate for SSRI-induced sexual side effects. *American Journal of Psychiatry, 156*, 156–157.

Rosenberg, K. (1999b). Sildenafil. *Journal of Sex & Marital Therapy, 25*(4), 271–279.

Seidler-Feller, D. (1976). Process and power in couples psychotherapy: A feminist view. *Voices, 12*(45), 67–71.

Seidler-Feller, D. (1985). A feminist critique of sex therapy. In L. Rosewater & L. Walker (Eds.), *Handbook of feminist therapy* (pp. 119–129). New York: Springer.

Solomon, S., & Cappa, K. G. (1987). Impotence and bicycling. A seldom-reported connection. *Postgraduate Medicine, 81*(1), 99–100, 102.

Stock, W. (1983). Sex roles and sexual dysfunction. In C. Widom (Ed.), *Sex roles and psychopathology* (pp. 249–275). New York: Plenum Press.

Tiefer, L. (1981). The context and consequences of contemporary sex research: A feminist perspective. In S. Cox (Ed.), *Female psychology: The emerging self* (2nd ed., pp. 23–41). New York: St. Martin's Press.

Tiefer, L. (1988). A feminist critique of the sexual dysfunction nomenclature. *Women in Therapy, 7*(2/3), 3–22.

Tiefer, L. (1996). The medicalization of sexuality: Conceptual, normative, and professional issues. In R. Rosen (Ed.), *Annual review of sex research* (vol. 7; pp. 252–282). Mount Vernon, IA: Society for the Scientific Study of Sexuality.

Wise, T. N. (1999). Psychosocial effects of sildenafil therapy for erectile dysfunction. *Journal of Sex & Marital Therapy, 25*(2), 145–150.

Zilbergeld, B. (1992). *The new male sexuality: The truth about men, sex, and pleasure*. New York: Bantam Books.

Carol Rinkleib Ellison, Ph.D.

Intimacy-Based Sex Therapy: Sexual Choreography

How we conceptualize and describe therapy issues shapes how we treat them. The intimacy-based sex therapy I have developed and practice is quite different from sex therapy in the world of formal psychology and medicine. There, success is typically defined in terms of enhanced or restored physical functioning (i.e., achieving and maintaining lubrication or erection, having intercourse or a same-sex equivalent, and achieving orgasm). In the intimacy-based model, success in a sexual interlude is defined not in terms of physiological functioning but in terms of creating erotic pleasure with outcomes of intimacy, satisfaction, mutual pleasure, and self-esteem. A couple is sexually successful when the partners create erotic pleasure, to whatever level and in whatever form they desire on that particular occasion, and each ends up feeling good about him- or herself and about the other; they both have a good time and enhance their relationship. This definition of success is the cornerstone of intimacy-based sex therapy. To facilitate such experiences is the guiding intention of the therapist.

☐ A Sex-as-Performance Model

The concepts and language of sex therapy as it is most widely practiced were formalized by William Masters and Virginia Johnson in their 1970 book *Human Sexual Inadequacy*. In their sex therapy, normal sex is considered to be sexual intercourse, and problems are called *dysfunctions*, defined by my dictionary as abnormal, impaired, or incomplete functioning of an organ or part. Those who do not function the right way—that is, according to their model of sexual responsiveness, the human sexual response cycle (excitement, plateau, orgasm, resolution)—are said to have a sexual dysfunction and to be *sexually inadequate*.

The reductionistic language of Masters and Johnson and the sexual response cycle as norm were formalized further in the 1994 *Diagnostic and Statistical Manual of Mental Disorders (DSM-IV)* of the American Psychiatric Association, in which sexual problems and concerns were labeled sexual dysfunctions and disorders:

> A sexual dysfunction is characterized by a disturbance in the processes that characterize the sexual response cycle or by pain associated with sexual intercourse. The sexual response cycle can be divided into the following phases: 1. *Desire.* . . . 2. *Excitement.* . . . 3. *Orgasm.* . . . 4. *Resolution.* . . . (pp. 493–494)

This modified version of Masters and Johnson's response cycle further diminishes sexual potential, since Masters and Johnson's *plateau* phase, an extended period of arousal and pleasure, was removed from the *DSM-IV* criteria for sexual health. It is no wonder, then, that treatment is conceptualized so often as penile injections, implants, and Viagra™ instead of as discussions about how to create and enhance erotic pleasure.

☐ The "Manufacturing Orgasms" Sexual Script

A Bit of History

While Masters and Johnson's classic book formalized the language, their thinking was not new. For over a century cultural and medical establishments have told us about the "right ways" to experience our sexuality. In the late 1800s, for example, some in the medical profession viewed sexual excitement itself as problematic and diagnosed masturbation and sexual desire as sexual disorders; by this definition, someone with a desire disorder was experiencing desire, not lacking it (Szasz, 1980). Between 1880 and 1900, some women were convinced to undergo mutilating surgery simply because they did not fit the sexual fashion of their times: clitoridectomy and female castration, removing women's ovaries, were vogue treatments for these medically defined problems (Barker-Benfield, 1976; Masson, 1986).

One of these imposed right ways to experience sexuality is the reductionistic construct referred to here as the manufacturing orgasms sexual script. This construct has been with us throughout most of the twentieth century. For those who think this way, the goals of sex are intercourse and orgasm. Success in sex is achieving orgasm, often with certain performance specifications for the orgasm. Few people raised in this culture have escaped the influence of well over a half-century of debate about clitoral and vaginal orgasms, for example, and both women and men have suffered trying to make women have the right kind. Obsession with clitoral and vaginal orgasms began with Freud in the early twentieth century. In marriage manuals and medical textbooks of the 1930s through the 1950s, vaginal orgasms (a woman's orgasms through intercourse) were said to be a sign of marital maturity; and simultaneous orgasms through intercourse were touted as the ultimate in lovemaking. While authors in that era did promote mutual pleasure, couples and therapists might read in the most widely read marriage manual of that time:

> [I]n ideal communion the stimulation will generally be focused on and in the vagina. . . . And this will be fully adequate for such a variety and intensity of sensation as will culminate in the orgasm.
>
> In the normal and perfect coitus, mutual orgasm must be almost simultaneous; the usual procedure is that the man's ejaculation begins and sets the woman's acme of sensation in train at once. (Van de Velde, 1926/1968, p. 165)

Similarly, "Both partners should, in coitus, concentrate their full attention on one thing: the attainment of simultaneous orgasm" (Chesser, 1947/1957). These statements epitomize the manufacturing orgasms sexual script/belief system: To be sexually successful, one *must* have an orgasm. The orgasm *must* occur in intercourse. And, according to some (like Van de Velde and Chesser), the stakes are even higher: The partners must have simultaneous orgasms.

Through the 1970s and 1980s, pressures to achieve vaginal and simultaneous orgasms were replaced by pressures, albeit unintended, to achieve other kinds of orgasms. Masters and Johnson introduced a new way for women to be inadequate in their classic *Human Sexual Inadequacy*:

masturbatory orgasmic inadequacy, that is, being able to have orgasms in intercourse but not from direct clitoral stimulation (1970, p. 240). There were books about total orgasms (Rosenberg, 1973); multiple orgasms (e.g., Hartman & Fithian, 1984); G-spot orgasms, with or without female ejaculation (Ladas, Whipple, & Perry, 1982); extended sexual orgasms (Brauer & Brauer, 1983); peak orgasms and valley orgasms (Rajneesh, 1976); and many others.

Sex therapists thinking in the manufacturing orgasms paradigm tend to focus their attention on dysfunctions and sexual performance—on achieving erections, ejaculatory control, and orgasms—rather than on the enjoyment and satisfaction of both partners. In this modality, for example, a woman whose vagina is spasming ("vaginismus") may be given dilators to stretch or force her vagina open rather than led, one step at a time, to the experience of desiring and welcoming her partner inside.

A manufacturing orgasms therapy approach sometimes leads to physical functioning "achieved" at the expense of intimacy, as in the case of the woman who, in individual therapy, learned to be orgasmic through masturbation. She and her husband came for couples therapy because she was unable to use that new skill in a satisfying sexual experience with him, and he had begun to experience performance anxiety because of her therapy. Their sexual times together had become awkward, and sex had begun to feel like work instead of fun for both of them.

☐ Intimacy-Based Sex Therapy

Intimacy-based sex therapy, in which the therapist thinks of sex as *creating mutual erotic pleasure in whatever form that might take,* is an alternative to this more traditional model of sex therapy. Intercourse and orgasms are choices, not requirements, for successful lovemaking. Variety in orgasmic experiences is welcomed. Intimacy-based sex therapy is a sex-as-experience model, not a work/performance one; in this model, sex is creating and experiencing erotic pleasure.

One of the first interventions with practically every couple is to talk about the definition of success that forms the cornerstone of intimacy-based sex therapy. To facilitate experiences successful in these terms is the guiding intention of the therapist. The intimacy-based therapist thinks and speaks in phrases that describe process or experience—creating orgasm, enhancing self-esteem, having orgasmic difficulties, experiencing erectile problems, ejaculating sooner than he or his partner would like, optimizing physical responsiveness, conditions for pleasure, continuum of erotic possibilities—rather than in nouns and adjectives that label the condition or the individual who has the experience; for example he or she does not use words like disorder, vaginismus, dysfunction, frigid, inadequate, or impotent. The therapist also avoids such work ethic/performance phrases as *achieve erection* and *achieve orgasm.*

I rarely call myself a sex therapist but, rather, a psychologist specializing in issues of sexuality and intimacy. I think of myself as a sexual choreographer™, a sexual detective, and a sexual problem solver. As choreographer, I help couples create a structure for their erotic spontaneity that will enhance intimacy and facilitate sexual experiences that meet my definition of success. As sexual detective, I might attempt to determine, for example, whether it is a medication, anger, attention on performance, or some combination thereof that is the basis of a man's erectile difficulties. As sexual problem solver, I might provide information on alternative medications and suggest specific experiments the couple might try in their lovemaking.

In the intimacy-based model, success does not depend on how stimulation occurs or on physical "functioning." Enhanced *sexual responsiveness*—a term more congruent with this approach than the more mechanical *physical functioning*—is likely to occur as an outcome of therapy interventions; but it does not define sexual success, nor is it the primary focus of attention for the therapist. Instead of goals of achieving intercourse or manufacturing orgasms, the primary goals of sex therapy are mutual pleasure, enhanced self-esteem, intimacy, and satisfaction. The relevant questions to consider during sex are not "How am I doing? Am I getting hard—or wet—fast enough? Am I going to make it?" but "Am I enjoying this? Am I enjoying what's happening right now?"

Concepts and Techniques of Sexual Choreography

Among the assumptions guiding this model are the notions that couples can create erotic experience, a process with building blocks or steps that we can understand and use, and that erotic experience occurs in many forms. The emphasis is on creating, facilitating, or enhancing—not achieving—pleasure, arousal, and orgasms.

During sex, attention may shift between our sensations, breathing, mental impressions, and emotions. We can sense physical tension developing, expanding, and releasing; we can experience pleasure and discomfort and pain. We may notice sexual energy intensifying, moving, and releasing. We also may be aware of a variety of emotions and of memories, fantasies, judgments, performance expectations, and other mental images.

The sexual choreographer acknowledges the multidimensionality of sexuality. The intimacy-based therapist considers the physical, mental, emotional, and spiritual/transpersonal dimensions of sexual responsiveness and interaction. She or he notes the presence and significance of physiological factors; of various emotional states such as anger, depression, and anxiety (including "performance anxiety"); and of concerns about such issues as trust, monogamy, and commitment.

Transitions—A Key to Creating Erotic Arousal

A sexual experience begins with a shift of attention and consciousness. Most people are most of the time in their not-doing-sex selves. A transition into one's doing-sex self can be practically instantaneous or occur gradually, over hours. It may be stimulated primarily through something outside of oneself or from hormones, physical changes, feelings, and images within (Ellison, 1984).

In partnered sex, individuals shift from their personal not-doing-sex selves into their doing-sex selves and also shift with each other from feeling separate to experiencing a sense of connection—togetherness. These personal and interpersonal transitions may seem to happen spontaneously or they might be made with effort (Ellison, 1984).

One role of the sexual choreographer is to help a couple facilitate effective transitions, both through specific suggestions and through working with the couple to develop their own rituals adapted to their specific life situations. The therapist detective will consider such questions as these: Is anyone initiating contact? Is there mutual intention to engage in sexual activity? Can they effectively develop—if appropriate for them—an *intimate trance*? (Ellison, 1986).

Transition, Physical Responsiveness, and Satisfaction

Many difficulties with physical responsiveness—lubrication, orgasm, erection, ejaculation—are related to or the result of skipping the crucial step of *transition* into the sexual process. Statements such as "I wish she would take more time," "I wish he would be more romantic," and "I wish we would spend more time on foreplay" indicate that more transition activities are needed or desired.

In 1993–1994, Bernie Zilbergeld and I conducted a national survey in which we asked college-educated American women about how they experienced and expressed their sexuality; 2,632 responded. We gathered information about how women experience and express their sexualities both in relationships and when alone. For these women, "feeling close to my partner before sex" was the top-ranked factor correlated with sexual satisfaction in an ongoing relationship. (Details of this survey are found in Ellison, 2000.)

To a client who reports tensing up or pulling away when touched or being unable to relax with a partner, I say something like, "Think about what your body is telling you. Such physical responses are signs that you are doing something you feel anxious about, do not want to do, or that would not be in your best interest." The role of the therapist is to determine several things.

For example, with the client just mentioned, I might ask some of the following questions, when appropriate:

- What is preventing you from connecting with your partner?
- What feelings and thoughts are pulling against a relaxed sensual response?
- Do you need to say "No, not right now," or negotiate for something other than what your partner is requesting?
- Are you needing more time for yourself instead of more closeness? Needing more privacy?
- Do you need to deal with birth control or protection against STDs?
- Are you afraid that allowing sensuous feelings to develop will result in your partner trying to be more *sexually* intimate than you want to be?

Sometimes the past interferes with responses and pleasure in the present. Pulling away may be a response learned long ago that has nothing to do with the current partner. Instead of an active response based on the present moment and the present partner, the response may be a reactive one—reactive to the situation and circumstances, but based in past experience. An individual may need to recognize that and learn to creatively act in the moment. In such a circumstance I might say, "When you notice your reaction, you might think *Isn't it interesting how this keeps happening?* Then take a deep breath and, as you let it out, look at your partner." Doing this will help avert self-judgment and shift that individual's attention back to the partner in the present moment.

Transition Activities

In recommending activities to facilitate individual and couple transitions, I might suggest that each individual warm up for sex—or for the therapy "experiments" they have agreed to do—by taking a shower or bath, for example, or by stretching and breathing deeply. Couple activities that are not specifically sexual can be excellent ways to begin feeling close. Such activities provide opportunities to weave in sexual innuendos and play, and can give interest and arousal time to build into full desire.

The ease with which individuals make sexual transitions is influenced by many factors and changes through the life cycle. Sex does not have to go away as couples get older, but it does change form; the suggestions therapists make to a couple need to be adapted to their ages and life situations.

An Attitude of "All the Time You Need"

No matter how much time is actually available, most people are able to respond most readily when they experience a sense that they have all the time they need for their attention to become focused in to sex and for their arousal to build. On one occasion a look or verbal suggestion might trigger a sharp rush of sexual desire in only a few moments. Another time, a relaxed, unhurried build-up of sexual tension might last an hour. Sometimes the pressure of a time limit does make sex exciting. Quickies can be very arousing and a lot of fun. Typically, however, feeling rushed and pressured to hurry interferes with the physical and psychological changes involved in sexual arousal. Feeling hurried, pressured, or like one is *trying* to make something happen can be in opposition to the body/mind state that lets one *surrender*. Even if they are at home and very busy, a couple may be well-advised to schedule a long-enough block of time so that they can feel they have all the time they need for feelings of mutuality and for physical arousal to occur.

Take Care of Details

I instruct clients that the transition into sex—or other sensual activities such as massage—can proceed more smoothly and effectively if distracting details are taken care of ahead of time. Some details might include putting on music and reviewing the ground rules set up in therapy. Others might be related to privacy, contraception, and disease protection (e.g., locking a door, unplugging a phone, getting a pillow, preparing a beverage, or opening a condom package).

Consenting to Be Intimate: Effective Sexual Negotiation

Consent of both partners is a prerequisite for mutuality and intimacy in sex. To consistently create satisfying sexual experiences, couples need to know how to make effective sexual invitations, and each partner needs to know how to successfully accept, reject, and negotiate the invitations the other makes (Ellison, 1987). A truly consenting adult knows how to say "No" or "As soon as I finish what I'm doing," as well as when and how to say "Yes." Mutual consent is a requirement for a sensitive intimate connection. Without consent, sensual pleasure cannot develop fully. Consent means "I agree to be here. I choose to be here. I'm doing this because I want to."

One aspect of low sexual desire may be an absence of full consent. A woman might say "I want to make my partner happy" to explain why she goes along with a partner's requests for sex at times when she doesn't really want to. At face value, it seems a good intention to do this and, in some relationships, going along with a partner's wishes succeeds in making both partners happier and enhances the relationship. In relationships where it does not do this, however, the partner who is only going along typically begins to avoid his or her partner eventually and to experience diminished sexual desire.

"Just say 'No' to sex" is at times good advice, even in an intimate relationship. Many people feel guilty about saying "No." They do not want to hurt a lover's feelings and believe it is their responsibility to take care of a partner's needs (e.g., "It's your wifely/husbandly duty"). With appropriate skills and a sensitive, cooperative partner, however, an individual can negotiate for outcomes that are mutually satisfying. Consider Josie and Joe (a composite of many couples I have seen in sex therapy):

> Josie never directly said "No" when Joe suggested sex, nor did she suggest some other activity she would prefer; but she would frequently participate only half-heartedly. When she did that, Joe assumed that she didn't really want to have sex with him. And, at those times, she didn't. He felt rejected and resentful. Joe had no way of knowing when Josie genuinely consented to sexual intimacy, and her passivity kept her from turning on very much. She was rarely orgasmic when they did have sex. She claimed that this didn't bother her, but it did bother Joe, who assumed her nonresponsiveness meant he was a less-than-adequate lover.

The partner who is unable to say "No" typically begins to avoid sex, and this was true of Josie. For awhile, Joe had seemed to be after sex all the time but, gradually, he began to initiate sex less and less often. By the time they saw me for sex therapy, they had not had intercourse in several months. Both were resentful and concerned about their low sexual desire.

From my perspective, neither Joe nor Josie was to blame. If they had known better ways to deal with sexual initiation, they would have been doing them. These were two people who wanted to have satisfying sex, but who had gotten into interlocking patterns or roles that kept that from happening. As their therapist, I considered where they were at the moment as their starting place, and then we talked about ways in which they might proceed from there to create the kinds of sexual experiences they wanted.

Even with the best of intentions, a person who frequently says "Yes" while actually meaning "No" and then thinks "I really hate this, but I don't want to displease you" sets up a situation that has negative consequences for both partners and for their relationship.

With respect to the partner who is saying "Yes" while experiencing "No," too frequently putting a partner's wishes before one's own leads to feelings of estrangement and resentment. A woman who almost always goes along with sexual invitations she does not genuinely want to accept (like Josie) will typically begin to tense up or pull away from her partner's touch, take measures to avoid or sidetrack his or her sexual invitations, or make other movements away from intimacy and pleasure. The verbal "Yes" will be denied by a subtle—or sometimes not-so-subtle—physical no. This means that sensual pleasure will be blocked; pleasure cannot develop fully because she is not surrendering to it.

From the other partner's point of view, it is painful to perceive the person with whom you are having sex as not really being with you, as resentful, or as only going through the motions. When your partner has sex with you half-heartedly or resentfully, you neither get your needs met nor are you set free by an honest "No" to fill them in a more satisfying way. Engaging in sex under such circumstances can be depleting rather than fulfilling.

In therapy, Josie and Joe learned how to more effectively make and respond to sexual invitations so that they could negotiate to mutually consensual sexual intimacy.

Ideally, when tendering a sexual invitation, you accept your lover's autonomy and right to have feelings different from your own. You could honestly say to your lover, "You can say 'No' to sex with me for right now and I won't stop believing that you love and desire me." I say "ideally" because so many of us have triggers that set off waves of hurt feelings as we reactively interpret our partners' responses as rejections.

"No" need not equal rejection, however. Although many people have never thought about what their assumptions are, each of us has some about what our partners' requests mean. There are also rules underlying our relationships that influence us when we initiate sex, either verbally or nonverbally. In the intimacy-based therapy model, the therapist helps the couple articulate the unspoken script.

An invitation can open a negotiation in which the partners know that they both share similar underlying assumptions. These assumptions might be, for example:

- *You will be completely honest in your responses to each other.* This assumption allows you to trust that neither of you will say "Yes" if you aren't really consenting. You can't fully trust a "Yes" from a partner who will never, under any circumstances, say "No" or "I'd like to wait until later."

- *There are an infinite number of ways to create pleasure together, and when you decline to have sex you are not necessarily refusing to have intimate contact.* You are, literally, just declining to have sex or, perhaps, just declining to have sexual intercourse or orgasm. You can talk further about what is possible.

- *In responding to a sexual invitation, you will clearly state your interest level.* If you are not interested at the moment, you will, if you can, suggest other mutual activities in which you might be interested or provide information about when you might want to have sex or spend time together.

Sexual invitations have underlying meanings. Each couple has their own implicit or explicit contract. An intimacy-based invitation might have an unspoken meaning something like the following:

- I'm interested in sexual/sensual activity, and I would like you to join me. Are you either in the mood or interested in getting that way?

- If I am more turned on than you are right now, my arousal level is not better than yours, it is only different. There is no need for you to rush to catch up. I can ease back the intensity of my arousal so that it more closely matches yours.

- I am making an effort to be aware of how you are feeling right now. I ask that you do the same for me. If I do not perceive your mood or feelings correctly, I trust that you will tell me.

Sometimes we want to give gifts to those we love, which may include occasionally having sex when we are not particularly interested. The key for evaluating how this plays out in a relationship is my guiding principle: Do the partners feel good about themselves and about each other afterward?

Putting a Structure Around Spontaneity

While more traditional sex therapy focuses on getting the genitals ready for action, intimacy-based therapy focuses on facilitating mutual interaction. I frequently suggest that a couple create rituals for relationship maintenance and enhancement. These are intended to set up their relationship in a way that will increase the likelihood that intimate feelings and sex will regularly occur. While many people believe that "sex should be spontaneous," the intimacy-based therapist understands that spontaneity actually is the outcome of a series of incremental steps in which one thing leads to another.

Two interventions I make within the first few sessions with a couple are to have them establish a goodnight ritual, if they do not have one already, and to explain my concept of weeknight sex.

The *goodnight ritual* is the realization of the couple's intention to affirm their loving and caring for each other as the last thing they do each night before falling asleep. This ritual is an expression of affection that might take only a minute or two or might be more prolonged. When the partners are not going to bed at the same time, the one not yet ready to retire can join the other in the bedroom to talk and touch with mutually focused attention. The therapist's role is more to help create the shared intention than to make specific assignments about how the ritual is to be carried out.

An image that is helpful as a couple begins to think about what the goodnight ritual might be is what I call *weeknight sex*, contrasting this image with the *fantasy/date sex* the partners might have on a weekend or when on vacation, when they are more rested and have more time. The weeknight sex concept frees couples from the limitations of the manufacturing orgasms sexual script and suggests other options.

In the Ellison/Zilbergeld survey, 67% of women with a sex partner in the previous year reported being "too tired" for sex, and 64% being "too busy" for sex sometimes, often, or all of the time. Excluding *sometimes*, 28% were too tired and 29% too busy often or all of the time. I suspect many of these women imagine that "having sex" includes starting from a place of utter fatigue with an alarm clock set to go off before she wants it to, and feeling obligated to get turned on, to have intercourse, and to have an orgasm. A woman's image of having sex may also include dealing with contraception and sexual safety and getting up to urinate and clean up afterward. No wonder she, in her exhaustion, would rather just turn over and go to sleep.

When couples think of sex as creating erotic pleasure, then sex is a continuum of possibilities and there are many ways they can express their affection through their sexuality, even when they're very tired. Low-key genital—or even nongenital—stimulation can be surprisingly erotic and relaxing. Weeknight sex for a couple might be, for example, a minute or two facing each other, legs wrapped around each other, cuddling or scratching each others' backs, and a brief "I love you"; or it might involve briefly caressing genitals and breasts without intention of peaking arousal or of orgasm; or lying in a "spoon" position and synchronizing breathing. It might be one partner holding and caressing while the other brings him- or herself to orgasm, or it might include joining together in intercourse, lying that way a few minutes, perhaps with a few gentle strokes. This contact does not involve trying to build arousal in a manner that would lead to tension and frustration if not released by orgasm. Weeknight sex can be a barely aroused expression of affection that involves sexuality. On occasion, one partner or the other, or both, might want to continue. Sometimes, both might be surprised as one thing leads to another and they become caught up in an intensely passionate moment.

Another ritual for relationship maintenance and enhancement is having a date once a week, during which the couple's intention is to create good feelings, with no griping allowed. If a couple wonders how they can possibly find the time or money to have weekly dates, I remind them that they are finding time and money for therapy, that there are many free and inexpensive activities, and that babysitters charge a lot less than I do. Also, dates don't have to be limited to a night out; a lunch-time affair with each other, for example, could be deliciously erotic.

A gripe session—or life maintenance session—once a week is as important as the date set aside for good times. Many couples are so busy with work, children, and other responsibilities that they have limited time to give each other undivided attention. It is almost impossible to have positive dates consistently if they are not balanced by opportunities to deal with the conflicts and life management details of the relationship. Couples who are unable to end gripe sessions positively may need to work in therapy on communication skills and fighting fairly.

Understanding and Accepting Differences in Sexual Styles

Many couples do not realize that differences in their sexual styles and expectations keep them from effectively making the transition to feelings of connection. Some of these include differences in how each thinks about sex and in what most effectively turns each on. One partner may have one script, one another. Neither is right nor wrong, but they do need to find ways to draw from and bridge their different styles. Metaphorically, sexual styles are like styles of dancing. You can teach your partner the steps you know or together develop others. Together, you can enhance your abilities to be aroused and to arouse each other.

Differing Sensory Styles

One way two individuals can differ is in their dominant sensory languages (Cameron-Bandler,1985). Most people are more developed in one or two senses than in the others. When partners' strongest senses differ, problems with sexual initiation, communication, and pleasuring may occur until the couple discovers satisfying ways to incorporate the dominant styles of both partners.

I listen for sensory style by noting which senses are referred to in the words clients typically use and by having them consider the relationship between their language and their sexual turn ons. Individuals might each make a list of favorite sexual turn ons. Each partner needs attention to his or her preferred senses to most readily turn on and fully enjoy sex. Together we consider how the couple can develop sexual invitations and transition rituals or activities that include the dominant sensory languages of both partners.

Focus of Attention During Lovemaking

Another realm in which partners might find themselves either similar in style and expectations or quite different involves their focus of attention during lovemaking and the sexual scripts that shape their expectations. Mosher (1980) discussed the dimensions of sexual role enactment, sexual trance, and engagement with the sex partner. I draw on his ideas and language here, and I highly recommend reading his article.

Some individuals and couples, for example, are drawn to active pursuit of novelty and excitement in their sex lives. A novel thrill or novel self-expression may seem more important in the sexual moment than whether sex is safe, comfortable, or sometimes even physically enjoyable. Sex may have a story line and fantasies may be acted out, perhaps with props and costumes (Mosher, 1980). Another, quite different sexual style involves attention drawn inward into sensation and, eventually, orgasm. Mental imagery may be scriptless sensory images rather than stories. "Receptive joy" may predominate over passion; sexual techniques may be less playful and emphasize repetitive, sensual pacing that draws the partners into an intimate trance (Mosher, 1980; Ellison, 1986). Attention during sex also may be predominantly absorbed into one's loving relationship with one's partner. Sex may be experienced as a loving merger, a momentary loss of self (Mosher, 1980), as described by a woman I interviewed (Ellison, 2000):

> I love, when I'm coming, to be able to look in his eyes and say "I love you" and just feel lost, merged with this person for a brief moment in time. I think this only happens now because I've a real clear sense of my own boundaries and he has a real good sense of his, so we are able to merge together and become one for a time, knowing that afterwards we will separate and become once again our separate selves. . . . There's a moment when I don't know where he leaves off and I begin and vice versa and we're merged and it has this real spiritual aspect to it. Participating in that experience is the most wonderful part of sex with love.

A client who reports needing to focus attention on other than her or his partner in order to become aroused may be offering a clue to the therapist about relationship problems. As one woman stated, "I had to use fantasy when I was having sex with my husband toward the end of our marriage because he didn't turn me on anymore" (Ellison, 2000).

Whether it is desirable that fantasies be shared and attention unified during sex has to be considered within the context of the individual partnership. If a difference in style or expectations is causing a problem, that difference can be addressed without one partner's style having to be right and the other's wrong. One approach to resolving problems is for the couple to share images of how each partner would like sex to be, and then to experiment with new sexual scripts. Sex might, for example, incorporate images and expectations from both partners (e.g., romantic poetry and sexy costuming); on other occasions one or the other might produce and direct the show. A couple might also seek out new images and experiment with ways of having sex that are entirely new to both, such as Tantric practices.

Differences in Addressing Differences

Another difference that might affect a couple's ability to bridge from separateness to the togetherness of sex is their individual styles of addressing the differences between them. These, too, may become a focus of the therapist's attention. John Gottman, for example, noted in *Why Marriages Succeed or Fail*—a good resource for understanding the various styles couples use in attempting to resolve their differences—that the survival of a relationship depends on "how well disagreements and grievances are aired . . . how [partners] argue—whether [their] style escalates tension or leads to a feeling of resolution" (1994, p. 173).

Intimacy Thrives on Separateness—and Togetherness.

In having sex, two individuals may seek to merge their boundaries to create a single pleasurable field of synchronized arousal. Couples who feel comfortably close much of the time might find it easier to make the transition into this state than, for example, partners who have a brick wall of resentments between them that they have to dismantle or get around before they can be close. It is possible, however, for a couple to have difficulties because the partners feel too comfortably close. Desire and sexual arousal require some separateness, some polarity, across which sexual tension can occur.

Initial interventions for some couples will include both suggestions to increase intimate activities that facilitate experiences and feelings of togetherness and individual activities that fill needs for more separateness. Other couples may need to focus first on either more intimacy or more separateness. A woman with a breastfeeding baby, for example, may feel so merged with her infant that she craves time just for herself.

☐ Sharon and Dave

Sharon and Dave,[1] a heterosexual couple, consulted me for therapy. They had had other couple's therapy in their 11 years of marriage, and now they wanted to focus on their sexual issues. They reported a lack of attraction to each other, although a 4-month separation earlier in the year had led to Dave "falling back in love with Sharon," experiencing a sexual awakening, and feeling hopeful about their marriage and sexual possibilities. He returned excited, with a lot of sexual energy and wanting to try new things. However, in the ensuing 6 months they had fallen back into old patterns, their sexual situation had deteriorated again, and Dave was currently feeling angry, resentful, and without much hope. Dave reported that Sharon would not respond, and he would withdraw. "What's the point of trying to be romantic—getting flowers?" he lamented. In creating the dance of sex, one thing leads to another. "Where are the steps where Dave and Sharon begin to get off the track?" was a question I would have to answer.

Sharon reported no desire to have sex with Dave and hardly ever feeling sexual with him. She found specific things unappealing, particu-

---

1. Sharon and Dave are based on a real couple, but in this chapter they are a composite of several couples with whom I have worked. This protects their identities and allows me to present aspects of intimacy-based sex therapy that did not apply specifically to them.

larly the way he kissed. She did feel sexual by herself, however, an indication to me that she was capable of sexual desire.

Sharon noted that in therapy in the past she had been resistant to exercises, but she was now willing to participate in them in an attempt to preserve the marriage. But, she emphasized, she wanted to start slowly. She had little faith either that sex would get better or that Dave would not attempt to turn anything they tried into sex, but she wanted to at least start.

I told her I did not think of what they would be doing at home as "exercises," but as "experiments" in which they would try to see what happened. We would figure out together what these experiments would be, discuss the outcomes, and proceed from there.

On Saturday mornings in the previous couple of months, Sharon and Dave had both enjoyed staying in bed talking, including sexual talk. But, they said, it hadn't "worked." Sharon reported that Dave would do things she didn't like; also, she didn't know what Dave liked sexually. I wondered—and asked them—what they imagined "working" would be. Neither could answer clearly, but the image their words created indicated that they both wanted more-or-less the same thing: That a situation like their Saturday mornings in bed together could evolve smoothly into mutually desired sex without Sharon feeling that Dave was pushing her for sex or Dave feeling that Sharon was pushing him away.

I told Sharon and Dave that I typically think of a couple as sexually successful when they create mutual erotic pleasure, to whatever level and in whatever form they desire on any particular occasion; each would end up feeling good about him- or herself and the other, realizing that they had a good time and enhanced their relationship. I pointed out that this definition of success addresses erotic pleasure but does not say anything about how stimulation occurs or include any particular aspect of physical responsiveness. Sharon felt relieved when she heard this, because it did not require her to have sexual intercourse.

I asked Dave and Sharon what they might do together during the next week that would leave them with the feelings described in my definition of success, and together we determined what that might be. Sharon said she was not ready for Dave to touch her, so I asked her for a starting place. She suggested—and both agreed—that she would spend 15 minutes touching him in ways that pleased her. I instructed them that Dave was to protect her from displeasing him by letting her know if she was touching him in any way that was uncomfortable or that he did not like. Other than that, she was to touch him for her own pleasure, and he was not to tell her how to do it.

I also talked about personal and interpersonal transitions. For Sharon and Dave, one aspect of the need for transition seemed particularly relevant. Sometimes stimulation that is too specifically sexual before an individual experiences consent and feels somewhat relaxed and receptive is irritating and unpleasant, causes her or him to pull away, and inhibits instead of facilitates arousal. I suspected that this explained some of Sharon's lack of receptivity for intimate touch.

Sharon and Dave—Session 2

A week later, Sharon and Dave returned for their second therapy session. Sharon had touched Dave for 15 minutes the previous night, and she described the experience as "better than I thought it would be." She told me she had put it out of her mind and been scared to do it the rest of the week. She was afraid of Dave's response—that he might try to turn the touching into "sex," and that it would not be enjoyable. She said she had watched the time and felt safe that way. We discussed how, in terms of my conceptualization of success, they had been successful.

Because one of Sharon's issues was the way Dave touched her, I guided them in doing hand and arm caresses, with Sharon the first to receive. I began by suggesting that they both take several slow, deep breaths and begin to focus their attention inward. I continued with images for relaxation, centering, and taking all the time they needed. Gradually I shifted Dave's attention to his hands. I had him rub his hands together to warm them and to experience the energy there, and then, very slowly—as I continued encouraging him to breathe deeply and remain centered—to place his hands on one of hers, shifting his attention between her hand and his. A step at a time, in a hypnotic tone of voice, I continued to guide him through an about-10-minute hand and arm caress, during which Sharon found she could enjoy his touch very much. They then reversed roles. I suggested that touching this way was kind of like a meditation, an image that Dave, especially, liked. I added that kissing, too, could be like a meditation.

Sharon's reaction to my description of "weeknight sex" was a realization that even genital holding or caressing was still too much for her, although she was ready for Dave to touch her. We ended the second session with an agreement that Dave and Sharon would exchange back rubs at some time during the week.

The transition into massage—or, for that matter, into sex—can proceed more smoothly and effectively if distracting details are taken care of ahead of time. I suggested to Sharon and Dave that for them some details might include putting on music, reviewing the ground rules we had set up, and talking about anything that was on their minds that might be making them feel unwilling to be close. This last item was particularly aimed at Sharon, who had a tendency to withdraw and think about something that was bothering her rather than letting Dave in on what it was.

Sharon and Dave Two Weeks Later—Session 3

In the two-week interim Sharon and Dave had experimented with affirming their loving and caring at bedtime, although not every night; they had not exchanged backrubs. Dave had noticed how busy they were; he was concerned about Sharon's lack of interest and said he was starting to push sex down; it took too much energy to carry this by himself, so he was trying not think about it; it was too frustrating. Sharon said that she wanted Dave to ask when he wanted a massage and not leave initiating up to her.

Where did they get off the track? I noted that they were having difficulties with initiation and transition, and that they needed to put structure around their spontaneity within their very busy lives. I had them mark specific times on their calendars to do the back massages, and left fewer decisions up to them about how they would be carried out. They went home with their massages planned in great detail. They knew who would go first, where their son would be at the time, who would turn on the music, who would warm the massage oil, and so on. I instructed them to begin either with a shared bath or by sitting on the edge of the bathtub talking for 10 to 15 minutes while they soaked their feet in warm water. We scheduled the next session in two weeks, but I told them to call me in one week if they were not back on track or if they were experiencing any problems.

To Get Out of Your Head, Start With Your Feet. Because Dave and Sharon had difficulty turning off their very active minds, I suggested that they start their massage activity—and later their sexual activity—with foot soaking or caressing. As they relaxed, attention and caressing could be moved up their bodies to their backs or, later, when their intention was sex, to their genitals. Sharon welcomed the images of soaking their feet and foot massages but knew she was not yet ready for genital caressing. I reminded them that what you do and how you do it are less important than that you are able to create an experience that enhances your relationship and leaves you feeling good about yourselves and each other.

Sharon and Dave Two Weeks Later—Session 4

They had done the massages, with Dave massaging Sharon first. Sharon had found the massage pleasant but had become somewhat frustrated when she sensed that Dave wasn't enjoying doing it. Dave had enjoyed massaging Sharon and using the oil, but about half way through he could tell that Sharon was not into it. Sharon said that, thinking about it now, she needed more transition; they had skipped the bath or foot soaking because they thought it would take too long. She liked the image of taking all the time you need and realized that talking and doing things together were ways for her to feel close. With respect to the complication of a teenaged son in the house she said. "It's nice to go away, or our son could go away overnight and we could stay home." Dave had enjoyed being massaged and had fallen asleep while Sharon was massaging him.

I worked with Dave and Sharon on the importance of speaking up when something was frustrating, telling them that speaking up was necessary both for intimacy and for getting what they wanted. Sharon's not speaking up, in particular, was one key to their difficulties, and at each session she presented me with at least one opportunity to model how she might speak up and redirect a situation so that it would not be displeasing or frustrating for her.

I again emphasized the need for transition. "Transition can take all day, and once you begin to massage—or to have sex—it's okay to stop in the middle," I told them. I repeated my earlier instructions: "You are each responsible for protecting the other from displeasing or frustrating you." Both specifically indicated they were still quite tense about having sex.

In therapy, I worked with Sharon and Dave on making and responding to sexual invitations more effectively so they could negotiate to mutually consensual sexual intimacy. I also gave them a handout with information on initiating and responding to sexual invitations. I occasionally give this handout to a thoughtful couple who, like Sharon and Dave, might benefit from taking it home and discussing its principles.

Sharon and Dave Four Weeks Later—Session 5

Dave and Sharon postponed this session because of the holiday season, and by the time they returned for therapy they had not only successfully exchanged massages, but also twice had engaged in mutually desired sexual intercourse. On the first occasion, their son was away overnight; on the second, he was asleep when they returned home from a Christmas party, where they had consumed a moderate amount of alcohol. They mentioned that Sharon had been dressed up both times, and Sharon made a comment about alcohol being "cheating." I noted that a glass of wine could be a very effective facilitator for sexual transition; given that neither had an addictive problem with alcohol, they might at times choose to use a moderate amount to enhance a sexual experience.

Sharon reported that she had particularly been helped by the concept of transitions and the idea that she could take all of the time she needed to get turned on. She was eager to plan something again soon; for her, such planning was better than spontaneity. Dave found planning helpful, but he also experienced it as creating some pressure. It was helpful to him also to know there was no hurry. Dave noted that the second time had been especially nice and that they had done a lot of kissing. Sharon said that kissing seemed a natural thing to do, and she had no complaints.

Dave and Sharon were interested in planning sexual opportunities and exploring new things, for example, the vibrator a woman friend had recently given to Sharon and the erotic video Sharon had given Dave for Christmas. They affirmed that they would continue to schedule weekly dates with each other and would see me once a month. The structure created by having a scheduled therapy session was helpful to them.

During this session I talked with Dave and Sharon about building arousal through simmering. *Simmering* is lighting a pilot light of arousal and keeping the arousal fueled—simmering it—in anticipation of later sex (Zilbergeld & Ellison, 1980). I suggested to Dave that some afternoon he call Sharon at work and suggest spending erotic time together later that evening. This would let their mutual arousal begin to build. Perhaps this would be a time when their son was out for the evening. When they got home, they might greet in a sexually suggestive way, touch, and give each other cues that said, I'm looking forward to later. And, I advised them: Don't stay up too late!

After five sessions, Sharon and Dave were once again having sex. They had progressed in the direction they wanted to go. Their sexual difficulties were not fully resolved, in that, for example, Sharon still withdrew at times without letting Dave know what was bothering her, and Dave still sometimes threw his hands up in frustration. But they had begun to learn and to experience the principles of sexual choreography and they had created a structure within which they could continue making progress toward their goal.

☐ Conclusion

What appears to be spontaneity is one thing leading to another, a step at a time. We can create a mood. We can create erotic pleasure. We do the best we can to create an erotic experience that flows freely without distraction by putting a structure around our spontaneity. We can establish the time and the place. We can enhance the setting and remove distractions. And then we can surrender control and be spontaneous as one thing leads to another. The sexual choreographer facilitates belief in this process and stimulates the imagination of the couple as to how they can create opportunities and let this happen.

Above all, the sexual choreographer focuses on enabling a couple to create erotic experiences—in whatever appropriate form their lovemaking may take—in which each feels good about her- or himself and about the other and has an enjoyable time.

☐ References

American Psychiatric Association (1994). *Diagnostic and statistical manual of mental disorders* (4th ed.). Washington, DC: Author.

Barker-Benfield. G. J. (1976). *The horrors of the half-known life*. NY: Harper & Row.

Brauer, A., & Brauer, D. (1983). **ESO: The new promise of pleasure for couples in love (*extended sexual orgasm)*. New York: Warner.

Cameron-Bandler, L. (1985). *Solutions: Enhancing love, sex, and relationships*. Moab, UT: Real People Press.

Chesser, E. (1947/1957). *Love without fear: A plain guide to sex technique for every married adult*. New York: Rich & Cowan.

Ellison, C. R. (1984). Harmful beliefs affecting the practice of sex therapy with women. *Psychotherapy, 21*(3), 327–334.

Ellison, C. R. (1986). Using intimate trance to increase sexual satisfaction. In B. Zilbergeld, M. G. Edelstien, & D. L. Araoz (Eds.), *Questions and answers in the practice of hypnosis* (pp. 211–218). New York: W.W. Norton.

Ellison, C. R. (1987). *Consenting to be intimate: Effective sexual negotiation*. Paper presented to the national meeting of the Society for the Scientific Study of Sexuality, Atlanta.

Ellison, C. R. (2000). *Women's sexualities. Generations of women share intimate secrets of sexual self-acceptance*. Oakland, CA: New Harbinger.

Gottman, J. (1994). *Why marriages succeed or fail*. New York: Simon & Schuster.

Hartman, W., & Fithian, M. (1984). *Any man can: Multiply orgasmic technique for every loving man*. New York: St. Martin's Press.

Ladas, A. K., Whipple, B., & Perry, J. D. (1982). *The g spot*. New York: Holt, Rinehart & Winston.

Masson, J. M.. (1986). *A dark science: Women, sexuality and psychiatry in the nineteenth century*. New York: Noonday.

Masters, W. H., & Johnson, V. E. (1970). *Human sexual inadequacy*. Boston: Little, Brown.

Mosher, D. L. (1980). Three dimensions of depth of involvement in human sexual response. *Journal of Sex Research, 16*, 1–42.

Rajneesh, B. S. (1976). *Tantra spirituality and sex*. San Francisco: Rainbow Bridge.

Rosenberg, J. L. (1973). *Total orgasm*. New York: Random House.

Szasz, T. (1980). *Sex by prescription*. New York: Anchor/Doubleday.

Van de Velde, T. H. (1926/1968). *Ideal marriage: Its physiology and technique*. New York: Random House.

Zilbergeld, B., & Ellison, C. R. (1980). Desire discrepancies and arousal problems in sex therapy. In S. R. Leiblum & L. A. Pervin (Eds.), *Principles and practice of sex therapy*. New York: Guilford Press.

9

CHAPTER

Jeanne Shaw, Ph.D.

Approaching Sexual Potential in Relationship: A Reward of Age and Maturity

A reward of maturity is the opportunity to reach for, and arrive at, sexual potential. Sexual potential is the highest mental, emotional, physical, and spiritual level to which we can aspire sexually. Although it may not be built into our reproductive code to take sex to the most intensely erotic level possible, the potential is there just the same. Individual limits to reaching sexual potential depend on our ability to soothe ourselves, tolerate anxiety, manage pressure to conform, observe and use contradiction and conflict, and feel autonomous in a committed relationship. Reaching for sexual potential requires us to acknowledge ourselves and our partners as whole and growing, not defectives who need to change.

Sandy and Warner are participants in a survey of sexually active older couples. They have been together for 49 years. When queried about the sexual aspect of their relationship, their self-satisfied smiles reveal that sex is as important to them now as it was in the beginning. Sandy reports:

> We were both young and naive when we got together. We learned with each other how to make sex work, there were no sex manuals in those days, and no information other than how babies are made. We didn't always agree about sex, money, energy, and time. If we hadn't each learned to stand up for ourselves, argue with good will, back off without resentment, and resolve our intolerable differences, we surely would have separated.

As it was, we each have felt enraged at major rough times along the way. We are both blessed with a good sense of the ridiculous and can laugh at ourselves. That helped us gain self-respect. I cannot say enough about how crucial self-respect was for our sex life, because in the early days it was just developing. We were sacrificing to please each other until that became tiresome, and anyway it didn't help. We had to take a good look at ourselves to discover that needing each other or needing the other to be different caused disrespect, which made sex feel sort of incestuous to me, young, clingy, and whiny.

But, *desiring* each other was an invitation, not a sneaky demand to be serviced, and desire could be accepted or postponed without guilt. It wasn't easy feeling guilt-free and grown-up in my generation, the 1940s war years. We both had to make a major effort to outgrow the notion of that time when couples' relationships were hierarchical, with the man at the helm. We had so much growing up to do; when I look back on it, I'm glad I'm not young anymore.

Even with all the hard work of growing up together, I think sex actually changed for the better after the initial rush wore off and disillusionment set in. That's when I knew I had to stretch my limits to get real, or feel controlled and miserable for the rest of my life. I wanted to see who the real Warner was, not my dream image. Another life-changing decision in the early days was deciding not to conform to both our families' rules about harmony: "Don't say anything, keep it in," or, "Don't rock the boat." As if another person's happiness or expression of anger were my responsibility. Going against ingrained values made us both plenty anxious, but we finally decided we were adult enough to follow our own values. It took us many years to go head-to-head with each other and both emerge feeling better than before. We still enjoy each other sexually; we feel real joy in connecting physically. Sex is very different, now than in our youth, or even 20 years ago. It is not so physically strenuous now, yet, in many ways, it is infinitely sweeter and more precious. At this stage, we are nearer the end, so we treasure what we have.

The feelings of Sandy and Warner reflect the behavior and feelings of couples who have the maturity and integrity to love intimately and erotically.

☐ The Person of the Therapist

My interest in learning from sexually active couples in successful working relationships evolves from the perspective that looking for health serves clients as well, if not better, than looking for pathology. The research I have conducted on the sexuality of older people (Shaw, 1994b) has informed my practice and affected the scope of my clinical objectives. It has led me to approach sex therapy from a different paradigm than I had between 1970 and 1990. The shift was as hard for me after 30 years of practice as the changes long-term couples must engender to create erotic sex. Consequently, this chapter is not focused on the "how tos" of doing sex therapy, but rather on the *person of the therapist* being with couples, making a difference. The key to my clinical approach is not only that I do not emphasize my clients' sexual techniques in relationship, but that I, too, am being as true as I can be to who I am without using the instructional techniques from my training. The basic theoretical principle that informs my work (and my living) is that the therapist's personal development, level of differentiation, and ability to connect with integrity are more significant to the outcome of therapy than skill at applying techniques (Kopp, 1977; Whitaker & Malone, 1953/1981).

The level of differentiation I am reaching through my own personal efforts and a new direction in sex therapy makes a profound difference in my work, not only with long-term results for couples but also with my own continuing enjoyment, increased energy, and expanding skill being a psychotherapist and sex therapist.

Strongly grounded in the theories of object relations, Gestalt, Transactional Analysis, Pesso System Psychomotor, and the multigenerational family therapy approach of Murray Bowen and others, the most lasting influence on my development as a therapist was cultivated from the early experiential school of psychotherapy with John Warkentin, Carl Whitaker, Richard Felder, and Thomas Malone. Each of these psychotherapists has had a different personal and professional influence on my life and work. Their most valuable lesson was that effective therapists are those who have had their own effective therapy and excellent supervision.

My approach to psychotherapy and sex therapy with couples rests on the philosophy that my task is to promote self-understanding and awareness in relationships. While I am in charge of the therapy process, my own presence, and attention for the therapy hour, couples are in charge of running their own lives. Because I am not attached to the outcome, the income, or their approval, I am free to be who I am instead of whomever couples wish me to be (e.g., an impartial judge, nurturing mother, benevolent teacher, or director of family in-service).

When couples present what they believe is a simple sexual problem, I no longer give them an opportunity to discover whether first degree change (e.g., a homework assignment) will resolve their sexual problem.

A new client, when queried, said he came to see me because his friend (a former client) had assured him I do not give advice. I have come to respect what I used to label *resistance,* that astute thing clients do to avoid the advice that will co-opt their integrity by doing for them what they could do for themselves. I do believe that problems, especially sexual problems, are gold mines for fostering maturity, nurturing integrity, and moving toward sexual potential.

☐ Promoting Sexual Maturity: A New Direction for Sex Therapy

The field of sex therapy began, and largely continues, with a primary focus on helping people overcome sexual dysfunction. The dysfunction model, with its aim of finding what has gone wrong and treating that and only that, has been the conventional sex therapy approach throughout more than this century. At present, conventional treatment options focus on goals such as increasing desire through hotter fantasies and more skillful genital stimulation, lengthening the time between arousal and orgasm, developing enough stimulation to have an orgasm, and getting more pleasure from the experience. These are fine goals, but goals are just the tip of the iceberg. Practicing therapy *without* goals is an experience many therapists seem reluctant to explore, especially in these times of goal-oriented, third-party reimbursement. Having goals is not inherently bad, it is only a way of *doing* something. The experience of *being* who you are in relationship to your life partner is not goal-friendly in a behavioral sense.

Goal-oriented sex therapy is no surprise, since the human sexual response cycle model (Masters and Johnson, 1966) that helped trigger a paradigm shift over 30 years ago is, itself, goal-oriented. Flaws in this model have been described by a number of clinicians, including Tiefer:

> Defining the essence of sexuality as a specific sequence of physiological changes promotes biological reductionism. Biological reductionism not only separates genital sexual performance from personalities, relationships, conduct, context, and values, but also overvalues the former at the expense of the latter . . . studying parts may be easier than studying people, but what do you understand when you're through? (1995, pp. 57–58)

Sexual behavior is not simply a physical act; it is a reflection of who we are and what is or is not happening in our relationships. Sex has generic and unique meanings to each partner; when we focus on techniques and behavioral goals before couples understand the meaning of sex, we interrupt or sidetrack their growth. We practice sex therapy as if the behavior we are treating is either functional or dysfunctional, when it might be more useful to couples if we look at what sex means and how that is reflected in their everyday relationship to each other. Exploring the reverse may be even more productive—that is, looking at what their relationship means and how that is reflected in the way they have sex. Sexual issues and relational problems are inherent in human development. They serve as a mighty impetus in pushing us toward maturity.

The premises that relationship problems and struggles are predictable and natural, and that sexual problems are fertile ground for growth, are not new; but they are concepts we have largely ignored, at least in the 25 years I have been in the field. A new direction in sex therapy is evolving that is less concerned with sexual frequency, behavior, and techniques and more concerned with promoting the treatment of sexual symptoms as a vehicle for, and a reflection of, personality development, maturity, and integrity (Schnarch, 1991).

Behavioral change may signify positive development (maturing), or not. Knowing the difference between maturing and behavior change, which may signify nothing more than compliance, is crucial to a relevant therapy outcome. While sex therapists cannot neglect goal-oriented behavioral change, we need to understand that it takes personal development and relational energy to move most positively toward sexual expression. When treatment ignores individual maturity, confuses genital skill with sexual energy, and disregards the meanings already present in sexual interactions, we miss very important points. We must not continue to separate sex from loving, sex from meaning, and sex from maturing. While skills and attitudes are undeniable developmental components, they are only basic building blocks to lifelong sexuality. With some exceptions (e.g., Apfelbaum, 1980, 1989; Malone & Malone, 1987; Schnarch, 1991, 1997; Shaw, 1997; Shaw & Erhardt, 1997; Tiefer, 1995), we have yet to observe and define the *advanced* skills that would allow us to move toward sexual potential.

The interventions for primary vaginismus and delayed ejaculation are examples of our progress in changing sexual *behavior*, but they also exemplify how we have ignored sexual *growth* (Apfelbaum, 1989; Shaw, 1990, 1994a). Our knowledge is currently at the level where we can teach women with primary vaginismus to permit vaginal penetration; however, if this is all we do, are we not providing simple symptom relief without offering partners the possibility of maturing sufficiently to enjoy effective, *lasting* sexual expression and erotic connection? Compliance with relaxation exercises that result in penile penetration rewards a woman and her partner with penetration, but it often neglects the steps that could help develop more effective ego boundaries (i.e., making firm decisions for herself without compliance to outside pressure or need for approval). Helping a woman take emotional charge of herself so that she decides *consciously* how, when, where, and with whom she will use her body to express her wholeness (and to receive love and whatever else she wants) is a step we should help her take *before* training her pubococcygeal muscles to relax.

We can teach a man with delayed ejaculation to avoid emotional pressure during penetrative sex with a partner, but we often neglect his conscious responsibility *to himself*. A man who gets erections automatically without sexual arousal has a compulsive need to please his partner and feels intense response anxiety (in this case, fear of not being aroused when he, in fact, is *not* aroused but thinks he should be because he has an erection); he is being over-responsible to his partner, but under-responsible *in his relationship to himself while he is with his partner*. Taking charge of himself consciously requires learning to respect his connection to himself, and thereby identify, decide, and express with intent to his partner what his body says so eloquently. Alerting him to the opportunity for sexual and personality growth seems more humane than giving homework techniques that may change his behavior but will not increase his ability to *feel himself in his own body* in relationship.

Thus, instead of learning only pubococcygeal muscle awareness, partners can begin to know and express their real selves, set appropriate personal limits and boundaries, and tolerate being loved in the face of whatever that love means. Partners learn to feel complete in relationship as opposed to being repaired defectives. Changing our models based on what works behaviorally, seeking to add depth to that as well as searching for new directions for what works poorly, and looking for opportunities to discover new possibilities seem like logical next steps.

☐ Shifting Paradigms

Sex therapy has consisted of behavioral or cognitive-behavioral approaches for half a century. It has been moving along in a considerably more humane direction than in preceding years, when a problem of desire meant a woman had some and masturbation was considered a mental disorder. To invite a change in paradigm, a crisis is needed. As therapists, we should look at our own levels of differentiation (maturity) and sexual potential.

With a shift from the skills-and-attitude model to one that moves beyond behavior and communication to personal growth in relationship, we discover new horizons in human sexual potential. Couples desire sexual experience that encompasses adequate genital functioning and moves beyond adequacy. After the brief stage of romantic love, when partners sincerely expect to feel attracted to each other for life, they are very often surprised at the force with which the inevitable power struggle shifts or shatters their early hopes and dreams. However, power struggles, and the clues they leave in their wake, are opportunities that offer at least two possibilities for change:

1. The disintegration of dependency fantasies often experienced as disillusionment, but actually normal and useful.

2. The opportunity to mature in relationship, increasing integrity and intimacy, often experienced as wholeness and renewed sexual energy.

Couples who use power struggles in the service of insight and growth rarely find their way to therapy. Those who do, come with the hope of being lovers again. They want to stop feeling like roommates with boring or no sexual behavior. Or, they want to stop feeling adversarial around sex ("Doc, our relationship is *perfect* except for sex. Fix *her/his* problem and everything will be great again.") These couples are understandably protecting their survival energies while they tirelessly avoid, deflect, deny, and refocus the anxiety they are paying us to expose. Instead of communicating somatically through arousal and orgasm problems, loss of sexual desire, passive withdrawal, and other means, when therapists (and ultimately the field of sex therapy) shift to a growth perspective, we encourage partners to be who they are in the relationship. When a sexual problem arises, it becomes the point from which partners increase their individual ability to support themselves, meet each other's energy face-to-face, and like who they are becoming in relationship to the other. Mediocre genital functioning, compromised integrity, and underdeveloped maturity need attention even after behaviorally successful therapy.

Our entire culture has been confused about adequate sex. We have long believed that orgasm is the primary measure of sexual satisfaction for both partners, no matter how nonerotic, merely adequate, or unremarkable those orgasms become. We have appropriately suggested puboccocygeal muscle exercises to strengthen orgasms, but how many couples understand what is happening in their relationship, or know what the language of their sexual behavior *means*? How many partners, without puboccocygeal muscle exercise, have you heard talk about puny orgasms at home and bed rocking orgasms during an affair? While orgasms are a delicious piece of the action, couples need more than orgasms to develop erotic sex *in relationship*. More than genital response, couples need the maturity that will guide them toward sexual expression as a reflection of who they are and how they bond.

Some of us are beginning to hear and heed the growing pains of couples with sexual dissatisfactions by attending to their next level of maturity instead of prescribing heavier fantasies, sexier lingerie, fancier vibrators, more explicit videos, more sexual adventures, more vacation time, and more genital mechanics to help revitalize sex. All of these techniques are described ad nauseam in self-help books that help only until they become boring, too.

We are beginning to listen for the meaning of sex to each partner at the same time we are noticing their levels of maturity. It is a rare long-term couple who comes to therapy knowing they have not yet matured enough to have really hot sex. Unfortunately, it is also a rare therapist who knows that hot sex happens between committed partners who have enough maturity to be deeply sexual in relationship *even, or perhaps especially, when they feel tremendous anxiety about being deeply sexual in relationship.*

☐ Increasing Sexuality in Relationship: Lessons from Sex Research for Sex Therapists

Early in 1990, I was working with a larger than usual number of post-midlife couples in sex therapy. These couples did not want stronger orgasms, they wanted erotic sex. Working with them led to the idea of collecting other people's stories about sex and aging as a way to widen my understanding of possibilities, to find out how and if older couples actually reached for sexual potential and what that experience was like for them. Furthermore, I hoped I could use the data to enhance my clinical work. Consequently, a query went out to people who might have answers: colleagues, friends, relatives, workshop and seminar participants, and whomever they recommended (over 50 years old).

The ensuing survey of self-described, sexually active older people (including 65 couples ranging in age from 50 to 93 years; Shaw, 1994b) made a strong case for differentiation as a major gateway to sexual actualization. The length of their relationships ranged from newlyweds to couples who had been together more than 60 years. Sexual orientation included 57 heterosexual couples, 4 male couples, and 4 lesbian couples.

Survey interviews were guided by the question, "To what do you attribute your present sexual growth and maturity?" The initial finding—that an easily located segment of older couples still have fulfilling sex—is important for what it can teach us about sexual attraction and sexual development in long-term relationships. Survey results question some of the inaccuracies about sexuality and aging, such as the celibacy stereotype or delicate-sex sentiment we have about older couples.

A highlight of the survey was that most respondents reported sexually active, sexually satisfying, surprisingly sweet, intense (if infrequent) *physical* sex. Not surprisingly, there was a high correlation between advanced age (over 87) and lower frequency of genital contact; but what was surprising was the fervor with which people of advanced age spoke or wrote about sex. If sexual energy is *not* unusual among couples who have been together for a long time, it raises the question of whether couples in therapy might want to consider this development for themselves. An obstacle may be a therapist who has no clue about the possibility of reaching sexual potential in such elderly couples and who therefore does not think to explore that topic.

Information gleaned from the survey helped shift my perspective about therapy outcome for all couples. Since erotic sex is possible and valuable in long-term relationships, a hard question arose: Is settling for less than what is possible acceptable for therapists of couples who are clearly looking for more than mere physical adequacy?

The survey helped in identifying the characteristics that lead to enduring sexual attraction, sexual energy, and actualizing sexual potential. In the case of sexual potential, the favorable conditions seem to include high levels of differentiation. Although some people may become mature enough to fulfill their sexual potential early in life, more of us take until midlife and beyond to develop such levels of differentiation.

On the other hand, some couples reach a certain level of intellectual maturity, eschew the risk of emotional growth, and experience change in any direction as though it were a threat to survival. We are all too familiar with the successful professionals and entrepreneurs who are brilliant in their fields and emotionally avoidant in their relationships, therapists included. To these couples, remaining the same—stagnation—seems the only logical choice until one partner notices and objects to the deadness that ensues with avoidance of change. It is unfortunate that therapists have more exposure to couples who are stuck in sexual and relational problems than to couples having glorious sex, although exceptions occasionally happen.

The survey couples' description of sexual potential confirms the maturing process of differentiation that Schnarch (1991, 1997) suggested is necessary for erotic sex between life partners. Survey participants illustrated the positive correlation between differentiation, continued sexual energy, and sexual potential.

Definition of Differentiation

Differentiation is an unwieldy family therapy term that, in layman's language, means consciously maturing—that is, defining who you are in relationship, thinking for yourself with consideration for your partner, soothing your own anxiety, and behaving with self-respect, responsibility, and integrity. The terms differentiation, maturity, and growth are used synonymously in this chapter. A differentiation or growth approach invites therapists of various theoretical persuasions to consider new perspectives for sexual relationships through claiming responsibility, consequences, and rewards for their own proactivity, reactivity, and projections.

Definition of "Sexual Potential"

Sexual potential is the height of your personal capacity for sexual pleasure and expression. The height of erotic sex requires conscious tolerance for high anxiety and a way to manage that in relationship, a measure of audacity, and the courage to love in the face of inevitable loss. Sometimes this means holding onto your sanity and calming yourself while your anxiety is high—then moving ahead, anyway. Ways to do this include breathing consciously, opening your mind to a real rather than a dreaded event, saying to your partner the very unspeakable truth you learned in childhood should never be uttered, convincing yourself that catastrophe is manageable, and meeting your partner's energy with your competent adult self.

Young adults who believe they have reached their sexual peak when they are intensely, uninhibitedly genital with each other do not realize that they are only beginning the journey from young adult sexual behavior to post-midlife sexual wisdom. The mature bonding of physical with emotional energy requires time to develop beyond the struggles inherent in the first decades of a committed relationship. Fulfilling sexual potential involves the nongenital, nonromantic, down-to-earth, ebb-and-flow aspect of human sexuality that comes with vintage living.

Being genital is different from being sexual. Being *genital* is a reflection of behavior, feeling "horny," wanting pleasure and release, a youthful desire also seen in old people. Being *sexual* includes genitality, but also is a reflection of who you are, your experience and expression of being alive and related. It is knowing the difference between doing and being. Both are lively feelings, but *being* sexual lasts for life and consistently nourishes one's individual growth and oneself-in-relationship.

Feeling sexual desire before, during, and after sex invites union, agreement, and maturity. A maturing partner can express the truth of his or her experience, such as: "I especially miss you when we're humping and I don't feel your presence. I have rethought my own tolerance for impersonal sex, and from now on I will make sure I am connecting with you mentally and emotionally, especially when I want to be physical with you." This unconventional perspective fosters presence, self-respect, and the *discomfort* of facing what you are, yourself, personally creating in your relationship. In the future, the nonphysical, nongenital aspect of a deeply sexual love connection and the sacredness of primitive sexual expression with a life partner may both be recognized as sexual potential.

Example of Actualizing Sexual Potential

Al and Dianna, survey participants, demonstrate how maturity, erotic sex, and the actualization of sexual potential go hand-in-hand. They also reflect the responses of survey couples who have the courage to love. Loving is a courageous act because loss is *always* the outcome. They have been married for more than 60 years, glad they stayed together through some "very tough times." Al says sex became better than ever after the first 27 years, when children were grown and gone, finances were better, careers were made, and the power struggle dispersed. This allowed them to be who they really were instead of who they thought they should be, and accept the "default" decision that, no matter what, they would spend the rest of their lives together. Al says,

> That "default" decision helped relieve us of the struggle for control. After that, sex got better than ever. On some occasions we began to melt into each other, and at those times it was especially erotic. We have always had sex for pleasure, fun, love, getting "down and dirty," relief, relaxation, and sometimes because there was nothing else to do. But for the last few decades, when we feel especially intimate, something else happens. When we are feeling particularly loving and attracted to each other, my–her–our sexual energy becomes so profoundly erotic—and merged—that it feels downright sacred. The feeling is indescribable. We both experience a kind of light shining around us. Dianna says she feels it streaming from her feet through her genitals to the top of her head, like cool sunshine, only brighter. Mine streams from my genitals out, down my legs and up my torso. We have talked about it, privately, at length. This might sound corny, but we think our lovemaking is so intense that we make light together, like we are making a blessing. Dianna is radiant for days after we make love in that special way. I am, too. We both have a few chronic health problems now, but our sex life is good.

This soulful revelation comes from a couple in their *late-80s* who still "neck" and sleep spoon-style, and whose sexual behavior includes fellatio, cunnilingus, and mutual masturbation, but not penis-in-vagina sex. The deep enjoyment older men can derive from nonpenetrating sex (Schiavi,

Mandeli, & Schreiner-Engel, 1994) can puzzle younger couples and therapists.

☐ Characteristics of Sexual Potential: Recommendations for Therapists

The most common responses of survey couples involved the ways people accumulate enough maturity and integrity to bring their whole selves into relationship with goodwill and good faith. The following is advice gleaned from the collective wisdom of this cohort. Their recommendations are addressed to couples (and therapists) who want to strengthen the meaning and energy of sex in lifelong relationships. These concepts are useful in couples therapy, not only when sexual issues come up but also in dealing with other issues. All quotes are from (disguised) clients, unless otherwise noted.

- *Know who you are and maintain your own identity when your partner wants you to be different, to do it his or her way.* Knowing who you are helps you to behave without pretense, including sexually.

> It was almost 30 years before I realized I wasn't letting Carter see the real me when we had sex. I was comfortable with our familiarity, I just felt anxious being, well, *me* during intense sexual arousal. I finally got past feeling rejected for my arousal, or rejecting my own arousal, really, to keep Carter comfortable. I made myself believe he wasn't rejecting me, and was that ever weird. His ultimate acceptance, and my finally accepting his acceptance, is a big part of who we are and how we share sexual feelings.

Malone and Malone described sexuality as natural energy: "True sexuality intimidates most of us because we are so far removed from our own real nature. We are frightened when a natural, open experience confronts us with our alienation" (1992, p. 14).

- *Soothe yourself in relationship when you feel anxious, fearful, helpless, insecure, and pressure to conform to ill-fitting demands.* Although anxiety may be contagious, you do not have to catch it, nurture it, surrender to it, or leave your partner when you have it. Presence prohibits your spacing-out when you imagine honesty might bring a punishing outcome or undesired result. Managing your own anxiety instead of leaning on a partner to do it for you requires self-support, self-respect, self-soothing, self-validation, and self-disclosure.

- Question: *"Why be in a relationship if I can do all that for myself?"* Answer: *"Because you're grown-up and in an intimate relationship with profound erotic potential you can do all that."* You stay in relationship because you decide to, have the courage to, and the maturity to—not because you need somebody to take care of you, as if you were emotionally deficient. You cannot delve into the potential of erotic behavior when your partner is somebody you need for support and reassurance. Taking care of yourself emotionally, being in charge even when you delegate care-taking to your partner (when he or she is willing), and behaving autonomously makes for profound bonding and greater sexual energy.

- *Adults may want but do not **need** a partner to do for them what they are capable of doing for themselves.* None of us is incomplete without a partner to fill in our deficits; we are complete because we are human. Actualization of sexual potential operates from self-respect by responding to and with one's own wholeness. Paradoxically, the more whole and emotionally separate (as in good ego boundaries, not isolation), the deeper the capacity for intimate connection.

- *Tolerate intense feelings—your own, your partner's, and others'.* Being able to stay connected with self while experiencing or witnessing intense emotions means we have a handle on responsiveness and, therefore, viable internal options. These personal choices seem, on some occasions, like pulling on a down jacket in a snowstorm, and on others like stripping naked to skinny-dip when we are modest but want to join the fun. A firm sense of self—feeling secure and clear about who you are—is the support you need to meet the (erotic) energy of your partner.

- *Self-support is easier when you are healing yourself of childhood wounds.* Being (or employing) your own healer means growing up enough to be in a *peer* relationship instead of a dependent one. Peers welcome sexual energy; nonpeers in hierarchical relationships hang old wounds on it. For example, the experience of the following clients I saw in therapy illustrates a shift from parent-child interaction to peer interaction:

Barbara and Jeff, married for 7 years with two children, were a sexual abuse survivor couple trying to put sexual energy back into their relationship. Barbara froze when Jeff touched her or looked as if he might want sex. If her guilt was great enough, she let him "do it" to her so he wouldn't bother her for another week. Jeff, in turn, was grateful for the handout and asked for sex only once a week, for fear Barbara would refuse him even that if he pushed her. Barbara had the ability to "space out" (dissociate) or leave her body while Jeff had sex with her ("does sex on her" like her father did). They came to therapy because Jeff wanted to be desired sexually and Barbara wanted to desire him, but incest "body-memories" got in her way.

They had benefited relationally, but not physically, from years of previous couples therapy and sex therapy. The changes in each of them during nearly 2 years of very hard personal work they did with me, *together*, happened as they decided they were, in fact, now adults in charge of themselves. How did they do this? They accomplished this through my (and, eventually, their own) consistent challenge to their beliefs that catastrophe was inevitable and unsurvivable and that anxiety should be avoided, and to their philosophy that the other one should be the soother. These changes came about as each partner began to claim his or her own projections and self-soothe. For example, Barbara began consciously to take charge of herself in bed and out. She said, "Yes" to herself, "Yes" to the wounded child inside who needed adult protection (her own, not Jeff's), and "Yes" to her ability to differentiate between sex as loving and incest as violence, especially in the face of childhood ambivalence around arousal dread and orgasm terror. Barbara learned in therapy to notice her own thoughts and feelings behind her behavior and attitudes, just as I noticed them clearly and directly in the beginning of therapy. She "bit the bullet" and tried the sexual behaviors that frightened her. She then became conscious of what frightened her. Instead of trying to get "violating sex" over with as soon as possible, Barbara learned to speak the unspeakable; she began "stopping herself in mid-air," giving words to freezing, spacing, and dissociating as, or before, she experienced them, starting in the therapy hour. She slowly began to soothe herself as an adult in present time, letting the little girl of the past release her constant survival-vigilance.

Jeff learned that sex without emotionally connecting violated his partner and cheated himself. He gradually learned to be with Barbara quietly, to hear her deepest hurts without trying to fix her. He also discovered how to recognize his own hurts, be with himself, and share himself with Barbara instead of protecting her from his own feelings of inadequacy, shame, and anger.

They learned irreverence from a respectful, irreverent therapist, which allowed them to unlock the transference of terror from her father's brutal incest to her husband's gentle, loving nature. They began timidly to touch each other sexually, to talk about it, and to tell me what happened when we next met. Part of their progress depended unconsciously on my being able to hear and accept their experience, thereby enabling them to hear and accept each other. Humor, laughter, and playfulness (modeled appropriately by me) helped Barbara out of her spacey, dissociative insulation. She actually laughed out loud the first time she opened her usually squeezed shut eyes to make eye contact (I contact) with Jeff during sex; she was surprised to find out how different she felt knowing and seeing her husband instead of dreading her father, who was becoming a bad memory instead of a present nightmare. Jeff learned to notice for himself when he felt disconnected from Barbara and to reject her appeasing handouts. Barbara learned to separate Jeff, her husband, from her father's violent touch and to welcome Jeff (Maltz, 1991). It seems simplistic, after 2 years of profoundly difficult personal growth, to say that each managed his or her own anxiety, became responsible and intentional about behaving, and thereby restructured a new marriage with erotic potential. But that is exactly what they did. The therapist's growth seems part of the process, too. For example, my increasing ease of discussing, asking, probing, and accepting the details of the sexual experience they designed for themselves created not only a safe holding environment but a new perspective from which they could individually create safety and pleasure instead of depending on the other to provide the holding environment.

Taking turns being unconsciously parental or childlike is fertile ground for differentiation. The *normal* fantasy that one partner should or could heal the other invites regressive behavior, disillusionment, and disempowerment. Destruction of this fantasy helps partners take charge of themselves—mature—in the relationship. Healing yourself does not mean isolating, it means being responsible for who you are *now*, with your partner. "A good love relationship can help heal many wounds of your childhood, but you must do considerable self-healing to be capable of a good love relationship" (Halpern, 1994, p. 258).

- *Risk knowing more about yourself and your partner every day.* Knowing yourself means you observe and claim your projections as your own instead of blaming your partner, and you use them for personal insight and change.

Sam came to therapy to help her partner, Corey, to change. A year later, she summed up her therapy and her growing ability to reclaim her projections:

I distanced Corey for years because I thought she was too demanding and critical of every little thing I did, especially sexually. It didn't occur to me that her criticism was warranted by my own silence that kept her effectively at arm's length and away from my heart. She was trying to connect with me verbally in the very way I could not tolerate. I was not yet open to my part,

I could only blame her and cringe. What a mess. Exposing my vulnerability to her is not easy, even now. It is embarrassing and dreadful but I am doing it, especially when she gets critical. We are improving and so is sex.

The trigger for Sam's change was my own willingness to notice out loud, in the form of a question, that she was neglecting herself to focus on her partner, that her projections were imaginary, not real, and that these observations were safe to make.

Knowing your partner means accepting him or her for who he or she is now, not trying to change him or her to be more to your liking. This is also true of therapy: Therapists must learn to accept the patient for who he or she is now, not trying to change him or her with goals for change. Corey responds this way to Sam:

I had always thought Sam was avoiding me because there was something wrong with me. When I heard more about her from her, I realized the issue was about Sam, not about me. I learned to listen without commenting on every little topic, and Sam's natural lovability became visible again. It was very hard for me to be accepting without trying to make her different or better.

This is a difficult task for therapists, as well. Being considerate but not responsible for your partner's needs, wants, and desires helps you both become autonomous and more deeply related.

Willingness to risk being sexual is part of how couples bond. This does not mean employing sexual fantasies or trying out sex toys. It means being in relationship with a conscious intent to know yourself and your partner profoundly, emotionally, physically, and in ways that enrich the relationship even as it causes anxiety. "To be fully sexual, we must feel accepted and unjudged. But we must learn to accept *ourselves* to escape being lulled into the ranks of the living dead" (Malone & Malone, 1992, p. 18). We can apply this to therapists, as well: that is, to risk *being with* patients without sexual goals or sexual advice as a way to empower couples to be themselves.

- *Cultivate the capacity to be caught off guard and enjoy the surprise and newness.* Jesse, a survey participant, said:

What I love best about Morgan is his capacity to love a surprise. His exuberance is contagious. Although some things we try turn out poorly, we do create delightful sex, playful feelings, and a continuous loving connection, in part because we can enjoy surprising each other and being surprised. Morgan's willingness to face something new and unexpected is very attractive to me. At 64, he is more desirable than when we got together 40 years ago.

- *Occasional longing for the presence and absence of a partner is healthy.* As Chris, a survey participant, noted:

Missing Pat helps keep my emotional welcome fresh. Sometimes I crave solitude and personal renewal time. Yet, sometimes even when I have not had enough alone time, I still long for Pat. We have very different needs for contact and solitude, and our years together have helped us make peace with the timing of our different cycles. At first, Pat thought I didn't care about our relationship because I needed solitude. I thought Pat was smothering. But we worked it out and my sexual energy stays fresh, most of the time.

- *The ongoing ability to be playful, curious, creative is essential.* Being sexually alive includes welcoming the unknown and delighting in new discoveries, especially sexually. Curiosity urges us to explore the unknown; playfulness helps us do it with relish and creativity. The ability to play allows partners to escape the downside of familiarity. Being sexual is play that allows partners to learn new aspects not only of the other but, more importantly, of themselves. Play helps partners develop goodwill and fair boundaries. Playfulness, curiosity, and creativity build enthusiasm for being alive and related. In a mature relationship, "Creative sexuality teaches us about death and ending. It is the only (good) experience we know that has an ending with no sense of loss, rejection, or separation in it" (Malone & Malone, 1992, p. 18).

- *Accept life's unchangeable rhythms and cycles.* Birth, death, and renewal are natural laws. Yet disillusionment seems both the curse and the blessing of human nature. Life (and most everything else) is impermanent. We do not often celebrate impermanence in America; yet we continue to feel surprised at its regular occurrence. Which of us past 60 has not looked with shock into a mirror? Letting dissatisfactions promote growthful change instead of resentment is one way to manage. Another is coming to terms with what is not going to change in you, your partner, and your relationship (or your clients).

- *Plan for the future.* Financial planning for old age is hard enough without planning together for one or the other's death. We rarely talk about how the surviving partner might live the rest of his or her life. The therapist who has done this with his or her own partner, parents, or grown child understands how painful it is to accept life's unchangeable rhythms, cycles, and unpredictability. But catastrophe happens. Joy happens. Wonder is wherever we look. Whether we dismay, ignore, or deny the inevitable, each response has consequences.

- *Acknowledge impermanence and loss, but love deeply, anyhow.* The tragedy of love is loss. Therapists must be willing to discuss this inevitable fact of life with couples. Whether couples are willing to have the discussion *is not relevant to the therapy.* It is enough that they become aware that they do not want to discuss loss. The tough decision is whether to love deeply, *now,* under the shadow of that loss, or to hold back so that less will have been invested when it happens. Knowing who you are as a separate person while you deeply value being with your partner indicates that you can love and lose that person. This capacity is evident in couples with intense erotic energy.

Therapists can do no more than elucidate the options and clear the way for partners to discuss the consequences of each choice. The rare therapists who have decided in their own relationships whether to love deeply or not enough to be devastated by loss know the potential for deadness in that choice. Loving in the face of loss reminds us that ending is tolerable if it is shared, that ending is part of nature's inevitable cycle, and that dying cannot, in fact, be separated from living.

Accepting death as part of life rearranges priorities. When this happens, couples no longer have to squeeze time from tight schedules to be together. They can *be* together. Understanding the difference between *doing* and *being* comes with maturity. Being who you are with a beloved partner can happen during an activity together; but it is not the activity but the *being with* that matters. The couples who can be with each other have learned, as Malone and Malone (1987) wrote, to be artists *in* their lives as well as craftsmen *of* their lives.

Although these characteristics might seem impossible to attain, they are results of the ongoing growth of couples who have lived them, maybe not all at once or not even all of them. To be grown enough to eroticize sex, sustain long-term sexual energy, and move toward sexual potential with a life partner, these qualities must at least be acknowledged, if not achieved (Schnarch, 1991, 1997; Shaw, 1997, 1998a,b).

☐ Therapist's Comfort Zone

The growth process in sex therapy includes maturation of the person of the therapist as well as the couple in therapy. The therapist's maturity and capacity for intimacy may be as crucial to the outcome of couples therapy as the growth process of the couple, itself. Schnarch (1992), like Bowen (1974) and numerous others, reminded us that the most effective therapy is practiced by therapists who have explored their own issues of sexual deadness (and aliveness), confronted their own status-quo behavior, claimed their own projections, reinforced their own integrity, and moved forward in their own living and personal development. Therapist growth and integrity, therefore, is relevant to couples' growth, sexual potential, and therapy outcome.

Correcting misconceptions by means of sex education is what we do very well; it is an arm's-length transaction, straightforward and cognitively based. Enlivening monotonous but functional sex is less of a struggle for therapists who are discovering *in their own lives* that better-than-adequate sex is not only a worthwhile possibility but a requirement for personal growth. Creating erotic sexual energy happens with maturation, not with techniques. In spite of therapy's impending manualization, or maybe because of it, therapists need to have the integrity to address sexual potential, the elusive quality that, someday in the future, may be seen as the right of every person just as manufacturing orgasms is now. The reason couples pay us, in spite of and because of their anxiety and yearning, is to help them find their erotic connection *without* the use of videos, sex toys, and disengaging fantasies.

Relying on personal maturation instead of behavioral devices can be as unsettling for therapists as it is for couples. The uneasiness that can accompany the step beyond what we now see as behavioral success—that is, what couples do *after* they learn the basics in sex therapy—is a signal to therapists to move beyond their own emotional comfort zones, contain and soothe their own unease, quell their free-floating anxiety, be aware of their defensiveness (including giving recipes for symptom relief), and maintain therapy as a place for couples to explore their maturity as much as their behavior.

When partners describe struggles with sex between sessions, especially if their energy in therapy is high, they can literally raise the temperature in the therapy room. Couples create intimate moments that may astonish them and also the therapist (and, in the following vignette, a cotherapist. Cotherapists were common in the 1980s; they are currently the exception rather than the norm, for financial among other reasons.):

Jamie and Ryan fidgeted during the first moments of our meeting, gearing up to report their failure to engage the previous night. This was odd, as we do not ask couples to report back to us, nor do we assign behavioral homework. Twenty minutes into the session, as they stumbled over words for body parts and functions, placating each other, being careful, the room began to heat up. The thermostat had been set at 72 degrees Fahrenheit, but the room registered *84 degrees*. My cotherapist was perspiring freely, and I felt as though I were in a steam room. What was going on under the surface? The couple said they felt a little stuffy (apt metaphor). Although I lowered the temperature, the room stayed hot.

We both noted that their high energy did not match their words or voice tones. I remarked on the temperature, asking my cotherapist if he thought it reflected anything about the couple's energy. He spoke to them through me, saying that perhaps their potential for erotic experience was now cooking on high. This apparently was a green light. Jamie confessed, for the first time, of feeling ashamed of a strong sexual urge, afraid it would go out of control. Ryan admitted, also for the first time, feeling afraid he might not be able to keep up if Jamie let loose instead of holding back her energy.

As they fantasized the consequences of specific sexual behaviors, each was able to stay in the conversation, feeling high anxiety. I began to feel mild sexual arousal, an internal signal that lets me know that the connection between partners is sexual and engaging. Jamie got clear that "steamy" did not mean "sleazy," and later in the week was surprised with delight in her newfound "sleazability." Ryan later discovered for himself that dependency on a functioning mind, heart, mouth, tongue, and hands prevented performance anxiety and, indeed, that genital performance was not an issue for Jamie. And we learned that an unreasonably overheated therapy room is predictive of intense unexpressed energy.

Therapists who are themselves differentiating, can handle the heat in therapy without using behavioral techniques. Although techniques may ameliorate therapist anxiety, they can interfere with the experience of self-discovery and growth, including the therapist's. Technical procedures that are devoid of personal feeling and participation by the therapist have little meaning and can become a barrier between therapist and couple, and between partners (Whitaker & Malone, 1953/1981). In managing a response to a couple's intense, unexpressed energy, seasoned therapists use their intuition and wisdom to risk the therapeutic unknown. It is the therapist's task to restore and promote partners' full participation in their own therapeutic process. To do this, the therapist must have his or her own self-support and a way to self-soothe through the unknown. Although modeling mature *behavior* comes with the therapy territory, moving through the experience of your own personal differentiation in your own therapy room is exquisite, nonverbal modeling of *growth*. The maturing therapist offers intimacy, vulnerability, and authenticity in therapy as part of the outcome that couples eventually take home.

When therapists witness couples having profound moments of emotional intimacy, they cannot help but be aware of their own experience of intimacy measuring up or falling short. This can and should be a wake-up call to therapists whose own sexual relationships are poor or nonexistent. In reference to relationship, your primary relationship is with *yourself*. I learned this actively during a session with a middle-aged couple:

This is the second session with clients Carter and Sydney, a mid-40s couple together 18 years, with three teen-age children. Their complaint is no sex since Carter's father died 4 years ago. They are stopping in to see me on the way to a divorce attorney. Half-listening to their continuous criticisms, complaints, and frustrations, I wonder what is underneath their empty chatter and why the discussion feels incongruent to me.

They are invested enough to seek couples therapy and persistent enough to have gone through three previous therapists. As always, I promise them nothing except my complete presence and attention (which is what they eventually learn to promise each other), to begin and end on time, and to collect my fee each visit. Their chatter is a sing-song that excludes me while it mesmerizes. I stop their concert by wondering aloud if they often hypnotize each other this way.

Ten minutes of exploring reveal a profound fear. Their loving is so strong that the thought of losing the other is unbearable; more so even than the loss of Carter's beloved father, whose death had triggered a search for meaning in their own relationship. The futility of their search is painful for both; it seems easier to squabble, criticize, and threaten divorce than to face the anguish of the other's death.

Meanwhile, from deep inside me comes a tide of sadness so intense that tears fill my eyes, almost but not quite spilling over. I am stunned by this sudden, unexpected surge of feeling. Ashamed that my countertransference is so *out here*, I do not speak, at least not in words. This entire revelation takes but a few seconds as I take a breath to collect myself. The couple does not consciously recognize that I resonate with the pain of their detachment and yearning. Their unconscious, spontaneous response is to reach across the sofa to each other, across 4 years, to hold hands for the first time since the death of Carter's father. This gesture, I discover later, enables them to create a more appreciative and uninhibited way to be together. I would not completely understand my own resonance with their connection to each other and my own post-midlife relationship grief until later; however, their reaching for each other indicates that my process has a concrete effect on their connection.

I do not fully understand transpersonal process or how one person's deeply felt, unspoken response can affect change in others, but it happens frequently to many psychotherapists. Whittaker and Malone explained therapy as a two-way process, that both patients and therapists grow from it. An example is the depressed therapist who wonders why clients are quitting or not following up on referrals.

Personal, private insight and self-awareness gained while working with couples are valuable additions to a therapist's growth. Therapist maturity expands with the ability to contain, manage, and direct emotional intensity, personally and professionally. Therapists do with couples what the couples could do for themselves if they believed they could manage without anxiety. We model for couples that life comes with anxiety and that we manage, anyway. When the therapist offers opportunities to differentiate, some partners, but not all, accept the challenge. Some do not even get the offer of a challenge.

An unknown number of therapists do not experience erotic sex with their own life partners after the initial romantic attraction wears down. Whether the therapist's personal history has an effect on the outcome of couples work remains both controversial and inadequately addressed, especially in the sex therapy arena. Nonetheless, sex and couples therapists should have more than a nodding acquaintance with the variety of meanings sexual behavior can have. Working with partners to eroticize adequate but mediocre sexual functioning requires a therapist who understands the association between adequacy in physical functioning and disappointment in normal sexual response; grasps the growth potential of the sexual symptom to both partners' personal development; and agrees to be present with them to their best possible outcome (if that is where they want to go), passing through his or her own anxiety along the way. What this means for therapists' sexual development is another entire book.

☐ Summarizing the Old Versus the New

Conventional perspectives such as the natural hunger model (Kaplan, 1979; Masters & Johnson, 1976) forged a new direction in their time, when the notion of sex purely for the pleasure of both partners was a radical departure from the then-popular notion that partners served each other's needs or, specifically in heterosexual relationships, that the woman served the man's sexual appetite. The idea of sex as a reflection of, and opportunity for, personal maturity and potential is an unfamiliar perspective. The following lists summarize and compare the conventional perspectives and a new approach for tomorrow's new directions.

Old Perspectives on Sexual Behavior

- Sex is a natural hunger.
- The focus is on body parts, genital techniques, positions, and toys.
- Fantasy and genital stimulation to orgasm is adequate sex.
- Desire is a function of one's need for sex.
- Anxiety reduction, relaxation, and comfort with sex is essential.
- Orgasm, even with minimal arousal, signals success.
- Interest in sex subsides over time and with age.
- Sexual problems are viewed as individual cause-and-effect issues.
- Partners validate, support, protect, and heal each other.
- Security is dependent on a partner's behavior.
- The contract for growth and change is between partners.

New Perspectives on Sexual Behavior

- Sex is learned; reproduction is natural.
- The focus is on connection with self and partner.
- Connection with a partner is arousing; fantasy is optional and nondistracting.
- Desire is a function of fullness, completeness, and self-respect.
- High levels of sexual tension and anxiety are tolerable and useful.
- Orgasms occur with intensity and without interference with desire.
- Interest in a partner remains or increases with increased maturity.
- Sexual problems are signals and opportunities for growth.
- Partners self-validate, self-support, self-trust, and self-heal in relationship.
- Security is dependent on one's own competence.
- Contract for growth is with oneself and takes place in relationship.

The new, or differentiation, perspective is an example of partners claiming responsibility for the kind of sexual relationship they have created and the kind they plan for their future. Some of the difficulty in a growth approach to sex therapy may be a result of romantic idealism. There is nothing inherently wrong with romance; however, the association of romance with dependency sabotages erotic potential. We are unfamiliar, as a culture, with partners who *in relationship* meet or delegate their own dependency needs, soothe their own anxiety and insecurity, validate and approve themselves, manage under pressure, balance when they are pulled off center, and feel and behave as whole adults who want to relate and develop further with other whole adults. When we assume, as therapists, that adults are already whole, that they are being sexually related in purposeful ways even when they report dissatisfaction, we begin to see the advantages of their symptoms as reflected in the hologram of sexual behavior, the key to their growth.

☐ References

Apfelbaum, B. (Ed.). (1980). *Expanding the boundaries of sex therapy* (rev. ed.). Berkeley, CA: Berkeley Sex Therapy Group.

Apfelbaum, B. (1989). Retarded ejaculation: A much misunderstood syndrome. In S. R. Lieblum & R. C. Rosen (Eds.), *Principles and practice of sex therapy: Update for the 1990s* (pp. 168–206). New York: Guilford Press.

Bowen, M. (1974). Toward the differentiation of self in one's family of origin. In F. Andres & J. Loris (Eds.), *Georgetown family symposium papers*. Washington, DC: Georgetown University Press.

Halpern, H. M. (1994). *Finally getting it right*. New York: Bantam Books.

Kaplan, H. S. (1979). *Disorders of sexual desire and other new techniques in sex therapy*. New York: Brunner/Mazel.

Kopp, S. (1977). *Back to one: A practical guide for psychotherapists*. Palo Alto, CA: Science and Behavior Books.

Malone, T. P., & Malone, P. T. (1987). *The art of intimacy*. Englewood Cliffs, NJ: Prentice Hall.

Malone, T. P., & Malone, P. T. (1992). Being sexual. *VOICES: The art and science of psychotherapy, 28*(1), 14–19.

Maltz, W. (1991). *The sexual healing journey: A guide for survivors of sexual abuse*. New York: HarperCollins.

Masters, W. H., & Johnson, V. E., (1966). *Human sexual response*. Boston: Little, Brown.

Masters, W. H., & Johnson, V. E. (1976). *The pleasure bond: A new look at sexuality and commitment*. Boston: Little, Brown.

Schiavi, R.C., Mandeli, J., & Schreiner-Engel, P. (1994). Sexual satisfaction in healthy aging men. *Journal of Sex & Marital Therapy. 20*(1), 3–13.

Schnarch, D. M. (1991). *Constructing the sexual crucible: An integration of sex and marital therapy*. New York: W.W. Norton.

Schnarch, D. M. (1992). The person of the therapist: Inside the sexual crucible. *VOICES: The Art and Science of Psychotherapy, 28*(1), 20–27.

Schnarch, D. M. (1997). *Passionate marriage: Love, sex, and intimacy in emotionally committed relationships*. New York: W.W. Norton.

Shaw, J. (1990). Play therapy with the sexual workhorse: Successful treatment with 12 cases of inhibited ejaculation. *Journal of Sex and Marital Therapy, 16*(3), 159–164.

Shaw, J. (1994a). Treatment of primary vaginismus: A new perspective. *Journal of Sex & Marital Therapy, 20*(1), 46–55.

Shaw, J. (1994b). Aging and sexual potential. *Journal of Sex Education & Therapy, 20*(2), 134–139.

Shaw, J. (1997). *Journey toward intimacy: A handbook for couples*. Atlanta: Couples Enrichment Institute.

Shaw, J. (1998a). *Journey toward intimacy: A handbook for gay couples*. Atlanta: Couples Enrichment Institute.

Shaw, J. (1998b). *Journey toward intimacy: A handbook for singles*. Atlanta: Couples Enrichment Institute.

Shaw, J., & Erhardt, V. (1997). *Journey toward intimacy: A handbook for lesbian couples*. Atlanta: Couples Enrichment Institute.

Tiefer, L. (1995) *"Sex is not a natural act" and other essays*. Boulder, CO: Westview Press.

Whitaker, C. A., & Malone, T. P. (1953/1981). *The roots of psychotherapy*. New York: Brunner/Mazel.

10

Karen M. Donahey, Ph.D.
Scott D. Miller, Ph.D.

"What Works" in Sex Therapy: A Common Factors Perspective

More than 30 years have passed since Masters and Johnson (1966) first proposed their model of human sexual response. Soon after came their landmark *Human Sexual Inadequacy* (1970), which proposed a treatment approach for male and female sexual disorders. The approach offered an alternative to the dominant psychodynamic perspective of sexual functioning along with hope that sexual difficulties could be treated effectively and efficiently (Heiman & LoPiccolo, 1983). Enthusiasm over Masters and Johnson's work gradually waned, however, as clinicians found themselves unable to replicate their reported success rates (Levin & Agle, 1978; Rosen & Beck, 1988; Zilbergeld & Evans, 1980).

At the turn of the millennium, serious questions remain about both the understanding and the efficacy of the treatment of sexual complaints. For all the growing complexity in the conceptualization of sexuality and sexual disorders, and in spite of the proliferation of models and techniques, there is "a paucity of controlled outcome research or studies of treatment process variables in sex therapy" (Rosen & Leiblum, 1995, p. 877). Where studies do exist, they typically find only moderate levels of success. More troubling, over the last several years there has actually been a dramatic decrease in the number of outcome studies and a growing medicalization of the field (Ackerman & Carey, 1995; Hawton, 1992; Leiblum & Rosen, 1989; Schover & Leiblum 1994). As a matter of fact, a recent issue of the

Journal of Sex Education and Therapy was devoted entirely to medical treatments heralded as a "turning point in the treatment of sexual dysfunction" (Plaut, 1998, p. 183).

☐ Been There, Done That

As unique as these observations about the proliferation of approaches and medicalization of treatment may seem to the field of sex therapy, they have an oddly familiar quality. Indeed, upon reflection, the history of sex therapy seems rather similar to the field of psychotherapy in general. In particular, the work of pioneering researchers and theoreticians was followed by a rapid proliferation of methods and techniques in the absence of virtually any empirical evidence of efficacy (Miller, Duncan, & Hubble, 1999). In the field of psychotherapy in general, a generation of researchers began putting the various approaches to the test, in essence pitting the warring factions against one another in a grand "battle of the brands."

As it turned out, the hope that one (or more) therapeutic approach would prove superior to others received virtually no support (Hubble, Duncan, & Miller, 1999a; Norcross & Newman, 1992). Indeed, aside from the occasional significant finding for a particular therapy, the critical mass of data revealed no differences in efficacy among the various treatments— from psychodynamic and client-centered approaches to marriage and family therapies (Hubble, Duncan, & Miller, 1999a; Lambert & Bergin, 1994; Miller, Duncan, & Hubble, 1997; Shadish, Montgomery, Wilson, Bright, & Okwumabua, 1993; Sprenkle, Blow, & Dickey, 1999). The same ideological battle was carried out with largely similar results in the field of sex therapy between the proponents of the psychogenic and organic perspectives. Subsequent research and clinical practice showed the dichotomy between the psychogenic and organic camps to be erroneous and the classification largely useful only in determining whether the client would be treated by a mental health professional or urologist (Althof, 1998).

While studies on psychotherapy in general provided little evidence of differential effectiveness, a mountain of data amassed showing treatment to be superior to both placebo and no-treatment control groups. Among other findings, literally hundreds of studies conducted over the last 30 years found the average treated person better off than 80% of those in a control group who received no treatment (Lambert & Bergin, 1994; Smith, Glass, & Miller, 1980). In spite of all the various shortcomings and problems in the research, reviewers Schover and Leiblum (1994) made similar observations about the field of sex therapy, noting in particular that, in spite of a dearth of quality research, "it remains one of the more effective psychotherapies, when practiced appropriately" (p. 24).

As early as 1936, Saul Rosenzweig wrote in the *Journal of Orthopsychiatry*, suggesting that the overall effectiveness of competing psychotherapy approaches had more to do with their *commonalities* than the divergent theoretical or technical factors on which they were based. Frank (Frank & Frank, 1991) picked up on this pioneering insight, applying the thesis across various forms of healing (e.g., groups, medicine, religious). His work stood virtually alone, however, until the 1980s, when an outpouring of writing began to appear on what came to be known as the "common factors"— features shared by all effective therapies (Strupp, Hadley, & Gomez-Schwartz, 1974; Weinberger, 1995). Lambert (1992) reviewed the empirical literature and proposed four such factors—extratherapeutic, relationship, expectancy or placebo, and model and techniques—as the principle elements accounting for improvement in those undergoing psychotherapy. Miller, Duncan, and Hubble (1997; Duncan, Hubble, & Miller, 1997; Hubble, Duncan, & Miller, 1999b) have since written extensively on these factors as the best bridge—the nouns and verbs, so to speak—between the various schools or "regional dialects" of therapy.

Unless revolutionary new findings emerge, a prospect that seems highly unlikely given the time and effort already expended in the search for superior treatment approaches, research supporting the common factors indicates that knowledge about what makes therapy effective is already in the hands of mental health professionals. The profession has labored far too long under the conventions of "it seems," "it appears," "another possible explanation could be," and "more research is needed" when interpreting available studies and describing therapeutic process. Even a cursory review of these customary prevarications leaves the impression that nobody wants to say, "this is it. This is in fact as close as we can come to it now, and here's what we do." As Kazdin (1986, p.102) ruefully wondered, what makes it so difficult to admit that "the absence of treatment differences reflects the true state of affairs?"

☐ From Sex Therapy to Therapy with People Who Present with Sexual Concerns

Research on the common factors suggests that successful "sex therapy" is more about therapy with people who happen to be experiencing sexual difficulties than about the application of a unique therapeutic modality or treatment technique (e.g., squeeze technique, sensate focus). As noted earlier, researchers point to the existence of four factors common to all forms of therapy despite theoretical orientation (dynamic, cognitive, etc.), mode (individual, group, couples, family, etc.), dosage (frequency, number of sessions), or specialty (problem type, professional discipline, etc.). In order of their relative contribution to change, these elements include:

1. Extratherapeutic (40%);
2. Relationship (30%);
3. Placebo, hope, or expectancy (15%); and
4. Structure, model, and/or technique (15%; Hubble, Duncan, & Miller, 1999c; Lambert, 1992; Miller, Duncan, & Hubble, 1997).

The language of the common factors dictates no fixed techniques, no certainties or invariant patterns in therapeutic process, no prescriptions for what should or need be done to effect good treatment outcome. Rather, clinicians learn to heighten the contribution of these factors by identifying the unique ways they operate in their own clinical work.

☐ Extratherapeutic Factors: The Role of the Client and Chance Change-Producing Events

Extratherapeutic factors are the single largest contributors to change and refer to any and all aspects of the client and his or her environment that facilitate recovery, *regardless of formal participation in therapy*. Curiously, most of the writing and thinking about therapy places the clinician at center stage in the drama of treatment. Clients, on the other hand, most often have been portrayed in the clinical literature as the bearers of family dysfunction, the manufacturers of resistance, and, in most therapeutic traditions, the targets for the presumably all-important technical intervention. As Held (1991) pointedly observed, most theories of therapy have actually been theories of psychopathology.

Research on the extratherapeutic factors literature makes clear, however, that clients are the true masters of change in treatment. Their strengths and resources, their world views, their perceptions of the therapist and what the therapist is doing, their social supports, and the fortuitous events that weave in and out of their lives matter more than anything therapists might do. By being mindful of the significant role such elements play in everyday practice, sex therapists can enhance their contributions to treatment outcome. Four suggestions can be useful in this regard.

Becoming Change-Focused

Heraclitis, the Greek philosopher (c. 500 B.C.), was known to say, "Nothing is permanent but change." Unlike diagnoses—static characterizations connoting a measure of constancy, even permanence, in clients' presenting complaints—the magnitude, severity, and frequency of problems are in flux, constantly changing. In this regard, clients will report better and worse days, times free of symptoms and moments when their problems seem to get the best of them. Without or with a little prompting, they can describe these changes—the ebb and flow of the problem's presence and ascendancy in their daily affairs.

To develop a change-focus, a therapist can listen for and validate change for the better, whenever and for whatever reason it occurs (Miller, Duncan, & Hubble, 1997). As just one example, consider studies that show 15% to 66% of clients experience positive treatment-related gains *prior* to the formal initiation of treatment (Howard, Kopte, Krause, & Orlinsky, 1986; Lawson, 1994). Obviously, such pretreatment change is extratherapeutic in origin, as it cannot be attributed to either the therapy or therapist. Whatever the cause, however, the high percentage reported indicates that clinicians can empower the contribution of extratherapeutic factors by listening for, inviting, and using the description of such change as a guide to therapeutic activity.

Therapists also can be changed-focused in their work when clients return for additional visits by heeding and then amplifying any references the clients make during the session to between-session improvement (e.g., clients reporting a sexual encounter with their partners). Also, in the opening moments of the session, therapists can directly ask clients about what, if any, changes have occurred since their last visit, with the simplest question coming in the form, "What is different?" or "What is better?" A sizable body of research literature shows that improvement between treatment sessions is the rule rather than the exception, with the majority of clients experiencing significant symptomatic relief earlier rather than later in the treatment process (Howard, Kopte, Krause, & Orlinsky, 1986; Reuterlov, Lofgren, Nordstrom, Ternstrom, & Miller, 2000).

Potentiating Change for the Future

Whether change begins before or during treatment, whether it results from the client's own actions or by happenstance, a crucial step in enhancing the effect of extratherapeutic factors is helping clients see any changes—as well as the maintenance of those changes—as consequences of their own efforts (Miller, Duncan, & Hubble, 1997). Naturally, a cardinal consideration is *perception*: specifically, the clients' perceptions of the relationship between their own efforts and the occurrence of changes. It is important that clients come to view the changes as resulting, at least in part, from something they did and can repeat in the future. Therapists, moreover, can support changes resulting from extratherapeutic factors in several ways. For example, they can spend time exploring the clients' role in changes that occur during treatment. Additionally, the therapist can ask questions or make direct statements that presuppose client involvement in the resulting change (Berg & Miller, 1992; Imber, Pilkonis, Harway, Klein, & Rubinsky, 1982; Walter & Peller, 1992). For example:

- How did you know to do what you did?
- What is it about you that helped you to do what you did?
- How did you figure this out?

As part of ending a visit, therapists may also summarize the changes that occurred during therapy and invite clients to review their own role in the change. Even if clients resolutely attribute change to luck, fate, the acumen of the therapist, or a medication, they can still be asked to consider in detail (a) how they adopted the change in their lives, (b) what they did to use the changes to their benefit, and (c) what they will do in the future to ensure their gains remain in place.

Minding the Client's Competence

As suggested, therapists can begin to cast their clients in the role of primary agents of change by listening for and being curious about their competencies (i.e., their part in bringing about and maintaining positive change). This approach requires a balance between listening empathically to their difficulties and being mindful of their strengths and resources. Approaching clients in this way not only helps to combat discouragement and instill hope but, as Adler noted, "make[s] it clear that the responsibility for . . . cure is the patient's business" (in Ansbacher & Ansbacher, 1956, p. 336).

Tapping the Client's World Outside Therapy

Clinicians also mind clients' contributions to change by incorporating resources from their worlds outside of therapy. Whether seeking out a trusted friend or family member, purchasing a book or tape, attending church or a mutual-help group, research indicates that the majority of clients both seek out and find support outside the formal therapy relationship (Garfield, 1994). This natural tendency can be facilitated by the therapist simply listening for and then being curious about what happens in the client's life that is helpful. Several questions are useful to keep in mind:

- What persons, places, or things has the client sought out in the past that were useful?

- What was different about those times that enabled the client to use those resources?

- What is the client doing now (in addition to therapy) that he or she considers helpful in understanding or solving the problem?

Case Example: They Say I'm Psycho

As an illustration of working to empower extratherapeutic factors in sex therapy, consider the dialogue taken from the case of a woman referred for therapy by her gynecologist (Miller, Duncan, & Hubble, 1997). The client had a longstanding history of dyspareunia accompanied by complaints of severe genital irritation and infection. Despite years of medical testing, no physical cause was ever identified for the client's complaints, and the latest in a long list of physicians suspected the problems were psychogenic. The client began the session by relating some of the history of her problems:

Cl: I have seen so many doctors over the last, well, several years. I have *had* this problem for 30 years. It's serious because, well, you see, I've been married twice and both times this problem . . .

Th: Uh huh.

Cl: It's a little embarrassing. I've, uh, had this redness and infection—well, the doctors have all said that I don't, have never had have any infection—but, on my genitals. I'm always swollen and irritated . . .

Th: Uh huh.

Cl: . . . and, well, it has always hurt to have intercourse, you know, because . . .

Th: (*finishing the sentence*) of the redness and irritation.

Cl: (*with relief*) Yeah. The doctor says I'm psycho . . . (*pauses*).

Th: Psycho?

Cl: (*nodding affirmatively*) Psycho . . . psychosomatic.

The client continued for several minutes, elaborating on her story and explaining that she had made the appointment for therapy following a recent visit to a new physician. Unable to find anything physically wrong with her, this latest doctor had said she should consider seeing a mental health professional. The therapist simply listened while the woman related these details. Following a natural break in the process, the therapist seized an opportunity to be change-focused in the interview by highlighting a statement the client had made in the opening moments of the session indicative of pretreatment improvement:

Th: You say that you have *had* this redness and irritation?

Cl: (*nodding affirmatively*) Mmm.

Th: Does that mean that there have been some changes for the better recently?

Cl: (*surprised*) Well, yes.

Th: What's been different?

Cl: I've tried almost everything. I tried almost every, well, the doctors have tried all the drugs—creams, steroids, antibiotics. Nothing has ever worked, at least not for very long.

Th: And lately?

Cl: Well, I have been applying a mixture of milk of magnesia and Benadryl, just a few drops topically, to the, uh, red, irritated areas.

Th: Hmm.

Cl: And it's much improved over the few weeks that I've been doing it.

Th: Is that right?

Cl: After 30 years, I'd almost given up hope of this ever, well, *changing*.

Th: Of course. And the mixture is helping?

Cl: Mmm.

As can be seen, exploration of the change occurring prior to treatment highlighted a dramatic difference in the client's perception of her sexual functioning. In an attempt to be mindful of her competence, the therapist and client continued the conversation by exploring the recent change as well as how she had discovered the present solution. The therapist also inquired about how the client knew the "appropriate dose" to use on any given occasion, as well as how she would know when the "medicine" was no longer needed. Thereafter, the conversation returned to the pretreatment change.

Th: Anything else that has been different or helpful lately?

Cl: (*surprised*) Well, yes. Right now, I find myself in a situation, well, with a man that I've known for most of my life and he's quite a wonderful person . . .

Th: (*pleased*) Hmm.

Cl: And now we, well, have a sexual relationship.

Th: (*curious*) That is different?

Cl: For the first time, last night, it didn't hurt.

Th: Is that right?!

Cl: (*proudly*) Yeah, for the first time.

Th: How do you think that happened?

Cl: Well, for three weeks . . . well, a lot has to do with Steven. We have, well, there hasn't been any pressure. We have gone very slowly, and the pain just hasn't been there.

Th: The pain isn't there?

Cl: I guess it helps that I'm in love with Steven, and I don't really think that I was in love with my husbands.

Th: Sure. What else might be making a difference?

Cl: Well, I'm not as guarded. He is so careful and, well, thoughtful of me. Early on, we talked and agreed that if there was any hurt then we'd stop and, oh, I think we spend a lot of time just, well, you know, touching and just, laying there, uh, being together.

In the excerpt, the therapist and client explored the changes the woman reported and began identifying and validating the role of others in the change process. Specifically, the client identified several differences in her own and her partner's behavior that were likely responsible for the recent changes. In the dialogue that followed, a considerable amount of time was devoted to the helpful ways the couple had discovered how to communicate with each other about their sexual relationship. In this way, the therapist empowered the extratherapeutic factors by tapping into the client's world outside of therapy. At the end of the session, the therapist and client agreed that no further sessions were needed. A routine follow-up with the referring physician several months later found that the woman had not presented with any complaints about her sexual functioning.

☐ Relationship Factors: The Client and Therapist Together

With the contemporary emphasis on models and techniques (as detailed earlier), attributions of success in something as seemingly vague and intangible as the "therapeutic relationship" cannot help but sound misplaced and simpleminded. For the last three decades, professional discourse has basically regarded the therapeutic relationship a "nonspecific factor"—the therapeutic equivalent to anesthesia before surgery (Strupp, Hadley, & Gomez-Schwartz, 1974). Common clinical expressions such as "I am establishing rapport," "fostering an alliance," and others convey a view of the relationship as a mere precursor to the "real" or "active" ingredients of treatment—namely, techniques such as confronting dysfunctional thinking, making transference interpretations, or teaching sensate focus activities (Bachelor & Horvath, 1999). However, the research is clear: As much as 30% of the variance in psychotherapy outcome is attributable to relationship factors (Lambert, 1992). The same is true for marital therapy (Estrada & Holmes, 1999).

Research on the power of the "therapeutic alliance" now reflects more than 1,000 findings (Orlinsky, Grawe, & Parks, 1994) and provides concrete guidelines for enhancing the contribution of relationship factors to treatment outcome. These guidelines include (a) accommodating treatment to the client's motivational level or readiness for change and (b) accommodating the client's view of the therapeutic alliance.

Accommodating the Client's Motivational Readiness or Stage of Change

Recent reviews of the research have found that accommodating treatment to the client's readiness for change facilitates the formation of a strong therapeutic relationship (Bachelor & Horvath, 1999; Prochaska, 1999). For decades, clients' levels of motivation have been dichotomized—either they were motivated or not. As it turns out, however, the idea of an unmotivated client is simply not true. Rather, it is more correct to say the motivation of "unmotivated" clients may not match the therapist's goals and expectations for treatment (Duncan et al., 1997). Further, no longer is motivation for change understood strictly as some trait or stable personality characteristic that passively tags along with clients. Instead, it is a dynamic process strongly influenced by others' contribution to the interaction (e.g., the therapist's).

This recent view of motivation is strongly reflected in the work of Prochaska and others on what has come to be known as the "transtheoretical" or "stages of change" model (Prochaska, 1999). The underlying premise of this approach is that clients will more likely engage in change projects when their therapists "assess the stage of a client's readiness for change and tailor their interventions accordingly" (Prochaska, DiClemente, & Norcross, 1992, p. 1110). Six stages have been identified:

In the *precontemplation* stage, clients typically have not made a connection between a problem in their lives and their contribution to its formation or continuation. Because of this, they usually are not in the mood either to participate in or to establish an alliance with a helping professional (Prochaska, 1995). Helping clients in precontemplation requires a light touch on the part of the therapist (Miller et al., 1997). The goal is *not* to make the client do something. Rather, the therapist's job is to create a climate in which the client can consider, explore, and appreciate the benefits of changing (Prochaska & DiClemente, 1992).

The second stage of change is *contemplation*. Clients in contemplation are renowned for their use of two words: "yes, but." Frequently, these clients recognize that a change is needed. They also may have a sense of a goal and even know what they need to do to reach it. Even so, they are unsure about whether the change is worth the costs in time, effort, and energy. In addition, they frequently are unsure or ambivalent about the losses attendant to any change they might make (Miller et al., 1997). Accommodating clients in this phase requires considerable patience, given their tendency to vacillate and be indecisive. An effective approach entails creating a supportive environment in which a client can carefully consider changing without feeling the pressure or need to take action (Duncan, 1989). In certain cases, the therapist might even actively discourage a client from taking action and, instead, simply encourage thinking or observation.

The third stage is *preparation*. In this stage, clients are actively considering the criteria and strategies for success. For the first time, therapists can assume a more active role in raising possibilities, presenting treatment options or change strategies, and constructively challenging the clients' problem-solving abilities. This phase is also characterized by the clients' experimenting with the desired change—trying it on for size, noticing how it feels, and then experiencing the effects. Therapists accommodate such clients when they encourage rather than downplay the significance of such early problem-solving efforts.

Following preparation, the *action* stage commences. Clients in this phase present with both a firm commitment and a plan for the future. In essence, therapists can stand by, offer measured emotional support, and help clients monitor, modify, or fine-tune their plans of action. Curiously, and unfortunately, a strong argument can be made that most traditional therapeutic approaches are based on clients being in the action stage. Anything short of this—and the majority of those seeking treatment are *not* likely to be in this stage—and clients are labeled "resistant," "in denial," or as "help-rejecting complainers." Tailoring treatment to the *client's* stage of change, however, enables the therapist to shift the grounding metaphor for clinical practice from one that emphasizes therapist power to one that stresses collaboration and facilitation (Miller et al., 1997).

Next clients move into the *maintenance* stage. As the name implies, the challenge of this particular phase is consolidating the changes that have been made and learning what needs to happen in order to maintain gains. Therapists accommodate clients' motivational levels by helping them anticipate the challenges that might provoke regression or relapse and develop prevention plans.

Finally, clients move into the *termination* stage. Here, there is "zero temptation to engage in the problem behavior, and there is a 100 percent confidence (self-efficacy) that one will not engage in the old behavior regardless of the situation" (Prochaska, 1993, p. 253). So defined, termination may be more of an ideal than an achievable stage. For many, maintenance is where they will stay. That is, they continue to be mindful of possible threats to their desired change and monitor what they need to do to keep the change in place.

Accommodating the Client's View of the Alliance

Closely related to accommodating clients' readiness for change is tailoring treatment to fit with their view of the therapeutic alliance or relationship. First and foremost, this means making a client's goals the focus of treatment *without* reformulation along doctrinal or diagnostic lines. Additionally, Torrey (1972) suggested that sharing similar beliefs with clients about the causes and treatment of problems is a prerequisite to successful psychotherapy. By listening and then amplifying the stories and experiences that clients offer about their problems—including their thoughts, feelings, and ideas about "where they want to go and the best way to get there"—therapists accommodate their clients' views of the alliance as well as take into consideration their beliefs about the nature of the problem and their ideas on how to solve the problem. Consider, for example, research from several fields that indicates that goals specified in small, concrete, specific, and behavioral terms and which clients perceive as both desirable and attainable are more likely to influence their behavior in the desired direction (Bandura & Schunk, 1981; Berg & Miller, 1992; Miller, 1987). Indeed, in one study researchers (Beyebach, Morejon, Palenzuela, & Rodriguez-Aris, 1996) found that the presence of treatment goals with such qualities increased the likelihood of a successful therapeutic outcome by a factor of two.

Therapists can help their clients describe their goals in terms that match these considerations by asking several questions:

- How did you hope that I might be of help?
- What is your goal for treatment?

- What did you hope/wish/think would be different as a result of coming for treatment?

- What would have to be minimally different in your life to consider our work together a success?

- How will you know when the problem has been solved? What will be happening?

Orienting treatment toward a client's goals, however, is only one part of a positive therapeutic alliance. Equally important is attending to the client's perceptions of the therapist and the relationship being offered. Estrada and Holmes (1999) found, for example, that couples in therapy expected their therapists to be active, directive, and focused while simultaneously providing an empathic and safe environment. However, in their comprehensive review of the research on this topic, Bachelor and Horvath (1999) reported that clients vary widely in their experience of the core conditions that distinguish good therapeutic relationships. They suggested, as well, that successful therapeutic relationships are those in which the definition of the therapist-provided variables are extended to fit with the client's own unique experience of those variables.

In practice, therefore, clinicians stand the greatest chance of enabling the contribution of relationship factors to outcome when they purposefully tailor their provision of the core conditions to their clients' definitions. Some clients, for instance, will prefer a formal or professional manner over a casual or warmer one. Others might prefer more self-disclosure from the therapist, greater directiveness, a focus on their symptoms or on the possible meanings beneath them, a faster or a more laid back pace for therapeutic work (Bachelor & Horvath, 1999).

Combining the findings on extratherapeutic and relationship factors reviewed up to this point leads to the conclusion that therapeutic success depends on enabling and confirming a client's resources in a partnership, informed by the client's goals and perceptions.

Case Example: Making Sex Fun

Consider the case of Robyn, a 40-something artist who presented for treatment of loss of sexual desire following problems she had had with dyspareunia. While the cause of the dyspareunia had been identified and resolved, Robyn continued to avoid sexual intercourse and participated only minimally in other forms of sexual intimacy. Robyn and her partner had not had intercourse for the last 2 of their 4-year marriage. At intake, she expressed a desire to be able to have sexual intercourse again. While her husband was very supportive, Robyn worried about the potential impact of the problem on their relationship. Clear about her goals and recognizing that the benefits of change outweighed the costs, Robyn was in the *preparation* stage of change. Recall that clients in this stage are actively considering the criteria and strategies for success. The question, of course, was which strategy would be most successful.

Near the end of the interview, the therapist asked Robyn to consider the criteria for assessing the qualities of a helpful intervention. In the ensuing discussion, it became clear that any approach had to "make sex fun." At the conclusion of the visit, the therapist agreed with Robyn's idea and scheduled another appointment. When she returned two weeks later, she reported having experimented with the changes she desired. In particular, she had taken out a sex board game she had purchased a year earlier but never played and invited her husband to play. Much to her delight, she found herself getting into the spirit of the game, feeling sexually aroused, and having fun. Consistent with treatment strategies appropriate for this stage, the therapist supported, even applauded, her idea and efforts to make sex more fun. The result was an immediate increase in Robyn's hope and expectation for a successful resolution to the concerns that had brought her into treatment. In the sessions that followed, Robyn and her husband worked together with the therapist to devise a further plan of action. The plan was then monitored and modified in response to the couple's feedback and experience.

☐ Placebo Factors: The Role of Hope and Expectancy

In early 1998, sildenafil citrate—Viagra™—was approved for the treatment of erectile dysfunction. Studies reported success rates of 75% to 80% in men taking the drug—even in populations with established organic pathology (e.g., spinal cord injury; *Clinician Reviews*, 1998). Generally lost in the media frenzy accompanying the event, however, was the finding that between 10% and 30% or more (mean = 24%) of those studied experienced significant improvement in their ability to achieve and maintain an erection *while taking a placebo* (*Clinician Reviews*, 1998). Even higher placebo rates were cited by Althof (1999). These figures are impressive even when concerns about flaws in the studies known to inflate effect sizes (e.g., use of an inactive placebo, highly select sample) are not factored into the results (see Greenberg, 1999). Although this does not mean the drug should be withheld, it reconfirms the strong role that hope and expectation play in treatment (Garfield, 1994). Moreover, it suggests that the actual or "real" effects of any given treatment can be augmented by attending to factors that influence placebo effects (Rodger, 1982).

The suggestions that follow should not be considered comprehensive or exhaustive. Nor do they possess any special curative powers on their own. Instead, their entire value resides in the extent to which they facilitate hope and a positive expectation for change.

Having a Healing Ritual

Rituals are a shared characteristic of healing procedures in most cultures and date back to the earliest origins of human society (Frank & Frank, 1991; Van Gennep, 1960). Whether giving clients a drug, telling them to chart their negative self-talk, or teaching the "squeeze" or "stop-start" technique, mental health professionals are basically engaging in healing rituals. Their use inspires hope and a positive expectation for change by conveying that the user—shaman, astrologer, or therapist—possesses a special set of skills for healing. That the procedures are not in and of themselves the causal agents of change matters little (Kottler, 1991). What does matter is that the participants have a structured, concrete method for mobilizing the placebo factors.

With myriad techniques from which to choose, the perennial question facing therapists is what particular ritual to use when working with an individual client. In this regard, therapists enhance the placebo component of the procedures they employ when they believe in and are confident that the procedures will be therapeutic. As Benson and Epstein noted, treatment professionals "who have faith in the efficacy of their treatments . . . are the *most* successful in producing positive placebo effects" (in O'Regan, 1985, p. 17). It is not surprising, for example, that recent reports have called into serious question the panacea status Viagra™ assumed when first released. As Sir William Osler once observed, "One should treat as many patients as possible with a new drug while it still has the power to heal" (Greenberg, 1999).

The placebo effects of a given procedure also are heightened when therapists show interest in the results of whatever technique or orientation they employ. It has long been known, for example, that people participating in research studies are more likely to respond in the predicted direction when they know the purpose of the experiment (Matheson, Bruce, & Beauchamp, 1978). Clinicians can put the same phenomenon to work by engaging in activities that convey a positive expectation of and hope for client change in the desired direction. For example, Asay and

Lambert (1999) suggested that therapists make a practice of asking about the beneficial effects of the therapy at some point during each session. A more proactive approach is to ask clients to notice and record any changes for the better that occur between sessions (Kral & Kowalski, 1989). Such a homework assignment conveys the therapist's hope for and expectation of improvement, which may in turn create an observational bias on the part of the client favoring therapeutic change.

Finally, procedures or techniques are more likely to elicit a placebo response when they are based on, connected with, or elicit a previously successful experience of the client. As just one example of this, consider research conducted by Batterman and Lower (cited in O'Regan, 1985), in which people suffering from rheumatoid and osteoarthritis were given placebo pain medication. Like many others conducting studies in this area, the researchers found that the people receiving placebos experienced significant relief from the pain often associated with these two debilitating conditions. More interesting, however, was their finding that people who had previously been treated successfully for pain with an active analgesic agent experienced *more* relief when given a placebo than those who had not been treated successfully for their pain prior to receiving the placebo. Similarly, the possible placebo effect of Viagra™ is suggested by the response to sildenafil citrate apparently continuing even after its known physiological effects have elapsed (Moser, 2000).

Having a Possibility Focus

Clients are best served by therapists helping them believe in possibilities— of change, of accomplishing or getting what they want, of starting over, of succeeding or controlling their own lives. There are a variety of ways for therapists to be more "possibility focused" in their clinical work. For example, treatment can be oriented toward the future. Traditionally, psychotherapy has been based on the idea that, for clients to have better tomorrows, they must first understand the past.

Assisting clients in describing the future they want tends to make that future more salient to the present (de Shazer, Berg, Lipchik, Nunnally, Molnar, & Gingerich, 1986; Kessler & Miller, 1995). The detail also lends an aura of reality, implying that the future the client is describing is possible to achieve in the present. In many instances, possibility even becomes connected with reality when the increasingly detailed description elicits recollections of having experienced all or at least part of what is being described (Miller & Berg, 1995).

Therapists also can work to enhance or highlight a client's felt sense of personal control. Research suggests, for example, that people who believe they can influence or modify the course of life events cope better and adjust more successfully when meeting adversity. This holds true whether the belief in personal control is accurate or not. As Taylor, Wayment, and Collins (1993) pointed out, simply believing one "has the means to influence, terminate, or modify a noxious event [helps one] cope better with those events" (p. 329). At the same time, research has established a link between a successful treatment outcome and clients' general belief in their ability to influence the course of life events (e.g., Beyebach, Morejon, Palenzuela, & Rodriguez-Aris, 1996).

Case Example: From Hard to Imagine to Imagine You're Hard

As an example of putting the placebo factors to work in sex therapy, consider the case of Bill, a 30-something software executive who sought treatment for erection difficulties. Although married nearly a year, Bill had been unable to have intercourse with his wife. While able to achieve and maintain an erection through oral or manual stimulation, he became flaccid when attempting penetration. In spite of repeated reassurance from his wife, Bill reported finding it "hard to imagine" that penetration would not hurt her. When several months of education, homework assignments, and cognitive/behavioral-oriented treatment resulted in no improvement, the therapist recommended an alternate approach. Specifically, the use of a future-orientation.

Th: It seems like you're already anticipating that you're going to fail before you do it. For example, when Michael Jordan goes for a layup, it would be disastrous if he were thinking that the ball wasn't going to go in. Instead, he is thinking, "The ball is going to go in." What we need to do is to begin to have you imagine yourself successfully having intercourse—to start thinking of yourself as a success rather than a failure at this. So, for the next couple of weeks, I want you two to refrain from trying to have intercourse. Then, I want you, Bill, to spend 5 to 10 minutes each morning and evening imagining that you are successfully penetrating and having intercourse with your wife. As you imagine this, I want you notice the smile on her face and how happy she is.

Bill agreed and for the next two weeks dutifully completed the assignment each morning and evening. When he returned at the next session, he reported having had an idea he thought would enhance the exercise as well as move the process to the next stage. He suggested buying a dildo similar in size to his own penis that his wife could insert in her vagina to test for pain prior to attempting intercourse. After a few weeks of watching her and practicing inserting the dildo inside his wife himself, Bill successfully managed to have intercourse. The couple terminated treatment soon thereafter.

☐ Models and Techniques: Structure and Novelty

Although the research conducted over the last 40 years suggests a much more modest appraisal of the differential effects of theory-driven models and methods, they still have value. Specifically, models and techniques help provide therapists with replicable and structured ways for developing and practicing the values, attitudes, and behaviors consistent with the core ingredients of effective therapy. In other words, the principle contribution of models and techniques comes through enhancing the potency of the other common factors—extratherapeutic, relationship, placebo, and hope and expectancy. Possibilities for how that occurs are discussed below.

Structure and Focus

Not surprisingly, the research literature indicates that focus and structure are essential elements of effective psychotherapy. In fact, one of the best predictors of negative outcome in psychotherapy is a lack of focus and structure. Failure to provide these crucial elements can have a greater impact on treatment outcome than the personal qualities of either the therapist or the client (Mohl, 1995). Here again, given the large number of choices available, the challenging question is which structure or focus the therapist should adopt when working with a particular client. In this regard, the data indicate that the particular orientation or technique is less important than the degree to which it helps the therapist develop and practice attitudes and behaviors consistent with the common curative factors (e.g., extratherapeutic, relationship, and hope and expectancy). Therapists can evaluate the degree to which a particular treatment approach will empower the common therapeutic factors by considering the following questions:

- Does the theory or intervention fit with, or can it be tailored to complement, the client's expectations and goals for treatment?

- Does the particular strategy capitalize on client strengths, resources, and existing social network?

- Does the method identify or build on the spontaneous changes clients experience while in therapy? How?

- Would the client describe the therapeutic interaction resulting from the adoption of the particular strategy or orientation as empathic, respectful, and genuine?

- How does the orientation or intervention increase the client's sense of hope, expectancy, or personal control? Can it be modified to do so?

Models and Techniques as Novelty

Another way models and techniques can be useful is by giving clinicians different options for case conceptualization and intervention, especially when little progress is occurring. Historically, treatment failures have been attributed to the client or the therapist. Clients were labeled either resistant to change or inappropriate for psychotherapy; therapists were considered inadequately trained or countertransferentially impaired. Once the fault was found, the integrity of the model or technique could be maintained.

Nowadays, however, with more than 400 therapy models and techniques to choose from, there is little reason for continued allegiance to a particular theoretical orientation when that way of thinking about or conducting treatment falters or fails. Instead, another model or technique can be considered. No blame need be assigned; therapists and clients can simply change their minds and make another selection. In this light, the different schools of therapy may be most helpful when they provide therapists with novel ways of looking at old situations, when they empower therapists to change rather than make up their minds about clients. This is not to say that therapists should switch orientations willy-nilly every time progress is not immediate. On the other hand, theoretical or technical orthodoxy should be considered secondary to whether progress is being made.

One way for therapists to determine whether a change of mind is called for is to be, as presented earlier, more change-focused in their clinical work; namely, to be mindful of—to listen for or inquire about—any changes that the client experiences before, during, or between treatment sessions. All large-scale, meta-analytic studies of client change indicate that the most frequent improvement occurs early in the treatment process (Howard, Kopte, Krause, & Orlinsky, 1986; Smith, Glass, & Miller, 1980). Similar findings have been observed in studies of sex therapy (Hawton & Catalan, 1986). Therefore, as far as timing is concerned, the data indicate therapists should consider doing something different when they fail to hear or elicit reports of progress from clients within a few weeks (rather than months) of beginning therapy. In this regard, orientations that help the therapist adopt a different way to identify or approach the client's goals, establish a better match with the client's stage of change, foster hope, capitalize on chance events and client strengths, and use or become aware of environmental supports are likely to prove the most beneficial in promoting progress.

☐ Summary

The development of the field of sex therapy has mirrored that of psychotherapy in general: a rapid proliferation of models and techniques claiming high success followed by research documenting modest results with little evidence of differential effectiveness and a growing medicalization of the field. While prompting concerns by some that the field of sex therapy is "withering on the vine" (Hawton, 1992), an alternate view is that factors common to all therapeutic approaches are more important to treatment outcome than strategies or techniques specific to sex therapy. Four common factors derived from 40 years of outcome research on psychotherapy in general have been presented here, along with suggestions for their application to people whose primary complaint regards their sexual functioning.

☐ References

Ackerman, M., & Carey, M. (1995). Psychology's role in the assessment of erectile dysfunction: Historical precedents, current knowledge, and methods. *Journal of Consulting and Clinical Psychology, 63*(6), 862–877.

Althof, S. E. (1998). New roles for mental health clinicians in the treatment of erectile dysfunction. *Journal of Sex Education and Therapy, 23*(3), 233–236.

Althof, S. E. (1999). *Viagra and couple satisfaction and the edits.* Paper presented at the annual meeting of the Canadian Sex Research Forum, October 1, Montreal.

Ansbacher, H., & Ansbacher, R. (1956). *The individual psychology of Alfred Adler.* New York: Basic Books.

Asay, T., & Lambert, M. J. (1999). The empirical case for the common factors in therapy: quantitative findings. In M. A. Hubble, B. L. Duncan, & S. D. Miller (Eds.), *The heart and soul of change: What works in therapy* (pp. 33–56). Washington, DC: APA Press.

Bachelor, A., & Horvath, A. (1999). The therapeutic relationship. In M. A. Hubble, B. L. Duncan, & S. D. Miller (Eds.), *The heart and soul of change: What works in therapy* (pp. 133–178). Washington, DC: APA Press.

Bandura, A., & Schunk, D. H. (1981). Cultivating competence, self-efficacy, and intrinsic interest through proximal self-motivation. *Journal of Personality and Social Psychology, 41*(3), 586–598.

Berg, I. K., & Miller, S. D. (1992). *Working with the problem drinker: A solution-focused approach.* New York: W.W. Norton.

Beyebach, M., Morejon, A. R., Palenzuela, D. L., & Rodriguez-Aris, J. L. (1996). Research on the process of solution-focused therapy. In S. D. Miller, M. A. Hubble, & B. L. Duncan (Eds.), *Handbook of solution-focused brief therapy* (pp. 299–334). San Francisco: Jossey-Bass.

Clinician Reviews. (1998). New options for erectile dysfunction. *Clinician Reviews Supplement, 6,* 3–7.

de Shazer, S., Berg, I., Lipchik, E., Nunnally, E., Molnar, A., & Gingerich, W. (1986). Brief therapy: Focused solution development. *Family Process, 25*(2), 207–222.

Duncan, B. L. (1989). Paradoxical procedures in family therapy. In M. Ascher (Ed.), *Therapeutic paradox* (pp.310–348). New York: Guilford Press.

Duncan, B. L., Hubble, M. A., & Miller, S. D. (1997). *Psychotherapy with impossible cases: Efficient treatment of therapy veterans.* New York: W.W. Norton.

Estrada, A. U., & Holmes, J. M. (1999). Couples' perceptions of effective and ineffective ingredients of marital therapy. *Journal of Sex and Marital Therapy, 25*(2), 151–162.

Frank, J. D., & Frank, J. B. (1991). *Persuasion and healing: A comparative study of psychotherapy* (3rd ed.). Baltimore, MD: John Hopkins University Press.

Garfield, S. L. (1994). Research on client variables in psychotherapy. In A. E. Bergin & S. L. Garfield (Eds.), *Handbook of psychotherapy and behavior change* (4th ed.; pp. 190–228). New York: Wiley.

Greenberg, R. (1999). Common psychosocial factors in drug therapy. In M. A. Hubble, B. L. Duncan, & S. D. Miller (Eds.), *The heart and soul of change: What works in therapy* (pp. 297–328). Washington, DC: APA Press.

Hawton, K. (1992). Sex therapy research: Has it withered on the vine? *Annual Review of Sex Research, 3,* 49–72

Hawton, K., & Catalan, J. (1986). Prognostic factors in sex therapy. *Behavior Research and Therapy, 24*(4), 377–385.

Heiman, P., & LoPiccolo, J. (1983). Clinical outcome of sex therapy. *Archives of General Psychiatry, 40,* 443–449.

Held, B. (1991). The process/content distinction in psychotherapy revisited. *Psychotherapy, 28*(2), 207–217.

Howard, K. I., Kopte, S. M., Krause, M. S., & Orlinsky, D. E. (1986). The dose-effect relationship in psychotherapy. *American Psychologist, 41*(2), 159–164.

Hubble, M. A., Duncan, B. L., & Miller, S. D. (1999a). Introduction. In M. A. Hubble, B. L. Duncan, & S. D. Miller (Eds.), *The heart and soul of change: What works in therapy* (pp. 1–32). Washington, DC: APA Press.

Hubble, M. A., Duncan, B. L., & Miller, S. D. (1999b). Directing attention to what works. In M. A. Hubble, B. L. Duncan, & S. D. Miller (Eds.), *The heart and soul of change: What works in therapy* (pp. 407–448). Washington, DC: APA Press.

Hubble, M. A., Duncan, B. L., & Miller, S. D. (1999c). *The heart and soul of change: What works in therapy.* Washington, DC: APA Press.

Imber, S. D., Pilkonis, P. A., Harway, N. I., Klein, R. H., & Rubinsky, P. A. (1982). Maintenance of change in the psychotherapies. *Journal of Psychiatric Treatment and Evaluation,* 4(1), 1–5.

Kazdin, A. E. (1986). Comparative outcome studies of psychotherapy: Methodological issues and strategies. *Journal of Consulting and Clinical Psychology, 54*(1),95–105.

Kessler, R. S., & Miller, S. D. (1995). The use of a future time frame in psychotherapy with and without hypnosis. *American Journal of Clinical Hypnosis, 38*(1), 39–46.

Kottler, J. (1991). *The complete therapist.* San Francisco: Jossey-Bass.

Kral, R., & Kowlaski, K. (1989). After the miracle: The second stage in solution-focused brief therapy. *Journal of Strategic and Systemic Therapies, 8*(2/3), 73–76.

Lambert, M. J. (1992). Implications of outcome research for psychotherapy integration. In J. C. Norcross & M. R. Goldfried (Eds.), *Handbook of psychotherapy integration* (pp. 94–129). New York: Basic Books.

Lambert, M., & Bergin, A. E. (1994). The effectiveness of psychotherapy. In A. E. Bergin, & S. L. Garfield (Eds.), *Handbook of psychotherapy and behavior change* (4th ed.; pp. 143–189). New York: Wiley.

Lawson, D. (1994). Identifying pretreatment change. *Journal of Counseling and Development, 72*(3), 244–248.

Leiblum, S., & Rosen, R. (1989). *Principles and practices of sex therapy.* New York: Guilford.

Levin, S. R., & Agle, D. (1978). The effectiveness of sex therapy for chronic secondary psychological impotence. *Journal of Sex and Marital Therapy, 4*(4), 235–258.

Masters, W., & Johnson, V. (1966). *Human sexual response.* Boston: Little, Brown.

Masters, W., & Johnson, V. (1970). *Human sexual inadequacy.* Boston: Little, Brown.

Matheson, D., Bruce, R., & Beauchamp, K. (1978). *Experimental psychology: Research design and analysis.* New York: Holt, Rinehart, & Winston.

Miller, S. D. (1994). The solution conspiracy. *Journal of Systemic Therapies, 13*(1), 18–38.

Miller, S. D., & Berg, I. K. (1995). *The miracle method: A radically new approach to problem drinking.* New York: W.W. Norton.

Miller, S. D., Duncan, B. L., & Hubble, M. A. (1997). *Escape from Babel: Toward a unifying language for psychotherapy practice.* New York: W.W. Norton.

Miller, S. D., Duncan, B. L., & Hubble, M. A. (1999). Some thoughts on the nature of therapeutic revolutions. In W. A. Ray, & S. de Shazer (Eds.), *Evolving brief therapies* (pp. 68–77). Iowa City, IA: Geist & Russell.

Miller, W. R. (1987). Motivation and treatment goals. *Drugs and Society, 1*(2/3),131–151.

Mohl, D. C. (1995). Negative outcome in psychotherapy: A critical review. *Clinical Psychology, 2*(1), 1–27.

Moser, C. (2000). *The effect of sildenafil citrate on middle-aged "normal" men.* Unpublished manuscript.

Norcross, J., & Newman, C. F. (1992). Psychotherapy integration: Setting the context. In J. C. Norcross & M. R. Goldfried (Eds.), *Handbook of psychotherapy integration* (pp. 3–45). New York: Basic Books.

O'Regan, B. (1985). Placebo: The hidden asset in healing. *Investigations: A Research Bulletin, 2*(1), 1–3.

Orlinsky, D. E., Grawe, K., & Parks, B. K. (1994). Process and outcome in psychotherapy—noch einmal. In A. E. Bergin & S. L. Garfield, (Eds.), *Handbook of psychotherapy and behavior change* (4th ed.; pp. 270–378). New York: Wiley.

Plaut, S. M. (1998). Editor's note: A new look at the biopsychosocial nature of sexuality. *Journal of Sex Education and Therapy, 23*(3), 183.

Prochaska, J. O. (1993). Working in harmony with how people change naturally. *Weight Control Digest, 3,* 249–255.

Prochaska, J. O. (1995). Common problems: Common solutions. *Clinical Psychology: Science and Practice, 2*(1), 101–105.

Prochaska, J. O. (1999). How do people change, and how can we change to help many more people? In M. A. Hubble, B. L. Duncan, & S. D. Miller (Eds.), *The heart and soul of change: What works in therapy* (pp. 227–258). Washington, DC: APA Press.

Prochaska, J. O., & DiClemente, C. C. (1992). The transtheoretical approach. In J. C. Norcross & M. R. Goldfried (Eds.), *Handbook of psychotherapy integration* (pp. 300–334). New York: Basic Books.

Prochaska, J. O., DiClemente, C. C., & Norcross, J. C. (1992). In search of how people change. *American Psychologist, 47*(9), 1102–1114.

Reuterlov, H., Lofgren, T., Nordstrom, K., Ternstrom, A., & Miller, S. D. (2000). What's better? Clients' reports of change in second and subsequent session. *Journal of Systemic Therapies, 19*(1), 111–115.

Rodger, B. (1982). Ericksonian approaches in anesthesiology. In J. K. Zeig (Ed.), *Ericksonian approaches to hypnosis and psychotherapy* (pp. 317–329). New York: Brunner/Mazel.

Rosen, R., & Beck, J. (1988). *Patterns of sexual arousal: Psychophysiological processes and clinical applications*. New York: Guilford Press.

Rosen, R. C., & Leiblum, S. R., (1995). Treatment of sexual disorders in the 1990s: An integrated approach. *Journal of Consulting and Clinical Psychology, 63*(6), 877–890.

Rosenzweig, S. (1936). Some implicit common factors in diverse methods in psychotherapy. *Journal of Orthopsychiatry, 6,* 412–415.

Schover, L. R., & Leiblum, S. R. (1994). Commentary: The stagnation of sex therapy. *Journal of Psychology and Human Sexuality, 6*(3), 5–30.

Shadish, W. R., Montgomery, L. M., Wilson, P., Wilson, M. R., Bright, I., & Okwumabua, T. (1993). Effects of family and marital psychotherapies: A meta-analysis. *Journal of Consulting and Clinical Psychology, 61*(6), 992–1002.

Smith, M. L., Glass, G. V., & Miller, T. I. (1980). *The benefits of psychotherapy*. Baltimore, MD: Johns Hopkins University Press.

Sprenkle, D. H., Blow, A. J., & Dickey, M. H. (1999). Common factors and other nontechnique variables in marriage and family therapy. In M. A. Hubble, B. L. Duncan, & S. D. Miller Eds.), *The heart and soul of change: What works in therapy* (pp. 329–360). Washington, DC: APA Press.

Strupp, H., Hadley, S. W., & Gomez-Schwartz, B. (1974). Specific versus nonspecific factors in psychotherapy: A controlled study of outcome. *Archives of General Psychiatry, 36*(10), 1125–1136.

Taylor, S. E., Wayment, H. A., & Collins, M. A. (1993). Positive illusions and affect regulation. In D. M. Wegner & J. W. Pennebaker (Eds.), *Handbook of mental control* (pp. 325–343). Englewood Cliffs, NJ: Prentice-Hall.

Torrey, E. (1972). *The mind game: Witchdoctors and psychiatrists*. New York: Emerson Hall.

Van Gennep, A. (1960). *The rites of passage*. Chicago: Chicago University Press.

Walter, J., & Peller, J. (1992). *Becoming solution-focused in brief therapy*. New York: Brunner/Mazel.

Weinberger, J. (1995). Common factors aren't so common: The common factors dilemma. *Clinical Psychology, 2*(1), 45–69.

Zilbergeld, B., & Evans, M. (1980). The inadequacy of Masters and Johnson. *Psychology Today* (August), 29–43.

CHAPTER

11

Alvin R. Mahrer, Ph.D.
Donald B. Boulet, Ph.D.

How Can Experiential Psychotherapy Help Transform the Field of Sex Therapy?

A few introductory points are called for in order to clarify the title of this chapter and to situate experiential psychotherapy in relation to most other therapies, sexual and otherwise.

☐ An Apology to Sex Therapists

We are not qualified sex therapists. We are not even unqualified sex therapists. We do not hold ourselves out as doing sex therapy or as specialists in sexual problems. We have no special background, knowledge, or training in sexual problems or sex therapy.

☐ Some Challenging Invitations to Sex Therapists

This chapter has a fair chance of being reasonably successful if some sex therapists are at least a little willing to accept the following challenging invitations:

234

- Are you reasonably willing to give this chapter a fair hearing, even though it does not conform to much of what is generally accepted in the field of sex therapy, and even though it may conspicuously depart from and violate many of the basic truths and foundational beliefs in the field of sex therapy?

- Can you set aside, for a while, the common framework of thinking of therapies as falling into a large matrix of what treatments are effective for what kinds of sexual problems (e.g., Leiblum & Rosen, 1989)? Instead, the invitation is to be at least a little open to the possibility that experiential psychotherapy may well accomplish some magnificent changes that most sessions of most sex therapies do not and cannot accomplish.

- Can you be open to the possibility of learning more about and actually trying out experiential psychotherapy if its way of thinking about human beings and psychotherapy and if what this therapy seeks to accomplish in a session are somewhat appealing and attractive?

- Can you be open to the possibility of allowing some transformational shifts in the field of sex therapy? The thinking underlying experiential psychotherapy is probably so alien to most sex therapies, and its positions on some basic questions are so distinctive, that you can use this chapter to open up the possibility of looking at these basic questions to find newer and better positions than those of experiential psychotherapy or even those of traditional sex therapies. One way of transforming a field is to play with altogether different positions or answers to basic questions.

☐ A Capsule Introduction to Experiential Sessions

The final section of this chapter gives a full description of an experiential session, but it is probably helpful to provide a snapshot here. Picture a person by oneself, in a session by oneself, or with a therapist; both have their eyes closed throughout the session, which usually lasts for an hour and a half, perhaps up to two hours. The session opens by searching for a scene, some time or situation when the feeling was very strong, a scene from recently or from some time ago. Now picture the person literally entering into this scene until it is exceedingly real and alive, and he or she locates the actual instant when the feeling peaks. By penetrating down into this instant, the person arrives at his or her inner world, a deeper world of hidden qualities and ways of being, different possibilities or potentialities for experiencing deep within, a world that is essentially unknown to the person him- or herself. This first step ends when the person touches, or is touched by, a deeper potential for experiencing.

The second step is a means for the person to welcome and love this deeper potential for experiencing that has been sealed off, kept down, hidden deep inside. In the third step, the person literally hurls him- or herself into the wholesale being of the whole new person who is this deeper potential for experiencing. This step is transformational; the person has become a radically new, qualitatively different person. The final step opens with this entirely new person tasting and sampling what a whole new world can be like, living and being in the imminent world of the immediate future of today and tomorrow and beyond. The final step ends when the whole new person, including what had been the deeper potential for experiencing, has a chance to rehearse, select, and commit him- or herself to a fitting, appealing way of being this new person in defined scenes in the whole new world that awaits.

If the opening scene were one of bad feeling, the qualitatively new person and world are essentially free of that scene of bad feeling. This is the bonus to the deeper and more profound change in the very person that the new person has become.

This chapter is organized around four questions:

- What are the significant changes a person can achieve in an experiential session?

- In the experiential framework, precisely what is "sexual"?

- In attaining the goals of an experiential session, are "sexual problems" and "sexual disorders" useful or essentially useless terms, and what is a preferable alternative?

- How do a therapist and patient proceed through an experiential session?

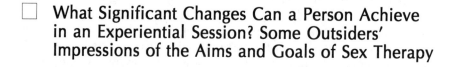

What Significant Changes Can a Person Achieve in an Experiential Session? Some Outsiders' Impressions of the Aims and Goals of Sex Therapy

In trying to become familiar with the field of sex therapy, our ignorance was punctuated by terms and phrases like meningomyelocele, dyspareunia, phocomelia, penile prostheses, pubococcygeal muscle, orgasmic platform, sexual surrogate, and paraphilia. What was not especially surprising was the technical knowledge in areas such as physiology, anatomy, neurology, and chemistry. Nor were we surprised that the field had a sophisticated category system of sexual problems, which sex therapy was to treat.

But three impressions about the apparent aims and goals were somewhat surprising and a little scary. One was that there seemed to be such collective agreement on what the aims and goals of sex therapy are, how people ought to be and behave sexually, what constitutes approved and disapproved sexual behavior, and how deeply ingrained were the do's and don'ts, the shalls and shalt nots, the values and moral-ethical judgments of so many sex therapists (Levine & Troiden, 1988). It was almost as if the professional attire hid the black robes of finger-wagging moral judges, contemporary ghosts of the Spanish Inquisition in the garb of sex therapists.

A second impression was the disturbingly deep and abiding differences separating a group labeled "males" and a group labeled "females." It seemed that differences within each group were dwarfed by the supposedly powerful and fundamental differences between these two categories, and that these differences were reflected in disturbingly different aims and goals of sex therapy for members of these two groups.

A final impression was the objective separation between the person and the sexual problem. It seemed as if the person was almost irrelevant or replaceable as the one who housed or owned the sexual problem that sex therapy aimed to fix.

On the other hand, these impressions may be explained away as either evidence of our ignorance of the field or reflections of our experiential way of looking at these issues.

Each experiential session is designed to enable just about any person to achieve two relatively general changes, which are described below.

The Direction of Change Is Toward Becoming a Qualitatively Transformed New Person

In each session, the person is given an opportunity to undergo a deep-seated change toward being the qualitatively transformed new person he or she is capable of becoming.

The session enables the person to probe deep inside and discover what lies there. In the experiential way of picturing a person, what lies deep inside are inner, deeper possibilities of experiencing, ways of being. They are called *deeper potentials for experiencing,* and they may consist of just about any kind of experiencing. For example, what lies deep inside may be a deeper potential for experiencing intimacy, closeness, and oneness; silliness, giddiness, and whimsy; being dominant, superior, and controlling; wonder, awe, and surprise; a sense of being stimulated, aroused, and excited. Once the deeper potential for experiencing is discovered, the person is enabled to welcome and love, to appreciate and cherish this deeper potential for experiencing. This is called *integration*. Even further, the person is provided an opportunity for this potential for experiencing to become an integral new part of the utterly new person he or she can become. Once this formerly deeper potential for experiencing becomes a part of who and what the person is, the person has undergone an utterly qualitative change into being an utterly transformed new person. This is called *actualization*.

The qualitatively transformed, new person acts and behaves, relates and interrelates, perceives and thinks, feels and experiences, and builds and constructs new worlds in new ways. Even further, there is a whole new person who acts and behaves, relates and interrelates, perceives and thinks, builds and constructs personal worlds, feels and experiences.

And there is a surprising bonus. Along with a transformed new person are actual bodily and physical changes in what is generally acknowledged as the sexual parts of the body, as sexual bodily structures and functions, as sexual anatomy, physiology, neurology, and chemistry. These deep-seated changes can and do include significant changes in the body that is the person.

The Direction of Change Is Toward Being Free of the Scene of Strong Bad Feeling

In the beginning of each session, the person looks for some scene of strong feeling, some situation or time when the feeling was powerful, intense, and saturating. The scene of strong feeling may be part of the person's current life, from relatively recently, or even from long ago. It may be a scene in which the feeling was pleasant and happy or (more often) painful, negative, awful, or bad.

By the end of the session, the direction of change is for the person to be free of the scene of strong bad feeling. It is no longer a part of his or her world, no longer a part of what life is for this person, no longer present in the person's ongoing world. Similarly, he or she is essentially free of the painful, strong, bad feelings that were a part of that scene.

Clinical and Research Criteria of the Effectiveness and Success of an Experiential Session

Suppose that, in the first part of a session, (a) we discover a deeper potential for experiencing being dominant, superior, and controlling, and (b) what was front and center was a scene in which her frail hopes were once again crushed in an attempt at love-making without even a whisper of sexual desire, and she is engulfed by awful feelings of self-doubt and gloomy guilt. What are the clinical and research criteria that the session was (or was not) successful?

There are two changes to look for, and each should occur by the end of the session and be present in the beginning of the next:

1. By the end of the session, even for just a few minutes, a qualitatively new person is present, one who includes the formerly deeper potential for experiencing. The criterion is the presence of a new person who radiates a new-felt quality of being wholesomely dominant, superior, and controlling. The more stringent added criterion is that the person who shows up for the next session is this continuing, qualitatively new person.

2. By the end of the session, the woman is free of the awful scene of desperately hoping for the preciously elusive sexual desire and the painful feelings associated with its absence. All of this is gone. Furthermore, neither the former painful scene nor the former painful feelings are part of the new person or the world of the new person who is here in the next session.

So, the stringent criteria for a successful experiential session are that, by the end of the session and the beginning of the next, the person has become a qualitatively new person and the new person's new world is essentially free of the old person's painful scene and the painful feelings in that scene.

A Friendly Challenge: An Experiential Session Is Better Than a Sex Therapy Session at Achieving These Goals

Most researchers have a mind-set in which therapies are compared by looking at posttreatment outcomes to see which is better in treating the pretreatment problem (Heiman & Meston, 1997; Kilmann, Boland, Norton, & Caid, 1986; Schover & Leiblum, 1994). Suppose we raise the stringency stakes. Experiential psychotherapy claims that it can achieve its two goals by the end of the session. The friendly challenge is for a session of sex therapy to show it can do better—that it can beat experiential psychotherapy in achieving these two goals by the end of a session.

Let's raise the research stakes even higher. Would you accept these conditions? If a sex therapy session can achieve these two goals better than an experiential session, we will do sex therapy. However, if an experiential session does better, you will replace sex therapy with experiential psychotherapy. Agreed?

The Purpose of Experiential Research Is to Improve Experiential Psychotherapy, Rather Than to Validate Its Effectiveness or Relative Effectiveness

Probably our main reason for doing research is to discover how to do psychotherapy better (Mahrer, 1996b), including experiential psychotherapy, rather than seeking to demonstrate that this therapy is effective, or is effective for this or that kind of sexual problem. We do not believe experiential psychotherapy is improved by research aimed at showing that it is effective, or is effective for this sexual problem, or is more effective than a rival treatment for some sexual problem. Of all the reasons for doing research, we prefer to do research to help make the psychotherapy better.

Experiential Psychotherapy Is for Most People, But Only for Some Practitioners

Just about any person can achieve the two valued changes by having a session with a fine experiential psychotherapist. An experiential session is appropriate for and can start from virtually any kind of scene of strong feeling. Regardless of what sex therapists would label the person diagnostically or label as a sexual problem, he or she will almost certainly be appropriate for an experiential session, and experiential psychotherapy will be appropriate for that person.

However, doing experiential psychotherapy is probably only appropriate for that small proportion of practitioners who share the experiential way of thinking about human beings and psychotherapy. Most practitioners do not share this way of thinking. That is, experiential psychotherapy is for most people, but only for some practitioners (Mahrer, 1996a).

Replace the Therapist Who Administers Treatment With the Teacher Who Teaches People How to Undergo Their Own Experiential Sessions.

What can sex therapists do if they themselves are genuinely interested in becoming more of what they can become and in being free of their own painful feelings in painful situations? Our answer is for sex therapists to become experts in undergoing their own experiential sessions. This opens up the exciting and bold possibility that sex therapists can also let go of their traditional role of the professional who administers the treatment and instead welcome the new role of the teacher who teaches interested individuals and groups how to become proficient in undergoing their own experiential sessions. The one who carries out the therapy is the "therapee," not the therapist! In this radical picture, sex therapists are still professionals with expertise, but what they do in their sessions is aimed at both achieving the two experiential goals and at teaching individuals and groups how to have their own personal experiential sessions.

☐ What Is the Experiential Meaning of "Sexual"?

Sex Therapists Would Probably Have a Hard Time Justifying Exclusive Ownership Rights of "Sexual"

It is probably unfortunate that groups are so clever in coming up with phrases that give the impression that they have exclusive ownership rights over their selected piece of the psychotherapy and counseling territory. "Sex therapy" is clever. But whatever "sexual" is can be owned by lots of other groups with their own clever phrases. When sexual involves behavior, sexual is owned by behavior therapy. When the sexual person is female, sexual can be owned by feminist therapy. When sexual involves two people, sexual can be owned by couples therapy. If sexual involves several persons, it can be owned by family therapy, group therapy, or even community therapy. If sexual occurs in the school, at work, or in a criminal context, it can be owned by school counseling, vocational or organizational counseling, forensic therapy, and many others. By giving up the myth of exclusive ownership over sexual, the field may be in a better position of moving forward as an enriched, broader, and more comprehensive field.

This brings us to the question of what is the experiential meaning of *sexual*.

Sexual Can Refer to the Scene in Which the Strong Feeling Occurs

The word sexual may refer to the scene of strong feeling that is front and center for the person and the therapist. If one scene is of two sweaty bodies on a bed, writhing in the ecstasy of intercourse, and another is of being locked onto the wheel of the sports car as it hurdles off the road and down the embankment, the first scene may be called sexual and the second scene not especially so.

Sexual may refer to the scene of strong feeling, but neither the person nor the experiential therapist does anything differently, whether a scene is called sexual or not. The point is that the word sexual may refer to something about a scene of strong feeling, even though calling a scene sexual is almost irrelevant in experiential psychotherapy.

Sexual Can Refer to the Immediately Ongoing Experiencing

The word "sexual" can refer to the nature of the experiencing occurring right now in the person. At this very moment, the experiencing in this person may be described with words such as sexual, romantic, lusty, erotic, or aroused.

The key is the sexual nature of the immediately ongoing experiencing, rather than what is talked about. A woman may well be talking about her sexual feelings or about how aroused she was with the right partner or during her most recent orgasm, but the immediately ongoing experiencing is not sexual if she is undergoing dispassionate withdrawal, distance, and objective analysis, or if the experiencing is one of being special, the precious jewel, the wonderful one. What is important is whether or not the immediately ongoing experiencing is sexual. If so, this is a second meaning of sexual.

Sexual Can Refer to the Deeper Potential for Experiencing

An experiential session starts by seeking to find a scene of strong feeling, and then uses that scene to discover the underlying, deeper potential for experiencing. The word "sexual" may refer to the nature of the scene of strong feeling, or to the nature of the immediately ongoing experiencing, or to the nature of something much deeper inside the person—a deeper potential for experiencing. It is an inner capacity for experiencing, an available kind of experiencing.

Usually, describing the particular nature of this deeper potential for experiencing in this person takes more words than merely calling it sexual. Here are some examples of more detailed descriptions of deeper potentials for experiencing, all of which may be loosely referred to as sexual: an experiencing of sexual giving in, passivity, surrender; an experiencing of sexual control, ownership, domination; an experiencing of showing, displaying, exhibiting sexuality; being sexually seductive, arousing, provocative; an experiencing of sexual oneness, intimacy, melding into one another; experiencing of sexual wildness, explosiveness, uncontained sexuality.

In the experiential framework, there are at least three quite different meanings or referents for the word "sexual." This raises the neighboring question: In other frameworks, such as sex therapy, precisely what does the word "sexual" mean?

☐ The "Scene of Strong Feeling" Is Exceedingly Useful: The "Sexual Problem" or "Diagnosis" Is Useless

One of the goals of an experiential session is to enable the person to undergo a deep-seated change, a qualitative shift into being a wholly transformed new person. The related goal is to become free of the scene or situation of bad feeling, so that neither the scene nor the bad feeling in that scene is part of this new person's new world.

In order to help achieve these two goals, it is important to find a scene of strong feeling. The feeling may be good or bad, but the work of the session requires that we start from some scene of strong feeling and not from what other therapies may rely on as some kind of "sexual problem" or sexual diagnosis, disease, illness, dysfunction, paraphilia, or disorder. In other words, experiential psychotherapy relies on the scene of strong feeling, often the scene of strong bad feeling, and declines any meaning or use of what other therapies call a "sexual problem, diagnosis, or disorder." There are several reasons for this.

Identifying and Getting Information About a "Sexual Problem" or "Diagnosis" Is Useless for an Experiential Session

Once a field buys the core notion that there are such things as sexual problems, sexual diagnoses, and sexual disorders, the field has bought a whole package of related things, such as identifying different kinds of sexual problems and disorders, having rules and guidelines for assessing and evaluating the presence of each kind (e.g., Charlton, 1997; Kaplan, 1995;

Schnarch, 1991; Wincze & Carey, 1991), and selecting and carrying out the appropriate treatment (see American Psychiatric Association, 1994; Rosen & Leiblum, 1995). It is then proclaimed authoritatively that professional sex therapists are to do an initial evaluation and assessment of the sexual problem or diagnosis/disorder. Experiential psychotherapy respectfully declines. In terms of the work and the goals of an experiential session, identifying and getting information about a sexual problem or diagnosis/disorder are essentially useless.

Not only does getting information about the patient's sexual problem or diagnosis offer practically nothing useful to the experiential therapist but, even more damaging, the very search for a so-called sexual problem or diagnosis tends to prevent the experiential session from being successful. It prevents finding the scene of strong feeling. It prevents discovery of the deeper potential. It prevents achievement of the goals of the session. The search for information about a sexual problem or diagnosis is not only useless for a successful experiential session, it is downright damaging.

Sexual Problems and Diagnoses Are Useless for Finding Sexual Scenes of Strong, Nonsexual Bad Feelings

Experiential work starts by finding a concrete scene of strong feeling. Many of these scenes are sexual, but the strong bad feeling is nonsexual. The whole enterprise of looking for and finding some sexual problem or diagnosis leaves the experiential therapist and patient with little or no idea of the sexual scene of strong, bad, nonsexual feeling.

When most therapists have labeled the patient the problem, and the diagnosis as a sexual addiction, the experiential therapist and patient still have the job of searching for a scene of strong feeling. It turns out to be this: He is watching a pornographic video from his secret cache in the basement, and he is knife-edged vigilant to the sounds from the garage, where his wife and son are returning from the school play. He is on edge that they might burst into the family room and catch him with the pornographic video. The feeling is strong, bad, *not sexual.*

It is almost impossible that a counselor calling the problem "sexual abuse" will ever find a scene of strong, bad feeling in which the 11-year-old girl is taking a shower, her mother's boyfriend comes in pretending he doesn't know she is in the shower, and her attention is riveted on the image of her mother outside the bathroom, complicit with his actions. Her thumping feeling is that she is just useable meat to her mother and her mother's boyfriend. Again, the feeling is strong, bad, and not sexual.

The very idea of sexual problems and diagnoses sends therapists on a chase that will almost certainly fail to find the experiential scene of strong, bad, nonsexual feeling.

Sexual Problems and Diagnoses Are Useless for Finding Scenes of Strong, Bad Feelings of Any Kind

The experiential quest is for scenes of strong, bad feelings, whether they are regarded as sexual or not. These scenes are almost outside the scope of what will be found when the search is for a sexual problem or diagnosis. Such a search is probably not going to have many sessions in which the emphasis is on scenes of his rising anxiety as he sees the elevator doors close and he is alone inside, or her heavy gloom as she sits on the cemetery grass, stroking the tombstone of her dead baby.

Even if the patient talks about sexual situations, the search for some sexual problem or disorder will almost certainly fall short of the experiential patient's actual scene of strong feeling. The nonexperiential therapist will search for evidence of the client's hypersexuality from her being aroused by men at work. However, in the experiential session a richly detailed scene is created: She is in the elevator of the government building, on her way to the 14th floor, where she works. Over there, among the seven or eight passengers, is that young good-looking fellow she has seen several times before. She is so aroused that she is trembling, acutely aware of the possibility that others might notice a sexual odor emanating from her genitals and her pointed glances at him. As the elevator stops at the 11th floor and he seems geared to leave, she closes her eyes, trying to summon her will to stay on the elevator, fighting her powerful impulses to follow him, to see where he works. She has done this before with other men, and she feels weak, nauseous, and disgusted as she opens her eyes and watches the back of his gorgeous head disappear.

Sexual Problems and Diagnoses Are Useless for Finding Scenes of Strong, Good Feelings, Sexual or Not

Not only does the search for sexual problems and diagnoses tend to lose scenes of strong, bad feelings, it also loses scenes of strong, good feelings, including scenes when the good feelings are sexual. Each experiential session starts by looking for scenes of strong feeling, and the menu explicitly includes good feelings. In perhaps 20% to 30% of experiential sessions, the scenes contain feelings that are delightful, happy, exciting, pleasurable. If we search for sexual problems and diagnoses, the chances are exceedingly low that we will look for, find, and work from scenes of strong, good feeling, sexual or otherwise. Yet these are as useful as scenes of strong, bad feelings in the work of an experiential session.

Sexual Problems and Diagnoses Are Useless for Discovering Deeper Potentials for Experiencing

In each experiential session, the first step culminates in the discovery of a deeper potential for experiencing. It is almost a truism that searching for the nature of a person's sexual problem is not going to bring the therapist or the person much closer to discovering the deeper potential for experiencing. Indeed, it is almost a sure bet that the whole process of treating a person's sexual problem will not bring the therapist or the person one inch closer to discovering the deeper potential for experiencing.

The Sexual Problem or Diagnosis Labels the Client Over the Whole Treatment Versus in Each Session the Person Finds a Scene of Strong Feeling

Once the sex therapist gets a solid grasp of the sexual problem or diagnosis, usually in an intake evaluation and psychodiagnostic assessment, the client is stamped with that continuing label over the course of treatment. If she is identified as a rape victim in the initial evaluation, she remains a rape victim. It is not especially common that each subsequent session starts with a fresh evaluation and assessment of the problem or diagnosis, although the therapist may later notice symptoms of something else, such as dyspareunia or low sexual desire.

In contrast, each experiential session opens with an opportunity for the person to find, focus on, and define whatever scene of strong feeling is front and center in this session. In the first session, the scene of strong feeling is right after her uncle taunts her, saying that she asked for it as he releases her from the kitchen floor. She is galvanized into grabbing the big knife and, in a state of glaring rage, guttural noises pouring from her throat, she waves the knife from side to side. In the second session, the scene of most powerful feeling is after the interview at the police station, when she and her mother are at her apartment and they share an incredibly powerful outpouring of rage at the uncle, and at men in general, and there is a whole new sense of bonded oneness between the two of them. In the third session, the scene of strong feeling is her as a child, proud of being fiercely independent, and never bothering her mother with worries and problems, like when the little boy next door accuses her mother of being dirty, and she sits at the kitchen table with her mother, determinedly not telling her what the boy said about her, except that she so wants to tell her mother what happened because she is so very scared.

In each session, to label the client with a sexual problem or diagnosis is not only useless but downright interfering with the important initial search for the important scene of strong feeling.

The Goals of "Fixing" Sexual Problems and Diagnoses Cannot Match the Goals of an Experiential Session

In each session, the experiential therapist and the person arrive at and move toward particular aims, goals, significant changes, and movement in the direction of optimal being for this person. It is almost certain that the aims and goals of assessing the patient as having some sexual problem or diagnosis cannot match the aims and goals of an experiential session. The aims and goals of the experiential therapist and the sex therapist are very likely to have almost nothing in common, with those of an experiential session probably being deeper and more comprehensive, and those of the sex therapist probably more superficial and truncated.

Perhaps the main reason is that each defined sexual problem or diagnosis includes its own particularized built-in aim and goal. Once you name the sexual problem or diagnosis, you have virtually defined the treatment aim or goal. If the problem or diagnosis is low sexual desire, then the almost automatic aim or goal is for the patient to have whatever is accepted as normal sexual desire. If the sexual problem or diagnosis is premature ejaculation, the patient is to have mature, not premature, ejaculations. If the sexual problem or diagnosis is sexual addiction or compulsive sexual behavior, the aim and goal is that the patient is not to be so addicted to sex and not to have a compulsion for sexual behavior. If the sexual problem or diagnosis is anorgasmia, then the almost automatic aim and goal is for the person to have orgasms. Whatever else is accomplished, once the sexual problem or diagnosis is defined, there is a built-in, automatic end-aim and end-goal.

In an experiential session, the aims and goals are not built into the sexual problem or diagnosis. They come from identifying the scene of strong feeling so that the goal is the washing away or the absence of that painful scene and the painful feelings in that scene.

They also come from digging down into the person's insides and finding a deeper potential for experiencing so that the aims and goals include the becoming of a whole new person with that deeper potential for experiencing a new part of the whole new person. The net result is that if a person somehow has an experiential session and a session with a sex therapist, the chances are exceedingly high that there will be almost no overlap between the two sets of aims and goals.

Even further, there typically is a flow of differing aims and goals for each successive experiential session, whereas in most sex therapies the aims and goals are largely set in the initial assessment of the sexual problem or diagnosis. These considerations make a case for saying that the aims and goals from sexual problems and diagnoses cannot match the aims and goals of an experiential session.

☐ How Do the Therapist and the Person Proceed Through an Experiential Session?

This volume is a forum for alternative and perhaps new ways of thinking about and doing what is generally called sex therapy. We believe that experiential psychotherapy qualifies. The purpose of this section is to provide an illustration of how to proceed through an experiential session with a person who might well be seen in the office of a sex therapist. This section is perhaps mainly for those who are in reasonable accord with the chapter so far, and who are therefore interested in what an experiential session looks like.

The Logistics

Picture a psychotherapist and a person, rather than a couple or a family, although these other arrangements are possible. Picture the person as the one who initiated the call for an appointment, even though a professional person or a relative or a friend may have told or encouraged the person to call the therapist. The telephone arrangements include letting the person know that the session is over when we both feel that it is over, whether that is under or over an hour, with most sessions being between one and two hours. Also, the therapist lets the person know that after the session we can decide if and when there might be a next session.

In the office, which is effectively sound-proofed, the person and the therapist sit in chairs that are large and comfortable, with large footrests, both chairs facing in the same direction, and quite close to one another. For therapists who are not comfortable with this arrangement, the chairs may be at some angle with one another. In either case, it is almost mandatory that eyes are to be closed throughout the session, both for the therapist and for the person. Typically, the therapist explains that it seems to be much easier to see what the person talks about if eyes are closed, and that is sufficient for virtually all persons, including patients who themselves are psychotherapists.

In the experiential approach, therapeutic work begins and ends with this session. In other words, each session is its own mini-therapy. Accordingly, the initial session is proceeded through as if this is the beginning and the ending of the therapeutic work. The initial session, in other words, proceeds through the same steps as any other session.

When Serge called for an appointment, he and the therapist agreed on an appointment about a week from then. The therapist provided the relevant information, and Serge showed up for the session. They go into the office, the therapist explains about having eyes closed, and the session is ready to begin.

The Person Is the One Who Does the Work; The Therapist Is the Teacher–Guide Who Accompanies the Person in the Work

Throughout the session, the therapist shows the person what to do, why to do it, and how to do it. The therapist is the teacher, the guide, and also accompanies the person in the work of the session. In turn, the therapist invites the person to be in the role of the one who carries out the work of the session. It is the person who carries out the actual work of change, rather than the therapist acting in the traditional role of therapist who administers therapy or who applies interventions onto the patient.

This means that the person's readiness and willingness to undertake each bit of work is uppermost. If the person is not ready or willing, that too is honored and we pause or stop. These therapist and patient roles essentially diffuse the typical sex therapist's concern about client "resistance" because there is essentially nothing for the client to resist (cf. Althof et al., 1989; Hartman, 1983; Kaplan, 1995). The person is the boss, not the therapist. If the person is not ready or is inclined to stop, that is what we do.

Therapist and Person Attend Mainly to the Person's Personal World

Throughout the session, the person's attention is almost exclusively directed at the person's personal world, at whatever is front and center for the person. Picture the person, with eyes closed, attending mainly to the objects and things of the person's world, to the scenes and situations that are immediately here for the person. Picture the therapist as doing the same. That is, the therapist's eyes are closed, and the therapist's attention is almost fully directed toward whatever is placed front and center by the person. Both therapist and person are concentrating on whatever is personally relevant and immediately here in the person's personal world.

This stance is in contrast to the ordinary stance in which therapist and patient are attending mainly to one another throughout most of the session.

Show the Person How to Find a Scene of Powerful Feeling

The therapist shows Serge how to find scenes when the feelings were truly powerful. Here are just a few of the ways of seeing what scenes, times, come to mind when either the therapist or Serge says aloud: (a) What is it that concerns me the most, the thing that bothers me terribly, the thing I worry about, feel awful about, the times and places when I feel so bad, so worried and bothered and concerned? What comes to mind? He answers himself: "It's when ... I was alone last week, at night, and ... I feel like crying, but I don't ... I am so depressed, nothing helps, may as well be dead ... Just feel so lost and ... depressed. I know I'm depressed ... " (b) When is it that the feeling in me was so powerful, so strong, inside, it was so bad, so awful, it hurts so much, one of the worst times? Serge answers, "Oh ... yes... Nadia, my wife, and we're talking. She is holding my hands, sitting on the bed, and she's just asking if I think we can ever have sex again ... She's so understanding, she knows I have depression, and she is just asking ... My depression stopped me and I have no sex feelings for years ... I want so much ... I try to tell her, and we talk ... This is so awful...." (c) When was it that I felt crazy, like falling apart, losing it, going out of my mind, when I hit bottom? "I think of when I was in Toronto last year, and this woman I met ... at the bar ... We went to her room and she touched me, and I think something snapped cause I started crying cause I had nothing. I don't even remember leaving. I felt like I wanted to be dead. In my hotel room. I just cried and it was the worst time in my life. That's when I came home and went to my doctor and ended up in the mental hospital."

The therapist asks Serge to decide which scene seems most compelling, most on his mind, the time that is pulling him most. "With Nadia ... On the bed. I'd do anything to get rid of this depression and have sex again..."

If a sex therapist were listening to an audiotape of the session up to here, she might announce that depression is a common comcomitant of low sexual desire in men, and quote people like Donahey and Carroll (1993) and Schreiner-Engel and Schiavi (1986). In contrast, those formal labels neither come from nor have any formal meaning in experiential psychotherapy. Second, the experiential therapist prefers finding out what is front and center for Serge in each session, rather than labeling him as having depression and low sexual desire as if they are to be his "problems" throughout all of the sessions. Third, the experiential therapist and Serge would carry out a session in the same way whether things called depression and low sexual desire were found to go together or to not go together.

Show the Person How to Live in the Scene and to Find the Moment of Powerful Peak Feeling

Serge is partly living in this scene. The therapist invites him to remain here, and to make the scene alive and real and very present, and for Serge to allow himself to be fully and completely in this scene of powerful feeling. He is to say aloud that he is to detail everything happening here, both outside him and inside him—every detail of the room, the bed, Nadia, all his thoughts and feelings, and he is to elevate his feeling state to its being powerful, booming, saturating. His job is to throw himself into a state of powerful, all-encompassing feeling. As he follows his own instructions, both he and the therapist are living and being in this scene. Serge puts himself into a state of elevated fear, near terror. He concentrates on Nadia's caring, concerned expression. He is sobbing.

Remaining in the state of strong feeling, he is to search for the exact instant when the feeling is powerful, at its peak. Details are filled in. He searches. Then he discovers the instant: "You're looking deep into my eyes! And you're saying something . . . 'I need it! I need it!' And you have a look on you! Oh God, yes! You got this look!"

Inside the Moment of Peak Feeling, Discover the Accessed Deeper Potential for Experiencing

The moment of powerful peak feeling is the doorway down into Serge's insides. Both therapist and Serge are to freeze this moment of peak feeling, live fully in this moment, and put themselves in the right position to receive, to touch, to be touched by, the deeper potential for experiencing. When the therapist and person are in the right position, when they deepen and intensify the immediate feeling, then the deeper potential for experiencing is received when they are touched by, when they undergo a state, an experiencing, a sense, that is (a) new, different, and (b) feels good, almost joyful, even for a precious moment.

Living fully in this exact frozen moment, what leaps out is this look on Nadia's face, a look of sheer animal lust, a sheer sexual wanting, a crazed and powerful craving, and something new rises inside Serge. For just an instant, there is something new, a steeling up, as if the whole body is clenched up, and out pours a piercing blast: "NOOOOOOOOOO!!!" The inner sense is a powerful experiencing of strength, of being invulnerable, of defiant, inviolate intactness. It is new, it is accompanied with wonderful feelings, and it lasts only a few seconds. But the therapist and Serge have been touched by, are in touch with, have discovered, a deeper potential for experiencing.

Show the Person How to Welcome, Appreciate, Love the Deeper Potential for Experiencing

Our best guess is that deep inside Serge has a potential for experiencing strength, invulnerability, defiant inviolate intactness. Both Serge and the therapist name what it is, identify it with these words, agree on just what it is. Since this experiencing is deeper within Serge, is alien to him, is not a part of who and what he is on the surface, and is probably something feared and hated by him, kept down, sealed off, Serge is now ready to undertake the big step toward welcoming, appreciating, having good feelings about, loving this deeper potential for experiencing.

The job of the therapist is to know the ways of enabling Serge to accomplish this change, and to invite Serge to use these methods in his own way and at his own pace. This step is done when Serge, perhaps for the first time in his life, can actually be on friendly terms with this deeper potential for experiencing, can welcome it, appreciate and love it, feel good about it.

Show the Person How to Undergo the Qualitative Shift into Being the Deeper Potential for Experiencing

Now that Serge can welcome and love the deeper potential for experiencing, the way is paved for him to undergo the massively radical shift out of the continuing person that he is and into being the qualitatively different person who is the live embodiment of strength, invulnerability, defiant inviolate intactness. This step is successful when Serge can be this whole new person (a) fully and completely, and (b) with absolutely wonderful feelings of happiness, joy, giddiness, and exhilaration.

To accomplish this, the therapist shows Serge how to locate scenes and situations from the past. Find past scenes from the recent and remote past, times when Serge may have had a soft beginning of this experiencing, times when Serge's whole world fell apart, times when he was overcome with the painful depression, times when he could or should have been powerfully strong, invulnerable, defiant, inviolate, intact, but was not. Find scenes from the period a few years before conception to some years after birth.

In these past scenes, Serge is shown how to live and be in the scene until it is alive and real, how to throw himself into being the radically and qualitatively different person who is fully and completely being strong, invulnerable, defiant, inviolate, intact. To make the transformation easier, Serge is shown how to be this whole different person with absolute power and energy, in a context that is wholly unrealistic, silly, whimsical, burlesqued, cartoonlike, and with feelings that are giddy, exuberant, joyful, buoyant, exhilarating, and sheer great fun.

This whole new Serge is also to be and to live in the painful scenes from the beginning of the session. He has raucous fun celebrating the experiencing of strength, invulnerability, defiance, and inviolate intactness in the scene where he was so depressed, so alone, where he may as well be dead, and in the scene in the Toronto hotel room when the attractive lady touched him and he sobbingly fell apart, and especially in the scene with his wife talking with him candidly about sex, and he is so guilty and remorseful about having no sexual feelings. In the scene with his wife, he reaches the ceiling of unbounded joy and unbridled fullness of experiencing as he screams: *"Are you kidding? No way! Noooo! No one can reach me. . . . I am powerful. . . . Go ahead and try. . . . HAHAHAHAHAHAHA!"*

By the end of this step, Serge is being the whole new person, but in the context of past scenes and situations.

Show the Person How to Be the Qualitatively New Person in the World of the Present

The final phase of the session opens with Serge continuing as this radically new person. What had been deeper inside is now a welcomed part of this qualitatively new person (this is called integration), and is also a part of who and what the new Serge is, how he acts and interacts, how he feels and experiences, how he creates and lives in his world (this is called actualization). The final phase enables this whole new person to be right here in the present world, the world outside the office, the world of today and tomorrow and beyond.

This final phase opens with Serge being the new Serge who is fully and joyously experiencing strength, invulnerability, defiance, inviolate intactness. Still in the context of absolute unreality, free of all realistic constraints, with wholesale unbounded playfulness and cartoonlike silliness, the therapist and Serge look for all sorts of scenes and situations in the world of today and tomorrow where the qualitatively new Serge might be the qualitatively new Serge.

When this is accomplished with feelings that are full and excitingly vital, alive, pleasant, wonderful, the therapist and Serge then move closer to reality. Is this new Serge ready and willing to be this way for real, in the real world of the present? They look for scenes and situations, perhaps lots of ready possibilities, perhaps just a few special times and places. When they find some scenes and situations from today, the therapist and Serge then get down to actual reality. This calls for rehearsal, actually trying it out, with plenty of room for refinement and modification. Here is where all parts of Serge are invited to voice their concerns, their objections, their reactions. Maybe being this new way in this forthcoming scene will be awful, will cause trouble. Maybe not. At least these other parts of Serge have plenty of opportunity to voice their feelings.

The work is done when this qualitatively new Serge is ready and willing and eager to be this new way, to do this new thing, to construct or reconstruct his personal world in ways that provide a wonderfully good feeling of strength, invulnerability, defiance, inviolate intactness. Serge is ready to commit himself, if it works out, to several new ways of being and behaving.

But what were these new possibilities, these forthcoming scenes and situations, these new ways of being and behaving that were so carefully found, rehearsed and refined, responded to by other parts of Serge? What are the ways that this new Serge committed himself to carry out in and from this newfelt experiencing of strength, invulnerability defiance, inviolate intactness? One is to have a serious decision-making talk with his business partner, and to resolve the division of responsibilities. It is about time to confront this issue. Serge had rehearsed this to a point where it was just right, felt good. Serge was also ready and eager to end the endless lending of money to his older brother, and this scene was also rehearsed and refined into a sound readiness and willingness. By the end of the session, the qualitatively new Serge was soundly geared toward entering the new world of the new present, and to be and behave in these new ways in these new situations coming from the newfelt sense of strength, invulnerability, defiance, and inviolate intactness.

This session allowed Serge to start with some scenes of powerful feeling, scenes of being engulfed by depression, a scene of painful absence of sexual feeling with his wife, a scene of chaotic falling apart with the attractive woman in the hotel room. By the end of the session, Serge had become a qualitatively new person, ready to enter a new personal world as this wholesome new person, and living and being in a world that is finally free of the old Serge's painful scenes and painful feelings in those scenes.

What Were the Practical Payoffs of the Session?

The next session, like every session, starts by opening up scenes of strong feeling. By starting this way, the next session provides a chance to see who is now present, compared to the person who started the previous session. It also provides a glimpse of what had occurred in Serge's post-session real world, and a chance to see what scenes of strong feeling are now front and center for him. Instead of the old Serge, the person who was now present radiated the newfelt sense of strength, invulnerability, defiance, inviolate intactness as he recounted how wonderful it was putting an end to the endless money-lending to his older brother.

And there were several bonuses. What about recent scenes of gloomy depression? There were none. Instead, what was front and center for Serge were strong-feelinged scenes from the last few days. He woke up in the middle of the night, oozing with explosive sexual feelings, and he and his wife had a festival of glowing sexuality. It was unbelievable. But the session focused on a scene later in the day, after a whole morning of pricelessly precious intercourse, when they are both in the shower, giggling and laughing about plans to enlarge the bedroom into a self-contained sexual sanctuary.

☐ Conclusions and Invitations

1. Each session of experiential psychotherapy offers the person a special opportunity to become the radically new person that the person is capable of becoming, and to be free of the old person's painful scenes and the painful feelings in those scenes. The invitation is for therapists in the field of sex therapy to learn and to practice experiential psychotherapy if this psychotherapy strikes appealing chords in the way the therapist thinks about what psychotherapy can be.

2. Virtually any genuinely interested person can learn to undergo one's own experiential sessions. Instead of the traditional role of the professional who administers treatment of sexual problems and disorders, the invitation is for sex therapists to learn how to undergo their own personal experiential sessions, and to adopt the role of teachers for

individuals and groups who are genuinely interested in learning to undergo their own experiential sessions.

3. Here are some invitations for radically altering the goals and objectives of sessions of sex therapy: (a) Determine the goals and objectives in and for each session, rather than from a pretreatment assessment that supposedly applies to the whole series of sessions. (b) Allow the goals and objectives to include an opportunity for the person to become a qualitatively new person, based on what each session discovers lies deeper inside the person. (c) Allow the goals and objectives to include genuine freedom from the old person's painful situations and the painful feelings in those situations. (d) Let the directions of change for this person come from this person's own inner deeper potentialities for experiencing, rather than from, for example, the values and moral judgments of the sex therapist.

4. Advance and expand the very meaning of sexual to include (a) the scene in which the strong feeling occurs, (b) the nature of the immediately ongoing experiencing, and (c) the nature of the deeper potential for experiencing in the person.

5. Provide room for the "scene of strong feeling" as a challengingly useful alternative to the traditional "sexual" problem or diagnosis. Let there be honest competition to see which alternative is more helpful for the person and for the field of sex therapy.

6. It is probably sensible to acknowledge that some "outside" therapies, such as experiential psychotherapy, not only constitute legitimate alternatives for what many sex therapies seek to accomplish, but aim at enabling some changes that are well beyond those offered by most sex therapies.

7. In addition to the common way of thinking of which treatments are appropriate for which sexual disorders and problems, provide room for thinking of which therapies, including experiential psychotherapy, are useful for the expanded goals, aims, and objectives of a boldly expanded field of sexuality.

☐ References

Althof, S. E., Turner, L. A., Levine, S. B., Risen, C., Kursh, E., Bodner, D., & Resnick, M. (1989). Why do so many people drop out from auto-injections therapy for impotence? *Journal of Sex & Marital Therapy, 15,* 121–129.

American Psychiatric Association. (1994). *Diagnosis and statistical manual of mental disorders* (4th ed.). Washington DC: Author.

Charlton, R. S. (1997). Evaluation of sexual disorders. In R. S. Charlton (Ed.), *Treating sexual disorders* (pp. 59–94). San Francisco: Jossey-Bass.

Donahey, K. M., & Carroll, R. A. (1993). Gender differences in factors associated with hypoactive sexual desire. *Journal of Sex & Marital Therapy, 19,* 25–40.

Hartman, L. M. (1983). Resistance in directive sex therapy: Recognition and management. *Journal of Sex & Marital Therapy, 9,* 283–29S.

Heiman, J. R., & Meston, C. M. (1997). Empirically validated treatments for sexual dysfunction. *Annual Review of Sex Research, 7,* 148–194.

Kaplan, H. S. (1995). *The sexual desire disorders.* New York: Brunner/Mazel.

Kilmann, B. R., Boland, J. P., Norton, S. C., & Caid, C. (1986). Perspectives on sex therapy outcome: A survey of AASECT providers. *Journal of Sex & Marital Therapy, 12,* 116–138.

Leiblum, S. R., & Rosen, R. C. (Eds.). (1989). *Principles and practice of sex therapy* (2nd ed.). New York: Guilford Press.

Levine, M., & Troiden, R. (1988). The myth of sexual compulsivity. *Journal of Sex Research, 25,* 347–363.

Mahrer, A. R. (1996a). *The complete guide to experiential psychotherapy.* New York: Wiley.

Mahrer, A. R. (1996b). Discovery-oriented research on how to do psychotherapy. In W. Dryden (Ed.), *Research in counselling and psychotherapy: Practical applications* (pp. 233–258). London: Sage.

Rosen, R. C., & Leiblum, S. R. (1995). *Case studies in sex therapy.* New York: Guilford Press.

Schnarch, D. (1991). *Constructing the sexual crucible: An integration of sexual and marital therapy.* New York: W.W. Norton.

Schover, L. R., & Leiblum, S. R. (1994) Commentary: The stagnation of sex therapy. *Journal of Psychology and Human Sexuality, 6,* 5–30.

Schreiner-Engel, P., & Schiavi, R. C. (1986). Lifetime psychopathology in individuals with low sexual desire. *Journal of Nervous and Mental Disease, 174,* 646–65l.

Wincze, J. P., & Carey, M. P. (1991). *Sexual dysfunction: A guide for assessment and treatment.* New York: Guilford Press.

CHAPTER

Wendy Maltz, MSW, LCSW, LMFCC, CST

Sex Therapy With Survivors of Sexual Abuse

The deeper that sorrow carves into your being, the more joy you can contain.
— Kahlil Gibran, *The Prophet*

☐ Introduction

Sex therapists face unique challenges when we treat survivors of incest, rape, molestation, and other forms of sexual abuse. With these cases, traditional sex therapy approaches and techniques often fall short. And no wonder. Clients who have experienced profound sexual violations early in life may have profound needs for healing as adults.

As a sex therapist who specializes in sexual abuse recovery, I find that focusing on sexual performance is not enough. I aim higher, aspiring to make sex not merely tolerable for my clients, but life-affirming, nurturing, joyous, and even beautiful. I teach *healthy sexual intimacy*, a type of sex very different from the lonely, destructive sex experienced in abuse.

This is not an easy goal. Many clients who have been hurt by sex have difficulty conceptualizing how it can ever be a positive experience. What's more, our sex-obsessed culture provides far too few models of healthy sexual intimacy. Instead, we get a steady diet of sex that is arousing and titillating, perhaps, but hardly instructive of a physical sharing that involves true caring, respect, and lasting satisfaction.

When I work with survivors, I step outside the limitations of traditional sex therapy and look at the whole person. Rather than focus solely on psychological and sexual functioning, I pay attention to a client's personal history, relationships, self-care activities, and quality of life. I help clients tap into and trust their own innate healing abilities. My role is that of a therapeutic guide whose knowledge and skills assist in advancing healing. I educate, ask questions, and offer solutions when clients feel "stuck."

My therapeutic style is eclectic and integrationist. This allows me to address the many facets of sexual abuse recovery work, from overcoming depression to establishing healthy sexual rapport. I choose healing techniques appropriate for each case based on what the client presents in session. An individual case might include self-esteem building, changing attitudes, cognitive restructuring, grief work, improving communication skills, relationship enrichment, physical/experiential learning, sex education, and problem solving. I notice that when I help a client in one area, there typically are positive repercussions in another. For example, when a survivor resolves anger toward a past perpetrator, he or she may suddenly feel more emotionally trusting of a present-day partner. And the increased emotional trust, in turn, may increase the desire for intimate sexual contact.

The cornerstones of my treatment approach are courage and creativity. It takes courage for survivors to face these issues. And, once faced, it takes creativity to discover a way to undo all the damage caused by abuse. As sex therapists, we play a vital role in supporting and empowering our clients so that they are not denied the pleasures of a satisfying sexual life.

When I became a sex therapist in the mid-1970s, I used standard sex therapy techniques to help people overcome embarrassing problems such as difficulty having an orgasm, painful intercourse, premature ejaculation, and impotence. I was impressed by how well these techniques worked. By combining sex education, relationship counseling, and progressive behavioral exercises, I often was able to successfully treat these problems within a matter of several months. As clients learned more about their bodies and gained confidence with their sexual expressions, they felt better about themselves in other areas of their lives.

But there were always a number of people in my practice who had difficulty with sex therapy and with the specific techniques I gave them as "homework." They would procrastinate and avoid doing the exercises, did them incorrectly, or, if they did manage some exercises, reported getting nothing out of them. Upon further exploration, I discovered that many of these clients had one major factor in common: a history of childhood sexual abuse.

I began to notice other differences between my survivor and

nonsurvivor clients. Many survivors seemed ambivalent or neutral about the sexual problems they were experiencing. Gone was the usual sense of frustration that could fuel a client's motivation to change. Survivors often entered counseling because of a partner's frustrations, and they seemed more disturbed by the consequences of sexual problems than by their existence. Margaret, an incest survivor, tearfully confided during her first session, "I'm afraid my husband will leave me if I don't become more interested in sex. Can you help me be the sexual partner he wants me to be?"

A number of the survivors who came to see me had been to sex therapists before, with no success. They had histories of persistent problems that seemed immune to standard treatments. What was even more revealing was that survivors kept sharing with me a set of symptoms, in addition to sexual functioning problems, that challenged my skills as a young sex therapist. These included:

- avoiding or being afraid of sex;
- approaching sex as an obligation;
- feeling intense negative emotions when touched, such as fear, guilt, disgust, or nausea;
- having difficulty becoming aroused or feeling sensation;
- feeling emotionally distant or not present during sex;
- having disturbing and intrusive sexual thoughts and fantasies;
- engaging in compulsive, risky, or inappropriate sexual behaviors; and
- having difficulty establishing or maintaining an intimate relationship.

Considering their sexual histories, problems with touch, and responses to counseling, I realized that traditional sex therapy was missing the mark for survivors. Standard treatments, such as sensate focus, often left survivors feeling discouraged, disempowered, and, in some cases, retraumatized. People who had been sexually victimized had an entirely different perspective on sex than other clients had. Thus, they required an entirely different style and program of sex therapy.

For the last 25 years, I have been specializing in sex therapy with people who have been sexually abused. I have discovered and developed several strategies and techniques that are very effective in working with this population (Maltz 1988, 1992/2001; Maltz & Holman, 1987). This chapter will provide an overview of these strategies and techniques.

In general, this model of therapy for survivors combines trauma recovery work with modified versions of sex therapy. The focus involves helping survivors change sexual attitudes and behaviors and learn a new approach to experiencing touch and sexual stimulation. This model addresses experience on mind, body, spirit, and relationship levels. It is an eclectic approach that integrates concepts and interventions from other models, such as client-centered, cognitive, Gestalt, humanistic, feminist, behavioral, and psychodynamic. This model empowers clients and addresses their needs on an individual, case-by-case basis. It challenges therapists to engage a therapeutic style that is less authoritative and prescriptive than has been suggested in traditional sex therapy. This model also takes into consideration the special feelings and needs of intimate partners.

Although I have developed professional training materials and written extensively on the subject, in this chapter the model will be condensed into 10 therapeutic recommendations.

☐ 1. Understand the Nature and Consequences of Sexual Abuse

To work effectively with survivors, the therapist must understand the nature of the sexual abuse and its impact on a client's sexuality. Sexual abuse is abuse to a person's sexuality. It occurs whenever one person dominates and exploits another by means of sexual activity or suggestion (Maltz 1992/ 2001, p. 31). Whether it is a gentle seduction by a loved relative or a violent rape by a stranger, perpetrators use their sexual body parts (hands, mouth, genitals) as weapons. They focus on the sexual body parts and sensations of the victims as their targets. Sexual abuse in childhood is highly stressful and usually traumatic because it affects a child's physical and psychological experience beyond the normal ability to cope.

Sexual abuse involves a loss of innocence and a betrayal of human trust. It is about one person exercising power and control over another. Victims are seen as objects for the perpetrator's self-gratification. The emotional experience and welfare of the victim is discounted and ignored. In addition, the years of secrecy, shame, emotional isolation, and feeling unloved and unprotected that often accompany abuse can damage the development of healthy self-esteem and lead to chronic depression, antisocial activity, and self-destructive behavior.

When sexual abuse occurs in childhood, it can seriously harm the natural course of sexual discovery and learning. Victims may end up hating their bodies for their sexual drives and responses, erroneously believing that something about their sexuality caused the abuse to occur. This can lead to avoiding and withdrawing from sex. On the other hand, some victims act out sexually with compulsive masturbation, indiscriminate affairs, and other forms of emotionally driven sex. Either way, survivors may have difficulty feeling comfortable with the natural ebb and flow of sexual feelings. And their ability to develop healthy, truly intimate relationships based on trust may be seriously compromised.

Given the wide range of possible sexual repercussions, it can be beneficial to identify the sexual impact of sexual abuse during the initial sessions of therapy. I often recommend clients take the *Sexual Effects Inventory* (Maltz, 1992/2001, pp. 62–69) and discuss their responses in therapy.

It is also important to assess how far a survivor has progressed in terms of his or her general recovery from the abuse. Sexual healing work is best undertaken only *after* a survivor has addressed other effects of sexual abuse, such as feelings of depression, self-blame, and unresolved anger toward the perpetrator and family of origin. Recovery from sexual abuse alone may take many months, even years, depending on the severity of the abuse and the extent of the repercussions (Bass & Davis, 1994; King, 1995; Lew, 1990). From the perspective of sexual abuse recovery, sexual healing is one of the last areas to be addressed. For survivors, sex is often the topic about which they have the most shame and fear. Talking about sex and exploring touch can rekindle traumatic feelings of powerlessness and overstimulation. It is important that clients doing this work already have in place a general understanding of what happened to them in the past, good skills for emotional and physical self-care, and a present lifestyle that is stable and relatively low in stress. Even when clients feel ready to do sexuality work, there may be times during the course of treatment when the sexual healing needs to be put on hold so that they can resolve more general repercussions of the abuse.

2. Reframe Sexual Dysfunctions as Functional

In general, traditional sex therapy views sexual dysfunction as bad, something to be cured as soon as possible. The emphasis is on increasing sexual activity and improving performance. But for many survivors, their sexual dysfunctions are, in fact, psychologically functional and important. At least for a while, some sexual problems may be working to help survivors avoid negative feelings and memories associated with past sexual abuse.

When Donna entered therapy for difficulty achieving orgasm, she had already exhausted a variety of exercises for improving orgasmic potential. She wondered if her inability to climax related to a strong suspicion she had that her father had sexually abused her as a child. Donna said that her father was an alcoholic whose personality changed when he was drunk. Although she had few memories of childhood, she did remember that she avoided her father's touch, and she had pleaded with her mom for a dead-bolt lock on her bedroom door when she was 11 years old.

Rather than work on sex therapy exercises, we decided to focus initially on her childhood relationship with her parents. After several sessions of this work, Donna told me about a very upsetting dream. In the dream her father took her to a mountain cabin to celebrate her sixth birthday. He filled the room with balloons and then laid her on a bed and performed oral sex on her. *Donna woke up from the dream having an orgasm.* In therapy, she sobbed and told me that she knew instantly, when she awoke from the dream, that it was a real memory.

No wonder Donna had been unable to climax. The physical experience of orgasm had been intimately associated with her past abuse. Her sexual dysfunction seemed to have been protecting her from the memory of her father's assault. After this dream experience, Donna was able to accept the reality of her abuse experience. She cried for her lost sexual innocence and expressed anger at how her father had exploited and betrayed her. Soon after, Donna began having orgasms with her husband. Emotional support and gentle explorations into her childhood experiences were essential to her sexual recovery.

In many other cases, I have encountered a similar process.

Steve, a 26-year-old recovering alcoholic, had a chronic problem with premature ejaculation. As we explored his inner psychological experience in therapy, he was able to identify that when he allowed himself to delay ejaculation, he would start to feel an urge to rape his partner. Premature ejaculation was protecting him from this very upsetting feeling. In therapy Steve realized that his mother had been acting out her anger at men on him as a child. He acknowledged his innocence and need for protection at that time in his life. Steve also allowed himself to feel the pain of not having been loved and truly cherished by his mother. Once he worked through his anger at his mother for the sexual abuse, Steve was able to comfortably prolong gratification with a female partner.

Impressing upon Donna or Steve the idea that their sexual dysfunctions were bad would have done them a disservice. In fact, their sexual problems were powerful coping techniques.

Furthermore, for survivors who have experienced little difficulty with sexual functioning, the onset of sexual functioning problems may actually signal a big step forward in their sexual healing.

Tony, for example, entered therapy as a 35-year-old single man. He had been in and out of abusive relationships for years. His partners were often sexually demanding and generally critical. Tony's father had raped him repeatedly when he was young, and his mother had molested him in his teens. As Tony resolved issues related to his past abuse, his choice of partners improved. But his sexual functioning became a problem. With a new girlfriend, he failed to sustain an erection. This was extremely unusual for him.

"She wanted to have sex, so she began to do oral sex on me," Tony explained. "I got hard and then lost it and couldn't get it back."

"Did you want to be having sex?" I asked him.

"No, I really wasn't interested then," he replied.

"Do you think your body might have been saying 'no' for you?" I asked.

"Yeah, I guess so," he said somewhat proudly.

"Wow, do you realize what's happening?" I declared, "you're becoming congruent! For all these years your genitals have operated separately from how you really felt. Now your head, heart, and genitals are lining up congruently. Good for you!"

While it felt funny for me as a sex therapist to congratulate a client on his sexual dysfunction, it was appropriate in Tony's case. In working with survivors to heal sexual hurts, the goal of treatment shifts from sexual functioning to improving self-awareness, self-care, trust, and intimacy skills. Insight and authenticity are more important than behavioral functioning.

Although healthy sexual functioning is a desirable long-term goal for survivors, we need to see sexual problems in context and find out how the client feels about a symptom before attempting to treat it. Therapists must respect dysfunctions, learn from them, work with them, and resist the urge to automatically try to "fix" them.

☐ 3. Avoid Negative Transference

The therapist's style is extremely important in working with survivors. It may, in fact, be more important to a successful outcome than any particular technique. Because sex is a loaded topic for survivors, there is a high possibility clients will transfer to the therapist the negative feelings they have toward the perpetrator and the past abuse. This process of negative transference is inevitable when you look at the psychodynamics of this kind of therapeutic relationship. As a sex therapist, you are interested in your clients' sexuality. You try to get them to desire and enjoy sex. You talk privately to them using sexual language that can be sensually stimulating. You attempt to diminish their defenses and influence their most personal thoughts, feelings, and intimate behaviors. Isn't that what perpetrators do, too? In addition, the techniques you encourage clients to use can sometimes feel overwhelming and upsetting. From the client's perspective, the sexuality focus can trigger negative feelings similar to what they felt during the abuse. The very process of sex therapy can strain a survivor's sense of control and protection.

To minimize negative transference, I suggest therapists adopt the following premise: *Do the opposite of what happened in the abuse.* For instance, because the victim was dominated and disempowered during the abuse, it makes sense that therapy should focus on empowering the client and respecting his or her reactions. Therapists need to explain techniques and interventions, encouraging clients to exercise choice at all times. This way survivors experience change occurring as a result of their own courage, initiative, and action. Therapists should offer suggestions, not give directions or prescriptions. Rather than admonish survivors for their resistances and relapses, therapists should reframe these as inevitable, seek to understand their reactions, and work with them to overcome challenges.

Because sexual abuse involves a traumatic violation of boundaries, it is important that sex therapists be good at maintaining clear emotional and physical boundaries. Talking about sex can stir up sexual feelings. It is inappropriate, and too confusing for the survivor, to combine sex-focused sessions (in which there are explicit descriptions of sexual activity or techniques) with touch. Therapy needs to be a safe place physically and psychologically—for everyone, at all times. Supportive touch, such as a quick end-of-the-session hug with an established client or briefly touching a client's hand or shoulder to offer comfort, should occur only after the subject of touch has been discussed and parameters agreed on between therapist and client beforehand. Other forms of touch, such as holding, rocking, or stroking, are never recommended.

It is also important for sex therapists not to dominate the content and course of therapy. Personally, I am most effective when I establish a therapeutic relationship with the client in which we are both working together. The client sets the pace and direction and presents the content; I provide encouragement, support, guidance, creative ideas, insight, information, and resources.

Similarly, I believe it is best that a therapist maintain a generally neutral position when it comes to resurfaced memories and reported recollections of sexual abuse. Although we do not want to discount a client's individual reactions and experience, we cannot presume to know what did or did not occur in his or her past. In general, I take clients' disclosures of past abuse seriously and work with them to better understand what happened and how they have been affected. For example, when Joani, a 30-year-old client, recalled her father orally sodomizing her as a child, we explored what this memory meant to her and how it might relate to problems with chronic jaw tension, fears of fellatio, and difficulty speaking up in public.

☐ 4. Improve Sexual Attitudes and Thoughts

Sex therapy with survivors differs from traditional sex therapy in that issues related to sexual attitudes and self-concept need to be significantly addressed before we can proceed with touch-related exercises. When survivors think about sex, they often confuse it with sexual abuse. When asked, "What is sex?" it is not unusual for survivors to respond "dirty," "painful," "overexciting," "out-of-control," "a power play," "an obligation," "bad," "disgusting," or "hurtful." This is understandable, since the abuse experience often provided a profound initiation into sexual sensations and interactions.

Survivors need to develop new attitudes about sex in the early stages of sexual recovery work so they can see it as something positive and worth pursuing. Abusive sex is exploitive, impersonal, impulsive, irresponsible, overpowering, and humiliating. Healthy sexual intimacy is something altogether different, involving mutual caring, respect, safety, trust, choice, and lasting pleasures. I frequently provide a number of written resources to help survivors learn the difference between healthy sex and abusive or addictive sex (e.g., Carnes, 1991, p. 255; Maltz, 1992/2001, 1995a; Maltz & Holman, 1987, p. 9).

I recommend that therapists make frequent distinctions between the types of sex that are being discussed in therapy. Thus, if a client says, "I hate sex," the therapist might help the client to identify what he or she dislikes (e.g., the negative emotions that get stirred up from certain kinds of touch or the interpersonal context in which the sex occurs). This approach leaves free the possibility that, under certain circumstances, sex could be positive and enjoyable.

Jane, a 23-year-old survivor of sibling incest, told me that, while she could entertain the notion intellectually, she had no idea what healthy sexuality would look like. Since she loved art, I suggested she make collages from magazine pictures: one to represent abusive sex and another to represent healthy sex. Collecting and discussing the images helped her to understand more deeply and conceptualize sex in a new, positive way. Other clients have benefited from reading descriptions of healthy sexual intimacy in poetry (Maltz, 1992/2001, 1996) and select romance novels. (Contemporary romance writers whose sexual descriptions often represent healthy sex dynamics include Jayne Ann Krentz, Elizabeth Lowell, Judith McNaught, Susan Elizabeth Phillips, and Mary Jo Putney.)

Before embarking on touch exercises, it also is important to identify and undo the survivor's negative self-talk concerning who he or she is as a sexual person. As a result of abuse, survivors often conclude that, sexually, they are bad; that they are objects for another's pleasure; that they are "damaged goods." They may carry around false beliefs, assuming that something about them or their sexuality caused the abuse or that changing the way they relate sexually would be impossible. It may be helpful to integrate cognitive restructuring work into the therapy at this stage (Jehu, 1988).

As therapists, we need to help people learn how to feel good about their sexual energies, body parts, passions, and expressions *in spite of the abuse*. I often find myself saying to clients, "You are not what was done to you." "You are not to blame for what was done to you." And "Your body's reactions and responses were normal, even necessary, under the circumstances." Gestalt dialogues and role-plays can help survivors develop compassion and reintegrate parts of their bodies they believe participated in or were responsible for the abuse. Similarly, survivors may need help resolving confusions and false conclusions related to their sexual orientation.

☐ 5. Stop Negative Sexual Behaviors and Identify Triggers

Before proceeding with specific exercises to relearn touch, survivors need to stop engaging in sexual behaviors that could undermine the healing process. These behaviors might include extramarital affairs, compulsive sex, unsafe and risky sex, violent sex, obligatory sex, or sex that mimics abuse dynamics (including dominance/submission, humiliation, or pain).

In discussing negative sexual practices, it can be helpful for the client to consider these questions: How does the behavior reflect, mimic, or reinforce sexual abuse? How does the behavior hurt me or others? How does the behavior interfere with developing a healthy intimate relationship? Why is it important to stop? What do I fear will occur if I stop?

Obviously, as with curtailing any habitual or emotionally driven behavior, the client's readiness and personal motivation are critical to success. Survivors who are engaging in addictive and compulsive sexual behaviors may need additional help through 12-step programs (such as Sexaholics Anonymous and Sex Addicts Anonymous groups, available in most major cities). Experience has taught that it is best not to pressure a client to reveal the full extent of his or her sexual acting-out behaviors. Minimizing, omission, and denial can function to protect survivors from feelings of shame or from being overwhelmed by the prospect of change. Disclosures often increase as emotional safety and trust increase in the therapeutic relationship. Thus, therapists are wise not to criticize clients' lack of candor in the early stages of therapy.

Although a survivor may see a sexual behavior as negative and even destructive, it may also be a source of great, albeit temporary, physical or emotional pleasure. Letting go of a negative sexual behavior may involve grieving its loss and the intensity of the sexual enjoyment it represented.

It is not uncommon or wrong for survivors to begin avoiding sex when they are involved in sexual abuse recovery work. Thinking about the past abuse and the perpetrator may stir up a host of posttraumatic stress symptoms (such as mood swings, flashbacks, insomnia, and depression). These naturally dampen sexual interest. Many survivors find that a period of sexual abstinence can be beneficial to their sexual healing. This "vacation from sex" (Maltz, 1992/2001) enables survivors to more easily resolve posttraumatic stress symptoms because they are less restimulated by sexual touch and partner demands. In addition, it can provide a clean slate for beginning new touch and sexual learning.

Many survivors experience automatic reactions to touch and sexual contact. Sometimes these occur as full-blown flashbacks, in which the survivor suddenly feels drawn back into the sex abuse experience. Automatic reactions also can occur in more subtle ways, such as a fleeting thought of the offender or a strange reaction to something a sexual partner says or does during lovemaking. Automatic reactions are experienced as sensations, emotions, and thoughts. These levels of experience are linked together in many unconscious ways. A particular sensation (say, being caressed on the cheek) triggers an emotion (fear) as well as a specific thought ("something bad is about to happen"). I encourage survivors to identify as many triggers or likely triggers related to the abuse as they can (Maltz, 1992/2001). Once identified, many of these triggers can be avoided. For instance, rough beards (that trigger memories of the perpetrator) can be shaved. If certain sexual positions (i.e., man on top) remind a survivor of abuse, they can be off-limits in lovemaking.

Survivors can learn numerous techniques to cope with unpleasant automatic reactions to touch and sex. I encourage survivors to develop compassion, understanding, and patience in regard to their own reactions. These reactions were originally protective mechanisms, common and unavoidable results of trauma. When a survivor encounters a reaction, he or she can learn to *stop*, become aware of the reaction; *calm*, reduce physical reactions using self-massage and breathing techniques; *affirm reality*, remind him- or herself of being in present time (i.e., older, bigger, with choices); and *alter activity*, either switch to a different behavior or adjust the present behavior to create new associations (e.g., if lightly stroking the arm is upsetting, try stroking more firmly or stroking another part of the body instead). Automatic reactions often diminish significantly or disappear over time as survivors become more aware of and responsive to when they come up and what they mean.

☐ 6. Include the Partner in the Process

The repercussions of trauma can create a crisis in intimacy for couples in which one or both partners were sexually abused in the past. Unwittingly, the intimate partner of a survivor becomes a secondary victim of the abuse. Unresolved psychological and sexual issues from the original abuse can harm the development of emotional trust and a mutually satisfying sexual relationship. Partners often misunderstand what's happening and worsen the situation by making sexual demands, blaming themselves or the survivor for problems, or refusing to participate in healing activities. When healing is not pursued, couples can get trapped in an unfortunate cycle of anger, emotional distancing, and alienation.

Intimate partners need to become well-educated about sexual trauma and its intimate effects. I often refer partners to several resources created specifically to address their questions and concerns (Davis, 1991; Maltz, 1992/2001; Maltz, Christiansen, & Joffee, 1988, 1995; Spear, 1991). When intimate partners understand the situation and what needs to occur to "fix it," they can work with the survivor as a healing team. This couples' approach becomes especially important when the survivor progresses to the level of doing exercises to "relearn touch." The partner's understanding and involvement are essential to a positive outcome in sexual healing therapy (Maltz, 1988). Depending on client needs, sometimes the therapist may want to meet alone with the survivor or the partner, and sometimes to see them as a couple. Partners may benefit from doing other individual or group therapy on their own, as well. Unresolved sexual and emotional issues from the partner's past often arise during the course of treatment.

When doing couples work, therapists need to resist unconsciously making alliances with either the partner (i.e., "We're healthy, we can fix her.") or with the survivor (i.e., "'Bad' partner isn't cooperating.").

Progress toward healing may involve some unexpected twists. As emotional honesty increases, new issues may surface.

Jonathan, a survivor of mother-son incest, finally felt strong enough to disclose a past affair to his wife, Angie. (He had been sexual with the other woman in his and Angie's bed). While the disclosure was a very positive step for Jonathan in his sexual recovery, Angie understandably responded with shock and anger. To her, it felt as if the infidelity had just occurred. She was so upset, she went home and dragged their bed out of the bedroom, sheet by sheet, blanket by blanket, then mattress by mattress. Several sessions were subsequently needed to rebuild trust in the relationship.

In another case, Ginny, a lesbian incest survivor, began emerging from long-term problems with depression and touch avoidance. Her live-in partner, Trish, began sharing more of her hurt and anger at how little sexual contact she had endured for so many years in the past. Although it was positive for Trish to begin sharing previously locked in feelings and sexual needs, to Ginny it felt like Trish was making it harder for her to move forward.

Double-survivor couples, in which both partners have histories of sexual abuse, present additional challenges in treatment. Sometimes these couples are more patient and understanding of the healing process. At other times, however, the increased sensitivity to touch and sex issues compounds the situation, slowing the couple's progress.

☐ 7. Teach New Skills for Approaching Touch

Sexual abuse seems to interfere with developing skills for enjoying intimate touch and sexual contact. Just being able to sit, breathe, feel relaxed, and stay present while touching one's own body can be a challenge. Comfortably touching a partner or feeling pleasure from a partner's touch also can be difficult. In addition, due to the shame, emotional isolation, and silence that surrounds much abuse, many survivors find it hard to communicate their feelings and needs during intimate, physical contact.

To avoid feeling overwhelmed, survivors need a lot of options for exercises that offer opportunities to heal. I rely on relearning touch techniques described in my book (Maltz, 1992/2001) and demonstrated in my videotape "Relearning Touch" (Maltz et al., 1995).[1] These exercises were developed to help survivors learn skills that are basic to enjoying physical contact, such as relaxing, staying present, and communicating.

The relearning touch exercises are "presensate focus." That is, they foster the development of skills that are prerequisites to standard sensate focus exercises. Survivors get the most out of the relearning touch exercises when they are undertaken during a vacation from sex. Intimate partners seem to cope better with this period of sexual abstinence and feel hope for future sexual sharing if they are having ongoing, active, physical sharing.

Relearning touch exercises are progressive. I recommend they be arranged in a sequence from playful, nonsexual touch to sensual, pleasuring touch activities. Some exercises can be done alone; others require a partner. Although it is important for the survivor to initially choose and

---

1. The video can be purchased from Independent Video Services: 1-800-678-3455.

control the exercises, in time roles can be switched, so that the partner can initiate and express creativity, as well.

Popular relearning touch exercises are:

- *Sensory basket:* The survivor interacts with a basket of sensual objects— such as an orange, spices, velvet cloth, a feather, silk fabric—one at a time while paying attention to smells, textures, colors, tastes, sensual feel, and so on.

- *Hand clapping:* The survivor teaches a simple hand clapping routine to his or her partner while the two are sitting facing each other in a comfortable setting.

- *Drawing on the body:* The survivor writes a message, letter by letter, on the partner's back, making a sweeping gentle hand stroke across the back between each word.

- *Safe nest:* The survivor creates a comfortable private space using blankets, pillows, and so on, and slowly explores self-touch in a safe and relaxed manner.

- *Safe embrace:* The survivor invites his or her partner to share the safe nest and they do resting and nonpressured touching explorations together.

- *Hand-to-heart:* In this meditation, the couple sits facing each other, placing right hands gently over each other's hearts, and focuses on sending and receiving feelings of appreciation, caring, and respect through the touch.

- *Magic pen:* The survivor tells his or her partner to hold onto one end of a pen, and then controls and designs the movement of the pen in space for both of them. Later, the survivor indicates when the exercise is over by telling the partner to let go of the pen.

- *Red light–green light:* The survivor looks at and then touches specific places on the partner's body, for limited periods of time, using a start–stop protocol for controlling touch.

- *Cleansing:* This touch exploration, alone or with a partner, takes place while bathing or showering.

- *Sensual body massage:* This exercise involves giving and receiving massages, with and without clothing, while focusing on safety, mutual pleasure, and increased communication.

Later-stage touch relearning resembles sensate focus in that it includes genital exploration, caress, and pleasuring.

A number of the early-stage relearning touch exercises—such as hand clapping, drawing on the body, magic pen, red light–green light, and hand-to heart—can be learned and practiced in the counseling office setting. The therapist can guide the couple step-by-step through an exercise, providing them with ideas and feedback to ensure success. At the end of an exercise, the therapist might ask: "How was your breathing?" "Were you relaxed?" "How able were you to stay present, communicate your needs, and have fun?"

These techniques can easily be modified, adapted, and rearranged in different sequences by survivors themselves, depending on their needs. For example, a survivor can vary the amount of clothing worn, the location in which the activity takes place, the part of the body being touched, the type of touch, and the amount of time spent touching. Survivors are encouraged to rest when needed, to become actively aware of what they are experiencing, to communicate openly, and to find creative ways to bridge and shift from one exercise to another, depending on interest and readiness.

8. Incorporate Traditional Sex Therapy as an Extension of Relearning Touch

When survivors express an interest in overcoming specific sexual problems (such as difficulty with orgasm, painful intercourse, premature ejaculation, or impotence), standard sex therapy techniques can be integrated during the advanced stages of relearning touch. Modifying traditional techniques gives survivors a sense of control over what they do and when, helps them deal with automatic reactions and abuse-related issues as they arise, and teaches them how to maintain emotional intimacy as sexual stimulation intensifies.

Barbara, a 30-year-old incest survivor, was upset that she could not climax from manual stimulation by her husband, Adam. In the past, when Adam had stimulated her, she flashed back to seeing her alcoholic father, with his red, bloodshot eyes looking at her as he touched her. This image was so distressing, she stopped and lost sexual interest.

To address this situation, Barbara spent time doing the "safe nest" exercise, exploring her own body, and eventually touching her genitals. As her comfort level increased, she incorporated standard preorgasmia exercises, including a genital self-exam and experimentation with different types of stimulation. These exercises helped Barbara gain a sense that her genitals belonged to her. She also learned how to relax as her arousal increased. Occasionally, she imagined that her husband was doing some of the touching. This safe nest setting stimulation sometimes resulted in a climax.

When Barbara felt ready, she invited Adam to join her in the safe nest to experiment together with relaxed genital touching. They used a red light–green light exercise format, so that Barbara could tell Adam when to start and stop touching her vulva through her underwear. Later, Adam rested his hand over Barbara's hand as she gave herself a genital hug to bare skin. This progressed to the point where Adam's hand was resting on Barbara's clitoral area while she gently rested her hand over his to stop or direct movement as she preferred. A variation of hand-to-heart was practiced in which they placed their hands on each other's genitals during the meditation. The focus of the exercises was always on relaxing, breathing, staying present, communicating, expressing love, and having fun. Eventually, Barbara was able to let Adam massage and stimulate her genital area on his own. Although she began enjoying their home sessions more and more, her arousal was not reaching orgasm.

In therapy I suggested we discuss the meaning and significance of orgasm. Because of the abuse, Barbara associated orgasm with capitulation, willing participation (in the abuse), humiliation, and loss of personal power. Barbara then did some role-play work to understand and "forgive" her body for physically responding during the abuse. (In abuse, orgasm is a natural response to stimulation and often a coping mechanism for the added emotional and physical stress of the trauma). We discussed new images and meanings for orgasm, using metaphors from nature (flowers opening to full bloom, waves cresting, etc.). A particularly profound moment occurred in couples therapy when Adam told Barbara that, when he had an orgasm, it was as if his "heart was spilling over with love" for her. Barbara began to sob. "It feels like I'm just starting to get it that orgasm can be an expression of deep caring for a partner," she exclaimed later, while patting her eyes with a tissue. Having recreated new, positive associations and meanings, Barbara was soon able to experience enjoyable climaxes from Adam's caresses and touch to her clitoral area.

Similar strategies of combining self-awareness and desensitization exercises with new insights and understandings can be used to treat other sexual concerns of survivors. A male with premature ejaculation may first want to do "stop–start" exercises (Zilbergeld, 1992, pp. 459–460) to an-

274 New Alternatives/Innovations in Sex Therapy

other part of his body, such as his arm. Later, relearning touch exercises involving caressing and massaging the genitals can be woven in with progressive experiences of increased stimulation and pleasuring. Psychologically based problems with impotence can be addressed similarly when the male survivor builds on relearning touch techniques to include relaxed genital touch and stimulation.

Women survivors who suffer from painful intercourse are often helped by integrating desensitization exercises using vaginal dilators (Maltz, 1992/2001, pp. 307–309).[2] For some women, such as those who were violently raped, the idea of the dilators may be very upsetting at first. It may be several months or longer before I mention them at all. Then it may be several months more before I show one to a survivor. One woman I worked with, who had been abducted and gang-raped during a 3-day ordeal, did not feel ready to address the possibility of therapy work with dilators until she and her boyfriend had done 6 months of relearning touch exercises and were beginning to explore genital pleasuring. I gave her the smallest dilator and suggested she just touch it from time to time at home. She and her boyfriend made up a game in which she pretended it was a wand and she was a conductor—she waved it around while her boyfriend whistled the *William Tell Overture*.

Creativity and fun are essential parts of sexual recovery, especially when survivors become more active sexually. Many couples find that certain lovemaking positions are easier than others and less likely to trigger abuse memories. The side-by-side, scissors position and the woman-on-top position seem especially helpful to women survivors who were held down and assaulted in the past.

☐ 9. Address Sexual Fantasy Concerns

Sexual fantasies can be extremely problematic for survivors of sexual abuse. It does not help, and in fact can be misleading, to respond to a sexual abuse survivor's concerns about sexual fantasies with comments such as, "Your [disturbing] fantasies are normal. Just relax and enjoy them. All your sexual thoughts are harmless."

Like dreams, our sexual fantasies can range from ones we enjoy and treasure to ones we find unpleasant and unwanted. Many of the survivors I have counseled and have spoken with at conferences have told me they suffer from abuse-related, intrusive, out-of-control sexual fantasies. In fact,

---

2. A set of four vaginal dilators can be purchased from Syracuse Medical Devices, 214 Hurlburt Road, Syracuse, NY 13224. Phone: 315-449-0657. Fax: 315-449-0756.

at a conference of 100 female survivors, 4 out of 5 raised their hands when I asked how many were having problems with unwanted sexual fantasies (Maltz, 1995b). Guilt, shame, and embarrassment about their most intimate thoughts often keep survivors from revealing sexual fantasy problems to their therapists. But addressing sexual fantasy concerns can be crucial to achieving a complete and lasting sexual recovery. When intrusive, unwanted sexual fantasies continue, they can function like unresolved nightmares, creating psychic stress, lowering self-esteem, harming the development and trust and intimacy with a partner, and essentially keeping the dynamics of the original sexual abuse alive.

I have developed a number of effective strategies for addressing sexual fantasy concerns (Maltz & Boss, 1997, re-released in 2001). Like dreams, unwanted fantasies can be analyzed in the light of conscious thought. Using a variety of expressive techniques, such as writing, drawing, and role-playing, clients can look closely at the story, characters, and symbols in the fantasy. Therapists also can help survivors explore when in the sexual response cycle the fantasy occurs. For example, does it increase excitement? Facilitate climax? Or alleviate other stresses? To identify how the fantasy may function, a therapist might inquire about how the client feels before and after the fantasy.

Through discussion and insight, survivors are able to see how their sexual fantasies may relate to past abuse. On a psychological level, unwanted fantasies often represent the sexualization of some kind of unresolved conflict related to past emotional injury, abandonment, and betrayal.

Nina, for example, avoided intercourse because she wanted to avoid the fantasies of anal rape that invariably intruded as she approached climax. Analyzing this recurrent fantasy, Nina discovered that it reenacted the humiliation she felt as a child when her father abused her by spanking her and anally penetrating her with his finger. Using role-play in therapy, she was able to express anger toward her father for betraying her trust and exploiting her innocence. She realized the shame and guilt all belonged to him. Nina imagined setting limits with him on how he could and could not touch her as a child. As a result, the anal rape sexual fantasy lost its power. Nina was able to climax without it.

In addition to analyzing their troublesome fantasies, survivors can learn other ways to loosen the hold of fantasy. Survivors can learn to stop and focus on the present moment whenever a fantasy begins to take over their thoughts. Clients can discover how to increase effective physical stimulation, improve communication with a partner, and reduce time and performance stresses in sex. Clients also can learn to bend the content of their sexual fantasies toward more healthy sexual expression. For instance, a client who fantasizes about sex involving a 70-year-old man and a 4-

year-old girl could deliberately change the fantasy to be about a 50-year-old man and a 15-year-old adolescent, and finally, to be about two 30-year-olds. Survivors can be taught to create new sexual fantasies with which they feel comfortable and that inspire lasting sexual pleasure and intimacy.

☐ 10. Practice Good Self-Care

Sex therapy with survivors of sexual abuse is more challenging for therapists than traditional sex therapy work. Not only do we need to be proficient in treating sexual abuse repercussions, such as posttraumatic stress, depression, and dissociative disorders, we also need to be very creative in how and when we integrate interventions that address sexuality concerns. Working with this population requires a therapist to be extremely patient. Unlike the relatively brief therapy format of standard sex therapy, it can take a long time (many months, sometimes even years) before clients report significant improvement in their sex lives.

Clients who are addressing these difficult issues often feel powerless, helpless, and overwhelmed. As therapists, we need to be steady and encouraging of even the smallest steps of progress. We need to offer them hope that recovery and healing are possible and that sex can be healthy and enjoyable. This means maintaining our own positive attitudes, even in the face of setbacks and frustrations.

As therapists, we also need to protect our own sexuality. Working with this population, we are exposed to horrific stories of sexual exploitation, violence, and harmful sexual practices. We need to learn to expect and handle occasional feelings of unwanted arousal or revulsion that may surface when a client is describing past abuse or present-day negative sexual behaviors. Sexual scenarios and images of any nature can be stimulating. Graphic sexual descriptions can effect physiological reactions even when we are averse to what we are hearing about. We can diffuse sexual energy by keeping ourselves calm (through relaxed breathing, sending unwanted sexual energy into the floor, mentally affirming our healing purpose, etc.) and keeping the client focused on the goals of treatment.

In addition, we need good support from other therapists to work effectively and take good care of ourselves emotionally. It is especially important to seek help from other therapists and advisors if you find yourself becoming preoccupied with sexual abuse images and thoughts away from work. On an ongoing basis, peer consultation and supervision can be helpful to maintaining perspective.

I recommend that therapists doing this work restrict their exposure to sexual abuse stories and descriptions in their private lives. If we are getting bombarded with images of abusive sex at work, it is especially important that we surround ourselves with stories and images of positive, loving sex at home. After hours, we can avoid or limit exposure to books, articles, movies, television programs, and so on that depict sex as exploitive or hurtful. We can keep certain areas of our homes (like the bedroom) as "abuse-free zones." Inside the zones, no materials or discussions related to sexual abuse are permitted. As therapists, we need to make a conscious effort to think about sex in positive ways and to find resources that validate and inspire healthy sexual intimacy.

☐ Conclusion

Doing sex therapy work with survivors of sexual abuse requires therapists to think and work creatively. We can empower our clients and work with them in developing a comprehensive healing program that is sensitive to their personal histories, present situations, and individual needs. As therapists, we cannot expect quick fixes for complex problems that may have originated in childhood trauma. But when survivors are able to use therapeutic help to heal their sexuality and to reclaim it as a positive life force, the results can be profound and rewarding for client and therapist alike.

These new approaches and techniques for treating survivors can also benefit many nonsurvivor clients. For example, the relearning touch exercises are helpful for anyone who wants to learn the skills necessary for experiencing emotionally intimate and deeply meaningful sex. And many people who come in for sex therapy benefit from looking more closely at (and perhaps changing) their sexual attitudes, behaviors, and fantasies.

Healthy sexual intimacy is infinitely joyful and rewarding. It is something everyone deserves. As sex therapists, when we are flexible in how we address sexual problems, we can help ensure that sexual healing is something everyone can achieve.

☐ References

Bass, E., & Davis, L. (1994) *The courage to heal: A guide for women survivors of child sexual abuse.* New York: HarperCollins.
Carnes, P. (1991). *Don't call it love: Recovering from sexual addiction.* New York: Bantam Books.

Davis, L. (1991*). Allies in healing: When the person you love was sexually abused as a child.* New York: HarperCollins.

Gibran, K. (1923/1973). *The prophet.* New York: Alfred A. Knopf.

Jehu, D. (1988). *Beyond sexual abuse: Therapy with women who were childhood victims.* London: Wiley.

King, N. (1995) *Speaking our truths: Voices of courage and healing for male survivors of childhood sexual abuse.* New York: HarperCollins.

Lew, M. (1990). *Victims no longer: Men recovering from incest and other sexual child abuse.* New York: HarperCollins.

Maltz, W. (1988). Identifying and treating the sexual repercussions of incest: A couples therapy approach. *Journal of Sex & Marital Therapy 14*(2), 142–170.

Maltz, W. (1992/2001). *The sexual healing journey: A guide for survivors of sexual abuse* (Rev. Ed.). New York: Harper Perennial.

Maltz, W. (1995a). The Maltz hierarchy of sexual interaction. *Sexual Addiction and Compulsivity 2*(1), 5–18.

Maltz, W. (1995b). *Sexual healing journey.* Paper presented at the Healing Woman Conference, May, San Francisco.

Maltz, W. (1996). *Passionate hearts: The poetry of sexual love.* Novato, CA: New World Library.

Maltz, W. (2001). *Intimate kisses: The poetry of sexual pleasure.* Novato, CA: New World Library.

Maltz, W., & Boss, S. (1997). *In the garden of desire: Women's sexual fantasies as a pathway to passion and pleasure.* New York: Broadway Books.

Maltz, W., & Boss, S. (2001). *Private thoughts: Exploring the power of women's sexual fantasies.* Novato, CA: New World Library.

Maltz, W., Christiansen, S., & Joffee, G. (1988). *Partners in healing: Couples overcoming the sexual repercussions of incest.* Eugene, OR: Independent Video Services (video).

Maltz, W., Christiansen, S., & Joffee, G. (1995) *Relearning touch: Healing techniques for couples.* Eugene, OR: Independent Video Services (video).

Maltz, W., & Holman, B. (1987). *Incest and sexuality: A guide to understanding and healing.* San Francisco: Jossey-Bass/Lexington Books.

Spear, J. (1991). *How can I help her? A handbook for partners of women sexually abused as children.* City Center, MN: Hazelden Foundation.

Zilbergeld, B. (1992). *The new male sexuality: The truth about men, sex and pleasure.* New York: Bantam Books.

Marny Hall, Ph.D.

Beyond Forever After: Narrative Therapy With Lesbian Couples

A dour pair stares out from the book jacket. Fastidiously attired in white lab coats, William Masters and Virginia Johnson might have been virologists on the track of Ebola or astronomers intent upon solving the riddles of the universe. But no, sex was their subject. In 1966, they published their pioneering work, *Human Sexual Response*. No sooner had they transformed all that swelling and sloshing and spurting into an elegant architecture of sex than a rogue theorist began dismantling it. The contemporary notion of sex, Foucault claimed, was nothing more than an elaborate fiction. It made it possible "to group together, in an artificial unity, anatomical elements, biological functions, conducts, sensations, and pleasures and it enables [us] to make use of this fictitious unity as a causal principle" (1980, p.154).

Soon after Foucault challenged the orthodox view of sex, a group of postmodernist-minded therapists began to deconstruct the sex problems of their clients. If sex was indeed provisional, fuzzy, a fictional event that was constantly being pummeled and tweaked by historical forces into novel shapes, these therapists reasoned, why not try to achieve this same sort of plasticity on a micro-level? When couples came to therapy complaining about inhibited or discrepant desire, why not intentionally destabilize their notions of sex? If the meanings of particular acts could be inflected differently—that is, if certain latent aspects of couples' sexual narratives could be teased out and emphasized, and other more central elements could be deemphasized—wouldn't formidable problems be reduced to insignificant footnotes in couples' sex narratives? Change our sexual stories, these narrative therapists claimed, and we change our erotic lives (Hall, 1991, 1993; McNamee & Gergen, 1992).

Lesbian, gay, bisexual, and transgendered (LGBT) populations are predisposed by their own experiences to find such a postmodern perspective congenial. In the process of coming out, of (re)defining themselves as sex and gender renegades, most have already stumbled upon the mutable nature of personal reality. In addition, they have discovered the enormous benefits that accrue to those who have found a way to rewrite their erotic narratives. But narrative therapy is a good fit for LGBT-identified therapy seekers for practical as well as philosophical reasons. It can provide queer clients with specific strategies necessary to rehabilitate widely discredited identities.

Once they declare themselves gay, bi, or trans, such outsiders must find a way to deal with negative cultural myths. In order to counter allegations that they are abnormal or immoral, they must be able to construct positive and legitimizing accounts about their sexual and gender preferences. It is just such account making—the manufacture of meanings that challenge the preexisting and widely circulating "truths"—that is at the heart of narrative therapy (Rosen & Kuehlwein, 1996). The following narrative-shifting strategies are designed to help therapists deal with the sexual presenting problems of one segment of the stigmatized LGBT populations: lesbian couples.[1]

☐ Lesbian Identity: The Forever-After Factor

Before lesbian couples make their first counseling appointment, most have already benefited from a collective form of narrative therapy. Thanks to the Gay Liberation Movement, the shadowy figures who, according to the

---

1. The suggestions for ways to change lesbian couples' sexual narratives come from a variety of sources. Some of my ideas are modifications of aspects of the sex therapy training I received at the University of California Medical School in San Francisco in the 1970s; other suggestions came from my work over the years with lesbian couples.

For details about the hit-and-miss nature of this work, see "Sex Therapy to Sex Therapy: Notes from the Margins" (Hall, 1991). Finally, my approach has been influenced by contemporary narrative therapists. An article by Robert Niemeyer entitled "Process Interventions for the Constructivist Psychotherapist" has been particularly useful (in Rosen & Kuehlwein, 1996).

lurid jacket of a 1960 paperback, inhabit "the dangerous half-world of forbidden love" (Bannon, 1960) have now come to believe they deserve the same rights and privileges heterosexuals enjoy. Perhaps most evident among these entitlements is the right to marry. Because contemporary laws lag behind gay partners' claims to legal recognition, lesbian couples have found alternative ways to certify the legitimacy of their unions. With whispered promises and public ceremonies, with planned futures and pooled assets, lesbian lovers show each other, their friends, and their families that they will be together for keeps. Weston summed up this legitimizing strategy nicely, pointing out that the dominant view of marriage is based on an axiom: What's real must last. With a great display of ingenuity, lesbians have turned the axiom into *what lasts must be real*. In our love stories, staying power replaces legal clout (Weston, 1998, p. 79).

Permanent partnerships are the central legitimizing strategy in contemporary lesbian identities. So central, in fact, that lovers do not necessarily part company when the high level of erotic arousal that fuels romantic twosomes fizzles. Instead, they bond more closely, determined to overcome whatever obstacle is impeding the progress of their partnership. Usually the obstacles these couples cite are psychological. Perhaps, couples speculate, the diminution of intensity can be explained by a partner's fear of intimacy, by a bout of depression, or by an intrusive memory of an early trauma. As well as being firm believers in psychological causes, lesbians also believe in therapeutic cures. In extensive surveys taken over the last two decades, 73% of self-identified lesbians have sought psychotherapeutic help—often for relationship problems (Alexander, 1996). Therefore, it is not surprising that, when couples need support that goes beyond the affirming slogans of Gay Liberation, they seek out a relationship expert/coach—the good fairy of the love story is summoned to lend a helping hand.

According to the dominant cultural script, lesbian couples are not—can never be—"real" twosomes. If partners no longer feel sexually aroused by each other, it may be hard for them to counter claims about their faux unions. And because they are same-sexed couples, they must also find a way to steer clear of the other ever popular "just friends" narrative. Because sexual functioning, liberation politics, personal identity, and self esteem are so inextricably entwined for lesbians, therapists working with partners cannot afford to restrict their focus to the inhibited desire that may be the presenting problem. In order for couples to extricate themselves from the identity quagmire nonsexual partnerships represent, couples and counselors must collaborate on forging new accounts—love stories that include updated versions of what it means to be normal, healthy, loving partners. These new accounts must normalize behavior previously devalued as unspontaneous, unloving, even "abnormal," both in and out of the bedroom. In addition, the new stories must legitimate couples whose relationships may not be permanent and whose sex lives, if they exist at all, are not based on passionate, mutual desire.

Before they can help their couples clients craft such radical, new accounts of their unions, therapists need to be conversant with the traditional stories many lesbian partners use to certify their togetherness. These stories often feature magical first meetings, earth-moving passion, and till-death-do-us-part commitments (Hall, 2000). As well as being respectfully aware of such romantic motifs, it is also important that clinicians have in their repertoires alternative stories that will help their clients go beyond the conventional happily-ever-after scenario.

In order to facilitate easy recall of both sets of love story themes—the conventional and the unconventional—I have used the following mnemonic device.

☐ The Mnemonic L.E.S.B.I.A.N. Guide to Forever After and Beyond

L—Long-Lasting Love

Finding Ms.(or Mr.) Right and living happily ever after is a universal favorite. As mentioned previously, this ideal is particularly important to stigmatized populations. Durable unions can lend credibility and legitimacy to the socially marginalized. On the other hand, if lesbians do not pair permanently—and statistics suggest that frequently they do not—they may feel doubly stigmatized (Kurdek, 1995).

Alternatives to the forever-after love story may include positive views of impermanent partnerships—that is, shorter engagements that are gratifying or enlightening. These can be viewed as passages or as present-oriented partnerships, rather than as failures.

E—Equality

Lesbians—often feminists—prize relationships that do not replicate heteronormative hierarchies and inequalities (Hall & Gregory, 1991; Johnson, 1990; Peplau, Pedesky, & Hamilton, 1982). But when it comes to sexual matters, it is unlikely that each partner will be equally libidinous or equally inclined to initiate erotic encounters. Consequently, it is useful for lesbian repertoires to include stories that normalize asymmetrical desires or roles. For example, it is perfectly normal if one partner tends to be the sexual initiator while the other is more passive.

S—Sex

The degree of arousal that would cause a woman to declare herself a lesbian is likely to generate a romantic story of cosmic inevitability in which love, sex, and ecstasy are all closely associated. Such a constellation, often indispensable to coming out and courtship, may prove problematic in later relationship phases. If passion and sex are fused, for example, the end of the honeymoon may also spell the end of sex. Consequently, it is important for lesbians to begin to develop other sexual stories. Such alternatives might include downsized erotic stories about sex as a diversion, as a way to relax, or simply as a way of making a signature statement about one's individuality.

B—Balance

According to the psychological narrative adopted by many lesbian couples, healthy lives are multifaceted. Sex is a key element, but so are recreation, spirituality, satisfying work, and good friends. In practice, however, it is imbalance rather than balance that characterizes most contemporary urban lives. There is simply not time to do everything—no matter how healthy such a regimen might seem. As a result, activities that are supposed to "just happen," like sex, simply don't.

In the alternative version of the balanced-life story, sexual spontaneity is replaced by conscious prioritizing of erotic encounters. These alternative stories might feature weekend getaways or once-a-week dates. In other words, sexual rituals or routines replace the old notion of spontaneous erotic combustion (Hall,1998, pp. 90–91).

I—Intimacy

Lesbian stories feature a special us-against-them realm shared by two lovers. Sex is part and parcel of this intimacy. Yet, intimacy between female lovers may be so nurturing, so companionable that it renders sexual connection redundant.

Erotic connection, paradoxically enough, may depend on the ability of partners—through role-playing or fantasy— to become strangers to each other (Hall, 1995, p. 209). Consequently, the alternative to the intimacy story may feature mutually agreed-upon distancing strategies.

A—Achievement

Another theme popular among couples under the sway of psychological narratives is "growth." In healthy relationships, so the story goes, partners resolve power struggles and come to understand and cherish each other more. Even after living together in a stable relationship for years, partners are to continue on mutual and individual creative paths. Such a relentless allegory of progress may end up triggering feelings of inadequacy in some partners. An alternative tale may give more credit to events over which neither partner has control. In the random universe posited by the alternative story, partners must make it up as they go along. In this improvised version, there is no goal to strive for, no pot of gold at the end of the rainbow. Rather, it is up to couples to invent and reinvent themselves and their sexual relationship.

N—Never Again

This part of lesbian narratives focuses on the past. Here we find relationships with parents or former partners that may have been abusive or exploitative. According to the conventional story, one should never repeat such patterns in present relationships.

In the alternate version, we stop trying to banish our nemeses. They are part of us. In fact, a conscious, stylized replay of old patterns can be a way to right ancient wrongs. Even violations we experienced as children can be transformed into sexual fantasies that we control. For example, if we imagine encounters between marauders and victims, we can turn the tables in our mind's eye. In the new imagined version, the victim can come out on top—both literally and figuratively. Or, by moving back and forth between the two roles, or choosing a position as outside observer, the former victim can undo some of the powerlessness she felt as a child. Such fantasy scenarios can be both arousing and healing (Morin, 1995).

This list of themes is partial, of course. It is based on the stories I have heard from lesbian clients who, for the most part, are ethnically diverse San Francisco professionals in their 30s and 40s. Other groups may favor other narratives. Geographical location, the era in which one came out, and membership in a particular generation are all factors that may contribute to the crafting of very different narratives. These narrative variations became evident recently when a colleague told me that her 20-year-old female client had just admonished her. The client had objected to being included in the catch-all term "lesbian community," which the clinician had been using loosely. "Don't call me a lesbian," growled the young client. "If you have to call me something, call me a dude or a dyke."

☐ Changing the Narrative

Changing clients' narratives may make it possible for couples to connect sexually in post-passionate ways. Or, such revisions may make it possible to legitimize nonerotic partnerships. But how do clinicians get from old narratives to new ones—from passionate, forever-after tales to stories that might normalize less romantic, less idealized partnerships? The following list of linguistic and performative strategies can help.

Context-Shifting Questions

Diminished or discrepant desire is a common presenting problem. Couples often initiate therapy because one or both partners have "turned off." Clinicians may begin to either narrow or expand the narrative horizon with the following series of questions about the problem. Can the clients be more specific about being turned off? What does it mean to be turned on? Is the absence of a turned-on feeling exactly the same as the feeling of being turned off, or is there a subtle difference between the two states? What are clients using as a baseline measure of desire? A previous relationship? The honeymoon phase of the current relationship? The way they felt last year at this time? Such questions suggest that the source of the problem may be certain unwarranted comparisons rather than the libido of either partner.

Other questions might zero in on particular episodes themselves. How is one disappointing encounter different from another? What were the particulars of each? Was one partner, or both, bored? Sleepy? Tense? What was each thinking? Expecting? Dreading? What happened then? These questions may lead the clinician and clients to collaborate on a more nuanced, less monolithic version of "turned off." Perhaps there are degrees of being turned off. Some turned-off states may, in fact, be more accurately labeled "indifferent" or "willing-if-I-don't-have-to-lift-a-finger." Ultimately, questions such as these may produce a more elaborate and multifocal view of erotic possibilities than the yes or no of the old on/off model.

The William Blake line about the world reflected in a grain of sand is a handy guide in this process. The more details the clinician can unearth, the more likely he or she will be able to construct a new tale about desire and its absence.

Untangling Story Snarls

Another way to suggest new narrative possibilities is to ask questions that hint at the influence of the past on the present, or the way in which one partner's story has affected the other. For example, the clinician might ask if a client felt turned off in other relationships. If so, was that diminution of sexual desire connected to the dissolution of the partnership? If the client answers affirmatively, the clinician might make the following observation: "If getting turned off meant the end of your last relationship, the feeling has become much more significant than a normal variation in desire. It is almost a self-fulfilling prophecy about the end. No wonder you are tense."

Or, perhaps one partner feels ashamed and guilty about not being turned on because she is certain she is hurting her partner's feelings. The clinician might direct the client to "notice how responsible you feel. Makes me think this kind of guilt has roots that predate this relationship. Give me a history of your responsibility for the happiness of others." Such exploratory questioning tends to open up the story horizon, allowing the main actor in the drama to shift roles and responsibilities. The new story about not being turned on acquires many more layers, meanings, and, hence, possible outcomes.

Inflection Strategies

Once new narrative possibilities have been suggested, they have to be developed and reinforced. Clinicians can use a number of strategies to accomplish this. One is to accentuate or emphasize previously uninflected information. For example, if a couple reports offhandedly that they comforted each other after a sexual disappointment, the clinician might say, "You know, it sounds as though you were very intimate—perhaps even more intimate than you would have been if you had had sex."

Resisting Narrative Pulls

Another strategy is to resist obvious narrative pulls in familiar directions. The first and most obvious of such pulls is a client's attempt to start a stampede toward a quick solution when feelings of frustration or disappointment seem unbearable. The clinician might resist such a tug by lingering with and naming painful feelings. For example, the clinician might say, "Not being turned on when you want so much to be sounds intolerable. More than intolerable . . . unbearable." Uncomfortably long pauses are good indications that the conventional narrative is being resisted.

Summary statements about a particular episode are additional clues that clients need help resisting narrative pulls. For example, a client might sum up her account of a disappointing sexual encounter with a brusque, "That's all that happened." Clinicians can challenge such faux endings by asking what happened next. And after that? This serializing of an episode by continuing to ask "what-then" questions may lead the couple to realize that the so-called ending was simply a transition to another form of closeness.

Disrupting Narratives

Predictable narratives can be disrupted as well as resisted. Let's use the example of both partners insisting that one partner's disinterest is the source of their sexual problems. If only the reluctant partner's libido could be rekindled, both insist, sex would resume as before. In such cases, the clinician might venture the following surprising, but plausible, hypothesis about who the actual problem partner is.

Say Kesha is the less libidinous partner, and Robin her unhappy mate. Turning to Kesha, the clinician might say, "You both agree that you, Kesha, are turned off and that you, Robin, are turned on. But couldn't it be that there is collusion going on, and Kesha has agreed to take the fall for both of you? Let me explain my reasoning. Robin, you know what Kesha's response to your overtures will be. Yet, even though you are absolutely sure of the outcome, you persist. In a sense, you are the one initiating nonsex, while seeming all the while to initiate sex. Do you think that's because it is easier for Kesha to take the rap as the nonsexual partner than it is for Robin?"

The point of venturing such alternative hypotheses is not to arrive at the truth, but to encourage clients to stray from their current narrative certainties. The more practice couples have at viewing their circumstances from novel angles, the easier it will be for them to tell their own ambiguous, multilayered love and sex stories.

Multiplying Narrative Links

Along with creating confusion about which of the two partners has the "problem," clinicians might also use the following interpretation to subvert the meaning of turned off. To Kesha, the less libidinous partner, the clinician might say, "It is obvious that you are acutely aware of your partner's feelings. You know how hurt she will be if you don't reciprocate her desire in the moment. But if you can say that you are suffering from some kind of numbness that is out of your control, then perhaps you won't hurt her so much. So, your being turned off is really a case of being turned on . . . too turned on to your lover's feelings."

Or the clinician might ask, "Has it occurred to you, Kesha, that your erotic life is delicate, composed of feelings and fantasies so subtle, in fact, that they disappear when compared with Robin's less subtle brand of eroticism? Do you think we can find out what your eroticism might consist of if it weren't constantly being overshadowed? First, let's figure out a way to construct a sort of bell jar that can protect it from comparison while we study it."

In short, therapists might profitably think of themselves as editors, who, with certain deft revisions, help clients change their life scripts and enable them to continue their legitimizing stories even if they are not swept away on a tide of desire.

Performance Strategies

By helping couples craft stories full of sexual asymmetries and ambiguity, clinicians can revise their forever-after tales. But clients also need to learn how to create such tales out of the office—that is, they must become accustomed to performing them on their own turf.

Dubbed *sensate focus exercises* by sex therapists in the 1970s, massage assignments are a good way to get clients in the habit of homework. At the same time, this exercise may help shift the sex narrative from genital, goal-oriented sex to more diffuse, full-bodied eroticism (Kleinplatz, 1996). Although there is no one way to assign massage homework, there are general guidelines: Erotic areas should be off-limits, at least in the beginning. Between turns, partners should have some sort of talking or writing exercise about how each felt in her role; the entire assignment should not last more than 45 minutes. The sort of sensate focus exercise I prefer adds a bit of mystery. The massaging partner divides her segment in half. One half of the massage is for her partner; that is, she touches her partner in the way she knows her partner prefers. During the other part of the massage, the masseuse will please herself. That is, as she is massaging her partner, she will pretend she is stroking herself in the ways she most enjoys being touched.

The masseuse does not reveal the sequence to the passive partner but, during the discussion break, they talk about it. The passive partner describes the difference between the two segments and guesses which segment was for her and which was for her partner. The masseuse confirms or denies her partner's speculation and explains the difference—from her point of view—between the two segments. Then, they can switch roles (or remain in the same roles if the clinician decides the couple's stories need to be asymmetrical).

Clients who live in cold (or glass) houses, or clients for whom massage exercises are contraindicated for some other reason, can be assigned spooning exercises. In these assignments, one partner curls—spoonlike—around her partner's back. Then, holding each other quietly for a few minutes, they breathe synchronously. Afterward, they can talk about the experience and then reverse positions. Another approach is to leave the activity unstated. The clinician may assign a placeholder exercise. In these fill-in-the-blank assignments, partners are to figure out some intimate activity to do for a brief period a few times a week. Ideally, partners will remain silent during the exercise. Instead of their usual conversations, they will engage in some sort of physical contact during the assigned time.

These exercises are designed to flush out information about otherwise inaccessible or unmentionable aspects of couples' private or conjoint narratives. The self-doubts, irritations, or secret wishes that may come to light can be explored and perhaps incorporated into partners' new erotic maps. Another goal of the massage or placeholder exercise is the staking out of a fresh physical and temporal zone. Uncontaminated by other commitments or obligations, or by the negative associations generated by past sexual disappointments, this space can be the *tabula rasa* upon which partners can begin to inscribe new forms of closeness and eroticism. In addition to the exercises, partners may (or may not) have sex as usual. But the newly designated time and space should be sex-free—reserved for as yet unnamed activities. Once in place, the zone can be used for further assignments tailored to narrative needs of clients. If, for example, a more nuanced, asymmetrical map of sexuality is the goal, one partner can be assigned masturbation somewhere in the vicinity of her partner. Perhaps in a nearby room, if the masturbator is self-conscious; or, if not, perhaps in her partner's arms. Half-sex exercises are particularly important strategies for partners with differential desires. The exercises demonstrate that sex partners need not always be equally engaged or aroused.

If one partner's sexuality seems to be overshadowed by her partner's more dramatic demonstrations of desire, the more obviously sexual partner can be given a record-keeping exercise. For a week, she is to keep track of the ebb and flow of her partner's tactile pleasures, fantasy life, and masturbation habits. Even reactions to films or novels will do. Obviously, such an exercise will require that both partners' attention be redirected in unprecedented ways. At the end of the week, the note-taking partner can read her report back to the subtly sexual partner, who may want to make additions or revisions to the account.

Plenty of starting-and-stopping exercises, regulated by a timing device with a beeper, are useful for sexual overachievers, codependent partners who are overly concerned about their partners' feelings, and turned-off clients. The overachievers will be reined in by the inexorable beep. The codependent can relax, trusting in the tick-tocking authority. The turned-off won't have time to get too turned off . . . and may even notice they are slightly less turned off at times. Because stop/start exercises break the rules about continuity and concentration and prevent the goal-orientation that so often characterizes sexual activity, they reduce performance anxiety. They may even generate a few giggles. The content of such exercises is not as important as the spirit in which they are co-created—"improv" rather than improve.

Perhaps the best way to illustrate how such strategies—both linguistic and performative—might be implemented is to describe a course of treatment with a lesbian couple who came to see me for sex therapy.

☐ Becca and Carmen[2]: A Never-Ending Story

Carmen, 32, and Becca, 30, met 4 years ago at a Silicon Valley mixer for gays who work in the computer industry. Within a year they had moved in together. When they first came to therapy, they were bitterly polarized over sex. According to Becca, Carmen was an insensitive, selfish lout who just wanted to "get her rocks off." Carmen, in turn, felt she had been swindled, lied to. She had always had a strong sex drive, she said, and was often disappointed by other lovers' flagging interest. Before she made a commitment to this relationship, she had been crystal clear. She really

---

2. Any information that might reveal the identity of these clients has been changed to ensure confidentiality.

needed a partner who could keep up with her sexually. In the first flush of romance, Becca had had no trouble making such a promise. But the two had polarized into yes and no positions shortly after they moved in together. They had tried therapy before for these issues, to no avail. In fact, they informed me, they had "fired" their last couples therapist for cautioning Becca never to say no in the bedroom. But since then, the yes/no impasse had become more intractable. And the stakes had gotten higher.

Even before they had met each other, each woman had expected to have a child. Because of her company's generous pregnancy policy, it made sense for Becca to inseminate first. After 6 months of visits to the sperm bank, Becca had become pregnant. As the prospect of having a child became a reality, Carmen was feeling more and more trapped in a sexless forever-after. Becca, who felt unloved and unnurtured, was afraid that Carmen would become so frustrated and impatient she would leave—a prospect that seemed unthinkable now that Becca was pregnant.

Despite their previous dissatisfaction with couples therapy, their apprehension about the looming family commitment and their deteriorating relationship induced them to give therapy another try.

I saw Becca and Carmen for 20 sessions, spread over a 6-month period. Their sexual complaints were very specific. Becca avoided sex because she felt objectified. Becca claimed that Carmen was not happy just holding her or making love to her. Instead of letting Becca savor her orgasm, Carmen would impatiently expect "her turn," which usually consisted of at least three orgasms. As a result, Becca said, she felt used.

Carmen, in turn, felt she had never misrepresented her sex drive. Carmen said she was happy to make love to Becca as often as she liked. Nothing, Carmen claimed, would make her happier. She pointed out that her three orgasms did not take any longer than Becca's single climax. As for Becca's need to "savor" her orgasm, Carmen was glad to comply. But Carmen claimed that if Becca was not prodded to reciprocate, she would simply roll over and take a post-climax nap. That would be the end of lovemaking. When that happened, Carmen said, she felt incomplete. Was it unreasonable, she asked, to expect her turn during lovemaking sessions?

Early Interventions

The first intervention was to tackle the inequity theme that was causing so much trouble in the relationship. I commented that it seemed as if each partner felt that, if she was not vigilant, her partner would get the lion's share. I wondered if there was some other context, one that predated their relationship, that prompted such vigilance. Perhaps the answer lay in their growing-up experiences. I asked them to tell me about their families of origin.

Becca was the oldest child in a middle-class Jewish family. Her father had a hair-trigger temper, Becca told me, and was constantly provoked by "others' mistakes." As a young child, she had adored him, imitated him, and tried to be "his helper" in his garage workshop. After the birth of a younger brother when Becca was 6, any hope of pleasing her father vanished. His attention—meager and conditional even before the birth of his son—shifted entirely to Becca's new sibling. Because her brother was frail, her mother's nurturing attention also shifted. But Becca said she never gave up the struggle for her fair share of her parents' attention.

Carmen's parents were working-class Nicaraguans who had immigrated to North America when Carmen was 2. When Carmen was 8, her mother divorced her father and married a man who had four children. Because Carmen's mother and stepfather both worked, the children were left on their own much of the time. Partly in defense against neighborhood gangs, partly because they were genuinely fond of each other, the siblings formed their own tight "pack." When the inevitable disputes arose, they relied heavily on notions of fairness to settle them.

This background information gave me an opportunity to reconfigure their 50:50 impasse, as well as the unflattering accusations each made about the other's "selfish" behavior. My goal was to incorporate all this background information into a more positive narrative. I observed that, for different reasons, as these two young women were growing up, there simply had not been enough attention to go around. In spite of their very different family constellations, social classes, and ethnicities, both had come to the conclusion that they would not get their fair share without a struggle. Therefore, their current impasses were not the results of selfishness, but of early training in scrappiness. Each had had to hold her own in a tough world. It was certainly valuable training to have acquired. Yet, possibly, because of having had such an intensive course in self-defense, each had been shortchanged in another area. I suggested that we work on another part of their skills—that we embark on a project we might designate as "tenderness training." Whenever the opportunity arose, I said, I would be a tenderness coach. Initially, they did not seem enthusiastic about my proposal, but they did not dismiss it.

Subsequent Interventions

Thereafter, small tenderness trainings punctuated most of the sessions. When they came in polarized, as they often did, I listened carefully to each partner's grievance and then restated it in a way that was not accusatory. These "edits" usually succeeded in garnering empathy from a previously defensive partner. When the conflict had been defused in this way, I gave them on-the-spot mini-assignments to say something sweet to each other. Sometimes these mini-assignments misfired. Carmen, for example, was offended when Becca complimented her on "your ability to get along with people whose values you detest." Carmen retorted that it sounded as if she was being praised for being an "A-1 ass-kisser." Hurriedly, Becca and I went back to the drawing board and fine-tuned the compliment until it emerged in a more palatable form: that Carmen had a knack for dealing with very difficult people. "Even me," Becca added ruefully. Carmen thanked Becca, and told her she loved her blue eyes.

Even though both partners always acted as though I was asking them for the declension of a particularly difficult Latin verb whenever I told them to say something sweet to each other, I persisted. With practice, both became more fluent in the language of positive regard. The honing and reinforcement of loving language, I hoped, would help shift their old 50:50 combat-zone cliffhanger into a narrative about a surplus of goodwill. In the new story we were crafting, positive feelings—even if slightly below the surface—were abundant. They could usually be tapped, but sometimes it would take effort. In this new story, scorekeeping was no longer necessary. They could redirect all the energy previously absorbed by such vigilance into their new tenderness project. I reinforced the motivation for this new narrative by emphasizing that sex therapy requires ample reservoirs of goodwill. We would dip into them regularly when we started the really challenging work on the ticklish and ever incendiary sexual impasse.

This gentler, kinder framework also gave me an excuse to interrupt their intermittent bouts of name-calling by reminding them they were backsliding on their tenderness curriculum. If they were angry, it was because they were hurt. I wanted their comments to reflect their vulnerability.

Sexual Histories

After I had heard about their families of origin, I asked Becca and Carmen to tell me about their sexual histories. As might be expected, they were dramatically different.

Becca's crushes on girls had begun when she was in her mid-teens. In college, she had been thrilled to find other lesbians, and had stitched together a very satisfactory erotic life from fantasies, sunset beach strolls, and love notes. In short, her affair recipe consisted of three parts romantic inspiration to one part sexual consummation. Her only heterosexual experience—motivated by curiosity—consisted of one encounter with a good friend.

In contrast, Carmen's background was singularly unromantic. She became orgasmic during petting sessions with boys in high school. In college, she had continued to date boys. She had not liked intercourse at first, but after a while compared it to sushi: "an acquired taste." After college, Carmen had discovered her attraction to women. Before meeting each other, Becca and Carmen had had a couple of other unsatisfying and short-lived lesbian relationships. When Carmen and Becca met each other, they felt they had discovered the soulmates they had yearned for. Both agreed that the relationship had been "hot and heavy for the first 6 months." Then Becca started saying no and making up excuses, and Carmen started pleading with Becca to "just do it."

After Carmen and Becca had described their histories, I emphasized the differences between Becca's desire for affection, closeness, and romance and Carmen's desire for down-and-dirty, orgasmic-focused sex. I commented that I was very impressed by their differences. I could certainly see how easily they could polarize. When one partner began to act upon her desires, the other would almost automatically feel ignored, unseen, and unheard. I told them about my private pet theory about lesbian sex—that many of us had an unusual capacity for passion. Why else would we forswear all the comforts of conventional lives? But the very passion that was our glory was also our downfall. In the beginning of relationships, it obscured differences, like theirs, that would cause problems later. And in their case, there was another complication. Because of the law-of-the-jungle tactics they had learned growing up, they simply could not risk paying close attention to the needs of others. In their case, what was most salient about their respective sexualities had been buried twice—first by passion, and then by their well-honed survival instincts.

At this point, we needed to pay attention to the long-neglected differences, but that would not be easy, I observed, because their differences had been denied and buried for so long that they had become inflamed. I said that what I would usually assign—massage homework designed to unmask differences—was too risky at this point. It might only aggravate their already overheated differences. Consequently, I emphasized the need to go slowly. I proposed what I would call a "placeholder assignment." That is, I wanted them to "hold a place for future erotic homework" by remaining quietly in each other's company—perhaps hold hands or spooning—for a few minutes a couple of times a week. After I explained the homework, Becca smiled and said she loved the idea of a nonsexual exercise. Carmen's reaction was less positive. She said it would be worth a try, but she was so deprived she worried she would get turned on and ruin it. But she could do it, she said, if she "vibed" first—that is, had an orgasm with her vibrator before the exercise officially began.

My interventions at this juncture—emphasizing their differences and the slow pace of the homework assignments—were intended to reinforce certain aspects of the new narrative. I wanted to inflect the tenderness narrative at the same time as I began to replace the old one-size-fits-all sexual passion theme with a more flexible erotic schema that allowed for differences and multiple forms of erotic expression.

When Carmen and Becca came back, they reported that, indeed, they had managed to have a couple of sweet times together. But the third time, Becca had decided she did not want to be part of Carmen's pre-exercise masturbation; she told Carmen to go do it somewhere out of sight. Carmen felt angry and rejected. Whereupon Becca felt that Carmen was violating the nonsexual spirit of the exercise.

When this mixed review was delivered, I remarked on the momentousness of their having had a couple of serene, close times together—the first time they could remember being close in months. I commented that the conflict that had reappeared was simply a useful reminder that their sexual styles were so distinct—like fingerprints—that, no matter what the shape of the exercise, the differences would eventually surface again. Could either, I asked, remember the first time in their relationship that their differences had surfaced? Becca said she remembered their first sexual fight. She explained that when they were still in swoon mode, both had participated in elaborate scenes, which she would choreograph. The scenes started in a local lesbian bar. They would enter separately and pretend to be meeting for the first time. Then, they would start to flirt. Several hours later, this slow seduction scene would shift to one or the other's apartment, where they would make passionate love for hours. Soon after they began considering themselves a committed couple, Carmen had complained about the length of these fantasy scenes. Becca had been so hurt that she had refused to do them anymore. "Yeah, and that was pretty much the end of sex," Carmen added glumly.

That had been a turning point, Becca said. If Carmen wasn't going to be sensitive to the kind of sex she wanted, then she wasn't going to be sensitive either. Carmen said that she had apologized to Becca for being insensitive, but it was too late. Becca wouldn't forgive her. Becca said she hadn't felt that Carmen was genuinely sorry. She just didn't trust her anymore.

By this time, both Carmen and Becca were tearful. I said it seemed that they were both sincere, but perhaps they were just now learning the tenderness language that could get them out of this particular cul-de-sac. I asked Carmen if I had her permission to play her role in a little psycho-

drama. After she said okay, I stood behind her chair and, addressing Becca
as a very passionate Carmen, I apologized profusely for having caused Becca
so much pain. I asked her to forgive me for being so insensitive. And I told
her I really loved and cherished her. I then turned to Carmen and asked if
what I was saying was true for her. She said it was all entirely true and,
while I returned to my own chair, Carmen repeated the same sentiments
to Becca in her own words. At this point, the differences—so painful to
both—provided another opportunity to reinforce the tenderness narrative. With a little cueing from me, Carmen and Becca were able during the
session to switch from the adversarial language to expressions of vulnerability.

The tenderness narrative continued to need reinforcement. Carmen
came in the following week fuming about the absence of sex. She had
been patient, she said, but nothing was happening. Her sexuality was her
core, and Becca seemed disgusted by it. She felt totally rejected and unat-
tractive. If Becca found her so repugnant, how could she possible love
her?

Becca responded defensively. She wanted a peer as a partner, she
said, "not someone who couldn't make herself feel attractive . . . whose
ego needed constant bolstering and who was constantly complaining of
'blue balls.'"

Carmen retorted, saying there was no point talking about feelings
with Becca. I interrupted to point out that, in addition to different sexual
styles, they both had dramatically different interpersonal styles. Carmen's
family motto had been, all for one and one for all. So she expected a certain kind of unconditional support which, as I gathered from Becca's account of her father, would have been unthinkable in Becca's family. Becca
talked about her father's contempt for vulnerability, his way of humiliating her if he spotted her lip quivering. I pointed out that she had identified
with him so thoroughly when she was young that she had become proficient with tools. In the same way she had mastered his drill set, she had
learned his tone. But she also could remember how devastating it was to
be on the receiving end of his critiques. Becca responded that she knew
she could be as biting as her father. I commented that her "zinger" tendency was a part of her—as much a part of her as the sensitive, empathic
side I had often witnessed. I assured Carmen that Becca was capable of
both kinds of responses. Keeping my fingers crossed, I asked her to tell
Becca—once more—how sad and unloved she felt when she felt rejected.
This time, Becca responded empathetically.

Given that our task was not to change their individual styles, but to
help Carmen and Becca understand and appreciate what seemed most
alien about each, I proposed an ambassador exercise. Carmen volunteered
to be the ambassador for the first week. I told her that she was to imagine

she was posted in an alien land with strange customs. She was to be as diplomatic as possible. She was to be of service. Even if her diplomatic toes got stepped on, she was to carry out her mission.

Once again, Carmen and Becca returned with mixed reviews. Carmen had been an attentive ambassador, running a bath and giving Becca a massage. But Becca had wanted Carmen to tell her a fantasy when she was masturbating, and Carmen hadn't done very well with that part of the mission. I said ambassadors sometimes needed cultural immersion tutorials, and asked Becca to give Carmen a quickie course in fantasy construction. Becca said Carmen made her the object of the fantasy, and she wanted someone else to be the object. She preferred to be the voyeur in the scene. When she had tried to correct Carmen, Carmen felt hurt and gave up. In addition to their sensitivity, I said that ambassadors also have to cultivate thick skins. Cultural misunderstandings were inevitable. What might seem like a zinger when translated into English, I said, may have started out as an endearment in Urdu. In fact, the exercise probably was not working unless someone got hurt some of the time. Such injured *amour propre*, in other words, was an inevitable byproduct of really sampling another culture.

After Becca had done her stint as ambassador, she reported that she had held Carmen several times while she "vibed" to orgasm. Indeed Becca had held her, Carmen agreed, but the episodes had been so unmemorable that she may as well have been alone. Plus, Carmen continued, "Ambassador Becca" had obviously been bored and impatient. Carmen had really wanted Becca to make love to her in a passionate, full-bodied way. By this time Becca was in her second trimester and visibly pregnant. She said the love-making position Carmen preferred was very uncomfortable for her now. Carmen said she would be happy to experiment with new positions—and I suggested that it would be good if they could come up with sexual positions for pregnant lesbians. Not just for the two of them. The community was desperately in need of just such a manual.

NarRATtive-magic

When Becca and Carmen came back for the next session, they had not experimented with alternative positions. But they reported having a surprisingly satisfying sexual experience. The prelude to the encounter had been the discovery, by Becca, of a dead rat in the kitchen. After she had disposed of it, she began to feel turned on. She came back to bed and woke Carmen. Delighted at the invitation, Carmen managed to spin a very convincing fantasy about a surprise visit from a sexy exterminator, a fantasy in which Becca was the voyeur instead of the object. Equally delighted,

Becca was an enthusiastic participant in Carmen's orgasms. It was the first post-honeymoon sexual encounter that had been pleasing to both. After some joking about rat-magic, I emphasized the way in which their hard work—their willingness to explore and tune into their respective sexual styles—had contributed to their ability to have a good time together.

After this, Carmen and Becca began to have regular sexual encounters. Sometimes these consisted of a quick, morning masturbation session, side by side, before they got up for work. Other times, their encounters were more fantasy-based. Sometimes, Becca simply held Carmen while she "vibed." Despite the fact that they were glad to be having sex again, they rarely agreed about how satisfying these encounters were. If Becca gave an encounter high marks, chances were good that Carmen barely remembered it; if Carmen had a good time, Becca usually complained about the encounter. On one occasion, Carmen said that Becca held her back in a way that prevented her having her usual orgasms. Becca said she was trying to "train" Carmen to be less orgasm-focused. As we explored what had happened, still more information about their differences emerged.

Becca's idea of ideal sex was that one person's orgasm—regardless of whose—was so sublime it should suffice for both. Therefore, Carmen's insistence on her orgasm somehow robbed Becca of the feeling of closeness and mutuality she wanted. If she could only slow Carmen down, Becca was sure Carmen would come to appreciate the mutual pleasure of interchangeable orgasms.

Besides their different pacing and preferences, I suspected that Becca and Carmen experienced mutuality differently. When I asked Carmen to explain what mutual sex meant to her, she said that she was really a "gay boy" at heart. Mutuality meant having simultaneous orgasms by some form of mutual friction. Since Becca could not come that way, Carmen had settled for a sort of syncopated simultaneity: "First you, then me." When it became apparent that what each had been construing as unmutual—even selfish—behavior could be reinterpreted as a difference in the way each expressed her desire to be close, the conflict dissipated.

The differences between Carmen and Becca were endless. Consequently, I advised them that there would always be surprises. New and jarring variations would continually pop up. That would probably mean they would never be 100% satisfied by any one sexual encounter. If one was pleased, the other was likely to be less content. But they had also found plenty of areas of overlap, and they had worked hard and successfully on developing a varied repertoire of erotic activities which, to a degree, each could enjoy at least some of the time. By wrestling with their demons and their differences, they really had reinvented their sexual life.

In the last part of therapy, the focus shifted from sex to family issues. Carmen and Becca came in with new disputes. They argued about whether

Carmen should go out to parties alone if Becca didn't have the energy to go, which set of grandparents they should spend Thanksgiving with, and which relatives should be present at the birth. They usually went toe to toe on each of these issues—often in hostile and accusatory ways. But with reminders of their different styles and with minimal tenderness coaching, they were able to be empathetic and come up with solutions.

In order to make sure their new, asymmetrical sex narrative was firmly in place, I gave them one more assignment. They were to stop having sex for a week. Since Becca's sexual rhythms were slower, subtler, and somewhat overshadowed by the urgency of Carmen's desires, Carmen was to keep a notebook detailing the ebb and flow of Becca's erotic life. The record-keeping seemed to reinforce their narrative about their different forms of sexual desire. Carmen reported how Becca had felt sensual on several occasions: After a bath and after seeing the lovemaking sequence in the film *The Governess*. Carmen reported that Becca felt sexual (without feeling the need to do anything about it) one morning when she woke up. I suggested that it would be a good exercise to repeat every couple of months, just as a reminder.

When Becca went into labor, the therapy ended abruptly. They called to tell me they were thrilled with their new baby girl, and that they were too tired to want anything more than to get an uninterrupted night's sleep.

☐ Forever After: Sex Therapists' Favorite Story

I tell myself that Becca and Carmen have the wherewithal to survive the inevitable turbulence that lies ahead. I also know that the happily-ever-after story is also a couples therapist's favorite narrative. This story is easier to sustain if, when our clients exit from the office, they depart from our lives. In this freeze-framed reality, our mission is accomplished and our clients have achieved their dream scenarios. Our faith in such happy endings erodes quickly, however, when clients and therapists are members of the same lesbian community. Chance encounters are inevitable. When we run into our clients at meetings or parties, we may discover that the relationships we struggled to maintain have dissolved. Perhaps the formerly loving partners are now bitter enemies . . . or best friends.

Such inadvertent follow-ups can be disappointing. We did not achieve what we set out to accomplish. Yet on another level—a collective narrative level—we may have succeeded beyond our wildest dreams. After all, it took thousands of stories—some painful, some triumphant—to spark the Gay Liberation Movement. The same may be true for lesbian love.

Before lesbians can feel safe enough to declare the diversity of their intimacies—to risk diverging from conventional, happily-ever-after scripts—they may have to tell many stories: stories about spells cast and broken, about magic beginnings and bitter endings, about short-term lovers and long-term companions. Narrative therapists can help lesbian couples develop just such repertoires.

In short, every couple with whom we work may not have passionate sex, or even stay together. But, they will probably be less susceptible to cultural clichés and more skilled at crafting new narratives about a wide array of lesbian intimacies. Even more importantly, these women's novel love stories may reshape the way still other lesbians—their friends and lovers—frame their own relationships. Eventually, this growing tide of new tales may change the way most lesbians think about intimacy. If, as narrative therapists, we have contributed to such a sea change, we have been profoundly effective.

☐ References

Alexander, C. (1996). The state of lesbian mental health. *In the Family* (January), 6.

Bannon, A. (1960). *Journey to a woman.* New York: Fawcett Gold Medal.

Foucault, M.(1980). *The history of sexuality (Vol. I): An introduction.* New York: Vintage.

Hall, M.(1991). Ex-therapy to sex therapy: Notes from the margins. In C. Silverstein (Ed.), *Gays, lesbians, and their therapists* (pp. 84–97). New York: W.W. Norton.

Hall, M. (1993). "Why limit me to ecstasy?" Toward a positive model of genital incidentalism among friends and other lovers. In E. Rothblum & K. Brehony (Eds.), *Boston marriages: Romantic but asexual relationships among contemporary lesbians* (pp. 41–61). Amherst: University of Massachusetts Press.

Hall, M. (1995). Clit notes. In K. Jay (Ed.), *Dyke life: From growing up to growing old, a celebration of the lesbian experience* (pp. 195–215). New York: Basic Books.

Hall, M. (1998). *The lesbian love companion: How to survive everything from heartthrob to heartbreak.* San Francisco: HarperCollins.

Hall, M. (2000). Scheherazade was a dyke: Storytelling in lesbian relationships. *Journal of lesbian studies.* Binghamton, NY: Haworth Press.

Hall, M., & Gregory, A. (1991). Love and work in lesbian relationships. *Lesbians at midlife: The creative transition.* San Francisco: Spinsters Book Co.

Johnson, S. (1990). *Staying power: Long-term lesbian couples.* Tallahassee, FL: Naiad Press.

Kleinplatz, P.(1996). The erotic encounter. *Journal of Humanistic Psychology, 36*(3), 108–123.

Kurdek, L. (1995). Lesbian and gay couples. In A. D'Augelli & C. Patterson (Eds.), *Lesbian, gay, and bisexual identities over the lifespan: Psychological perspectives* (pp. 243–261). New York: Oxford University Press.

Masters, W., & Johnson, V. (1966). *Human sexual response.* Boston: Little, Brown.

McNamee, S., & Gergen, K. (1992). *Therapy as social construction.* London: Sage.

Morin, J. (1995). *The erotic mind.* New York: HarperCollins.

Peplau, L., Pedesky, C., & Hamilton, M. (1982). Satisfaction in lesbian relationships. *Journal of Homosexuality, 8*(2), 23–35.

Rosen, H., & Kuehlwein, K. (Eds.). (1996). *Constructing realities: Meaning-making perspectives for psychotherapists.* San Francisco: Jossey-Bass.

Weston, K. (1998). *Long slow burn: Sexuality and social science.* New York: Routledge.

CHAPTER

Alex Carballo-Diéguez, Ph.D.
Robert H. Remien, Ph.D.

Sex Therapy With Male Couples of Mixed- (Serodiscordant-) HIV Status

A sexual act between two individuals is, by necessity, much more than a physical act. It involves a plethora of cognitions, emotions, and symbolic meanings that may facilitate or interfere with sexual behavior. When the two individuals in question happen to be of the same sex, sexual interaction becomes a stigmatized behavior. Furthermore, when only one of the partners is infected with the *human immunedeficiency virus* (*HIV*), many issues related to health and risk of contagion come into play. In this chapter, we focus on topics to be considered in therapy with male couples of mixed- (or serodiscordant-) HIV status. The psychotherapist who sees these couples in consultation may have to deal with specific sexual problems (e.g. diminished desire, erectile dysfunction, or premature or delayed ejaculation) that may constitute the focus of the work. Yet, for the therapy to succeed, the therapist must consider the wider context in which such sexual problems are embedded. We use quotes both from patients in our clinical practices and research participants to illustrate some of the issues discussed.

☐ Psychological Issues for the HIV-Positive Partner

Studies have shown that HIV-seropositive men are more likely to experience sexual dysfunctions than seronegative men (Brown & Pace, 1989;

Jones, Klimes, & Catalan, 1994; Meyer-Bahlburg, Exner, Lorenz, Gruen, Gorman, & Ehrhardt, 1991). Furthermore, as HIV illness progresses, loss of sexual interest, erectile dysfunction, and endocrine abnormalities are likely to appear. These changes and the impact they may have on the relationship of a mixed-status couple are not widely known to the population at large. For example, a decrease in sexual interest and function in the infected partner could be a correlate of testosterone deficiency. This can be treated with testosterone replacement, which results in improved sexual interest, erectile function, and satisfaction with sexual life among symptomatic HIV-infected men (Wagner, Rabkin, & Rabkin, 1997a).

Although some questions have been raised concerning the ethics of helping HIV-infected individuals regain sexual functioning (because of public health concerns about infection transmission; Fisher, 1997), we believe, with Wagner, Rabkin, and Rabkin (1997b), that this view is erroneous and misguided. There is no scientific evidence that people who experience sexual dysfunctions are less likely to engage in sexual risk behavior. For example, an HIV-positive gay man with erectile failure may engage in receptive anal sex; conversely, if he no longer experiences erectile problems or anxiety about them, he may be more likely to use condoms. Furthermore, as clinicians, rather than prolonging a distressful symptom in a patient, we should strive, when the means are available, to both solve the symptom and promote other measures that may contribute to the larger goal of ensuring public health.

The progression of HIV disease may also bring physical changes to the infected person, such as wasting syndrome (which involves an uneven pattern of weight loss) or the now less frequently seen Kaposi sarcoma (a form of skin cancer). These symptoms affect not only an individual's general level of energy, including his libido, but also his self-image and feelings of attractiveness. In addition, the uninfected individual may or may not be turned off by the appearance of his partner. These issues, which are difficult for the couple to discuss because of fear of hurting the infected partner's feelings, may lead to sexual inhibition or lack of sexual interest in both partners.

☐ Medication Side Effects

In the developed world, individuals with medical coverage can benefit from many new drugs that inhibit or slow the progression of HIV disease. Many of these drugs are taken in combination, as "cocktails." Although indisputably beneficial, the currently available treatments are cumbersome, intense, and generally associated with unpleasant physical and psychological side effects. The former include nausea, vomiting, headaches, skin rash, numbness of extremities, fever, and diarrhea. One of our patients reported that his drug regimen required him to take protease inhibitors three times a day, and that he experienced an urgent need to defecate immediately after each dose. This had a serious impact on his prior preference for receptive anal sex.

Psychological side effects include nightmares, depression, and psychotic manifestations. If these symptoms are treated with psychotropic drugs, additional sexual impairment may ensue. Sexual dysfunctions caused by psychotropic drugs can be classified into two groups: sexual inhibition (of desire, arousal, or orgasm) and increased sexual function disorders (increased sexual desire, priapism, and premature ejaculation).

Furthermore, there are indications that antiretroviral drugs used in combination with Viagra™ (sildenafil) may increase the risk of adverse events. These include priapism and, in one case, cardiac arrest.

Therefore, it is important for both members of a couple to be aware of the possible side effects of medications, interaction between medications, and the impact these may have on their sexual lives, so that they can learn to accommodate.

☐ Emotional Issues for the HIV-Positive Partner

Two decades into the epidemic, practically all gay men in the United States are aware of how HIV is transmitted and how transmission can be prevented (Ames, Atchinson, & Rose, 1995; Chang, Murphy, Diferdinando, & Morse, 1990; Díaz, 1997). Nevertheless, many men encounter difficulties adhering consistently to safer sex practices because of emotional issues and drives, low risk perception, trust in a partner, or lapses of control (Boulton, McLean, Fitzpatrick, & Hart, 1995; Carballo-Diéguez & Dolezal, 1996; Dowsett, 1993; Ross, 1990). In other cases, men assume that if a partner is willing to have unprotected sex, he must be HIV-positive (or negative), as they themselves are (Klitzman, 1999). Finally, we have seen mixed-status couples in which concerns about HIV transmission are overpowered by the desire for sexual pleasure and intimacy, the love for the partner, or cultural issues such as machismo and gender roles (Carballo-Diéguez, Remien, Dolezal, & Wagner, 1997; Remien, Carballo-Diéguez, & Wagner, 1995).

Those who have unprotected, penetrative sex know that there is risk involved, and that they may become infected. Yet, when the HIV-antibody test shows a positive result, thus signaling infection, most individuals react with shock and disbelief. This is illustrated in the following vignette from a research participant:

Investigator: When was the first time you thought you might have gotten infected?

Participant: I had unprotected intercourse. Then, I developed a fever, and I had swollen glands. I stayed home for a few days, and I called my AA sponsor. He was reassuring . . . [but] nevertheless, I did call my MD and had an HIV test.

Investigator: What was your expectation?

Participant: My expectation was that it would be negative.

Investigator: What happened when the results came back?

Participant: When the results came back . . . the doctor foolishly called me at my office late in the day on a Monday, which is not something you are suppose to do. . . . He called me, [and] my heart started racing. He asked me to come in the morning. [That night], I remember walking up to the car, and it was early November because the leaves were off the trees and the wind was blowing and everything looked surreal. . . . The cold seemed strong. . . . Everything felt kind of . . . unsettled, unhappy. I drove the car . . . and the thoughts that were going through my head were: God, this really is, this is it? . . . . I'm going to die . . . . This is the end. . . . I have really done it this time. I went home, called my three closets friends, and . . . cried a lot that night. I got a few hours sleep, but was very tormented. . . . And then the next day, I went to see the doctor in his office. He had a nurse [or] caseworker, a specialist there . . . and she was very reassuring about the disease, talking about the progress they've made and the hope that they have for people's future and that I would probably never get sick. She suggested that I become my own advocate and try to learn much about HIV, . . . call around, see different doctors and get different opinions, and check out in the market the different clinical studies.

Investigator: How did you feel during this process of finding out what was available?

Participant: On a very functional level [it] is very good to become my own advocate. I went on . . . and advocated for myself quite clearly and very efficiently to get all the information that I needed. Of course, it was a very lonely time. I felt frightened, I felt dejected, the world turned against me, and I was very alone.

The initial shock and disbelief are compounded by guilt. Many gay men think that, two decades into the epidemic, they should have known better and protected themselves more efficiently. A young male patient reported the following:

Patient: I had cocktails with one manager who works in another restaurant. He had lost his lover two years ago to AIDS. [We] started to get on a conversation about it, [and] he actually comes out and says how stupid it is if people get infected now. I just stood there like amazed, because here's somebody who originally I was going to tell. . . . Now, here's someone who's telling me, "it's something you can control" and "how wrong it is," and I do feel like that, I do kick myself a lot, but at the same time, I have it now so either I kick myself for getting it or I accept the fact that I have it.

Being informed that one is infected with a virus that is transmissible through bodily fluids forever taints all future sexual encounters. Some individuals attempt to deny the implications of the infection. Those who start antiviral treatment and respond to it quickly may think that the absence of detectable signs of viral replication renders them noninfectious. Yet, we have found that even these individuals have some awareness of the risk they may pose to noninfected partners; they demonstrate a need to create elaborate justifications in order to fend off anxiety and guilt and enjoy or even engage in sex.

Other individuals have reported going through periods of abstinence following notification of their positive HIV status. Still others curtail their range of sexual activities, for example, by limiting sex to mutual masturbation, by avoiding even deep kissing, or by avoiding emotional involvement with other men, as illustrated in the following vignette.

Patient: Well, sexually it sort of took . . . I had a very limited libido anyway and it completely went away [when I found out I was HIV-positive]. So, sex for a long time wasn't something that I was interested in very much. [Then] it was more me gratifying them and not letting them really contact me at all. You know, keeping myself pretty much away from people sexually. . . . I had an orgasm . . . but never . . . so that anybody would ever be close to me. You know, if I saw somebody and then we had sort of quickie sex, it was more like let him get his and then I'll worry about mine later. That type of thing. I mean, I wouldn't let anybody get to have oral sex with me or anything. It is not something that at that time I would even allow.

Therapist: So what were you doing?

Patient: I was basically performing oral sex on them.

Disclosure of positive HIV status is not an easy subject (Klitzman, 1998). Some men tell any prospective sexual partners that they are infected, and many HIV-positive men prefer to restrict their dates and sexual encounters exclusively to HIV-infected individuals. In this case, they feel there is a greater commonality of circumstances, and that the possibility of passing the infection becomes a nonissue. A vignette from an HIV-positive patient illustrates this point.

Patient: I'd been looking for a normal guy, but it's hard to find. So we talked for hours. We went out to dinner, and . . . it was raining so we went to his apartment, we talked further, and I said, "I'm going to go," because I knew he had an early morning. As I was leaving, no touching, no anything, I leaned over to give him a kiss goodbye and he was very weird about it. He said, "Well, I have to tell you something." All of a sudden I just knew. He said, "I'm HIV-positive, and I want you to know that before we go further, because I like you and I know that we will see each other again." I just smiled. It was such a relief to the point where I felt like crying. It was such a relief for him also.

Yet, it is often the case that, in a new encounter, men do not immediately discuss their HIV status. Infected individuals fear the rejection that disclosure may bring.

Therapist: What did [the man you were dating] say when you told him?

Patient:	He said that he'd been tested in his life, and it had been negative. . . . He was great when I told him, like he was very concerned for my health, which I look at as a lie now because he just never called back. I tried to call him again. He just disappeared.

HIV-infected men often say they are more than containers for a virus, and that they want to be appreciated for the full range of their intellectual, emotional, and physical capacities. In our clinical practice and in community meetings, we frequently hear that many individuals think, as long as they behave safely in the sexual encounter, they are under no obligation to disclose their serostatus to a new partner. They also think that the responsibility for safer sexual behavior is shared by the partner, as well; if the latter does not pose the question, an HIV-positive individual may not feel obligated to disclose his status as long as he behaves safely. The challenge many men report is that the "stakes are higher once you start liking someone," that there is more to lose if rejection occurs. Yet, if a relationship develops, sooner or later most HIV-positive men disclose their serostatus to their partners.

Therapist:	How did you deal with the issue of your HIV status?
Patient:	Well, he's from Latin America, so it was not something that I thought was going to be a long-term thing, neither of us really did, so the whole issue was never brought up while he was here. It was after he left that we realized there was a bigger attraction than we had initially thought. So, I told him over the phone that I was HIV-positive.
Therapist:	What happened when you told him?
Patient:	Well, he started crying, and he told me he had to call me back. He called me back like three hours later, and he said okay, you know, big deal. And I was like, yeah, but you were crying before, what's up with that? And he was like, I thought that you were going to tell me that you had met somebody else. Because I had told him that we needed to talk, he just assumed that I had met somebody else, so he was crying out of relief. He was upset that I hadn't told him, but he understood why.

The source of the infection may become an issue for men in couples. In the particular case of a serodiscordant dyad, the HIV-negative partner is clearly not the source of the infection. The HIV-positive partner may have become infected prior to entering the relationship with the HIV-negative one or through sex outside of the relationship. Sex outside the relationship may or may not be known or suspected by the other partner. All of these possibilities affect how the serodiscordant status is dealt with within the relationship and how it affects the sexual interaction.

☐ Emotional Issues for the HIV-Negative Partner

We have observed a wide range of reactions in HIV-negative men who find out that their partners are HIV-infected. Some decide the relationship is no longer viable and break up. Others continue in the relationship; their behavior then may range from obsessive attention to avoid becoming infected to a nonchalant involvement in sexual acts that could result in viral transmission. If they have been involved with their partners for some time and have had unprotected sex without becoming infected, some individuals assume that they have some natural immunity and eschew condom use. Others think that being the insertive partner means there is less risk for them, such as in the following example of a Puerto Rican couple. (The verbatim transcript in Spanish is below and is followed by our translation.)

(+):   (*Dirigiéndose al terapeuta*) Yo preferiría que él se pusiera un condón cuando me lo mete. Él no quiere.

(-):   [Me] corta la inspiración, me quita la nota. . . . [Además] no es que te disguste que yo no lo use. Te preocupa, pero no es que te moleste. Yo estoy feliz sin usarlo.

(+):   Es que si te obligo a usarlo, nunca más me lo metías.

(-):   Exacto! (*ríe*)

(+):   Para él no hay tanto riesgo de contagio. Si él exigiera que yo se lo metiera sin condón, yo no lo haría. Punto. Pero como yo ya estoy infectado, yo pienso que él no me puede infectar con otro virus o "strain" porque [él] es negativo. Entonces, lo acepto. Pero pienso en las laceraciones que puede tener en el pene. . . que se puede infectar.

Investigador: ¿Qué haría que tú, Pedro, usaras condón?

(-):   Si yo fuera positivo. Ahí tendría que cambiar la conducta, por poco placentera que fuera para mi.

****

(+):   (*Addressing the therapist*) I would prefer him to use a condom when he screws me. But he doesn't want to.

(-):   It cuts my drive, it turns me off. . . . [Besides], it's not that you are displeased that I don't use one. You are concerned, but it's not like it bothers you. I am happy not using one.

(+):   If I forced you to use one you wouldn't screw me anymore.

(-):   Correct! (*laughs*)

(+):   For him, there isn't as much risk of contagion. If he demanded that I screw him without a condom, I would not do it. Period. Since I am already infected, I don't think that he can infect me with another virus or "strain" because he is negative. Therefore, I accept it. But I think about the lacerations that he might have on his penis and that he might become infected.

Investigator: Pedro, what would make you use a condom?

(-):   Being positive. Then, I would have to change my behavior, even if that were unpleasant for me.

In some cases, two men become involved with each other knowing from the beginning that they have opposite serostatus. This is a difficult situation. Although initially the mutual attraction and the feelings they develop may overpower concerns about HIV transmission, sooner or later those concerns show up and cause strain in the relationship.

In other cases, men who are HIV-negative have been said to experience "survivor guilt." They ask themselves why they have not become infected despite having engaged in sexual risk behavior. Feelings of guilt have been postulated as one force underlying the continuation of unprotected sex.

☐ Determining What Is Safe and Pushing the Limits

Most gay men are aware that not all sexual acts between an infected and an uninfected partner carry the same level of risk. Deep kissing is at the negligible-risk end of the spectrum, although some may worry that open wounds in the gums and bleeding may pose risk. Anal intercourse in which the HIV-positive man ejaculates in the rectum of the HIV-negative one is generally classified at the opposite, extreme-risky end of the continuum. Different levels of risk are attributed to all the in-between behaviors, and the partners may choose to draw the line of what is acceptable at different places. For example, some individuals consider that it is "not too risky" for the HIV-positive man to engage in unprotected anal penetration as long as it is only for the brief moment before he gets too excited and produces preseminal fluid. Others think that unprotected oral sex is safe as long as no preseminal fluid is seen at the end of the urethra.

Furthermore, with the advent of new drugs that drive viral replication below detectable levels, some couples may consider that unsafe sex is less risky than before. They may believe that reduced viral load means lesser (or no) chance of transmitting the virus, or that science is closer to having a cure for HIV and therefore it is "less serious" to become infected (or reinfected) today than it was in the past. One or both members of the couple may feel this way, but they may have avoided talking about it and are, therefore, unclear about how to behave sexually with each other.

Interestingly, when these men are questioned about the level of certainty they place on their theories of reduced risk, most acknowledge that there is a wide margin for error. Yet, the issue is not so much whether they are justified in their beliefs but the strong drive they experience to have unhindered sex. This creates certain cognitive dissonance by which, although they recognize the risk, they report extenuating circumstances that justify their behavior.

The initial boundaries of what is considered safe may relax over time. A wish for intimacy may overpower caution. We have seen couples of known HIV-discordant serostatus who engage in unprotected anal sex despite being fully aware of the risks involved (Carballo-Diéguez & Dolezal, 1997). Our research has shown that, in general, the HIV-positive partner tends to be more conservative than the HIV-negative partner when it comes to unprotected, penetrative sex: It is much less likely that an HIV-positive man will ejaculate inside the rectum of an HIV-negative man than vice versa (Carballo-Diéguez, Remien, Dolezal, & Wagner, 1999).

Patient: When we're in a relationship, we're consumed by it. . . . It drives me crazy because they know I'm HIV-positive and they want to do things that . . . it's like I'd say to them, you can't play in my playground, I don't want you to, you have to stay on your side of the fence. And they still want to do stupid stuff.

Gold (1993) pointed out that there are differences between decisions made in a nonsexual situation, with time for cool reflection on advantages and disadvantages, and impulsive behavior that may not be mediated by reasoning in a sexually charged situation.

☐ Condoms

Most men dislike condoms, which are perceived as a barrier that decreases sensation, may retard ejaculation, and can cause irritation (Carballo-Diéguez & Dolezal, 1996; Feldblum, Morrison, Roddy, & Cates, 1995). The act of putting on a condom is seen as an interruption of the normal crescendo of sexual tension. Furthermore, some men consider semen exchange an essential component of sexual intercourse, one that indicates commitment to the partner (Prieur, 1990). Decades of efforts to eroticize condom use have produced little progress, as it continues to be seen mainly as a method of disease and pregnancy prevention. Although about half of the men who have anal sex use condoms consistently, most admit that they do it out of necessity rather than pleasure. Only a few individuals see secondary advantages to condom use, such as improved hygiene and less messiness (Carballo-Diéguez & Dolezal, 1996).

In the case of mixed-status couples, condoms are frequently perceived as unwelcome reminders of the infection of one of the partners (Remien, Carballo-Diéguez, & Wagner, 1995). By contrast, having unprotected sex is sometimes used by the negative partner as a sign of love and acceptance of his positive counterpart.

Putting on a condom may also be a serious problem for men who have erectile dysfunction. These men report that the process of reaching out for the condom, opening the envelope, finding which side of the condom is up, and unrolling it on the penis is complicated enough to result in a loss of erection. Fear of being unable to regain the erection may ensue. This creates a vicious circle that interferes with condom use on future occasions. Some men try to deal with this problem by "dipping in," or having a few thrusts of unprotected penetration before actually putting the condom on. This, of course, involves risk.

Men who have premature ejaculations may be concerned that the manipulation of the penis will result in an early orgasm. Although safer sex campaigns have stressed, as an added benefit, that wearing condoms makes men "last longer," we have yet to hear a man afflicted by premature ejaculation report that condom use has helped him with his problem.

Finally, men with delayed ejaculation generally feel that they need extra stimulation, and condoms are seen as decreasing sensation.

☐ Other Sexual Problems

Both the presence of HIV and its associated symptoms as well as the secondary effects of antiviral and psychotropic medication may affect sexual desire and functioning. It is not an easy task to establish the differential diagnosis between sexual problems stemming from such sources and others related to emotional and systemic problems in the relationship with the partner. For example, the HIV-negative member of a couple may complain of insufficient frequency of sexual intercourse, and the HIV-positive man may reply that he just does not feel the desire for it. How are we to interpret the situation? There are no shortcuts; we must examine and rule out the multiple, possible sources of the symptoms.

A paradoxical issue that emerges in response to the new antiviral therapies is that many infected individuals experience a renewal of sex drive and an improvement in sexual functioning, while their partners may have become accustomed to a reduced level of sex. The new situation may require a readjustment and changes in the sexual behavior of the HIV-negative partner, who now feels under pressure to be more responsive.

Alcohol and Recreational Drugs

The use of alcohol and recreational drugs is popular among gay men (Paul, Stall, & Bloomfield, 1991). Bars are typical places of encounter and socializing for gay men, and alcohol is used to reduce anxiety and fear of rejection. Furthermore, gay men who favor "the party scene," especially European-American gay men, often use so-called designer drugs to boost their energy in order to spend all night (or even entire weekends) dancing and partying. Some of these drugs affect sexual functioning. For example, "ecstasy" (methylenedioxymethamphetamine, or MDMA) is known to result in erectile dysfunction ("crystal dick"). Some men use ecstasy in combination with Viagra™ (sildenafil citrate) to counteract the undesired effects.

Alcohol and drug use combined with sexual activity may be an integral part of the sexual life of a couple. However, we have seen cases in which individuals with long histories of substance use suddenly stopped when they were diagnosed as HIV-positive. This generally follows a desire to "clean up one's act"—that is, a kind of bargaining with fate to regain health. A situation like this may alter the previous sexual balance and behavioral patterns of a couple and result in maladjustments that become the focus of treatment. As with all couples, honest dialogue about changing sexual needs and expectations need to occur over time, particularly if significant shifts take place.

"Extramarital" Sex

Gay men in relationships tend not to be monogamous. In our study of 75 mixed-status couples (Wagner, Remien, & Carballo-Diéguez, 1998), 50 (67%) were nonmonogamous, with either one or both members reporting outside partners. A quote from a participant in another study illustrates this point.

Participant: [Before testing positive,] I got into a relationship for about 6 years. We [used condoms] for a while and then we both were tested. I made that choice of doing it without a condom with him after a while, even though it is wrong because later [I found out] he cheated. I also cheated, but I never let anyone penetrate me at these times, it was a fooling around kind of thing.

In 41 of the 50 couples in our study, both partners described the relationship in the same way: 31% said it was open, with both members acknowledging outside sex; 27% did not refer to the couple as open, but reported knowledge of some sexual partners outside the relationship; 24% said the outside sex was kept secret. In the remaining 9 couples, partners had discrepant views of the nature of the relationship.

In the case of mixed-status couples, sex outside the relationship is often seen as a way to deal with sexual and emotional problems within the couple. For example, if the HIV-positive man feels a lack of sexual interest or is just too ill to have sex, he may disregard or even encourage the sexual activity his partner has with other men. Some HIV-positive men have reported going to "jerk-off clubs" to take care of their sexual needs. These are environments where sexual activity is permitted but limited to mutual masturbation.

☐ Psychotherapeutic Approach to Mixed-Status Couples with Sexual Problems

We have discussed that the sexual symptoms of a couple may be related to biological factors in either partner, medication side effects, emotional issues, cognitive factors, substance use, and a wide array of contextual factors. In the examples presented, we have also shown how the interactions between partners may result in the establishment of particular systems that perpetuate symptoms in the couple. As we take the next logical step—that is, trying to help the couple deal with its problems—we often find ourselves drawing insights from several different psychological theories that may help to explain the phenomena under observation. We have found that, rather than zealous adherence to one particular theory, what works is an integrative approach such as the one described by Nichols (1998). From an integrative perspective, therapy deals with both the individuals' feelings, thoughts, and dynamics, as well as the major systems and subsystems in which the couple functions. It "has both process and product aspects; it is a process of problem discernment and intervention/solution, combined with incremental and systemic enhancement aimed at producing more effective marital relationships" (Nichols, 1998).

The initial step is to identify whether an organic problem is present that requires attention. If the symptom manifests itself in the HIV-negative individual, a detailed analysis of his health status is as necessary as if the symptom appears in the HIV-positive man. The problem in the latter case is that it is frequently difficult to disentangle the possible effects of the viral infection itself from medication side effects, psychological symptoms, and interpersonal problems. A careful tracking of the dates at which symptoms appeared or became more serious and other concomitant events may help facilitate the differential diagnosis. Ultimately, even if the symptoms are biologically determined or are side effects of medication, they always involve a psychological and interpersonal component that can be the focus of the psychotherapeutic process.

Throughout this process of differential diagnosis, we are attentive listeners, providing information when necessary and listening to *what is not being said but would be expected* from a mixed-status couple. Opening the dialogue on sexual problems is key to the progress of the treatment. Often, even in the course of a couple's treatment, sexual symptoms are not spontaneously discussed and require prompting by the therapist. It is important to elicit frank and direct information on sexual behavior, including its frequency, type of acts favored and rejected, couple satisfaction, and knowledge and thoughts about what sex life should be for a mixed-status couple. The therapist may need to raise unexpressed issues (i.e., concerns about

HIV transmission, sexual dissatisfaction, potential illness, and loss) as well as facilitate direct discussion about sex behaviors in explicit ways. This directive approach is often necessary to facilitate discussion of otherwise avoided topics. It involves a careful balancing of HIV-related and nonrelated issues. While HIV concerns are often avoided, it is also common for couples to blame HIV for all of their interpersonal and life difficulties. The therapist must pay attention to this phenomenon and point it out when it is observed. Conversely, although HIV cannot and should not be the sole focus of the therapy, key HIV-related challenges must be addressed. The timing of these particular discussions will vary, and is up to the clinical judgment of the therapist (Remien, 1997).

Sexual matters cannot be addressed in a vacuum. Rather, the broad context of the relationship must be considered. By the time the couple presents for treatment, there often has been a buildup of many unexpressed feelings, concerns, and conflicts. The therapist should strive to create a safe environment in which difficulties can be confronted. For a while, the therapy room can become the container for tremendous fears, rage, and despair that are too frightening or overwhelming to be communicated outside. At the onset of treatment, many couples find it useful to be told by the therapist that they can now discuss some of the difficulties they face in the consulting room and *avoid* talking about them at home temporarily. This contributes to establishing the therapy space as one in which the couple can confront difficult feelings without conflicts spilling over to and interfering with the couple's everyday functioning.

We also seek to understand the complementarity of both members of the couple: How they fit together, what attracted them to each other initially, and what holds them together. We also look at the complementarity of the symptoms, what they mean for each member of the couple, and what secondary benefits, if any, are derived from them.

We see most of our interventions with couples as a type of hypothesis testing. We share with the couple our view that a particular problem may be interpreted in a certain way and let the couple analyze, criticize, reject, or accept our hypothesis, carefully observing throughout this process the consistency (or lack of it) between overt and covert narrative and behavior.

Occasionally, we have had the chance to work with several mixed-status couples in a group format. This is a challenging endeavor, as problems can be addressed at the individual, couple, interpersonal, or group-as-a-whole level (Coché & Coché, 1990). We have found the "fishbowl technique" to be very powerful in working with serodiscordant couples. We ask the couples to sit in two concentric circles, with the HIV-positive men inside and the HIV-negative men surrounding them, or vice versa. (They are told that in a subsequent session the seating arrangement will be reversed). The inner circle can speak, while the outer circle is asked to listen only. We ask the men in the inner circle to speak about how they feel about themselves when it comes to sex, difficulties they experience, and what their wishes are. Subsequently, the men in the outer circle are asked to comment on what they heard and to react to it. It is generally the case that the men in the inner circle find commonalities with one another and comment freely on their thoughts and ideas, almost forgetting the presence of the outer circle. Often, when their turns come, the previously silent partners state that they had never known their partners felt that way. Most of the time, this technique initiates a dialogue that continues later within the couple and allows for a more honest and direct discussion of problems.

The following is a brief case study of the treatment of a couple of mixed-HIV status.

Case Study

Sam and Peter were referred for couples therapy by Peter's individual therapist. Peter was a 34-year-old journalist; Sam, a 36-year-old accountant. They had been together for slightly more than 6 years.

The presenting problem was lack of sexual activity and emotional distancing for the prior year, with escalating arguments about everyday events and concerns about the future of the relationship. Sam felt reluctant to undergo couples therapy and attended only with Peter's persuasion. The therapist acknowledged this resistance by pointing out that frequently one member of the couple is more motivated than the other to enter couples treatment. He recommended that they start to talk and see what issues came up; they could reconsider Sam's reluctance down the road.

During the initial sessions, the early years of the relationship were reviewed, including what attracted them to each other, how they decided to be in a "steady" relationship, and what made them unique as a couple. They mentioned that they had found out they were a mixed-HIV-status couple 6 months into the relationship. Before that, neither man had been tested in several years, and both knew there was a chance they could be infected. Therefore, they had practiced safer sex with each other from the start. As the bond between them became stronger and they started to see their relationship as long lasting, they decided to get tested for HIV. At that time, they found out that Peter was HIV-positive. Although this did not necessarily shock them, they were very disappointed with the news and needed a period to adjust to it.

As they began to focus specifically on their problems, they discussed their disagreements about the choice of friends with whom they wanted to spend time, who was responsible for household chores, Sam's apparently increasing alcohol abuse, Peter's mother's terminal illness, and Peter's diagnosed depression.

Although the reference had been made to their serodiscordant-HIV status, the therapist purposely did not have the couple focus solely on issues related to HIV in the early sessions. The couple did indicate that they wanted to be sexual with each other and that each man was feeling some internal pressure about it; yet, they did not know how to reinitiate sex after months of avoidance. The onset of the sexual symptoms did not coincide with changes in the health status of the men or in the medication Peter was taking. Rather, it appeared that emotional factors, still vague at this stage of the treatment, had resulted in progressive sexual distancing. Acknowledging the internal pressure the men manifested about reinitiating sex, the therapist took a systemic approach to alter the situation and asked the couple to refrain from having any sex with each other until they had spent some time discussing specific issues related to sex. This was done primarily to ease the pressure they were experiencing and to let them know they would indeed spend time in therapy focusing specifically on sex.

During the session that followed this discussion, the men sheepishly reported having had very pleasant and satisfying sex with each other. It had occurred very naturally on a Sunday morning while they were reading the newspaper in bed. They said that it happened, in part, because there was no pressure to have sex as a result of the "prescription." Sex was reportedly satisfying and very affectionate. Subsequently, the men found themselves having "romantic" conversations over the telephone with each other when Peter was out of town on business for several days.

During the next several sessions, the psychotherapy focused on sex. The men talked explicitly about oral sex, including their concerns about possible transmission of HIV, questions of sores in the mouth, bleeding gums, flossing, and so on. They also talked about how each felt about Peter's performing intense, uninhibited fellatio on Sam, without Sam reciprocating. The couple talked openly about likes and dislikes, about ways of having anal sex, their *true* feelings about the use of condoms, and ways of having them available and of initiating their use. The therapist posed many questions and encouraged a frank and open discussion. Sam expressed how he had always been reluctant to talk about these issues, particularly for fear of making Peter feel like a "pariah." Peter was able to say that he felt like "contaminated goods," and that he had been feeling hurt and rejected because of some of Sam's behaviors. Over time, the therapist helped the couple discuss the underlying anger with empathic comments like, "Boy, it seems like this damned virus has taken a lot of the freedom away from the sex you used to have with each other." The patients were able to give voice to their anger "at the virus" and the losses it presented, which led to diminished anger toward each other. Most of their internal feelings and concerns were not different from one another. Both men felt anger and fear and were unable to express these emotions out of a wish to protect each other. Voicing them out loud diffused the negativity of their feelings and reopened the sharing of intimacies between them.

The couple also addressed the diminished sex drive that Peter was experiencing. There were questions as to whether this was related to HIV, side effects from antiviral combination therapy, or his antidepressant medication. They decided that Peter would discuss this with his physician during his next visit. Finding Peter's testosterone levels low, the physician prescribed low-dose testosterone replacement therapy. The combination of the testosterone replacement treatment and the discussions the partners were having in the psychotherapeutic sessions opened up a renewed sexual interest for both of them.

☐ Conclusion

Male couples of mixed-HIV status who consult a psychotherapist are likely to have their sexual interactions intimately affected by their health condition. The impact may be overt or covert, may constitute the reason for the consultation, or may be a problem the partners are afraid to discuss. In this chapter, we have presented a number of points the psychotherapist should take into consideration in the course of treating with such couples. Furthermore, the psychotherapist ought to be attentive when these issues are not discussed in treatment, since they may constitute an area of problems that is being avoided.

We have briefly mentioned that, in addition to dealing with male couples of mixed-HIV status individually, group work can be a potent technique to speed up the emergence of intimate issues, to help couples feel less isolated and different, and to enhance the empathy that is at the heart of all psychotherapeutic processes.

Finally, we want to encourage psychotherapists to work in a sex-affirmative mode, even in the case of couples of mixed-HIV status. A healthy sexual life is central to the happiness of individuals and couples. Those who believe that helping an HIV-positive individual regain sexual functionality constitutes a public health risk, and who would rather condemn the sufferer to his symptoms, are abandoning the traditional, clinical mandate to cure, and are instead adopting a moralistic view tainted with prejudice. Under the pretense of defending public health, some individuals are espousing punitive, segregationist measures that are unlikely to work in the case of an illness with a long incubation period, like HIV disease, especially in the context of the democratic societies where we have the privilege to live. We believe that an empathic treatment of HIV-infected and affected individuals and couples, as well as an open attitude to discussing the many axiomatic issues posed by HIV and sex, is always beneficial to those involved and to society in general.

☐ References

Ames, L., Atchinson, A., & Rose, D. (1995). Love, lust, and fear: Safer sex decision making among gay men. *Journal of Homosexuality, 30*(1),53–73.

Boulton, M., McLean, J., Fitzpatrick, R., & Hart, G. (1995). Gay men's accounts of unsafe sex. *AIDS Care, 7*(5), 619–630.

Brown, G. R., & Pace, J. (1989). Reduced sexual activity in HIV-infected homosexual men. *Journal of the American Medical Association, 261,* 2503.

Carballo-Diéguez, A., & Dolezal, C. (1996). HIV risk behaviors and obstacles to condom use among Puerto Rican men in New York City who have sex with men. *American Journal of Public Health, 86*(11), 1619–1622.

Carballo-Diéguez, A., Remien, R., Dolezal, C., & Wagner, G. (1997). Unsafe sex in the primary relationships of Puerto Rican men who have sex with men. *AIDS and Behavior, 1*(1), 9–17.

Carballo-Diéguez, A., Remien, R., Dolezal, C., & Wagner, G. (1999) Reliability of sexual behavior self-reports in male couples of discordant HIV-status. *Journal of Sex Research, 36*(2), 152–158.

Chang, H., Murphy, D., Diferdinando, G., & Morse, D. (1990). Assessment of AIDS knowledge in selected New York State sexually transmitted disease clinics. *New York State Journal of Medicine, 90*(3), 126–128

Coché, J., & Coché, E. (1990). *Couples group psychotherapy.* New York: Brunner/Mazel.

Díaz, R. (1997). Latino gay men and psycho-cultural barriers to AIDS prevention. In M. Levine & P. Nardi (Eds.), *In changing times: Gay men and lesbians encounter HIV/AIDS* (pp. 221–244). Chicago: University of Chicago Press.

Dowsett, G. W. (1993). Sustaining safe sex: Sexual practices, HIV, and social context. *AIDS, 7*(1), S257–S262.

Feldblum, P. J., Morrison, C. S., Roddy, R., & Cates, W. (1995). The effectiveness of barrier methods of contraception in preventing the spread of HIV. *AIDS, 9*(suppl. A), S85–S93.

Fisher, W. (1997). Do no harm: On the ethics of testosterone replacement therapy for HIV+ persons. *Journal of Sex Research, 34,* 35–38.

Gold, R. S. (1993). On the need to mind the gap: On-line versus off-line cognitions underlying sexual risk taking. In D. J. Jerry, C. Gallois, & M. McCamish (Eds.), *The theory of reasoned action: Its application to AIDS-preventive behavior* (pp. 227–252). Oxford: Pergamon Press.

Jones, M., Klimes, I., & Catalan, J. (1994). Psychosexual problems in people with HIV infection: Controlled study of gay men and men with haemophilia. *AIDS Care, 6*(5), 587–593.

Klitzman, R. (1998). Disclosure. In R. Smith (Ed.), *Encyclopedia of AIDS* (pp. 181–182). Chicago: Fitzroy Dearborn.

Klitzman, R. (1999). Self-disclosure of HIV serostatus to sexual partners: A qualitative study of issues faced by gay men. *Journal of the Gay and Lesbian Medical Association. 3*(2), 39–49.

Meyer-Bahlburg, H., Exner, T., Lorenz, G., Gruen, R., Gorman, J., & Ehrhardt, A. (1991) Sexual risk behavior, sexual functioning, and HIV-disease progression in gay men. *Journal of Sex Research, 28*(1), 3–27.

Nichols, C. (1998). Integrative marital therapy. In F. Dattilio (Ed.), *Case studies in couple and family therapy* (pp. 233–256). New York: Guilford Press.

Paul, J., Stall, R., & Bloomfield, K. (1991). Gay and alcoholic: Epidemiologic and clinical issues. *Alcohol Health and Research World, 15*(2), 151–160.

Prieur, A. (1990). Norwegian gay men: Reasons for continued practice of unsafe sex. *AIDS Education and Prevention, 2*(2), 109–115.

Remien, R. (1997). Couples of mixed HIV status: Challenges and strategies for intervention with couples. In L. Wicks (Ed.), *Psychotherapy and AIDS* (pp. 165–177). Washington, DC: Taylor & Francis.

Remien, R., Carballo-Diéguez, A., & Wagner, G. (1995). Intimacy and sexual risk behavior among serodiscordant male couples. *AIDS Care, 7*, 429–438.

Ross, M. W. (1990). Reasons for non-use of condoms by homosexually active men during anal intercourse. *International Journal of STDs & AIDS, 1*, 432–434.

Wagner, G., Rabkin, J., & Rabkin, R. (1997a). Effects of testosterone replacement therapy on sexual interest, function, and behavior in HIV+ men. *Journal of Sex Research, 34*(1), 27–33

Wagner, G., Rabkin, J., & Rabkin, R. (1997b). Response to commentaries. *Journal of Sex Research, 34*(1), 37–38.

Wagner, G. J., Remien, R. H., & Carballo-Diéguez, A. (1998). "Extramarital" sex: Is there an increased risk for HIV transmission? A study of male couples of mixed HIV status. *AIDS Education and Prevention, 10*, 245–256.

15

Gina Ogden, Ph.D.

Integrating Sexuality and Spirituality: A Group Therapy Approach to Women's Sexual Dilemmas

I am the Goddess, I am the Mother
All acts of love and pleasure are my ritual.
—Doreen Valiente, "The Charge of the Star Goddess"
as adapted by Shawna Carol for *Goddess Chants*

It has long been clear to me that women who enter sex therapy may be searching for more than information about the physiology of sexual response or directives for behavior modification (Ogden, 1988, 1999a, 1999b). Even when they are not able to articulate it at the outset, they may be concerned with broader, qualitative issues I have identified as the spiritual intangibles of sexual relationship. By spiritual, I do not necessarily mean religious. I mean a range of nonphysical experiences that includes intentions, emotions, wishes, dreams, expectations, memories, values, and meanings. While at least some of these are intrinsic to all sexual interactions (Daniluk, 1998; Heyward, 1989), the cultural dualism of the last two millennia dictates that we compute them separately from the information we receive through our physical senses—what we see, hear, smell, taste, and feel kinesthetically (Eisler, 1995). Consequently, despite sex therapy's assertion that the brain is the most important organ of sexual response (Allgeier & Allgeier, 1988), "sexual" has come to be associated exclusively with the body, and "spiritual" to be associated exclusively with realms beyond the body, those which are intangible or extraordinarily subtle. Omitting such spiritual data from the sex therapy equation simplifies how clinicians approach sexual problems, but it also narrows the options for clinical success.

In my practice of sex therapy since 1974, I have observed that almost every one of the women clients, students, and interviewees with whom I have conversed has described experiencing sex as being more than physical, perceiving the ups and downs of sexual relationship as possessing spiritual aspects as well as bodily ones. These women range from their teens to their 80s and include heterosexual, lesbian, bisexual, and transgendered women. Women in my clinical practice have been mostly middle-class and Caucasian, but the above observations are confirmed by other women with whom I have been in contact over the years: students, workshop participants, interviewees, and survey respondents from a range of ethnic backgrounds and religious traditions. Together, these women represent a variety of sexual dilemmas, ranging from the devastating effects of childhood abuse or negative cultural messages to relationship impasses caused by boredom, affairs, or clueless partners to the social difficulties implicit in exercising sexual options such as celibacy, polyamory, or changed orientation. Their issues have ranged from terror of physical contact to the longing for hot, passionate touch, and from emotional starvation to the craving for intimacy, to know and be known.

But the complexity of these ongoing themes in women's lives does not fit neatly into a category of sexual "function" (e.g., ability to be interested in, aroused by, and orgasmic on intercourse or genital stimulation) or "dysfunction" (e.g., anorgasmia, dyspareunia, vaginismus, or inhibited desire). True to a dualistic world view, accepted clinical definitions of sexual interaction focus on only the physical and quantifiable aspects. For example, sexual arousal is generally defined by sexual scientists only in biological terms: increased breathing, heartbeat, blood pressure, vasodilation, pupil diameter, and lubrication. Similarly, sexual satisfaction is generally defined only as physical satisfaction: the muscle spasms of orgasm, complete with pulses, flushes, and emissions that can be counted and measured.

These definitions are so universally accepted in our culture that they have become standard criteria for "normal" and "functional" sex. As such, they form the traditional clinical foci for behavioral change. They lend themselves to increasing medicalization—witness the recent Viagra™, for women as well as men. In fact, sex therapy has retained its narrow focus with such integrity since Masters and Johnson introduced their methodology in the 1960s, that it leaves out much of what is crucially important for women's self-esteem, pleasure, satisfaction, and even "function." If the

frigid woman served as a clinical stereotype for the first half of the twentieth century, the rigid sex therapist may well be on the way to becoming a
clinical stereotype for the first half of the twenty-first.

The good news is that this leaves a broad field of clinical inquiry
untapped by traditional sex therapy. This chapter looks beyond stereotypical sex therapy to propose a group approach to addressing the complexities of sexual dilemmas presented by women. It discusses the spiritual intangibles of sexual relationship and the characteristics of spiritual sex. It
applies these to a model for conducting group therapy and offers illustrations to assess the efficacy of this approach. Finally, this chapter discusses
the applications of this approach to therapy with individuals and couples.

☐ Spiritual Intangibles of Sexual Relationship

It has been my experience that sexual issues about which women clients
most often have questions or unresolved feelings fall into five broad categories, which frequently overlap. Each category is complex in itself, involving cultural issues as well as personal and relational ones, and inter-
weaving physical, emotional, mental, and spiritual responses to sexuality.
Information from the present may be informed by the past and even by
anticipation of the future.

1. *Safety:* This means how to maintain appropriate physical, emotional,
   and spiritual boundaries without blocking enthusiasm for intimacy and
   desire for physical touching and orgasmic satisfaction.

2. *Self-image and body-image:* These issues concern how to develop sexual
   self-worth in a culture (and possibly a relationship) that seeks to control how women look, dress, act, think, speak, eat, smell, and make
   love.

3. *Nurturing:* Dilemmas of nurturing involve how to balance the ability to
   give and receive love, comfort, and joy, despite mixed messages about
   the rights and roles of women, and despite past and present relationship imbalances in giving and receiving.

4. *Power:* The question here is how to cultivate sexual energy and initiative in a society (and possibly a relationship) that still views women as
   the second sex.

5. *Pleasure:* Pleasure issues involve how to rethink erotic experience in a

world in which women are not supposed to define sexual pleasure. Also, how to cultivate the freedom to enjoy sexual interaction, or even to talk or think about sexual interaction, without shame, guilt, or negative repercussions.

It is important to emphasize that these issues are intangible, not because they are unreal in women's lives, but because science cannot yet measure them. Consequently, they lie beyond the physical focus and performance-oriented goals of traditional sex therapy. Yet any or all of these issues may present crucial clinical themes, guiding the course and outcome of therapy. I have observed that when these spiritual intangibles are left unaddressed, they can dramatically lengthen the necessary number of sessions or undermine therapy altogether. But when they are appropriately addressed at the outset of therapy, the number of sessions may be reduced and outcomes may be positive, even surprisingly so. For, when clients fully understand and integrate these spiritual intangibles, shifts occur in sexual awareness and attitude that inevitably bring about behavioral changes. These changes include the letting go of self-protective denials and deceptions and the opening of energy that allows women to connect body and soul within themselves and with their partners, if they have partners. There is a sense of multidimensionality and freedom from cultural restraint (Bonheim, 1997). This free, multidimensional experience is what some women call spiritual sex.

Characteristics of Spiritual Sex

The following characteristics of spiritual sex emerged from women's descriptions (Ogden, 1999a, 1999b):

1. *Oneness:* Spiritual sex is a whole-person process, an intimate merging of body, mind, heart, and soul that melts artificial boundaries implanted by cultural dualism. A primary characteristic is a sense of oneness—with one's self, one's partner, nature, and the Creator of the universe (by whatever name one chooses). A retired social worker, 76, described the sensation as oceanic: "Like being liquid and alive. It's knowing that you're one with every blade of grass and pine needle. It's relaxing all over, letting go. The sensation of being breathed. Of joining the pulse of the planet."

2. *Heightened senses:* For sex to be spiritual does not mean turning away from the senses. Rather, it means embracing the senses fully and even

heightening them. Women spoke of mountaintop sensuality and excitement, and also of the down-to-earth ordinariness of the sex–spirit connection: a familiar smell, a whispered name, a tender (or not-so-tender) touch that extends the senses beyond their usual boundaries. Many women described exquisite sensuality as a path to God.

3. *Transcendence:* Spiritual sex is characterized by a sense of timelessness during sexual interaction, and an ability to travel across limitations of space and time. "We called each other by our Greek names," reported a 51-year-old career counselor. "I can literally feel my soul being touched and moved," reported a 41-year-old nurse-practitioner: "It's like that sense of coming home after you've been away—where everything is totally familiar, yet at the same time so filled with brilliance and color that it's like being transported to another planet."

4. *Love and partnership:* Spiritual sex nourishes relationships, functioning like yeast that activates and reactivates intimacy, both with a partner and with one's self. It is in the growth of love that many women find the embodiment of spiritual sex. This includes passionate falling-in-love experiences as well as the more complexly woven fabric of long-term partnership, the commitment and intimacy that sometimes connect sex even more poignantly with spirit. A 30-something Episcopal priest described the synergy she experienced with her partner in terms of her ability to be wholly present with herself: "When I open myself to warmth, desire, depth, expansion, and trust, there is no separation between sex and spirit."

5. *Increased energy:* Spiritual sex is often accompanied by a flood of extraordinary energy—the energy otherwise chronically employed in the cultural business of separating body and soul. Women described this, variously, as a sense of wonder and self-esteem that lifted their hearts, rocked their bodies, and touched their souls. This energy often lasts well beyond a specific sexual encounter to inform the rest of a woman's life. In the words of a 60-year-old educator, "I can take it on the bus with me every morning when I go to work, and my whole day is wonderful."

6. *Ecstasy:* Women reported an ecstasy connection through their senses and emotions, through all aspects of relationship, and through imagination and memory. Connection scenarios range from the purely physical ("my vibrator") to flights into nonordinary reality. Many are directly spiritual, as in this letter from a 36-year-old colleague describing a relationship that had felt both erotic and sacred to her: "It was like

being touched by God," she wrote. "Not that my *partner* was God, but that the intensity of our lovemaking was proof that God existed; that only God could have created anything so powerful and positive. Sexual pleasure and sexual love are, for me, *evidence* of God." Some women said they have experienced this connection quite spontaneously while making love, or while meditating or dreaming. Some have actively sought it through bodywork, energy healing, yoga, or Tantric exercises, all of which use breath and movement to open pathways between body and spirit. Some have discovered the connection through reading, listening to music, or working the Internet; others through religious practices, such as Wicca, which honor the erotic energy of all living things.

An Operational Definition of Spiritual Sex

Because the scope of sexual satisfaction so often reaches beyond physical parameters, it is necessary to find more all-encompassing ways to define sex so that we can discuss all of its aspects in clinical sessions. When I am with clients, I talk about sex as energy—specifically, as embodied energy that moves us to reach out, makes contact, and let go. By the same token, I also talk about spirit as energy—specifically, cosmic energy that moves us to reach out, make contact, and let go.

For clinical purposes, I offer an operational definition of spiritual sex. This differs from biologically driven definitions of human sexuality in that it incorporates the multidimensional nature of sexual relationship: Spiritual sex is erotic interaction in which the quality of desire, arousal, and satisfaction is determined by thought, emotion, and meaning as well as by here-and-now physical sensation.

☐ A Group Approach to Women's Sexual Dilemmas

A clinical conundrum in helping women move through their sexual dilemmas has to do with the relational limitations of one-on-one therapy. By its doctor–patient contract, it presents an unequal power dynamic between client and therapist, one that prevents some women from engaging in therapy at all. This contract also sets rigid personal boundaries around emotional sharing and physical touching. Although such boundaries may be necessary safeguards to deter abuses of power, they also block spiritual intangibles such as nurturing and pleasure in the relationship and the self-esteem that arises from more fluid kinds of give and take.

Because my original therapy training was in family systems therapy, it was natural for me to lean toward group sessions as an alternative to one-on-one therapy for certain kinds of women's sexual dilemmas. By observing master therapists like Whitaker, Minuchin, and LaPerriere, I had seen the systemic changes that could occur simply by gathering related people in a room together with a common purpose (or complaint) and a skilled facilitator (Haley, 1987). I reasoned that women's sexuality groups could function as similar containers for systemic change, requiring only subtle intervention once a group had been gathered and given a safe place in which to relate. Consequently, throughout my career as a sex therapist, I have conducted periodic group therapy sessions, most often in a weekend workshop format.

For these groups I drew from several models: women's consciousness-raising groups of the 1970s (for their open sharing of feelings), the preorgasmic women's groups of the 1970s (for their focus on sexual issues; Barbach, 1975), and family systems work.

There are a number of reasons I have chosen to focus this chapter on a group approach rather than on individual or couple therapy. First, the group contains within its structure heightened potential for all the spiritual intangibles of sexual relationship (Daniluk, 1998). For many women, safety is the most crucial of these. The act of creating "woman only" space allows participants the freedom to speak without having to filter their responses through men's, which are dominant in our culture (Daly, 1978; Eisler, 1995). Once it is established that a group is free of the usual gender role-playing dynamic, it is already acting as a change agent. Ingrained cultural habits begin to dissolve and clients can use the group to find new ways to take responsibility for the rest of the spiritual intangibles of sexual relationship: self-image, nurturing, power, and pleasure.

Further, because group members may represent many points of view, groups can be as widely educational as they are directly therapeutic. I have witnessed particular richness in the layering of sexual information on both cognitive and emotional levels. When the group focus is to educate about pleasure, it is possible to incorporate into the group process beauty, comfort, sensation, humor, fun, and play. Often it is the zany, unpredictable moment or the moment of unexpected understanding that creates the most profound burst of change.

I have found that working with women in a group setting can more fairly equalize the roles of client and therapist. Therefore, I find conducting groups gratifying because I can challenge belief systems without being in a one-on-one power position with clients. Often, I can take greater therapeutic risks with clients because the resources of the group—the intelligence, experience, and energy in the circle—create their own checks and balances on me and provide a safety net for both client and leader, so that even difficult experiences become opportunities for group exploration rather than potential control-and-power trips.

Also, leadership boundaries are different than in a one-on-one therapy situation. Within the circle of the group, peer relationships are possible, even to some extent for the leader, particularly when group leadership is shared. This sense of sudden sisterhood is another factor that allows clients the freedom and support to move beyond predetermined roles and fly beneath their defensive radar.

With these factors in mind, group workshops are an ideal vehicle for creating a bridge between sexuality and spirituality. Postgroup feedback reinforces these assertions. Although I do not routinely track participants following a workshop, participants often contact me later, come to subsequent groups, or arrange reunions to which I am invited.

This said, I offer a strong caveat about conducting groups, especially when dealing with such stereotype-shifting material as sexuality and spirituality. Dedicated victims, narcissists, and borderlines do not fare well in group therapy and, under certain kinds of stress, they have the emotional energy to undermine the group and undo the therapist. Successful participants have to be able to listen and to share both the leader and the experience with others in the group. They must be ready to move beyond dense levels of self-involvement, anger, and fear. Since it is not always possible to screen participants (and even when it is I have been fooled), I find it important to use introductions as a vehicle through which to carefully assess clients' readiness. If I am in doubt about a participant's capacity to handle group activities, I can suggest her right to pass on certain activities, and also offer personal support in the form of eye contact, verbal encouragement, and any interventions that will reinforce her safety and the safety of the group. Also, I routinely introduce protective ground rules the entire group can monitor, such as confidentiality, "I" statements, respectful listening, and taking responsibility for one's own feelings.

☐ A Weekend Group: "Journey to Sexual Wholeness"

To address the spiritual complexities of women's sexual dilemmas, I have developed over the years a group therapy experience for women entitled, "Journey to Sexual Wholeness." Although the focus of the group is on sexuality, spirituality is built systemically into the weekend. Throughout this workshop, powerful symbols, images, and ceremonies—both traditional and innovative—are combined to create an atmosphere in which women can discover their sexuality anew, free of stereotypic associations. Placing sexual content within the context of spiritual ritual allows for a mix of information far more rich and complex than is found within the bounds of traditional sex therapy. This helps women engage all aspects of their being—body, mind, heart, and soul.

Pivotal to setting up this group journey is the creation of tangible safe and sacred space, using symbols common to both religious worship and sexual romance, such as candles, incense, and a profusion of flowers. Equally important to weave into the fabric of the weekend are ritual elements common to both religion and romance, such as music, dancing, singing, special foods, words of love and comfort, and noncoercive touch—literally laying on of hands. These elements act as a tangible bridge by which participants can move back and forth from the dictates of culture, where sexuality and spirituality are artificially divided, to a place where sexuality and spirituality naturally meet.

Also important for group set-up is a resource section with books, articles, bibliographies, and videos (along with a VCR and monitor), and sex toys, if appropriate. This allows participants to research subjects from sexual abuse to sexual ecstasy independently and at their own pace.

What follows is an outline of a weekend group conducted at Rowe Conference Center in Rowe, Massachusetts, in June of 1998. The location and time of year meant we could spend some of our time outdoors, but I have run similar groups in the city. I have also run such groups alone, though in this instance I had the luxury of two coleaders: Prue Berry, musician and codirector of Rowe Conference Center, and Katja Esser, artist and teacher of ritual. Having worked with each of them previously, I chose them to share music, ceremony, logistics, and the sheer joy of this creative work. The 24 women present included 5 married women, 6 partnered women (2 of them lesbians), 10 single women (3 of them lesbians), a woman in a polyamorous relationship, and a lesbian couple. Two of the women were African-American, two were from the Netherlands, and the rest were Caucasian women from the northeastern United States. Ages ranged from 24 to 63. Occupations ranged from student to concert cellist to physician to writer to horse trainer.

Progression and Process of the Group

Session 1: Friday Evening—Invocation and Introduction

On Friday evening, as participants entered, we formed a silent ring around the candle-lit space set up beforehand—in this case, a circle of flowers, candles, shells, stones, feathers, and other objects. At the outset, I made clear that this space was interactive, inviting participants to add meaningful items of their own to enrich the mix. A brief welcome and outline of the weekend stated that the focus would be on the spiritual aspects of women's sexual issues, and that spiritual traditions of many cultures would be used to create a container for our journey to sexual wholeness.

We consecrated the workshop space, literally and figuratively, by burning sage, ringing Tibetan bells, and calling on spirits of the seven directions—North, East, South, West, Above, Below, and Center—and of the elements—Air, Fire, Earth, and Water. To introduce therapeutic tradition, we called on the senses and the emotions to help guide our journey. This introductory process provided both protection and focus, and also offered spontaneous opportunities for participants to speak of the changes they wished for their sexual lives.

The group was asked to protect the space by taking a vow of confidentiality—that is, not to reveal anyone else's personal information shared during the weekend. (Women whose stories appear in this chapter have given specific, informed consent, and their real names have not been used.) Each woman then introduced herself formally, stating her intention for the weekend journey. Intentions ranged from "gaining information about sex" to "understanding the links between sex and spirit" to "touching and nurturing," to "more ability to cope with being single" to "ability to cope with partnership and intimacy." It is noteworthy that these goals are considerably broader than those most often defined when clients present for conventional sex therapy.

At the close of this first session, women added objects to the space in the center of the room. This was a tangible way for them to join the group and at the same time to claim ownership of some part of this public space, an action that may have been difficult for them in their daily lives. In a dramatic instance, one women placed her wedding ring in the center, stating that she was ready to think of herself as a sexual woman again for the first time since her husband had committed suicide more than a year before, on Valentine's Day.

Session 2: Saturday Morning—The Element of Air: Understanding the Issues

The morning session focused on the element of air, which we used as a metaphor for the intellectual and emotional awareness of the connections between sexuality and spirituality. A thorough check-in with participants' feelings was followed by a lecture and discussion of the spiritual intangibles of sexual relationship, the role of various religions in separating sex from spirit, and the symbols and rituals that join sexual romance and religious worship—the candles, incense, flowers, and so on, described above.

The group then divided into subgroups of three, giving each woman 10 minutes to relate her personal experiences of connecting sexuality and spirituality—what helped her and what were deterrents. Another hour's group sharing served as a clearinghouse for information, along with the fears, angers, anticipations, and questions women had brought with them.

Several women mentioned that this session was crucially important for them, enabling them to take risks and develop trust in themselves and in each other. As the stories informed one another, they began to weave an emotional fabric that helped sustain participants during the weekend and, for some women, long afterwards. For instance, Sibylle, a 36-year-old dancer and performance artist, volunteered her impressions in long-term follow-up 7 months after the workshop. Listening to one of the other women during this session had moved her to rewrite her own sexual script when she returned home and to become much more assertive in asking directly for what she wanted. Her sexual dilemma had centered around how to be fully herself in her relationship without feeling "on stage," and how to make her wants known to her partner, whose own sexual performance anxieties clouded his abilities to listen to her.

> Adele's story really inspired me. Understanding that spirituality has to be part of sexuality. That sex doesn't have to be just boom boom. How Adele said what she went through in her relationship—all the different levels so that I could understand what's possible for me. Now I'm more sure of where I want to go with my own relationship. I feel more alive and connected. Yes, it's created some disruption between me and my partner. I want him to share the vision with me, to cooperate. I have become more demanding. I don't accept the way things are.

It was evident that the impetus for Sybille's change was another participant's forthrightness rather than some intervention from the therapist. This points up one of the prime advantages of group work—the interaction with peers that provides both role models and support to move beyond old patterns.

Session 3: Saturday Afternoon—The Elements of Earth and Water: Grounding and Dissolving

The afternoon session took place outdoors and focused on the senses. To honor the element of earth, we began by walking a labyrinth, an ancient symbol of the Divine Feminine. Although at first glance a labyrinth looks like a maze, there are no dead-ends. It has only one continuous path, which weaves and winds around on itself many times before it reaches the center. In some early traditions, this represented the womb of the Goddess, the Great Mother (Lonegren, 1996). For our weekend of journeying to sexual wholeness, it provided the geometry of sexuality and spirituality as well as evocative symbolism and gave women a tangible image-in-motion for sexual changes they sought. Participants offered insights such as these: "The journey to sexual wholeness is not a straight line." "I had to trust that I was on the right track even though I didn't know exactly where I was." "The way in is the same as the way out—and vice versa."

The twofold purpose of this labyrinth journey was to move clients' awareness into their bodies and to encourage self-direction in dealing with individual sexual dilemmas. When information initiates through the body rather than solely through cognitions, it is impossible to stay locked into the intellectual dimension so prominent in many forms of therapy, or into behavioral techniques so prominent in traditional sex therapy.

In the center of Rowe's labyrinth the group gathered to ground their sexual fears ("I send my terror of pleasure into the receiving earth.") and once again to invoke their desires for sexual wholeness ("I take on the delight of being a fully satisfied woman.").

From the labyrinth, we went to a nearby stream to honor the sensuous and purifying element of water. Those who chose to "baptized" themselves into sexual wholeness by dunking in an icy natural pool. The group then gathered in a giant hot tub, where we splashed, played, and fed one another sensuous foods. I hoped this activity would reach beneath defense systems concerning body image, homophobia, and even childhood trauma. In fact, this session was fun for the women who were used to this degree of physical honesty with one another. For other women it presented a challenge. For those who had been forced to grow up prematurely, the playfulness was a stretch. For others, the physical closeness and sensuality with other women was initially uncomfortable. As participants relaxed, several women commented in amazement that this afternoon did not turn into a sexually compromising situation as it might have if men had been present or if the focus had been on more stereotypical sexual behaviors.

Session 4: Saturday Evening—The Element of Fire: Journey to Sexual Wholeness

The evening session presented another shift for participants, this time from body to mind. The evening was designed as an exploration of the element of fire, both tangible fire and the fire of the imagination. It was an opportunity for participants to move beyond ordinary patterns of organizing sexual information by journeying to the sound of a drum into "nonordinary" realms, a spiritual tradition practiced by many indigenous cultures. Research on drummed journeys by cultural anthropologist Mircea Eliade (1972) and healer Sandra Ingerman (1991, pp.137–158), among others, has revealed such journeying to be a genuine and healthy opening to the awareness of subtle energies. These traditional rituals are designed to promote mystical experiences that might bring new insights and radically change the way participants viewed their sexuality.

This journey into the mind of sex and spirit was framed by physical experiences intended to open participants up beforehand and to ground them afterward. Before the journey, women entered the candle-lit room with rhythmic music playing, where they were handed scarves and invited to move and dance for about 10 minutes as sensually as they wished— as if they were snakes, shedding their skin. The drummed journey began with participants lying in a circle, feet facing toward the center space. The instruction was, "Close your eyes, follow your breath inside yourself. Now journey to find your own internal Keeper of the Flame of Sexuality and Spirituality. Allow your Keeper to lead you through the paths of a labyrinth, at the center of which you will meet the Goddess of Sexual Wholeness, who will invite you into her womb." The drumming lasted about 15 minutes, followed by enough time for women to share all that they wished, first in dyads and then with the whole group.

Stories that emerged ranged from being rocked in the arms of the Goddess to encountering a sacred bull to being rebirthed as a fully sensual woman. Linda, who had placed her wedding ring in the central sacred space, relived a deeply felt sexual dream of her adolescent years and received a radiant message that she was now mature enough to implement it. Andrea reported that she missed the touch and sensuality of the afternoon and felt quite alone during the journey session, imprinting into her body–mind how much she needed to incorporate more touch and sensuality in her life.

Finally, we held a ceremonial candle-lighting in which each participant reiterated her intention for her own growth and offered it as light and flame to others. The evening ended with a candle-lit procession through pine woods to a bonfire, where we sang, shared stories, and laughed.

Session 5: Sunday Morning—Affirmation and Closure

Sunday morning began with unstructured sharing, which both richly informed the group and also highlighted its diversity. One woman spoke of her long-term marriage, in which she and her husband were experimenting with celibacy in order to deepen their spiritual commitment to themselves and each other. Adele demonstrated the sensual Tantric breathing she had practiced in a polyamorous group. Andrea spoke of her addiction to food as a displaced need for nurturing—and was able to ask for, and receive, hugs. Linda spoke of the grief that still wracked her and of her growing ability to own her strength without denying the sadness and loss connected with her husband's suicide. A number of women spoke of the terror of sexual expression, a legacy of childhood and adult abuse. Several spoke of feeling outrageously sexy, describing sexual ecstasy as a gift connection of body and soul. By now, the atmosphere was one of openness, respect, and deepening awareness.

The final ceremony was a trust walk in which each woman asked for and received affirmations of her own choosing. This exercise reiterated the major themes of the weekend: intention, giving, receiving, safety, positive self-image, power, pleasure, and the possibility of transformation that seemed magical rather than strictly logical. As each woman reached her turn, she stated what she had learned and her personal intention for continuing her journey to sexual wholeness. She then requested a specific affirmation from the group, which was whispered to her as she was guided, eyes closed, through the double line of group members. At the end of this final journey a warm hug awaited her.

Women spoke of feeling held by the group; of having sensations so deep that they lasted long beyond the weekend. One woman said, "My affirmation was said back to me in so many ways I had to believe it. By the time I reached the end of the line, I had a sense that it was already happening." Another woman related, "I'm going to take you all with me so the next time I have doubts I'll hear you all saying, 'You are a tower of strength.'" Giving the affirmations proved to be educational, as well. One woman said that once she had gone down the receiving line, she realized how stilted her own affirmations to others had been, and she began making them much more personal. For closure, we formed a final circle, offering appreciations to one another and to the space.

Participants seemed to be glowing by the end of the weekend. Big hugs and soft eyes prevailed. There was also much laughter. For some, this laughter was the relief of finding community and a new direction.

☐ Long-Term Feedback from Participants

While feedback immediately following a group of this sort is usually enthusiastic, even euphoric, it is the long-term feedback that reveals how effective the methods actually are in precipitating attitudinal and behavioral changes in participants' lives.

Following are illustrative histories of two participants. What about the process helped in dealing with the spiritual intangibles? In what ways did this group experience reach deeper than traditional one-on-one sex therapy? Their feedback indicates that some events were more moving than others, yet that the group created a cumulative momentum that superseded any single aspect.

Andrea

This 51-year-old Caucasian educator presented her sexual dilemma as isolation and a yearning to be more open about her sexuality. Her professional goal was to acquire information about the connections between sexuality and spirituality so that she could incorporate them into her teaching career. Her personal goal was to feel safe enough to embrace what she called "the wounded part of myself," the child who was emotionally rejected by her mother when a sibling was born and who was thereafter used as a sexual toy by her father and older brothers. Now she was ready to fully own the "goodness and wholeness" of sexual pleasure by putting to rest the shame associated with her "bad-girl" feelings around the abuse. However, the feelings were complex and difficult to resolve. She felt humiliated and responsible for having allowed the abuse, and at the same time sexually aroused by the memory of the attention and stimulation.

In the course of the weekend, more of Andrea's sexual history emerged. The sex in her 20-year marriage had been devastating for her: "I was never kissed, just fucked for 30 seconds." Toward the end of this marriage, a brief affair taught her that sex could be sensuous, intimate, and empowering. About 10 years ago, the affair ended, she became suicidal, entered therapy, and finally left the marriage. In the last 15 years, much therapy, along with self-help books and a great deal of her own work, has enabled her to become aware of her early abuse and to resolve many of its effects, which included an eating disorder. But the sexual effects remained: negative body image, low self-esteem, and terror of intimacy, along with a doomed sense of longing for a sexually nurturing relationship. Two years before the workshop, Andrea entered sex therapy to try to resolve desire discrepancies with an equally terrified woman partner. The therapy emphasized mechanics and seemed to miss the point. Andrea continued to feel unseen, unheard, disempowered, oversexed, and unsatisfied, as she had as a child.

She described the differences between that individual sex therapy and this group experience as "night and day." She pointed out that, as much as she had needed one-on-one therapy in her early years of recovery, it had eventually fostered a tendency to be self-absorbed in her pain and abuse. But the ceremonial quality of the group left no room for self-absorption, which allowed her to reach a new level of personal development: "There was no constant focus on me, but on the issues. Therefore growth was magnified by the number of women present." She related that the entire weekend was both personally and professionally "transformative," that it "catapulted" her forward, helping her embrace her sexuality and affirm the value of her life's work.

Andrea identified several elements of the group as helping her feel this way: The first was contact with other participants and leaders. This involved exposure to both information and emotional experience, which helped her feel "safe, heard, and embraced" in her vulnerability. Also, being in this setting with professionals linking sexuality and spirituality made her feel less alone, affirmed her "values, dreams, and visions." A second element of enormous significance for Andrea was safe touch—holding hands in the circle, doing the snake dance, and slithering among other participants. She described the afternoon session at the brook and hot tub as particularly moving:

> It was significant in terms of my body issues. It was a safe environment without focus on the thought of orgasm or performance. Being in the company of women, experiencing the sense of touch, taste, and laughter was a great adventure in body self-acceptance. I was not treated differently as a large woman. Carrying 100 extra pounds didn't make a difference. I was enjoyed as a spirit and a human body. I felt fear and good feelings, and I chose the good feelings. The fear didn't have to be there.
>
> It was truly transformational. This feeling has been retained for almost a year now. I open up more to thoughts, awareness, enjoyment of the sensual part of my humanness. It's the first time in my life I've moved beyond guilt and shame. I'm so excited. I never felt this before.

This group was a vehicle for Andrea to review her old, fear-based processes in terms of the opportunities and challenges in her present life. Clearly, she had learned much from the group's information, pleasure, and fun. But even the parts of the group that had been difficult for her had been opportunities to replicate old processes in enough safety and support so that she could simply observe them, let them go, and move on. In that sense the group had been an important passage on her journey to sexual wholeness.

Loren

For this 48-year-old Caucasian journalist who had engaged in a great deal of spiritual growth in the last decade, the sexual dilemma was typically complex and woven into her history. Raised a Roman Catholic, she had been carefully taught that her body was a source of shame, that sexual desire was a source of guilt, that sexual pleasure was more important for a man than for a woman, and that procreation was the purpose of sex. All of these added up to the resounding message that "good girls don't." She reported, "I actually felt I could not be myself and be loved. It was either/ or." When she came to the workshop, she had been divorced for 4 years after a 23-year marriage, which she described as "intense and passionate," but during which sex had become a cause for anger, arguments, recriminations, and finally repeated affairs by her husband. Her goal for the weekend was to bridge what she saw as a chasm between sexuality and spirituality so that she could move beyond feeling ashamed of her own sexual nature and withdrawing sexually.

For Loren, it was the Saturday evening journey that was particularly transformative. Her response to the journey was immediate and dramatic. Members of the group remarked that her voice and her whole physical body became larger, more powerful and confident. These responses withstood the test of time. A letter she wrote 6 weeks after the workshop was reaffirmed in a conversation 5 months later:

> One of the reasons that the drummed journey was so powerful for me is that the images of Mother and Goddess of Sexual Wholeness came together for me. My personal mother was deeply ashamed of her sexuality. The extent of it only became apparent to me after her death a year or so ago. She could never admit that she had ever loved sex. I had no role model for loving myself as a sexual being.
>
> When you asked us to contact the keeper of the flame of our sexuality and spirituality, she was immediately present to me—a naked, dancing, playful, pagan priestess. She fairly leapt and skipped ahead of me through the labyrinth. At the center was the Goddess of Sexual Wholeness, whom you had said would invite us into her womb. At first she looked like a Botticelli Venus and I thought—"No, she doesn't have to be blonde and classically beautiful. She could look more like me." Then she shifted through all colors of skin and hair and was very big and imposing. . . . And I realized I could crawl up inside her womb. . . . When I did it was a large space, very dark yet also comfortable and safe.
>
> It was then my body began to sob and shake as I felt what it was like to have a mother who was strong and powerful enough to really take care of me, to give me what I needed in a way my personal mother had not been fully able to do. And perhaps most important, since she was the Goddess of Sexual Wholeness, she was not ashamed and she could birth me without shame. I could come into my life without the burden of shame about my

body and sexuality. The energy in my body continued to move with shaking and sobs as I felt the full impact of these images . . . [including] an image of being held against her breast and soothed. It feels like a touchstone I can return to when I come up against fear, doubt, and shame on my journey to fully claiming my sexuality.

> I am very grateful for this journey, for this experience. To have the chance to redeem the ideal of Mother as Virgin and replace it with the experience of Mother as wholly, holy sexual Goddess.

> I know all this inner work and allowing myself to slowly come out more as a sexy woman, a woman who wants to be seen in her fullness, who is not afraid that being sexual somehow diminishes or negates all the other aspects of her self-expression will help me connect on a deeper level with a partner in the future. It gives me such hope that I will have the opportunity to share the bigger self that I am becoming with a new lover/partner in a way that will allow my sexuality, my spirituality, my creativity to shine.

Like Andrea, Loren relived a significant piece of her history in the group. In her case, that history that was at once archetypal and deeply, specifically personal. The depth of her "rebirthing" as a sexual woman was a function of the safety and support of the group along with the full, counterculture permission to link sexuality and spirituality in all their earthiness and (w)holiness.

☐ The Significance of Integrating Sexuality and Spirituality

The clinical significance of integrating sexuality and spirituality is at least five-fold, in no particular order of importance. There is some overlap in each of these categories.

First, linking physical and spiritual responses broadens the discourse on sexuality beyond the mechanics to a larger model that can encompass a variety of cultural contexts and religious traditions. It broadens accepted definitions of sexual satisfaction beyond the medical model by substantiating that mind–body connections are as valid as physical goals. It broadens the discourse on sexual desire beyond its biological components by placing that desire within the spectrum of emotional and even mystical experience. Once these definitions are broadened, it is possible to focus on the spiritual intangibles of sexual relationship: safety, positive self-image, nurturing, power, and pleasure.

Second, integrating sexuality and spirituality challenges dualistic belief systems that insist on separate roles and functions for body and soul, male and female, gay and straight, and so on. Once one holds the intention of integrating sexuality and spirituality, one is already incorporating into sexual relationship spiritual values such as connection, wholeness, intimacy, and cooperative partnership. These may move clients to explore realms beyond their socio-religious conditioning, setting the stage for unlimited personal growth and change.

Third, integrating sexuality and spirituality validates empathic, relational sex, whether the relationship is with a partner or one's self. When sexual response emerges from the energetics of relationship rather than from the playing out of cultural roles and power dynamics, there is an inevitable softening of boundaries and a recognition of one's own and one's partner's intrinsic value. This can facilitate the teaching not only of deepening personal erotic potential but also of tangible alternatives to relationship disconnection and violence.

Fourth, integrating sexuality and spirituality connects sexual pleasure with overall healing. Because all levels of the personality are involved, patterned defenses may be caught off guard, bypassed, or reprogrammed altogether. As in behavioral sex therapy treatment, there may be temporary relief of symptoms, but there is also likely to be more wholesale and permanent change. Conversely, when only the physical or behavioral aspect of sexual experience is addressed, clients are more likely to continue feeling symptomatic and needy, potentiating a seemingly narcissistic attachment to endless personal growth.

Finally, as demonstrated in the examples above, healing may be fast, sometimes even spontaneous. This presents a distinct boon in this age of quick fixes and short-term therapy allowances of managed care.

☐ Integrating Sexuality and Spirituality in Nongroup Sessions

The examples in this chapter derived from group therapy, but aspects of this approach to integrating sexuality and spirituality can be adapted for use in sessions with individuals or couples. To help create the kinds of complexity afforded by group, I sometimes find it useful to layer different techniques, drawing upon traditional sex therapy along with every other modality in which I am trained, such as family systems, Gestalt, bioenergetics, psychodrama, play therapy, visualization, energy healing, and spiritual healing.

Specific elements of the group approach I have used consistently and successfully in individual and couples sessions include asking clients to state and restate intentions and encouraging them to share feelings with their partners or friends, to ask directly for what they want, and to search out the spiritual lessons in their past sexual experiences. Also, especially for dilemmas of low self-esteem and negative body image, I have regularly helped clients develop self-affirmations. Above all, I have asked clients to listen deeply to themselves and to their partners and to hear the spirit revealed in each other's desires.

With clients who are open to it, it is possible to develop specific rituals and ceremonies to help dissolve sexual dilemmas. Within a session, I have used breathing exercises and intoning words or vowels. These methods are designed to shift clients from habitual responses of linear problem solving into more fluid, body-centered modes of accessing information.

Visualizations have been helpful in moving many clients beyond cultural stereotypes and reminding them of natural and ancient contexts of sexuality and spirituality.

For therapy homework, I have supported clients in developing their own ceremonies for a variety of sexual dilemmas. These include exorcising a critical mother from the bedroom, permission-giving for self-pleasuring, and using extended eye contact and breathing techniques borrowed from Tantric rituals. I have suggested that clients ally with the elements of air, fire, earth, and water to enhance the sex–spirit connection with a partner—cavorting in a ceremonial bath, rolling around before a roaring fire, and so on. In particular, I have suggested that clients make the connection between sexuality and spirituality by acknowledging that many of the rituals and symbols of sexual romance are also time-honored rituals and symbols of spiritual worship. Specifically, I have encouraged them to connect sex and spirit intentionally by incorporating candles, flowers, incense, special foods, wine (if appropriate), and music into their lovemaking. I have suggested that they speak lovingly and comfortingly, dance, lay hands on one another in a nongoal-oriented way, and offer each other massages by way of anointing each other with oil. I have supported them in making as much joyful noise as they can muster—as long as the neighbors don't complain.

In preparation for sessions with clients, I have often used ceremonies with myself, which vary from meditation and prayer to visualizing clients and asking for guidance in their behalf. When my intention has clearly been to give over control rather than to give up power, this has always been effective. Afterward, clients have taken uncanny leaps forward in some spiritual intangible of sexual relationship. In fact, I find that the more I personally connect with the spiritual dimensions implicit in sex therapy, the more deeply I understand that therapy that is egoless for the therapist becomes most self-responsible for the client, and ultimately most empowering.

☐ Conclusions

From more than 25 years of clinical practice, I know how unlikely it is that transformations of the depth, speed, and complexity reported above could have taken place within the context of traditional sex therapy. Wonderful things happen in the therapy room, but not this. The container is too small. The intense interaction with others in the group is missing. How could Sibylle have changed her self-imposed performance tripping so immediately without that flood of information, or Linda have recommitted her wedding ring to herself without that flood of support? The empowering peer relationships with the group leaders are absent. In a one-on-one contract, the playful outdoor interactions on Saturday afternoon could never have occurred, and anything approaching them would most certainly carry with it the sticky stamp of transference/countertransference and create a distracting subplot all its own. In one-on-one sex therapy, there would never have been the constant tangible presence of spiritual symbols and rituals—the flowers and candles, dancing, chanting, and drumming. In a dozen therapy sessions strung back to back, there would not have existed the fortuitous moments that enabled Andrea and Loren to walk through their defense systems unimpeded, like Alice through the looking glass.

Traditional sex therapy provides acknowledged relief for problems that require simple permission, specific information, structured homework, or a monitored behavioral method such as the squeeze technique. But for many sexual dilemmas, especially the complex ones that women typically present, a more encompassing approach is helpful and sometimes necessary. Integrating sexuality and spirituality, particularly in a group therapy setting, creates a bridge that can help clients with a variety of presenting problems transcend sexual stereotypes and connect more profoundly with the erotically complex relationships in their lives. Moreover, it can free therapists to move beyond the goal-orientation of traditional sex therapy to present clients—and themselves—with less directive, more creative options.

☐ References

Allgeier, A. R., & Allgeier, E. R. (1988). *Sexual interactions*. Lexington, MA: D.C. Heath.

Allison, D. (1994). *Skin: Talking about sex, class, and literature*. Ithaca, NY: Firebrand Books.

Anand, M. (1989). *The art of sexual ecstasy: The path of sacred sexuality for western lovers*. Los Angeles: Jeremy Tarcher.

Angier, N. (1999). *Woman: An intimate geography*. Boston: Houghton-Mifflin.

Barbach, L. G. (1975). *For yourself: The fulfillment of female sexuality*. Garden City, NY: Doubleday.

Bass, E., & Davis, L. (1988). *The courage to heal: A guide for women survivors of child sexual abuse*. New York: Harper & Row.

Belenky, M. F., Clinchy, B. M., Goldberger, N. R., & Tarule, J. M. (1986). *Women's ways of knowing: The development of self, voice, and mind*. New York: Basic Books.

Berman, L. A., & Berman, J. R. (2000). Viagra and beyond: Where sex educators and therapists fit in from a multidisciplinary perspective. *Journal of Sex Education and Therapy, 25*(1), 17–24.

Bishop, C. (1996). *Sex and spirit*. Boston: Little, Brown.

Bonheim, J. (1997). *Aphrodite's daughters: Women's sexual stories and the journey of the soul*. New York: Fireside.

Bornstein, K. (1995). *Gender outlaw: On men, women, and the rest of us*. New York: Routledge.

Boston Women's Health Book Collective. (1998). *Our bodies, ourselves for the new century*. New York: Touchstone.

Brennan, B. (1987). *Hands of light: A guide to healing through the human energy field*. New York: Bantam Books.

Brock, R. N. (1988). *Journeys by heart: A Christology of erotic power*. New York: Crossroad.

Bruyere, R. (1994). *Wheels of light: Chakras, auras, and the healing energy of the body*. New York: Fireside.

Budapest, Z. (1989). *The holy book of women's mysteries*. Berkeley, CA: Wingbow.

Camphausen, R. C. (1996). *The yoni: Sacred symbol of female power*. Rochester, VT: Inner Traditions.

Chalker, R. (2000). *The clitoral truth: The secret world at our fingertips*. New York: Seven Stories.

Christ, C. P. (1987). *Laughter of Aphrodite: Reflections on a journey to the goddess*. San Francisco: Harper & Row.

Classen, C. (1993). *Worlds of sense: Exploring the senses in history and across cultures*. London: Routledge.

Combs-Schilling, M. E. (1989). *Sacred performances: Islam, sexuality, and sacrifice*. New York: Columbia University Press.

Couninan, C. M. (1999). *The anthropology of food and the body: Gender, meaning, and power*. New York: Routledge.

Culpepper, E. (1997). Missing goddesses missing women: Reflections of a middle-aged Amazon. In K. L. King (Ed.), *Women and goddess traditions in antiquity and today* (pp. 426–443). Minneapolis: Augsburg/Fortress.

Csikszentmihalyi, M. (1990). *Flow: The psychology of optimal experience*. New York: Harper & Row.

Damasio, A. (1999). *The feeling of what happens: Body and emotion in the making of consciousness*. San Diego: Harcourt.

Danielou, A. (Trans.). (1994). *The complete kama sutra*. Rochester, VT: Park St. Press.

Daniluk, J. C. (1998). *Women's sexuality across the life span*. New York: Guilford.

Davis, E. (1995). *Women, sex, and desire*. New York: Hunter House.

Decosta-Willis, M., Martin, R., & Bell, R. P. (Eds.). (1992). *Erotique noire: Black erotica*. New York: Doubleday.

Dodson, B. (1987). *Sex for one*. New York: Crown.

Dodson, B. (1991) *Self-loving: Portrait of a woman's sexuality seminar* (video). www.Bettydodson.com.

Eisler, R. (1995). *Sacred pleasure: Sex, myth, and the politics of the body*. San Francisco: HarperCollins.

Eliade, M. (1972). *Shamanism: Archaic techniques of ecstasy*. New York: Princeton University Press.

Ellison, C. (2000). *Women's sexualities: Generations of women speak about sexual self acceptance*. San Francisco: Jossey-Bass.

Eriksen, J. A. (1999). *Kiss and tell: Surveying sex in the twentieth century*. Cambridge, MA: Harvard University Press.

Espin, O. M. (1997). *Latina realities: Essays on healing, migration, and sexuality*. Boulder, CO: Westview.

Faludi, S. (1991). *Backlash: The undeclared war on American women*. New York: Crown.

Faludi, S. (1999). *Stiffed: The betrayal of the American man*. New York: William Morrow.

Fausto-Sterling, A. (2000). *Sexing the body: Gender politics and the construction of sexuality*. New York: Basic Books.

Feinberg, L. (1997). *Transgender warriors*. Boston: Beacon.

Fisher, H. E. (1992). *The anatomy of love: The natural history of monogamy, adultery, and divorce*. New York: Norton.

Francoeur, R. T., Cornog, M., & Perper, T. (Eds.). (1999). *Sex, love, and marriage in the 21st century: The next sexual revolution*. Lincoln, NE: iUniverse.com.

French, M. (1992). *The war against women*. New York: Summit Books.

Freud, S. (1916). Three contributions to the theory of sex. In A. A. Brill (Trans.), *The basic writings of Sigmund Freud*. New York: Nervous and Mental Disease Publishing Co.

Gimbutas, M. (1989). *The language of the goddess*. San Francisco: Harper & Row.

Goldner, D. (1999). *Infinite grace: Where the worlds of science and spiritual healing meet*. New York: Hampton Roads.

Goodison, L. (1990). *Moving heaven and earth: Sexuality, spirituality, and social change*. London: Women's Press.

Grant, L. (1993). *Sexing the millennium: A political history of the sexual revolution*. London: HarperCollins.

Grosz, E. A. (1994). *Volatile bodies: Toward a corporeal feminism*. Bloomington: Indiana University Press.

Guy, D. (1999). *The red thread of passion: Spirituality and the paradox of sex*. Boston: Shambhala.

Haley, J. (1987). *Problem-solving therapy*. San Francisco: Jossey-Bass.

Hall, M. (1987). Sex therapy with lesbian couples: A four-stage approach. *Journal of Homosexuality, 14*(1/2), 137–156.

Herman, J. L. (1991). *Trauma and recovery*. New York: Basic Books.

Heyn, D. (1992). *The erotic silence of the American wife*. New York: Turtle Bay Books.

Heyward, C. (1989). *Touching our strength: The erotic as power and the love of God*. New York: HarperCollins.

Hite, S. (1976). *The Hite report: A nationwide study of female sexuality*. New York: Macmillan.

Hooks, B. (2000). *All about love: New visions*. New York: William Morrow.

Hyde, J. S. (1996). *Half the human experience: The psychology of women* (5th ed.). Lexington, MA: D.C. Heath.

Jacobs, S. E., Wesley, T., & Lang, S. (1997). *Two-spirit people: Native American gender identity, sexuality, and spirituality*. Chicago: University of Illinois Press.

Jordan, J. V. (1987). Clarity in connection: Empathic knowing, desire and sexuality. *Work in Progress No. 29*. Wellesley, MA: Stone Center for Developmental Services and Studies.

Kaplan, H. S. (1979). *Disorders of desire.* New York: Brunner/Mazel.

Kasl, C. (1989). *Women, sex, and addiction.* New York: Tichnor & Fields.

Kinsey, A. C., Pomeroy, W. B., Martin, C. E., & Gebhard, P. H. (1953). *Sexual behavior in the human female.* Philadelphia: W.B. Saunders.

Kitzinger, S. (1983). *Woman's experience of sex.* New York: Putnam.

Koszeki, M. A. (1994). *Sexuality, religion, and magic: A comprehensive guide to sources.* New York: Garland.

Lanier, J. (1989). From having to being: Toward sexual enlightenment. In G. Feuerstein (Ed.), *Enlightened sexuality: Essays on body-positive spirituality.* Freedom, CA: Crossing.

Laumann, E. O., et al. (1994). *The social organization of sexuality.* Chicago: University of Chicago Press.

Lorde, A. (1978). *Uses of the erotic.* Trumansburg, NY: Out and Out Books/Crossing.

Lonegren, S. (1996). *Labyrinths: Ancient myths and modern uses.* Glastonbury, UK: Gothic Image.

Mains, R. P. (1999). *The technology of orgasm: Hysteria, the vibrator, and women's sexual satisfaction.* Baltimore: Johns Hopkins University Press.

Maltz, W., & Boss, S. (1997). *In the garden of desire: The intimate world of women's sexual fantasies.* New York: Broadway Books.

Masters, W. H., & Johnson, V. E. (1966). *Human sexual response.* Boston: Little, Brown.

McCormick, N. (1994). *Sexual salvation: Affirming women's rights and pleasures.* Westport, CT: Praeger.

Moore, T. (1998). *The soul of sex: Cultivating life as an act of love.* New York: HarperCollins.

Nelson, J. B., & Longfellow, S. P. (Eds.). (1994). *Sexuality and the sacred: Sources for theological reflection.* Louisville, KY: Westminster/John Knox.

Ogden, G. (1988). Women and sexual ecstasy: How can therapists help? *Women and Therapy,* 7(2–3), 43–56.

Ogden, G. (1994). Women who love sex. *On the Issues,* 3(2), 44–45.

Ogden, G. (1995). Media interruptus: Sexual politics on the book-tour circuit. *Ms.* (Nov./Dec.), 86–87.

Ogden, G. (1998a). How sex can be spiritual. *New Woman* (July), 105–109.

Ogden, G. (1998b). Sex as a path to the soul. *New Age* (Jan./Feb.), 56–60.

Ogden, G. (1999a). *Women who love sex: An inquiry into the expanding spirit of women's erotic experience* (Rev. Ed.). Cambridge, MA: Womanspirit.

Ogden, G. (1999b). Sex and spirit: The healing connection. *New Age* (Jan./Feb.), 78–81, 128–130.

Ogden, G. (in press). Sexuality overview. In S. Gamer et al. (Eds.), *International encyclopedia of women.* New York: Routledge.

Reich, W. (1942/1973). *The function of the orgasm.* New York: Farrar, Straus, Giroux.

Savage, L. E. (1999). *Reclaiming goddess sexuality: The power of the feminine way.* Carlsbad, CA: Hay House.

Schnarch, D. (1997). *Passionate marriage: Keeping love and intimacy alive in emotionally committed relationships.* New York: Norton.

Shaw, M. (1994). *Passionate enlightenment: Women in Tantric Buddhism.* Princeton, NJ: Princeton University Press.

Somé, S. E. (1997). *The spirit of intimacy: Ancient teachings in the ways of relationships.* Berkeley, CA: Berkeley Hills Books.

Starhawk. (1989). *The spiral dance.* San Francisco: Harper.

Tavris, C. (1992). *The mismeasure of woman.* New York: Simon & Schuster.

Taylor, E. (2000). *Shadow culture: Psychology and spirituality in America.* New York: Counterpoint.

Tiefer, L. (1995). *"Sex is not a natural act" and other essays.* Boulder CO: Westview.

Timmerman, J. H. (1992). *Sexuality and spiritual growth.* New York: Crossroad.

Tolman, D. L. (2000). Object lessons: Romance, violation, and female adolescent sexual desire. *Journal of Sex Education and Therapy, 25*(1), 70–79.

Torgovnick, M. (1997). *Primitive passions: Men, women, and the quest for ecstasy.* New York: Knopf.

Vance, C. S. (Ed.). (1984). *Pleasure and danger: Exploring female sexuality.* London: Routledge & Kegan Paul.

Whipple, B., Ogden, G., & Komisaruk, B. (1992). Physiological correlates of imagery-induced orgasm in women. *Archives of Sexual Behavior, 21*(2), 121–133.

Wilber, K. (1995). *Sex, ecology, spirituality.* Boston: Shambhala.

16

CHAPTER

Peggy J. Kleinplatz, Ph.D.

Conclusions:
Advancing Sex Therapy

In Part I of this book, contributors identified many of the problems and criticisms facing the field of sex therapy. The chapters comprising Part II suggest that there are solutions at hand, although these solutions would not uniformly point us in the same direction.

The conclusions we may reach from the criticisms, the proposed alternatives, and the innovations are as follow:

1. *Sex therapy should aim for more than remediation of symptoms of sexual dysfunction.* Treatment of the symptom alone may dishonor and dehumanize the individual or couple. Our goals should extend considerably deeper, to deal with underlying issues—and not only when "necessary," because the symptom seems intractable (see Kaplan, 1974). We can also aim considerably higher, to help our clients attain insight; increase self-esteem; improve body-image; and experience pleasure, intimacy, joy, connection, erotic potential, empowerment, mutual resonance, and ecstasy (Apfelbaum, Aanstoos, Kleinplatz, Ellison, Shaw, Hall, Maltz, and Ogden).

2. *Sexual problems can provide opportunities to aim for profound change for the individual or the couple* (Kleinplatz, Shaw, and Mahrer & Boulet). Instead of attempting to eliminate the troublesome symptom, the pre-

senting problem can be seen as a precious doorway to fundamental personality change: for example, authenticity, maturity, transcendence, the ability to be present, integration, and transformation. We will never discover the full depth and breadth and height of what sexual beings can become in therapy unless we explore what lies within them (Mahrer & Boulet).

3. *The kinds of sexual issues that concern our clients may be much broader than what currently exists or is envisioned in our taxonomies.* Such concerns include wanting greater partnership, safety, spiritual fulfillment, fun, a sense of aliveness, and an opportunity to triumph over past experience (e.g., childhood sexual abuse). In order to know the full range of what sexual beings aspire toward, we should ask them (Tiefer and Ogden). Individuals are likely to have a range of different answers. Qualitative research will be required to find out what clients really seek.

4. *Sexual dysfunctions, disorders, and the paraphilias must be understood in the contexts in which they arise and come to be seen as problematic.* Symptoms (e.g., difficulties with erection, lubrication, pain, or lack of desire) are virtually unintelligible if viewed in isolation. We tend to focus unduly on the performance problems of the genitals, ignoring the persons attached and the world in which the problem is identified and defined. Difficulties in sexual performance, high or low desire, and unusual sexual interests do not necessarily indicate that something is "wrong" (Apfelbaum, Moser, Stock & Moser, Shaw, Maltz, and Hall). The context required to make sense of sexual problems may include personal and cultural values (Apfelbaum, Brooks, Tiefer, Kleinplatz, Moser, Stock & Moser, Ellison, Hall, Carballo-Diéguez & Remien, and Ogden), the relationship, (Apfelbaum, Brooks, Stock & Moser, Ellison, Hall, Shaw, Carballo-Diéguez & Remien, and Ogden) and subjective experience (Aanstoos, Kleinplatz, Mahrer & Boulet, Maltz, and Hall).

5. *Sex therapists can and should assume a greater role in shaping the public discourse surrounding sexuality.* Sex therapists deal with a class of problems that stem from and are directly affected by social values and attitudes surrounding sexuality. As such, we have a critical role to play in preventing rather than simply treating sexual problems. Rather than adopting mainstream values as a way of furthering our professional credibility, we can provide resistance to those beliefs and attitudes which generate sexual difficulties. This may entail targeting broader, more public venues. We can affect prevailing norms and influence our society's entire sexual discourse through educational outreach, community intervention, group therapy and workshops, and selective use of the media

(Brooks, Tiefer, Kleinplatz, Moser, Hall, Carballo-Diéguez & Remien, and Ogden).We cannot be value-neutral; we will have to choose sides in favor of either validating the status quo or facilitating diverse choices.

6. *The person of the therapist plays a significant role in sex therapy, but it is a neglected variable in our literature.* The personal development of the therapist has implications for how far he or she can take (or accompany) clients on their sexual journeys. Although therapists must bring a set of skills and knowledge to the clinical endeavor, their efforts will be limited or enhanced by their maturity and their abilities to be fully present and engaged during therapy sessions. Such abilities may be more important than any applications of technique (Shaw). In order to become better therapists, we should consider undergoing our own, personal changes (Mahrer & Boulet).

7. *Sex therapy can consist simply of interventions the therapist performs upon the patient, or it can be conceived of as the therapist helping the client to mobilize resources that already lie within.* If sex therapy's inceptions involved the therapist as expert in a white coat (Masters & Johnson, 1970), the alternative entails eschewing the role of authority and becoming the agent who facilitates clients' abilities to discover and implement their own solutions (Shaw, Donahey & Miller, Mahrer & Boulet, and Ogden).

8. *We have much to learn about how to be more effective clinicians by studying what works in psychotherapy per se.* Sex therapy has often been regarded as a unique clinical modality, separate from the field of psychotherapy in general. It is as though we have a domain set off from the world of other human issues and concerns, just as sexual functioning is often viewed apart from the rest of a person's experience, relationships, and society. Professional isolation has restricted our field. Research into and the study of what works in psychotherapy in general can advance greatly the practice of sex therapy (Donahey & Miller).

9. *Sex therapists must look beyond the medical to see the whole person.* Sex therapists must be attuned to the impact of medical innovations and interventions on our patients and on our field. However, it is illusory to think that we can break a person down into distinct component parts, that is, psychological versus organic. The best therapy is accomplished by working with the person within (Aanstoos, Mahrer & Boulet). Even when medical concerns are a component of what brings the patient to the attention of the clinician, it is essential that the therapist deal with the whole person who has the problem (Tiefer, Stock & Moser, and Carballo-Diéguez & Remien).

10. *Technical solutions may be useful for treating technical difficulties. However, in order to help individuals and couples attain optimal sexual development, we need more innovative methods.* The goals determine the means, whether in bed or in sex therapy. If the aim is mediocrity, mediocre means will suffice; if the aim is extraordinary, methods will have to be designed accordingly. These solutions may include some of the approaches described here that have not been typical of conventional sex therapy (e.g., Mahrer and Boulet's Experiential Psychotherapy; Hall's application of narrative therapy; and new types of and uses for group therapy, as described by Carballo-Diéguez and Remien and by Ogden). New approaches that have yet to be envisioned and created also will be needed. Good thinkers and researchers will have to come up with these methods to fulfill a grander agenda.

If the vision of sex therapy implied by these conclusions appeals to you, I hope you will contribute to improving our field. The changes called for are neither minor in scope nor incremental in kind. We need changes in the core assumptions and treatments of sex therapy—changes that go to the essence of the conventional theory and practice of sex therapy. The choice ahead is akin to that which confronts our clients: We can either risk change, even when what we already do works so expediently, or we can risk stagnation. The criticisms, innovations, and alternatives in this book point toward choosing fundamental change in the hope of future growth. If you feel excited by how much stronger this field can become, please consider this invitation to join the authors of this book in this endeavor.

☐ References

Kaplan, H. S. (1974). *The new sex therapy.* New York: Brunner/Mazel.
Masters, W. H., & Johnson, V. E. (1970). *Human sexual inadequacy.* New York: Bantam Books.

INDEX

ABOUT THE EDITOR
AND CONTRIBUTORS

About the Editor

Peggy J. Kleinplatz, Ph.D., is a clinical psychologist, certified sex therapist, and sex educator. Since 1983, she has been teaching Human Sexuality at the School of Psychology, University of Ottawa, where she recently received the Prix d'Excellence award for her teaching (2000). She also teaches sex therapy at the affiliated Saint Paul University's Institute of Pastoral Studies. Kleinplatz deals with sexual issues in individual, couple, and group therapy. Her work focuses on eroticism and transformation. Her email address is *kleinpla@uottawa.ca*

About the Contributors

Christopher M. Aanstoos received his Ph.D. in Phenomenological Psychology from Duquesne University. Currently he is a Professor of Psychology at the State University of West Georgia. He is a Fellow of the American Psychological Association and has served as president of its Division of Humanistic Psychology and Program Chair of its Division of Theoretical and Philosophical Psychology. Aanstoos has contributed to more than 80 publications. He edited the books *Exploring the Lived World* and *Studies in Humanistic Psychology*. He is also the editor of the journal, *The Humanistic Psychologist*.

Bernard Apfelbaum, Ph.D., is Director of the Berkeley Sex Therapy Group. He is a certified sex therapist and a certified analytic therapist whose primary contributions have been in three categories: general therapy issues, sex and sex therapy, and analytic therapy (ego analysis). For a more extensive biography, bibliography, and selected papers, see his Website at *www.bapfelbaumphd.com*

Donald B. Boulet, Ph.D., has been an Associate Professor with the School of Psychology at the University of Ottawa, Canada, since 1975. He is a former Director of the Centre for Psychological Services, University of Ottawa, an APA-accredited internship training unit for doctoral interns in psychology. Boulet is involved in clinical supervision, research, and teaching and maintains an active private practice working with adults utilizing an experiential approach.

Gary R. Brooks received his Ph.D. from the University of Texas at Austin in 1976. He currently is the Director of Training at the Central Texas Veterans' Health Care System in Temple, Texas. He is an Associate Professor in Psychiatry and Behavioral Sciences with the Texas A&M University Health Sciences Center, Adjunct Faculty member at Baylor University, and Instructor of Men's Studies with Texas Women's University. He has authored or coauthored five books: *The Centerfold Syndrome* (1995, Jossey Bass), *Men and Sex: New Psychological Perspectives* (1997, Wiley), *Bridging Separate Gender Worlds* (1997, APA Press), *A New Psychotherapy for Traditional Men* (1998, Jossey-Bass), and *A New Handbook of Counseling and Psychotherapy for Men* (in press, Jossey-Bass). Brooks received the 1996 Distinguished Practitioner Award of the APA Division of Men and Masculinity and the 1997 Texas Distinguished Psychologist Award.

Alex Carballo-Diéguez received his Ph.D. in Clinical Psychology in 1986. He is currently an Assistant Professor of Clinical Psychology at Columbia University and a research scientist at the HIV Center for Clinical and Behavioral Studies of New York State Psychiatric Institute and Columbia University. His research activities focus on HIV prevention and factors associated with sexual risk behavior among gay men and serodiscordant couples. In 2000, Carballo-Diéguez was elected fellow of the American Psychological Association in recognizion of his "outstanding contributions to psychological science." He is a member of the editorial review of the journal *AIDS and Behavior* and has been an ad hoc editor of numerous other scientific journals. He is also a private practitioner who sees individuals and couples for psychotherapeutic treatment.

Karen M. Donahey, Ph.D., is a licensed clinical psychologist. She is an assistant professor and the Director of the Sex and Marital Therapy Program in the Department of Psychiatry and Behavioral Sciences at Northwestern University Medical School in Chicago. Her email is *k-donahey @mwu.edu*

Carol Rinkleib Ellison, Ph.D., is a psychologist in private practice and author of *Women's Sexualities: Generations of Women Share Intimate Secrets of Sexual Self-Acceptance.* She is an Assistant Clinical Professor with the Department of Psychiatry at the University of California, San Francisco, and an Adjunct Faculty member at the Institute of Imaginal Studies in Petaluma, California. A Fellow with the Society for the Scientific Study of Sexuality, Ellison is also an esteemed researcher and regular instructor of human sexuality courses for mental health professionals.

Marny Hall, Ph.D., psychotherapist and author, specializes in sex therapy with lesbian couples. She has presented aspects of her work at conferences and seminars in North America, the Netherlands, Italy, and the United Kingdom. Her publications include numerous articles and three books: *Sexualities, The Lavender Couch,* and *The Lesbian Love Companion.* Hall lives and works in the San Francisco Bay Area.

Alvin R. Mahrer, Ph.D., is a Professor Emeritus at the School of Psychology, University of Ottawa, Ottawa, Canada K1N 6N5. He is the author of 11 books and more than 200 other publications, and he was recently recipient of the American Psychological Association Division of Psychotherapy's Distinguished Psychologist Award. Mahrer is probably best known for his experiential psychotherapy, his experiential model of personality, his discovery-oriented approach to psychotherapy research, and his philosophy of science for the field of psychotherapy. His email is *amahrer@uottawa.ca*

Wendy Maltz, MSW, is Clinical Director of Maltz Counseling Associates in Eugene, Oregon. She is a licensed marriage counselor and certified sex therapist with more than 22 years of clinical experience in sexual abuse treatment. She is the author of *The Sexual Healing Journey: A Guide for Survivors of Sexual Abuse,* coauthor of *Incest and Sexuality: A Guide to Understanding and Healing,* and several other books. She produced *Partners in Healing* and *Relearning Touch,* two highly acclaimed videos for couples addressing the sexual repercussions of abuse. Maltz is an internationally recognized conference presenter, workshop trainer, and public speaker on sexual recovery and healthy sexuality. For more information on her work, visit her Website at *www.HealthySex.com*

Scott D. Miller, Ph.D., is a cofounder of the Institute for the Study of Therapeutic Change, a private group of clinicians and researchers dedicated to studying "what works" in treatment.

Charles Moser, Ph.D., M.D., is a Professor of Sexology at the Institute for Advanced Study of Human Sexuality in San Francisco. He is board certified in Internal Medicine and maintains a private practice in San Francisco. He focuses his practice on the sexual aspects of medical concerns and the medical aspects of sexual concerns. He is the author of *Health Care Without Shame* (1999, Greenery Press) a guide to communication by and to healthcare professionals about sexual issues. Moser is in the process of forming the American College of Sexual Medicine and Health, a professional organization for healthcare providers concerned with the medical aspects of sexuality and the sexual aspects of medicine.

Gina Ogden, Ph.D., is a licensed marriage and family therapist, a certified sexuality therapist, and author of *Women Who Love Sex: An Inquiry into the Expanding Spirit of Women's Erotic Experience.* Her survey on integrating sexuality and spirituality is the first to investigate nationwide responses to this subject. She is presently a Visiting Scholar at the Radcliffe Institute, Harvard University, where she is completing the survey analysis.

Robert H. Remien, Ph.D., is a Research Scientist at the HIV Center for Clinical and Behavioral Studies and an Assistant Professor of Clinical Psychology (in Psychiatry) at Columbia University. His research is currently focused on primary and secondary prevention interventions for HIV+ individuals and HIV-serodiscordant couples. He is the chair of the New York State Psychological Association's Task Force on AIDS, a member of the New York City Department of Health Prevention Planning Group, and senior faculty for the American Psychological Association's HIV training for psychologists. Remien provides clinical supervision to psychology and psychiatry residents in training and volunteer group facilitators in community-based organizations, and he maintains a part-time private practice in clinical psychology in New York City.

Jeanne Shaw, Ph.D., is a licensed psychologist, clinical nurse specialist, AASECT-certified sex therapist, mother of four, and grandmother of seven. She has conducted sexuality workshops, seminars, consultation and supervision in the United States, Australia, Israel, and Canada since 1976. Her publications include the *Journey Toward Intimacy* handbooks for singles and gay, straight, and lesbian couples, and numerous professional articles. In the independent practice of psychotherapy in Atlanta, Georgia, for more than 25 years, she now travels around the country in her motorhome, writing, working occasionally, and playing.

Wendy Stock, Ph.D., is a clinical psychologist and a member of the teaching and research adjunct faculty of California School of Professional Psychology–Alameda. Her areas of specialization are human sexuality, sexual abuse and trauma, gender issues, and feminist issues in clinical psychology. Stock's research has focused on women's experiences of pornography and psychophysiological and subjective responses to erotica and pornography. Her publications include feminist analyses of sexual dysfunction, sex therapy, and power dynamics in heterosexual relationships. Stock currently teaches courses in Feminist Therapy and Feminist Research Methods at CSPP and maintains an independent practice.

Leonore Tiefer, Ph.D., is a clinical psychologist and sex therapist in New York City. She holds appointments in the Departments of Psychiatry at the New York University School of Medicine and the Albert Einstein College of Medicine. She was Codirector of the Sex Therapy and Gender Disorders Clinic at Montefiore Medical Center from 1988 to 1996. She has many publications in theoretical and empirical sexology, and her 1995 collection of essays, *Sex Is Not a Natural Act* (Westview Press), is widely used on college campuses. She is also very active as a feminist, Unitarian-Universalist, and as vice-chair of the Board of the National Coalition against Censorship.